The Collapse of State Socialism

The Collapse of State Socialism

THE CASE OF POLAND

Bartłomiej Kamiński

PRINCETON UNIVERSITY PRESS

PRINCETON, NEW JERSEY

Published by Princeton University Press, 41 William Street,
Princeton, New Jersey 08540
In the United Kingdom: Princeton University Press, Oxford

Library of Congress Cataloging-in-Publication Data

Kamiński, Bartołomiej, 1944–
The collapse of the state socialism : the case of Poland/Bartołomiej Kamiński
p.   cm.
Includes bibliographical references and index.
1. Communism—Poland—History—20th century. 2. Poland—Politics and
government—1945– 3. Poland—Politics and government—1989– I. Title.
HX315.7.A6K36   1991   335.43'09438—dc20   90-21737   CIP

ISBN 0-691-07880-7 (acid-free paper)—ISBN 0-691-02335-2 (pbk. : acid-free paper)

This book has been composed in Linotron Times Roman

Princeton University Press books are printed on acid-free paper
and meet the guidelines for permanence and durability of the
Committee on Production Guidelines for Book Longevity of the
Council on Library Resources

Printed in the United States of America by Princeton University Press,
Princeton, New Jersey
10 9 8 7 6 5 4 3 2 1
10 9 8 7 6 5 4 3 2 1
(Pbk.)

To Matthew

Contents

Tables

Preface

THE ORIGINS of this book go back to the mid-1970s when I was involved in a large research project on global models of the international system. Having analyzed the assumptions and simulations of the then well-known book *Limits to Growth* (Meadows et al. 1974), I concluded with my friend and co-author Marek Okolski that Communist countries are more likely to experience "limits to growth" problems than market-oriented systems. We then pledged that once our other joint research projects on the world economy were over we would write a book on the absence of self-recuperating mechanisms in a Communist system. Those projects, which resulted in several books and articles, were more time consuming than we had anticipated, however. I began the project only in the 1980s. The Solidarity period and then Solidarity's struggle for survival after the imposition of martial law kept my interest alive.

The view I had from my Polish experience was that both rulers and ruled were enslaved by the system. As a student of Western economics, I was also aware of the fuzzy or even nonexistent boundaries between economics and politics. Having lived in both Communist and non-Communist countries, I saw that there was a more fundamental difference between those two worlds than that suggested by most observers. It was more than a matter of different mixtures of market and command.

These observations led me to develop a method to analyze the Communist system, which promised to explain a wide range of processes. The concepts of "fusion" and "negative legitimation" made it possible to integrate problems of economic growth, the functioning of the economic system, and political management. These problems have been, as a rule, studied seperately.

Glasnost and *perestroika* in the Soviet Union, the emergence of the Solidarity-led cabinet and the collapse of Communist regimes throughout Central Europe did not destroy the structure of the book. To the contrary, they vindicated my analysis of systemic flaws of state socialism. I have to admit that I did not expect any of those developments to occur during my lifetime, however.

The Department of Government at the University of Maryland provided a particularly favorable environment. George Quester in his capacity as chairman was greatly supportive of my enterprise in a variety of ways. I persevered in my project thanks to the encouragement of Davis Bobrow, Karen Dawisha, Stephen Elkin, and Karol Sołtan. I also derived considerable benefit from long discussions with scholars from Central Europe visiting the Woodrow Wilson Center. Earlier versions and drafts presented at various conferences benefited enormously from comments and suggestions by Keith Crane, James Depleth, Peter Dombrowski, John Hardt, Robert Janes, David Kemme, Mario Nuti, Paul Marer, and Linda Roccioppi.

The first draft of the manuscript was read carefully by Karol Sołtan, who made so many incisive comments and suggestions that I restructured it almost entirely. The restructured version was then critically assessed by Roger Kanet, Arthur Rachwald, and Aron Wildavsky. I am greatly indebted for their critical comments.

Last but not least, I am indebted to my wife Eva and my son Matthew who had to put up with the almost endless noise of my computer and with my prolonged absences from active participation in family life.

The Collapse of State Socialism

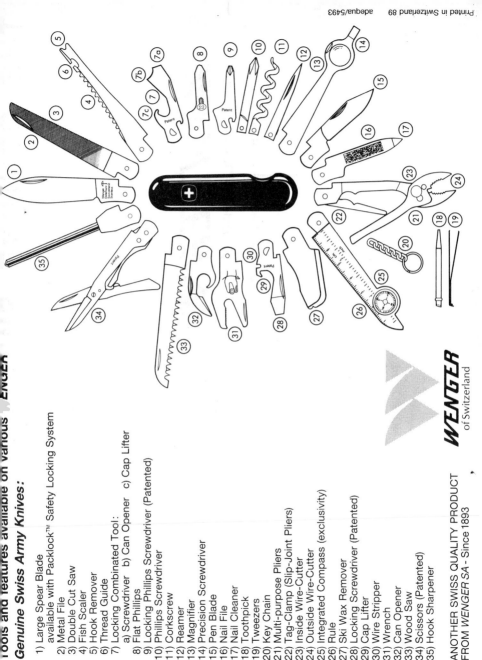

Tools and features available on various WENGER

Genuine Swiss Army Knives:

1) Large Spear Blade
   available with Packlock™ Safety Locking System
2) Metal File
3) Double Cut Saw
4) Fish Scaler
5) Hook Remover
6) Thread Guide
7) Locking Combinated Tool:
   a) Screwdriver b) Can Opener c) Cap Lifter
8) Flat Phillips
9) Locking Phillips Screwdriver (Patented)
10) Phillips Screwdriver
11) Corkscrew
12) Reamer
13) Magnifier
14) Precision Screwdriver
15) Pen Blade
16) Nail File
17) Nail Cleaner
18) Toothpick
19) Tweezers
20) Key Chain
21) Multi-purpose Pliers
22) Tag-Clamp (Slip-Joint Pliers)
23) Inside Wire-Cutter
24) Outside Wire-Cutter
25) Integrated Compass (exclusivity)
26) Rule
27) Ski Wax Remover
28) Locking Screwdriver (Patented)
29) Cap Lifter
30) Wire Stripper
31) Wrench
32) Can Opener
33) Wood Saw
34) Scissors (Patented)
35) Hook Sharpener

WENGER
of Switzerland

ANOTHER SWISS QUALITY PRODUCT
FROM *WENGER SA* - Since 1893

SWISS

THE GENUINE SWISS ARMY KNIFE

➕ **WENGER W**
of Switzerland

Official supplier to the Swiss Army since 1908

LIMITED LIFETIME WARRANTY

All *WENGER* Genuine Swiss Army Knives, which are purchased in the USA and its territories and possessions, are warranted for the lifetime of the original purchaser, against breakage or malfunction, under normal use, due to defects in material or workmanship. We will repair or, at our option replace any defective knife with the same or a comparable model. We will refund the purchase price if repair or replacement is not commercially practicable or cannot be made in a timely fashion. This warranty will become null and void if the knife is misused, abused, tampered with or taken apart. It also does not cover any ornamentation, imprint or inlay applied to the knife. **We will not be liable for any incidental, consequential, or special damages arising from any and all uses of the knife.** Some states do not allow the exclusion or limitation of incidental consequential or special damages, so the above limitation or exclusion may not apply to you. This warranty gives you specific legal rights and you may also have other rights which vary from state to state.

For warranty service, please send the knife with a US return address and $ 3.00 (for return postage and handling) to WENGER Swiss Army Knife, 15 Corporate Drive, Orangeburg, NY 10962.

WENGER Swiss Army Knives... the first Swiss Army Knife good enough to carry a limited lifetime warranty.

HOW TO CARE FOR YOUR HIGH QUALITY PRECISION INSTRUMENT

Please oil lightly all the pivot points on your knife. When storing your knife, be sure it is free from moisture and lightly oil all metal parts. Make sure you wipe the knife dry before returning it to your pocket. Follow the procedures and your Swiss Army Knife will give you a lifetime or trouble-free cutting pleasure.

OLD COMMUNISTS desperately seeking to reconcile with the abrupt collapse of Communist regimes in Eastern Europe are quoted as saying that communism remains a wonderful concept, but either people have not lived up to it or there were serious errors in its implementation. This book argues the opposite: communism, or state socialism,[1] was a *terrible idea but awfully well implemented.*

Because institutional arrangements deprive state socialism of the capacity to channel self-interested behavior into socially beneficial performance and condition its survival on a base of direct coercion, the whole concept of politico-economic order is fundamentally flawed. By eliminating autonomous sources of economic growth and innovation, it makes the state directly responsible for the provision of goods and services. Because it deprives policy makers of information and tools to elicit the most productive behavior from themselves and other actors, the economic system fails to secure efficiency in the use of resources that would guarantee its long-term viability. The institutional design of state socialism creates a paradox: policy actions designed to improve performance only accelerate its decay.

State socialism was too well implemented. It managed to survive beyond a point when accumulated shortcomings made economic recovery extremely difficult to obtain. Although it was based on an institutional design doomed to failure in the world of rapid change, it lasted long enough to destroy the economies and natural environments of countries that had lived under it, to ruin the lives of millions before its final collapse, and to spoil the moral environment, as President Vaclav Havel put it.[2] Communism succeeded in attracting some of the best minds and through a combination of repression, cooptation, and corruption disarmed a majority that quickly became silent and apathetic. It survived because so many people were willing to compromise their principles: "None of us is merely a victim, because all of us helped to create it."[3] Communism also succeeded in alienating, almost as quickly as attracting, intellectuals and professionals. The system encouraged mediocrity and loyalty and rejected boldness and innovativeness.

[1] I shall use the term "state socialism" throughout this book. To avoid terminological confusion, the term "socialist state" will refer here to a state in a Soviet-type society. The term state socialism has several advantages: it identifies the state as a major actor; it is more narrowly focused than Soviet-style economies (or societies); it is not normatively loaded like the widely used term "centrally planned economies (or societies)," which implies rigidly and effectively enforced central controls. On the other hand, it is not misleading like the term "communism." Communism belongs to the realm of ideology and identifies the goal not praxis.

[2] New Year's Day Address, *New York Times*, 2 January 1990.

[3] Vaclav Havel quoted in Andrew Nagorski (1990b, 22).

Current debate on the origins of the collapse of communism that assigns primacy to either economic or political factors is ill-founded because neither politics nor economics exists under state socialism. Under state socialism, everything is politicized except politics, which is almost completely depoliticized. People are banned from voicing their opinions. They have to repeat party slogans and follow the party line. Under state socialism, everything focuses on the economy except economics, which is utterly de-economized, and as a result, is fully politicized. Although products and services are in short supply, producers are not required to follow the rules of economic efficiency that would ultimately increase their availability. Because prices reflect bureaucratic preferences and bear little relation to relative scarcities, they provide neither planners nor producers with information conducive to subjecting decision making to economic efficiency.

Thus the roots of the collapse of state socialism are neither economic nor political—they are institutional and systemic. They stem from the destruction of both politics and economics.

Systems born of Western political tradition have displayed enormous diversity and capacity to respond to changing domestic and international challenges. The secret of this flexibility lies in an institutional design that recognizes the relative autonomy of politics and economics and of actors as well as various public domains. As a result, it allows self-interest to become a driving force of change. In the great triad comprising the state, society, and economy, the functions of each are limited by design, and each performs a different set of roles. The rules governing interaction among them recognize the autonomy of each of them.

Despite their enormous political variations, the "organizational map" of non-Communist societies exhibits some basic institutional similarities among them. Their organization of politics separates legislative, executive, and judicial institutions. Various codes and rules governing those institutions and their interactions are responsible for significant political variations within the institutional perimeter of the separation of powers. The way that the state interacts with the economy is also similar. Although non-Communist economies exhibit differences in the size of state-owned sectors, in the ways that link business with government, in dominant market structures, and in levels of economic development, the state authority to intervene *directly* in the economy is subject to legally codified structures and processes. The diversity of arrangements and domestic structures generated by similar institutional parameters also reflects a whole gamut of economic and political performances ranging from failures and political instabilities to successes and prosperity.

In stark contrast, the institutional arrangements of state socialism do not allow a similarly wide range of variations. Had it not been for the diverse histories of respective countries, and the impact of that diversity on domestic political cultures, the world of state socialism would have been extremely dull.

The variations, as limited as they were, were the product of the factors that affected the strategy of Communist takeovers and subsequent strategies used to assure the survival of Communist regimes. Differences in history (most notably, the heritage of autocracy versus democracy), levels of socioeconomic development, and other political and cultural circumstances prevalent during Communist takeovers all accounted for the survival of some pre-Communist institutions and traditions. The Soviet Communists did not bother to maintain other parties; German or Polish Communists allowed their existence, strictly supervised by the Communist party.

However, the most significant differences between Communist countries were the result of strategies pursued by Communists to assure the legitimacy of their rule. Except for Czechoslovakia (1968), Hungary (1956), and Poland, which was notorious for its defiance of state socialism, Communist regimes did not experience serious challenges until the "springtime of nations" in the fall of 1989. Polish Communist authorities had to cope with a whole series of upheavals in 1956, 1970, 1976, and 1980-1981. Although the Czechoslovakian political system returned to "normalcy" after a short-lived Prague Spring that was crushed by the Soviet-led military invasion, Hungarian and Polish Communist regimes became significantly less oppressive in response to upheavals and aspired less to total control. Polish Communist authorities, for instance, had to accept the existence of an independent Catholic church and scrap agricultural collectivization programs. Bowing to social demands, they also had to make other concessions throughout the 1980s that eventually culminated in the establishment of the first non-Communist government in Eastern Europe in August 1989.

Otherwise, despite significant differences in levels of economic development, in their economic and historic circumstances, and in political cultures, they exhibited remarkably similar domestic structures (Comisso 1986) that subjugated the economy to the state. Consequently, they can be lumped together on several counts. First, there was not a single success story under state socialism. After an initial success in extending the industrial base, they all experienced a protracted growth slump—the more developed the economy was when a Communist takeover took place, the sooner it occurred.

Second, state socialism created everywhere an environment conducive to social, economic, and political decay. It evolved from—to borrow loosely from Brzeziński's (1989, 41) description—a Leninist totalitarian party through a Stalinist totalitarian state to a Brezhnevite totally stagnant state dominated by a completely corrupt totalitarian party. The institutional environment of economic activities favored sectors producing resource-intensive goods, discriminated against consumer goods, and generated a path of development leading to economic self-strangulation.

Third, the state, broadly defined as encompassing all political institutions including the Communist party, was by design to assume a dominant position vis-à-vis the economy and society. The state assumed functions reserved under a Western system to the economy and independent institutions regulating social interaction. Consequently, the state was assigned by Communists the role of sole agent of change and the status of social production organizer. In contrast to a Western order, the socialist state had the authority and responsibility to control production.

Fourth, the principle of separation of executive, legislative and judicial powers was de facto replaced by the principle of unity of powers. The existing government structures, which often paid lip service to the separation of powers, were of no consequence to the domestic political process. Although the states all had constitutions and legislatures, and some of them had several political parties and some variety in institutional forms, the Communist party was firmly in control. Except for periods of upheavals, legislatures acted like rubber stamps for current policies of the Communist party.

Thus incomparably smaller variations in institutional arrangements and performances of countries under state socialism suggest that state socialism cannot be conceptualized in similar terms. There are fundamental differences between Western style goverments and state socialist politico-economic orders, although they share many parallel traits. State socialism has developed, for example, giant bureaucracies (see, for instance, Meyer [1961]); yet to portray the system as a bureaucracy that displays patterns of behavior similar to those of any large organization does not offer any insights about its evolution. Military procurement, with its absence of competition and the propensity of participants to distort information and inflate cost, is reminiscent of behavior under central administrative planning, yet nobody would identify it as the most relevant feature of Western politico-economic systems. Charles Lindblom (1977) argued that all politico-economic systems existing in the world can be characterized by different mixes of government and market. He would be right if he qualified "the world" with the adjective "non-Communist." A market is more than a place where buyer and seller meet. A market is a human artifact that incorporates contractual relationships, interdependencies between buyers and sellers, and competition compelling autonomous economic actors to respond to price signals. And such a market has never been compatible with state socialism.

The idea of a "continuum" of various mixes of government and market also underlay much of the Western sovietological thinking about state socialism, which after years of tinkering with the Friedrich-Brzeziński "totalitarian model" switched to the explanations that neglected the role of the state and elevated economics and society as major domains that allegedly explain the workings of the system. Then, indeed, the only difference between capitalism and socialism boiled down to different proportions of the same components. These approaches, labeled institutional pluralism, modernization, and so forth,[4] logically paved the way for the long-forgotten convergence theory, which had a lot of intellectual appeal in the West in the 1960s.[5] Its major prediction that the clusters of capitalist and socialist systems will merge into a third approach that will combine the best that the two systems offer totally missed the point. The reason, as I shall argue, is that convergence cannot occur when there is a discontinuity, or when the major institutional traits are not shared. Not surprisingly, the official Soviet Communist ideology rejected convergence—as it turned out rightly, although for wrong reasons—as a possible future because the only future for the world was communism.

The continuum approach is conceptually flawed because it mistakenly suggests the possibility of easy movement from one point to another characterized by a different mix of government and market. This view implies that conversion of state socialism into a Western democracy would involve a simple reshuffling of the institutional arrangements. If this were the case, why then did state socialism fail to respond to new challenges by simply reorganizing itself? Why did the Hungarian economy after more than two decades of "market-oriented reforms" or the Polish after a decade of similar reform effort display drawbacks, such as shortages and inefficiencies, which were much more similar to economies under state socialism than under capitalism? Finally, why does the debate now focus on the transition and what is so difficult about it if the challenge consists only in slightly modifying the proportions? These questions cannot be even asked when a "continuum" approach is adopted. They only emerge if we allow for a discontinuity between the two clusters of politico-economic orders.

A claim by Communist ideologues that state socialism is a distinct politico-economic form was probably their only "finding" that accurately reflected the reality. Former East German General Party Secretary Erich Honnecker was right when he declared that capitalism and communism "were as different and incompatible as fire and water."[6] Communists indeed succeeded in creating a system that is unique. State socialism is a distinct system: its institutions *explicitly* reject the autonomy of society and the economy. Its institutions are predicated upon aspiration by the state to total control of both society and the economy.[7] The state socialist economy, as we shall see, is *not a mixed economy but a fused economy*. For that reason alone, it belongs to a different set of politico-economic systems—to a set where political and economic components cannot be separated.

Thus what sets apart state socialism from other politico-economic systems lies in the unique symbiosis of the state with society and the economy, which

---

[4] For a review, see White et al. (1982, 14–23).

[5] For a review, see Meyer (1970) and Brzezinski and Huttington (1963, 421–34).

[6] Quoted in Kovrig (1988, 9).

[7] It is important in this context to stress the word "aspiration" as an expression of the goal of institution building.

I call here the *fusion principle*. As a result of fusion, both politics and economics lose the distinctive features characteristic ofr Western societies. Fusion determines the political and economic logic of state socialism. A socialist state aims to control directly all economic activities, the process of economic growth, and capital formation. Its political aspiration is to extend its rule over all domains of public life and to suppress group and individual interests.

There is little if any room for democracy in a politico-economic system where the economy is inseparable from the state; at best, there may a "socialist" democracy deprived of the institutions that would ensure full accountability of the rulers. Subjecting the economy to the administrative rules makes the state responsible for the burden of distribution. Although a significant portion of distribution is effected through money and prices, shortages—according to Kornai (1982), the characteristic that defines a state socialist economy—of allocation criteria are inevitably based on nonpecuniary and noneconomic efficiency considerations that are subject to arbitrary politically driven decisions.

Because external and politically neutral criteria are absent, politicization of resource distribution is a source of conflict. A farmer, an industrial enterprise, or an individual seeking to obtain some desired products all, more often than not, have to curry favors from the state administration. As a result, transactions become highly personalized and subject not to purchasing power but to "political" peddling. Because of the secondary role of "objectivity" introduced by money in a market economy, they are conflict generating. These conflicts destabilize the relations between rulers and ruled; if unchecked, they would lead to anarchy. The only way to ensure stability is to erect a political regime capable of destroying liberty. Freedom is to state socialism what water is to fire: it destroys it. Therefore, the institutional design of state socialism calls for a full suppression of individual freedoms: as the late general secretary of the Soviet Communist party Konstantin Chernenko succinctly observed, "Practice shows that where 'pluralism' flourishes it leads only to the loss of the party's fighting efficiency, to the erosion of its ideological foundations."[8] The system that Stalin headed was the closest to this ideal. Yet evolution has pushed it in another direction, toward liberty and crisis.

The paradox of the evolution of state socialism is that to ensure its survivability the authorities have been under pressure, generated by either domestic or international challenges, to reconcile with their incapacity to control everything, a privilege implicit in the way that the politico-economic order was set. All attempts to improve the system defied, as a rule, the original institutional design; they ran against the institutional logic. Actions meeting societal aspirations and rational from the point of view of stimulating economic performance ran counter to the ideological foundations of state socialism.

[8] Quoted in Kovrig (1988, 14).

The evolution has been characterized by a search for substitutes for mechanisms and institutions that were rejected by Communists—the market mechanism, the rule of law, and the institutional form of an effective interest mediation. But without autonomy and competition market instruments are useless. Without the separation of powers and direct accountability of the government, the establishment of either *rechstaat* or effective interest mediation is not possible. Instead this search undermines the capacity of the state to suppress individual interests and to direct the economy. Loosening the controls only leads to a loss in the party-state's fighting efficiency and the erosion of its ideological zeal, to loosely paraphrase Konstantin Chernenko.

The withdrawal or limited exit of individuals from the spheres controlled by the state is a symptom of the decay of state socialism. According to Albert Hirschman (1970), efficiency can be restored through a combination of voice (articulation of dissatisfaction), loyalty (a belief in reformability "from within"), and exit (withdrawal). When the belief in reformability of the system is eroded by a series of unsuccessful reform attempts, loyalty to the institutions of state socialism is also undermined. When voice is either suppressed or simply ignored by the authorities and there is no loyalty, the only reaction to a deterioration in performance is exit or withdrawal. The individuals can exit (though not all of them, as the case of East Germany illustrates). On the other hand, the state cannot withdraw from various domains of public life without establishing institutions that assure at least the viability of the relatively autonomous economic system and the emergence of institutional procedures for copying with diverse interests. In the absence of democracy, the withdrawal of the state exacerbates individual and group demands for resources and leads to conflicts and inefficiencies. In the absence of a market mechanism, which is the only institutional device available to substitute for the exit of the state from the economy, the state's withdrawal only increases chaos. Thus the process cannot be completed without destroying state socialism; it only prolongs the decay.

State socialism's "stage of decay" is characterized by the loss of control by the state over the allocation of resources as well as over rewards and penalties. The capacity of the state to suppress individual and group interests significantly weakens.[9] Within the state various quasi-representative institutions with some authority and competing power centers emerge. They operate, however, in an ill-suited institutional framework, which by design allows only for moncentrity, and thus produces internal tensions and difficulties in implementing policies (B. Kamiński 1989a). Thus because there is no alternative political party and economic bargaining becomes less constrained, the polit-

---

[9] In an article coauthored with Karol Sołtan, we have described this evolution as a movement from a rigidly constrained to a weakly constrained bargaining regime (Kamiński and Sołtan 1989).

ico-economic system is deprived of internal mechanisms to restore discipline and to return economic performance to a satisfactory level.

The discipline can be restored either by a recentralization of controls or the introduction of the institutional framework that explicitly recognizes pluralism. The former is often not a viable alternative especially when Communist ideology has lost its appeal because of unfulfilled promises. The latter is outside the institutional boundaries of state socialism. As Kamiński and Sołtan have argued elsewhere, the solution "lies . . . not in more rigid control of every sphere of social life, but in a more rigid refusal to control at least some spheres. . . . It rests on Schelling's paradox that the ability to constrain oneself may be a source of power."[10] In other words, a strong commitment not to do certain things allows more effective control in other areas. But without the depoliticization of the economic system, that is, eliminating fusion and ensuring state autonomy, this control cannot obtain.

Given the Marxian origins of the ideology of state socialism, it is paradoxical that Marx's laws of motion for social systems have turned out to be more applicable to the offspring of Marxist ideology. According to Marx's historical materialism, each successive socioeconomic formation would inevitably fall except communism, the ultimate stage in the development of humanity. The irony is that the law of inevitable demise applies more to a formation that has emerged as a result of the Soviet Communist Revolution than to capitalism, its alleged predecessor. State socialism, rather than capitalism, is torn apart by the contradictions between productive forces and the relations of production, and between base and superstructure. Alienation of workers is felt more acutely in state socialism than in capitalism (Coleman and Nelson 1984). The institutional framework of state socialism, based on utopian assumptions that everything can be directly controlled from above and that all concerned will offer the best response to state directives, plants the seeds of its own destruction in the world of rapidly expanding technology and production.

In contrast to Marx's vision of linear progression in history, the destruction of state socialism marks a return to a Western-type system. "The crisis consists," Italian Marxist Antonio Gramsci (1971, 26) once observed, "in that the old is dying and the new cannot be born." But the solution to the crisis of state socialism does not imply that—in broad institutional terms—something new will be born. To the contrary, the objective of the transition currently debated and implemented in some East European countries is to establish free markets and democracy.

The contradiction—revealed by poor economic performance and increased social dissatisfaction—that cannot be solved in state socialism is not between productive forces and relations of productions. These are not Marx's contra-

---

[10] Kamiński and Sołtan (1988, 27). For a discussion of this method of enhancing one's bargaining power, see Schelling (1963, 22–28).

dictions that are responsible for the disintegration of state socialism, and the East European workers rose not to build communism, but to bury it. The reasons are rooted in the flawed institutional design of state socialism, which—in an ironic twist of Marx's concept of an extra space offered by each successive formation to develop productive forces—failed at the outset to create conditions for a long-term sustainable growth.[11] The institutional design is responsible for erecting domestic structures that leave little room for adaptation to the external non-Communist world, and, more significantly, attempts to adapt and correct various problems that undermine its underpinnings. Although communism and its applied version of state socialism were born in the West, they have rejected major Western political and economic innovations, such as democracy and the market. The rejection of democracy deprived the state of the institutional potential to solve social conflicts and to mediate among competing interests, and thereby, to evolve in response to new social demands. The rejection of the market has been responsible for extreme politicization of economic processes and involved the state in the day-to-day operation of the economy. The result is that economics is politicized, and politics is depoliticized. The suppression of both economic and political freedom, characteristic of state socialism, accounts for a system's inability to adapt to the international economy and thus challenges state socialism's economic viability. Suppression is also responsible for the state's inability to respond to social demands for participation—the result of changes in the composition of society.

Both the rise and the fall of state socialism can be traced to the destruction of domains that were beyond the direct reach of the state, especially the economy. Appropriation of the economy gave the state the control over resources and a seemingly enormous capacity to shape its political and economic predicament. This turned out to be an illusion because the fusion of the state and economy is a crisis-generator in a triple sense: first, it allows only a limited institutional adjustment; second, it limits the range of feasible development strategies; and, third, feasible crisis management strategies undermine the economic viability of state socialism. Because options involving various mixes of state and market are simply not available, fusion curtails the scope for institutional adjustment and accounts for the extremely limited reformability of state socialism. The fusion also excludes all alternatives that are based on varying degrees of the openness of the economic system to the outside world and thus subjugates decision makers to what I call the *closed system logic*.

Fusion is thus responsible for a path of development that depletes growth potential and is economically inefficient. This path may be sustained only by

[11] Economic growth in Poland was obtained thanks to the reserves accumulated under capitalism and access to Western technology and capital (see chap. 3).

keeping the consumption of consumer goods in check. As a result, if a regime is forced to make economic concessions to consumers to assure political stability when massive repression is not an acceptable alternative, its long-term economic viability weakens. The increased provision of economic goods becomes more difficult, because the closed system logic discriminates against consumer goods and makes it impossible to exploit opportunities offered by international markets. Such a legitimating strategy only brings closer the day of reckoning with economic realities.[12]

Yet contraction in physical output did not cause Communist regimes to fall in 1989. The self-anointed authorities did not have to bow to public will. They could have again survived the people's withdrawal from acceptance of authority. Instead they gave up power, but under considerable pressure from Moscow. The collapse of Communist regimes in Eastern Europe proved that state socialism could have been neither established nor maintained without Soviet bayonnets. Mikhail Gorbachev's decision to let the peoples of Eastern Europe choose their political destinies instead of restoring central controls through overt, massive repression to suppress their growing dissatisfaction with the inevitably deteriorating economy was clearly prompted by his conviction that state socialism had become obsolete and its disintegration could not be reversed without economic and political catastrophe. He was probably caught by surprise, like everybody else, by the speed with which Communist regimes fell once Moscow declared its exit. Indeed, except for Hungary and Poland, nowhere in the Communist world was the potential for disintegration so visible.

Yet very similar processes, although spread over a much shorter time span, had been at work. The collapse was caused by the same institutional factors. In contrast to Hungary or Poland, other Communist regimes more effectively suppressed individual interests early. They avoided the futile exercise of experimenting with various economic and political innovations that would only aggravate the crisis and raise the economic cost of overcoming the legacies of state socialism.[13] On the other hand, the disintegration of state socialism spread over a longer time allowed the emergence of alternative social arrangements outside the direct reach of the state that have already proved extremely useful in assuring political stability while state socialism is dismantled in Poland.

Because of the duration of the decay stage, the case of Poland offers unique insights into the workings (or rather, mal-workings) of state socialism. The

[12] Gierek's policies pursued in the second half of the 1970s, when Western credits were increasingly used to sustain consumption in excess of the productive capacities of the Polish economy, are not the only illustration. Similar policies were pursued by Brezhnev and other Communist leaders, though without reliance on Western financing.

[13] The exception was Romania where a combination of suicidal economic policies and massive repression ruined the economy and moral fiber of the people.

deficiencies of the institutional design were most clearly visible in Poland. So were the limitations imposed by the system logic that practically enslaved even genuine Communist reformers. Although East European countries affected by the 1989 upheaval were spared Tocqueville's dangerous stage of a bad government reforming itself, the case of Poland has broader theoretical implications for possible futures for those governments that do quickly dismantle state socialism.

Poland has always been the weak link, to borrow a term from Lenin, in the state socialist world. The authorities' efforts to extend state controls over all domains of public life have been neither vigorous nor successful. They had to accept that their capacity to govern depended on coexistence with the church (Korboński 1988). Consequently, their pretense to control all sources of social values was quite limited. The shortcomings of state socialism, such as microeconomic inefficiencies, low international competitiveness, poor quality of products and services, and the disintegration of work ethos surfaced sooner than in other countries. No other state socialist country has gone through so many political upheavals and economic crises. No other country has come so close to a collapse.

Poland's movement away from state socialism has broader international implications. The reasons are strikingly similar to the ones that induced Karl Marx to declare Poland the key "revolutionary" linchpin in nineteenth-century Europe. As Marx expressed it in a letter to Engels on 2 December 1856:

> What has decided me definitely for Poland, on the basis of my latest studies of Polish history, is the historical fact that the intensity and vitality of all revolutions since 1789 can be gauged pretty accurately by their attitude to Poland. Poland is their "external" thermometer. (Kandal 1989, 45)

Much has changed over the last century. Marx had in mind a democratic revolution against feudalism not state socialism. He could not predict that a hundred years later the struggle would be against the politico-economic order that had been inspired by his writings and that the struggle would be for democracy and markets. Nonetheless, Poland's fate has remained linked to Russia, or rather, the Soviet Union. But in another ironic twist of history, this time it may be in another way—the success of Poland's struggle with dismantling state socialism will boost Mikhail Gorbachev's efforts to build a Western-style politico-economic order in the Soviet Union.

This study proceeds on two levels. On one level, it is a theoretical inquiry into the characteristics of state socialism, its principles of organization, and its disintegration. The theory underlying this study, although focused on the case of Poland, has a much broader range of applicability and offers insights into processes occurring in all societies under state socialism. It answers such questions as Why has a system that is flawed on so many counts managed to survive for so long? Why has it been losing its ability to adapt to the changing external environment? Why has it come so close to economic disintegration without eliciting a prompt viable response from the ruling elites, as the case of Poland clearly shows? The hypotheses and answers are derived from the institutional characteristics of state socialism, its utopian aspiration of the state to control everything, and its inherent inability to create conditions conducive to productive activities at all layers of society and the economy.

On the second level, this book is empirical; it attempts to integrate a theoretical framework of state socialism with an empirical analysis of developments in Poland. Thus the hypotheses derived from a set of institutional arrangements are tested empirically whenever possible.

The organization of the book reflects the theoretical and empirical purposes outlined by division into two parts. The first part traces the institutional sources of state socialism disintegration, whereas the second shows how the attempts that go beyond primitive coercion actually accelerate the demise of the system. The logic of state socialism is coercion and direct central controls; its political and economic performance cannot be improved by introducing instruments of Western provenance while rejecting its concepts of division of "labor" in political and economic spheres.

The first chapter sets forth a general intellectual perspective on state socialism and its underlying concepts for management of social interaction and the economy. It explores the institutional framework of state socialism from the point of view of its impact on the capacity of the socialist state to solve social and economic problems and to steer development. Despite the enormous powers accumulated by the state (or perhaps because of those powers), its capacities have weakened with the modernization of the economy. I argue that the institutional design of state socialism is basically flawed, and that even the brightest rulers could not infuse economic and social vitality once the revolutionary fervor is gone without totally abandoning the system. Although their power is institutionally unlimited, they are enslaved by the poverty of the institutional design, which dramatically curtails ways to adjust to domestic and external demands.

The analysis in chapters 2 and 3 demonstrates how these basic institutional flaws have affected political and economic developments under state socialism. The empirical illustrations are derived from the case of Poland. The main proposition in chapter 2 describes the limited "reformability" of the economic dimension of state socialism. To demonstrate it, I establish a conceptual framework for the comparative analysis of economic institutional "innovations" and then apply these concepts to the study of economic innovations implemented in Poland from 1981 to 1988. The innovations that were effected, similar to those introduced in Hungary, represent the ultimate institutional innovation possible within the confines of the fusion principle. They show the limited institutional capacity of the socialist state to redesign itself and establish a viable economic system that would assure the best response to external stimuli.

The central thesis of chapter 2 is that features of economic development common to all socialist states can be explained by the limitations imposed on central planners by the institutional design. In chapter 3, analyze the forces that shape the evolution of the state socialist economy and the limits they have imposed on development strategies. Because of domestic arrangements, the strategies are bound to be inward-oriented, favoring the choice of import-substituting activities. They also discriminate against the production of consumer goods because of the institutional closeness of the economic system. The inability to assure economic efficiency combined with the pressures to generate economic growth lead to the neglect of the natural environment, infrastructure, capital assets, and so forth, which inevitably depletes the potential for future growth. As in chapter 2, the discussion of constraints set by the fusion principle on the choice of development strategies is followed by an examination of developments in Poland in the 1970s and the 1980s. Gierek's import-led growth strategy in the 1970s illustrates an attempt to defy the closed system logic, whereas Jaruzelski's adjustment strategy (if it deserves this name) in the 1980s shows the institutional limitations to integration with the world economy. Poland is clearly an extreme case, but other East European countries have not had much success in becoming competitive in international markets. Neither have they avoided destroying their natural and man-made environments.

In chapter 4, I show how the crisis management contributes to the disintegration of state socialism. Deteriorating economic growth performance erodes the ideological basis of the system and increases the potential for political instabilities. What distinguished Poland from other state socialist societies was the cycle of political upheavals. Each upheaval brought political concessions from the authorities; some of them were contained by granting economic concessions. Each of them weakened the capability of successive regimes to suppress workers' interests. The paradox of Polish state socialism was that attempts to assure minimum legitimacy led to the workers' veto over economic policies, thus fulfilling, in an ironic twist, the ideological claim of the dictatorship of the proletariat.

In chapter 5, I discuss the reasons why the option of restoring central political and economic controls through massive repression (in line with the institutional arrangements of state socialism) was not available to the "architects" of martial law imposed in December 1981.

The only way out of Poland's predicament was an overthrow of state socialism, as explained in the concluding two chapters. In chapter 6, I examine the Jaruzelski regime's response to decline, which illustrates the limited range for political experimenting within the institutional limits of state socialism. Various innovative measures were introduced by the regime as it attempted to withdraw from some of the ideological pretenses of state socialism and to reconcile with the accelerated withdrawal of people from the system, while retaining its core. A rapid expansion of civil or alternative society, as it was called in underground Solidarity publications during martial law in the early 1980s, increased social apathy and indifference and, more significantly, showed the insolubility of the problem of genuine political participation under state socialism.

In the concluding chapter, I identify major systemic incompatibilities caused by the absence of both a market and a political mechanism of conflict mediation. I analyze the barriers to and forces of transition from state socialism to parliamentary democracy and a market economy.

The book has two appendixes. The first gives an account of major political and economic developments in Poland from 1982 to 1989, and the second discusses Poland's debt crisis.

CHAPTER ONE

The Institutional Sources
of Crisis-Generating Tendencies

THE STATE socialist world today is collapsing. The root of its disintegration is the institutional structure of state socialism. The collapse of state socialism is of its own making. Its institutional structures are inadequate to cope with external and internal challenges. The promise and threat of the crisis is that it cannot be solved without overhauling the basic institutions of a socialist society.

State socialism is set apart from other politico-economic systems by its institutional framework based on the fusion of the state and the economy as well as of the state and society. As such, it is a continuation of earlier political systems dominated by patrimonial bureaucracies and traditional hierarchies. This fusion defies economic and political rationality in the contemporary external environment characterized by rapid change. The design assumes away self-interest as a driving force of social change and puts the burden of responsibility for virtually everything on the state. The crisis is a failure of the state to respond to demands of society and the external environment. In other words, given the institutional constraints, a viable politico-economic order cannot be born without eradicating state socialism.

Many analysts of the institutional underpinnings of state socialism have directly transplanted Western political and economic concepts. This approach to the analysis of development is a mistake. The focus on apparent similarities has accounted for flaws and weaknesses in many of these analyses. Charles Lindblom (1977, ix), for instance, has sought to analyze all existing contemporary politico-economic systems in terms of varying proportions of state and market. He writes, "The greatest distinction between one government and another is the degree to which market replaces government or government replaces market." The existing continuum is marked at one end by a laissez faire competitive system; but at the other end one cannot place state socialism, as Lindblom and many others, explicitly or implicitly, do.

Politico-economic systems differ not just in how much of state and market they put into their mixtures but also in the extent to which these elements can be separated at all. State socialism is not characterized by a dominant share of government and a miniscule share of the market. Instead, it is characterized by a qualitatively different interaction between the state and the economy. Lev Trotsky criticized Stalinist central planning for "freeing itself from monetary (tsennostnyi) control, just as bureaucratic arbitrariness frees itself from political control."[1] What Trotsky failed to note is that the economy has become part of the state. This is not a question of different proportions of government and market but of a qualitatively different arrangement.

The institutional arrangement of state socialism is the outcome of a fusion of state and economy. Neither the state nor the economy can be separated. Economic, political, and social components are blended.[2] The weakness of Lindblom's analysis of communism stems from a failure to recognize that the symbiotic relationship between economy and state gives rise to a different set of characteristics and calls for different theoretical concepts. This does not necessarily imply that they do not share some common social phenomena and pathologies (Kamiński 1989a).

The fact that in spite of frequent reform attempts the institutional design of state socialism survived almost intact is often regarded as a proof of the built-in bias against any change or of state socialism's nonreformability (Tatu 1987). As Poland's former prime minister Mieczysław F. Rakowski noted:

> For almost forty years, the factors determining the party's position in the system, and indirectly in the society, have been rooted in the sphere of the economy. The party, in fact, or rather to be precise its leadership was in charge of means of production and exercised control over their utilization. Every government and Planning Commission played to a great extent the role of an official distributor of the above mentioned means. (Rakowski 1987, 50)

This citation suggests that direct controls over the economy were crucial for the party-state apparatus to defend its privileged position.

Yet state socialism has clearly changed, although the evolution circumvented the design granting the party-state institutional omnipotence. It has become softer, leakier, and less oppressive. An extreme centralization has given way to deconcentration of power: managers of large state-owned enterprises and local party-state officials have acquired a certain level of autonomy. But those deconcentrated "smaller units" have remained organized around the fusion of the state and the economy, and their interactions have been more or less strongly subject to the center of power. All the modifications have been moving the party-state closer to the very concept of social order that its founders rejected. In its decay, state socialism has become a caricature of democracy and of the market economy because the emerging pluralism was not

[1] Leon Trotsky, "Chto takoye SSSR i kuda on idyot?" (What's the Soviet Union and where is it going?) mimeo., 1936, quoted in Nove (1986, 60).

[2] A good analogy, for which I am indebted to Karol Soltan, is as follows: Put cucumbers (market) and tomatoes (state) into a blender. Some mixtures will be cucumber heavy, others tomato heavy, which represents various proportions of the ingredients. But, if you turn on the blender, although the proportions do not change, the ingredients fuse. State socialism is the result of blending, not of different mixtures of state and economy.

matched by institutional changes that recognized the autonomy of self-interested behavior.

The objective in this chapter is to identify and assess the impact of the institutional arrangement of state socialism on its political and economic dynamics. I address two major themes here: first, the institutional framework of state socialism, and, second, its inherent limitations in controlling economic performance and sustaining political stability. The common denominator is the link between institutional design and the increasingly limited capacity of the socialist state to adapt to societal aspirations and exigencies of the international political economy. The first theme, the original institutional design of state socialism, as it emerged in the Soviet Union under Stalin in the 1930s, has continuing relevance for the study of contemporary state socialism. In spite of substantial changes, its essential features have survived sturdily. Although the economic system has become a caricature of command planning, and its polity has become a caricature of totalitarianism, the mechanisms have remained essentially intact, particularly in the economic system.

The second theme that I address is the impact of the institutional arrangements on the capacity of the socialist state to adapt to domestic and external challenges. The ability of the state to collect information about economic opportunities, to enforce its preferences, and to adjust its structure is strongly curtailed by ideological and political constraints. Those constraints are the product of a social fabric created by the institutional design of state socialism.

This substance that locks together the rulers and the ruled has not been resistant to change. The modes of governance have evolved since Stalin's death. Brutal, random, and indiscriminate repression has given way to more sophisticated methods of control. Repression has become more selective. Society has regained some autonomy. In the economic system, planning procedures have been vastly improved. Yet, this fabric, combined with the dominant Soviet position in Eastern Europe, has not provided a fertile ground for inventing and implementing institutional changes that would reverse the process of decay. This chapter sets a theoretical framework for the analysis of the disintegration of state socialism.

THE INSTITUTIONAL DESIGN OF STATE SOCIALISM: THE END OF POLITICS AND ECONOMICS?

The institutional design of state socialism resulted from a Marxist vision of a Communist social order adapted to the conditions prevailing in a relatively backward country, Russia. Preoccupied with the theoretical account of processes that would lead to the fall of capitalism, neither Marx nor Engels devoted much attention to specific features of a transition to communism. They highlighted the modus operandi of communism only by showing how the contradictions of capitalism could be removed. The task of designing the intermediate order "until the higher phase of communism arrives" was left to Lenin and his followers.[3]

Marx's and Engels's vision was predicated upon a total rejection of capitalism once it had fulfilled its "historic mission" of developing the forces of production. A revolutionary eradication of all its institutions was to put an end to all social problems. The source of evil was private ownership. As they stated in *The Communist Manifesto*, "The theory of the communists may be summed up in the single sentence: abolition of private property" (Nove and Nuti 1972, 19). This has been the core of Communist ideology.

Viewed against a broader background of Marxism, the abolition of private property was thought to have several important implications for the "new society." First, private ownership was regarded as the only source of antagonistic social relations. It gave rise to exploitation and, together with the development of productive forces, was responsible for the growing alienation of workers. As Engels wrote in *Anti-Dühring*, the abolition of private property would amount to "the genuine resolution of the conflict between man and nature and between man and man" (Nove and Nuti, 1972, 24). Engel's analysis suggests that in communism there would be *no room for politics*.

Second, the disappearance of private property was to put an end to civil society. Economic relations (civil society) would wither away for "the producers do not exchange their products."[4] The state, as the instrument of class repression, would also disappear in the absence of classes. The pervasive view expressed in Marx's, Engels's, and Lenin's writing was that the state was the "executive committee" acting on behalf of the capitalists to ensure the reproduction of the relations of production based on private ownership and, therefore, exploitation.

By the same token, money was to be abolished, and then the economy would become demonetized. When everything became everyone's property and allocation was according to one's needs, then direct exchange would replace the use of money. As a result, *economics would also disappear* because resources would be allocated not by markets and prices but by the conscious decisions of the society. Thus the abolition of private property in the conditions of material abundance would produce a harmonious society in which there would be no room for either politics and the state or the economy and the market.

Although Russia after the Revolution was a long way from material abundance, the intermediate order that was founded for the "lower phase" of communism[5] has retained some major elements of the vision of communism.

[3] V. I. Lenin, "Session of All-Russia C.E.C., 29 April 1918" quoted in Nove and Nuti (1972, 20).

[4] Marx, "Critique of the Gotha Program" quoted in Nove and Nuti (1972, 22).

[5] This phase precedes, according to Marx, the "higher phase" of material abundance and of new social consciousness liberated from the legacy of superstructure of the capitalist formation.

The underlying assumption was that capitalism could contribute little to economic modernization. This task was to be undertaken by the Communist party. True to their ideology, the Communists adopted an institutional design that totally rejected democracy and the market. In addition, they also *repulsed the rule of law*. Lenin, discussing Marx's comments on "parliamentary cretinism," argued that the dictatorship of the proletariat should be a system of rule "unrestricted by any laws" (Parkin, 1979, 180).

The abolition of the market mechanism liberated state socialism from the control of the "invisible hand," whereas rejection of democracy put it beyond social control and direct accountability for the actions of its elites. A market, in its obfuscated form, was allowed to operate only during a short period of the New Economic Policy (NEP). The state, which assumed direct control over the economy, also assumed full responsibility for effecting change. Democracy was replaced by hierarchical subordination; all activities were to be controlled from above.

The notion of democracy was rejected even within the party, as Lenin's ban on factions and his concept of "democratic centralism" demonstrate. This institutional design allocated the leading role in society to the party. The state was to be its instrument for mobilizing society to construct the material foundation for communism. Command planning based on accounting and control was to become a major tool of state control over the economy. As Lenin described it:

> Accounting and control—that is mainly what is needed for the "smooth working," for the proper functioning, of the first phase of communist society. *All* citizens are transformed into hired employees of the state, which consists of the armed workers. *All* citizens become employees and workers of a *single* country-wide state "syndicate."[6]

The assumption underlying Lenin's vision was that the state would be responsible for solving all problems related to coordination of activities throughout the whole economy. The market and money as devices for allocating resources and goods were regarded as inferior to the party and its administrative arm, the state.

The claim of the superiority of order based on state ownership, command planning, and the party's leading role has been at the heart of Communist ideology. Therefore, it is scarcely surprising that Communist takeovers have always resulted in the imposition of a one-party rule and the seizure of direct control of the economy. The nationalization of almost all capital assets including banks and trade organizations, the introduction of state monopoly over foreign trade, as well as the establishment of one-party control through a nomenklatura have been among the measures that completed the process of Com-

[6] V. I. Lenin, *State and Revolution* quoted in Nove and Nuti (1972, 26).

munist takeovers. Even though a small private sector survived in some countries, the state's monopolistic position as a supplier, buyer, and rule generator gave it controlling powers. By owning most of the capital assets, the state has become, as Lenin suggested, the main employer, thus controlling who would be employed and promoted. By virtue of its aspiration to full control over the economy, that is, the rate of accumulation and production and the distribution of goods and services, the party-state has become the locus of decision making. And because it seeks legitimation in Communist ideology this system has earned the title of state socialism.

The idealized institutional features of state socialism compared with bourgeois democracy are presented in table 1.1. (The major organizing principles of state socialism discussed in this book are summarized in table 1.1.) By contrasting their institutional features, one may see that state socialism is a symmetrical negation of the Western order based on the rule of law (rechstaat), rulers' accountability (democracy), and autonomy of the economy (civil society). The contrast between the two orders is particularly visible in the markedly different ways the two designs suggest to organize the fundamental interactions between the state and society and between the state and the economy.

TABLE 1.1
Contrasting Features of Democratic and State Socialist Institutional Design

Issue-area	Liberal "Bourgeois"	State Socialism
State vs. society	State as its agent	Society as an object
	Civil society	Autonomy rejected
	Conflict mediation	Conflict suppression
	Political pluralism (diversity)	Political unity (homogeneity)
Accountability	Voters	Party hierarchy
Law	Autonomous (as a constraint)	Purposive (as a tool)
Mechanism of mass compliance	Legal-rational legitimation	Direct coercion and/or "bribing"
State vs. economy (organizing principles)	Exclusion (macrointervention)	Inclusion/fusion (microintervent.)
	Stability of the rules	Variability of the rules
Mechanism of allocation	Market/state (prices)	State/quasi markets (directives)
Economy	Horizontal links Contracts Demand-constrained	Vertical links Plans Supply-constrained

Under state socialism, the socialist state aspires to assume all functions, whereas in a Western system the division of functions is clear cut.

The Western design, which leaves the future open and stresses personal freedoms, is rules oriented. The state socialist design determines the future and subordinates means to its attainment. It is tasks oriented. The former holds "means" invariant, whereas the latter subordinates means to a goal. The former is expected to create conditions for decentralized actions that will contribute to welfare maximization, whereas the latter assumes the task of doing so. The future social order orientation of Communist ideology legitimates the state's activity insofar as it is conducive to the construction of a Communist society; the ends justify the means.

The Western design seeks to control effects of freedom through the political system. Noting that factions (or interest groups) are the product of freedom, James Madison (1787) writes, "But it could not be a less folly to abolish liberty, which is essential to political life, because it nourishes faction than it would be to wish the annihilation of air, which is essential to animal life, because it imparts to fire its destructive agency."[7] The state socialist design destroys liberty for the sake of "genuine" liberty and a conflict-free society in the future.

Suppressing economic and political freedoms has several implications for the modus operandi of state socialism. With the declining appeal of the promise of a better future, economic performance becomes essential to state socialism's legitimacy. By becoming the direct organizer of economic activity, the state assumes the sole responsibility for economic performance. Given the fact that the institutional design is based on the assumption that rapid economic development will almost immediately generate an abundance of material goods, there is little institutional room for making adjustments unless the goal is achieved within a short time, as the Russian revolutionaries hoped would be the case.[8]

The elimination of the market not only limits innovative potential and removes the opportunity for entrepreneurship, it also eliminates a very wide range of possible adaptive responses. The burden of adjustment falls on the state, which then has to set tasks for individual actors. In contrast with modern societies, which can cope with crises by either manipulating macroeconomic parameters, by changing the scope of the market, by extending or curtailing the state administrative mechanism (regulation versus deregulation), state socialism can only improve procedures of administrative intervention. Because the institutional requirements of a successful adaptation to the international economy call for flexibility, this deprives state socialist societies of a whole

---

[7] Madison, "The Federalist Paper #10," in Rossiter, *Federalist Papers*, 78.

[8] Some of them were allegedly aware of the advantages of a market. For instance, Lenin's experience with war communism led him to reassess his view of the market at the sunset of his political career (Nove and Nuti 1972).

array of public policy instruments that indirectly encourage a decentralized response.

The elimination of the market reduces economic mechanisms available to the socialist state to an administrative mechanism, while simultaneously creating what Nove (1986, 163) described as "the impossible [in terms of information processing] scale of centralized micro-economic planning." Although fusion of the state and economy may temporarily increase the capacity to mobilize and extract resources, it also deprives the state of the possibility of controlling economic processes by altering the government/market mix. Note that when capitalism was faced with the Great Depression of the 1930s, it responded by changing the respective roles of the *existing* institutions: the state intervened in the economy while the scope of the market was reduced. As long as a national economy is not distinct from the state, the option of moving from more government to less market, or vice versa, is not available to the authorities.

Marketization as an option to adjust the economy is not feasible within the institutional parameters of state socialism. Because a market is a way to organize society that is essentially different from state socialism, its introduction amounts to no less than the elimination of state socialism. Leaving aside a minor argument that according to Communist ideology the evolution under a state should lead away from the market, which in turn erodes the legitimating function of the ideology for the rulers and their supporters, the problem is that the very source of power is the state's *direct* involvement in the economy. The verdicts of a market are usually different from the state's rulings; the former rewards efficiency and the latter loyalty. And the market cannot exist without the autonomy of economic actors and competition.

Even assuming political willingness and the absence of resistance to the introduction of a market, a market society cannot be created instantaneously. As Karl Polanyi wrote in his classic study of the transformation of modern society: "The fount and matrix of the system was the self-regulating market. It was this innovation which gave rise to a specific civilization. . . . The liberal state was itself a creation of the self-regulating market. The key to the institutional system of the nineteenth century [as well as the modern one] lays in the laws governing market economy" (Polanyi 1957, 3). The rejection of a market and of other institutions indispensable for its existence (e.g., law) amounted to the rejection of a Western politico-economic order, which was precisely the objective of the Communists.

By putting all its eggs into one basket, the quick achievement of communism, state socialism severely impaired its adaptive capacity. *By rejecting a market environment, state socialism put the full burden of economic management on the party-state. As a result, any revealed conflict related to dissatisfaction with economic performance becomes a direct challenge to the state and consequently to the political order.* The socialist state is "besieged" with claims on the economic resources of which it is the ultimate distributor, and to avoid economic chaos it must suppress group interests. By adopting Marx's view that conflicting interests are caused mainly by private property, the designers of the system have deprived it of a political mechanism for conflict mediation. By subordinating law to changing purposes, the designers of the system have curtailed its capacity as a tool to regulate human behavior. Consequently, as will be demonstrated, its capacity for survival has been strongly dependent on the ideological zeal of its supporters and its ability to repress contending views.

IMPLICATIONS OF FUSION: FEATURES OF STATE SOCIALISM

Although total "etatization" of the society and the aspiration to an unconstrained capacity to control fully all domains of public policy have turned out to be illusions because the socioeconomic reality has proved to be much more complex than assumed in the institutional design, the established politico-economic order has retained the principle of fusing the state with the economy and society. As a result, the social fabric has become organized around the socialist state, assuming functions that in market societies are carried out by actors operating outside the state.

Some functions are shared by all states[9] independently of the political order they maintain; others are unique to socialist states. In the broadest terms, the primary functions of the state include preventing society from breaking apart and losing independence. The state has to have access to economic resources to fulfill these functions. Therefore, making sure that the performance of a domestic economy is adequate to reproduce the existing political system remains one of the major functions of the state. Although the reasons for this interest may vary across the spectrum of political regimes, they all boil down to threats to the state's survival from the social, economic, and security consequences of depressed economic performance.

In modern capitalism, the state has no authority to control economic processes directly through microeconomic intervention (Offe 1975). The state is, however, responsible for sustaining conditions conducive to economic expansion. Although the state is not directly involved in the economy, it is, nevertheless, held accountable for providing economic prosperity and social stabil-

---

[9] Because the purpose of the present discussion is to highlight the modus operandi of state socialism, such widely discussed theoretical issues as "autonomy" of the state, the state as an instrument of dominant class, the extent of integration of various social groups in economic policy making, methods of interest intermediation, and so forth, will be referred to only as far as they help explain the interaction of the state and the economy. These features are an elaboration of a twofold functional description of a capitalist state in terms of accumulation and legitimation maintenance developed by the German school of political economy. For an excellent review of German debate on the theory of the contemporary capitalist state, see Carnoy (1984).

ity. The survival of the state depends upon the presence and continuity of the accumulation process. And finally, the state, shaping economic processes mainly through the market, tends to rely on mechanisms of mass compliance based on legal-rational legitimacy, that is, autonomous law.

In the most general terms, these features distinguish the capitalist state from other states, but they are of little use for comparative studies among capitalist states. All they imply is that the economy is autonomous from the state, which, in turn, is held responsible for creating an environment conducive to economic prosperity and social stability.

The nationalization of the productive means and the imposition of direct administrative controls have given the socialist state the status of production organizer and manager. In contrast to the capitalist state, the socialist state has assumed the authority and responsibility to control production, although it may choose to delegate some of its authority to enterprises because of incentive or information considerations. However, no matter what formal or real autonomy exists for economic actors, the predicament of the socialist state stems from its direct involvement in the economy. Thus, in contrast to the capitalist principle of exclusion, the underlying principle of state socialism is the fusion of the economic sphere with state power.[10]

With some qualifications, the second feature pointing to the state's responsibility for economic prosperity is also present among functional requirements of state socialism. A necessary condition of economic development is the capacity to transfer to the future the ultimate use of resources presently available. In this sense, any state determined to stay on the path of economic growth must sustain conditions of accumulation, that is, conducive to capital formation.

Economic performance has been an important (increasingly the only) source of legitimation for socialist regimes. These economies have traditionally displayed a strong bias in favor of accumulation. In contrast to capitalism where competition weeds out the inefficient and rewards the efficient and innovative, no similar mechanism exists in state socialism. As many observe, in the absence of market competition, capitalism is devoid of its vigor and creativity. The source of forces generating new technologies, production, and investment is competition in capitalist societies. The same cannot be said about state so-

---

[10] One may note in passing that descriptions of the Soviet Union and Eastern European systems as "state capitalist societies" are methodologically erroneous. (See, for instance, Cliff [1974]. For a brief survey of literature criticizing this approach to state socialism, see Nuti [1979] and Lane [1985].) The differences between capitalism and state socialism are not quantitative but qualitative and stem from contrasting principles of organizing the economy—the principle of exclusion in the former and of inclusion in the latter. They relate to fundamental differences in the roles of law, administration, scope of pursued policy objectives, institutional ways of articulating interests, and ensuing modes of controlling the society and the economy.

cialism; the only instrument to combat inertia in state socialism is a "taut plan," that is, administrative coercion.

Under state socialism, the state enforces its preferences through a hierarchically organized bureaucracy endowed with coercive powers. Not surprisingly, the state economic administration tends to display all the drawbacks of any large organization, regardless of its social setting, with one qualification—they are exacerbated. Among the most conspicuous bureaucratic diseases are secrecy, formalism, proliferation of cumbersome procedures, rigidity, the tendency to destroy all those components in environment that require undertaking organizational changes, and the tendency to concentrate on control rather than performance. Bureaucratic diseases are not confined to selected aspects of social life but are omnipresent. The democracy and accountability that check expansion of bureaucracies in Western societies are not present in the Soviet-style socialist order. Excessive bureaucratization destroys both social life and the economy. We have, therefore, an interesting question: Why has the bureaucracy not expanded to the point that it fully paralyzes socialist societies?

Studies on the power structure in socialist countries indicate that the party apparatus that holds the dominant position within the state functions as a substitute for public control.[11] As Romanian political scientist Sylviu Brucan (1983, 39) noted, "Those who man the commanding positions in the state system (government and administration and its machinery, including the military and coercive machinery) are recruited from the party apparat." The party apparatus controls promotions to higher positions through a hierarchically organized nomenklatura system and plays a twofold role as controller and stimulator of the state administration, although both roles are part of the same state structure.[12] In addition, both control and stimulation are hierarchically organized with internal procedures typical for any large organization. From the point of view of the functioning of the socialist state, the nature of interaction between the two is crucial, demanding a clear-cut subordination of the state administration to the party apparatus.

The party apparatus is usually beyond not only social but also party member control; it controls itself. As a rule, a substantial number of members of a Communist party central committee, an organ that is supposed to monitor activities of the party, are those employed in the apparatus. Jadwiga Staniszkis

[11] The dominant role of the party apparatus is stressed particularly by the authors who used to hold high party and administrative posts in Eastern Europe, for example, former Romanian deputy prime minister Brucan (1983) and Ota Sik (1981), deputy prime minister during the Prague Spring.

[12] Maria Hirszowicz (1980, 138) succinctly describes their mutual relation and its functional equivalent to other forms of control over bureaucracy when she writes, "The 'bureaucracy-against-bureaucracy' system can be considered a substitute for many alternative mechanisms for curbing the power of bureaucracy and stimulating its performance."

(1984, 93) estimated, for instance, that employees of the party apparatus accounted for more than 50 percent of the Central Committee membership of the Polish United Workers' Party (PUWP) in the 1970s. It is, perhaps, even more significant that they accounted for 83 percent of the members of the commission charged to organize and draw up the agenda for the 9th Extraordinary PUWP Congress convened in 1981, during the Solidarity period. Thus, they were also supposed to achieve the impossible task of "reforming themselves."

To be effective, the party apparatus must be in a position to temporarily revoke the formal procedures of the economic bureaucracy, to bypass usual lines of communication, and to intervene directly and across institutional lines. Put differently, the party apparatus has the authority to revoke temporarily various legal procedures that would otherwise limit its scope of action. Suspension or selective observance of rules is not only part of its normal mode of operation but is crucial to the survival and effective functioning of state socialism. The socialist state can easily discard the straightjacket of law and regulations by claiming that the fulfillment of a vaguely defined common interest requires a different set of rules. In the absence of democratic institutions with which to control administration, the proliferation of rules and penalties would reach the point where governing would become very difficult, if not impossible.

The key to an effective fulfillment by the Socialist state of its administrative and managerial functions is—to use Maria Hirszowicz's (1980) term—the duality of informal and formal procedures that, taken together, produce the principle of "rule bending." The coexistence of informal and formal procedures is a source of internal tensions. Although it allows some things to get done, the victims of this arrangement are the professionalism of the bureaucracy and the integrity of those who are beyond the rule of law.

Another victim is the quality of the legal order. The principle of rule bending combined with the state's direct microeconomic intervention is an invitation to lawlessness. Yet, the law is indispensable for a clear definition of the actions that will be penalized. The result of those conflicting forces is vagueness, unclear wording, loopholes, and so forth, which allows for an arbitrary interpretation of legal acts. For instance, many pieces of legislation contain a provision that in "the socially justified cases," a given law may be suspended. This gives the local authorities the power to decide whether a given act applies to a particular situation or person. These cases are not specified but are left to the discretion of the local administration.

The effectiveness of this dual legal and political order, which implies the existence of a dividing line between power and authority, is critically dependent on the integrity of the party and its apparatus. Any weakening of internal discipline inevitably leads to abuses that serve local ends.

The fusion of the state and the economy creates an environment conducive to the pursuit of local ends at the expense of public objectives. Although the essence of capitalist state policy is to provide guidance in economic issues with minimal central controls,[13] the absence of a market mechanism in socialist states requires administrative "rationing." Under rationing, the access of consumers to goods and services ought to depend on demonstration of the proof of public desirability and the need for required allotments. In practice, however, access depends upon establishment of a network of personal contacts with those in charge of rationing.[14] With the growing complexity of the economy, this produces a gigantic hierarchically organized system of "mutual exchanges of favors" that—as will be demonstrated later—becomes one of the dominant modes of ensuring mass compliance. This may be a source of political stability, but it simultaneously breeds alienation and dissatisfaction.[15]

The exception in capitalism has become a rule in state socialism. Although some bureaucratic procedures have been developed to handle rationing on the basis of impersonal rules (e.g., methods of capital project evaluation), the verdicts of these procedures are usually not followed. The reason is not only that information on which decision is based is of such low quality (in part because of the lack of "good" prices and in part because outcomes in the future are uncertain) but mainly because economic actors have no formal autonomy to make decisions, and other noneconomic aspects are taken into account. In fact, commands (directives) must be crafted to individual conditions of actors; they are personalized, and the content of a message changes depending on the addressee. This modus operandi may be called the "principle of rule variability." Its by-product is that the whole process of economic management becomes extremely politicized.

In all, blending of the state and the economy produces a unique politico-economic order in which politics becomes fused with economics. The scope of functions that the socialist state assumes is incomparably wider than in those orders where the economic system is legally separated from the state. Its

[13] This should not imply that capitalist state actions are confined to manipulating impersonal market forces and never infringe on private autonomy. However, when such infringement occurs, it often contributes to the politicization of the economy and, consequently, weakens legitimacy and administrative competence. This view seems to be shared by both radicals and neoconservatives. See Offe's (1984) essay " 'Ungovernability': The Renaissance of Conservative Theories of State." The politicization of resource distribution erodes consensus and introduces conflict, which ultimately results in the erosion of democracy (Usher 1981).

[14] This paves the way for patron-client relationships (Hough 1969; Skilling 1966; Oi 1967; Wilkerton 1979).

[15] This is well documented by Coleman and Nelson (1984). Cross-country analysis leads them to support the validity of the following hypothesis: "The more obtrusive the state's role in structuring, managing, and "resolving" social conflict, the greater the tendency of dissatisfied workers to attribute responsibility directly to the state for conditions held objectionable on normative grounds" (p. 3).

power attributes including ownership of all (or almost all) productive assets,[16] provision of employment to a majority of employed, control of mass media, and control over an extensively developed apparatus of repression surpass even those held by authoritarian regimes. Thus, on paper, the socialist state has a great potential to impose its will. Yet, these impressive power attributes are also a source of its weaknesses when confronted with the imperatives of the contemporary international economy.

POTENTIAL FOR DECAY

Deviations from rational and efficient behavior of individuals and organizations occur under any politico-economic system. The institutional arrangements of state socialism leave little room for their correction. The fusion of the state and the economy replaces economic efficiency with political criteria subject to whims of the regime. Deviations from economic efficiency feed upon themselves and, therefore, lead to a general decay. Because the powerful mechanism of autonomous self-recuperation operating through competition is not available, the task of correcting the behavior that is undermining social and economic viability is placed exclusively on the state. The ''etatization'' of society reduces the capacity of a regime to identify problems and to marshall forces to overcome them. State socialism has limited homeostatic controls. I shall demonstrate that this institutional design curtails a range of regime-preserving solutions to crises and that some solutions actually exacerbate the process of decay.

The institutional design of state socialism is based on utopian assumptions about human nature, society, and, consequently, the forces underlying socio-economic development. Its social and political evolution is predicated on the assumption of continual progress towards harmony. In the course of development, the society should become more and more homogenized. Individuals, families, and social groups should lose their distinct identities and merge into an indistinguishable whole. The state would then also wither away.

But economic modernization pushes towards diversity and increasingly elaborate division of labor, and individuals refuse to have ''the same opinions, the same passions, and the same interests'' (Madison 1987, 78). Conflicts do not disappear once private property is abolished. Individuals and groups occupying different economic positions have diverse interests, whereas the institutional design deliberately neglects their existence.

Nothing in the Leninist institutional design would allow it to cope politically

---

[16] Even if there is a private sector, the state's monopolistic position as a supplier, buyer, and rule generator gives it controlling powers over it. For a discussion of private sector-state interface in Poland in the 1980s, see Kamiński (1989c).

with the absence of consensus.[17] Even assuming societal consensus on the ideologically determined goal, the creation of communism, there may be differences on the best way to reach this goal. The only options open to rulers are to "buy" cooperation of dissenting groups, although adhering to the Communist ideology, or to coerce them.[18] Either option undermines the system's legitimacy. Stalin favored the latter; his successors have relied more on the former. Thus, even assuming that all individuals share Communist ideals, the institutional design provides no room for the advantages derived from exploring their knowledge and expertise to select the best path leading to communism.

Politics, that is, the art of compromising, is assumed away, not because there is always a unity of interests but because interests are to be suppressed for the sake of creating a Communist society.[19] The institutional suppression of criticism (or "voice" in Hirschman's [1970] terminology) deprives state socialism of a mechanism for self-recuperation if anything goes wrong. When voice is blocked, there is no opportunity to resort to "political channels" because there is no politics. Therefore, when coercion is not effective, it is virtually impossible for rulers to obtain a measure of political consensus from the population. In addition, information about failures is also blocked, which makes changing the "course" more difficult if not impossible.

The socialist state has implemented various forms of quasi participation, for example, "transmission belt" organizations as a means to channel discontent and control dissent. These forms of participation, although poor substitutes for democratic processes, contribute to political stability by providing the state with additional channels of communication. Nuti (1982) claims, for instance, that the abolition of workers' councils was a factor contributing to the eruption of strikes in Poland in 1980. On the other hand, some of these organizations, such as writers' unions in Czechoslovakia in 1956 and in Poland in 1956 and 1968, may contribute to crises. Although the skillful use of quasi participation as a part of social engineering may have contributed to the superior stability

[17] It is worth noting that Rosa Luxemburg (1961) challenged Lenin's concept of building communism by suppressing such characteristics of bourgeois democracy as free speech and free press. Her line of argument was that the institutions should not be predesigned but evolve as a result of political process.

[18] Lenin's principle of democratic centralism does not provide a solution to this problem because, even if fully adhered to, it hinges critically on the ability to link all partial measures to the adopted goals. But in any complex situation, there is a hierarchy of means and ends. Means at a higher level are goals for lower levels. In addition, there is a time span between the party congresses that according to this principle adopt strategy subject to the critical evaluation of delegates. The principle forbids those who discover discrepancies between applied measures and the program to voice their opinions.

[19] In marked contrast, the "bourgeois" institutional design fully accounts for self-interested behavior and mechanisms of conflict mediating.

and longevity of state socialism as compared to authoritarian or Fascist regimes, it offers no protection once social dissatisfaction erupts.

The serious consequence of the suppression of voice—the elimination of the feedback loop between the rulers and society—usually results in apathy and indifference. Apathy may provide stability and flexibility, but only if voice is not fully blocked (Hirschman 1970, 14). Although mass organizations controlled by the party provide limited opportunities for unblocking voice, the lack of social enthusiasm in following state directives undermines the economic viability of state socialism. The state can dominate apathetic and indifferent society, but it can hardly mobilize it to pursue economic tasks.

Because the state monopolizes all initiatives, its ability to effect change is critically dependent on mobilizing society. Society can be mobilized through terror or around some shared goal of constructing communism in a hostile environment. For instance, Stalin's strategy of industrialization was compared by the Soviet writers to a war campaign with Stalin as a field commander facing specific objectives with limited means (Hardt 1976). Because of the organizational impossibility to focus on all objectives, it is suited to handle one emergency but not several emergencies.[20] In other words, the design does not allow for effective functioning when terror and ideology lose their mobilizing capability and when the objectives are multiple. Because the socialist state is the ultimate organizer of economic activity, the design does not leave much room to produce behavioral characteristics that would *internalize* the propensity to produce and generate new technologies and products. This is so because no one but the state can compel producers to produce or adopt new technologies.

The ideological assumption is that central planning more than compensates for the loss of dynamism caused by the deliberate rejection of the market.[21] As in the society-state interaction, a unity of will and action has been assumed. By the same token, the institutional design takes for granted that the party-state has perfect, total knowledge and can, therefore, elicit maximum efforts from all individuals. But unless they all are ready to forego private interest, information is likely to be subject to distortion or deliberate withholding. The assumption of perfect information can be met only in a very static and simple environment, which is not what a modern economy is. In addition, as we have seen, the capacity to mobilize society may be severely hampered by political arrangements conducive to a society's indifference and apathy.

The assumption of the superiority of the fusion of the state and the economy over other politico-economic systems is justified only if the following four conditions are simultaneously met: (1) the state has a perfect knowledge of all

[20] Or as Nuti (1988, 370) noted, socialism is only good "at handling *priority* but not priorities."

[21] For a superb discussion that contrasts central planning with a market, see Wildavsky (1979).

available options and means at its disposal; (2) it has the ability to fully enforce its preferences; (3) it can create motivations so that all actors are willing to cooperate even at the expense of their self-interest; and, (4) it has the ability to "reform itself" to improve its adaptive capacity in response to changes in external and internal circumstances.

The first three conditions could be met only in a politico-economic environment where a full political hegemony exists, as defined by Antonio Gramsci. According to Gramsci (1971), full political hegemony occurs when the party-state apparatus becomes fully merged with civil society; the ruling oligarchy (or the leader) exercises control through the imposition of its world view (ideology), which in turn is fully internalized by society; and, the rulers control political consciousness, and thus their rule is fully legitimated.[22] In this context, hegemony implies social acceptance of the superstructure of state socialism. Although the extent to which state socialism succeeded in establishing hegemony varied from one country to another, political hegemony has never been full—if anything, it has tended to decline. In the course of evolution and economic modernization, satisfying Gramsci's conditions for full hegemony becomes virtually impossible, which increases the crisis potential. In addition, the party-state does not have perfect knowledge and cannot elicit maximum effort and the best response from all individuals.

Limits to Information and Preferences Enforcement

Information is not readily available. It has to be retrieved by higher levels of the state hierarchy from lower levels down to economic actors. Information withholding is a very important component of bargaining between the authorities and economic actors over the distribution of resources and planned tasks, as many authors have argued (Birman 1978; Kornai 1986a; Laky 1979). In the absence of the market, the main mechanism for allocating resources is bargaining.[23] When central planners know the production functions of enterprises, they can easily determine feasible plan quotas. However, with the increase of informational complexity due to economic modernization, the relative bargaining position of local authorities and producers vis-à-vis central authorities increases because of the inability of the central planners to process the information needed to monitor economic activities. Distortions in information originating from lower levels of the hierarchy weaken the effectiveness of the planning process. Because economic actors seek to secure the most easily attainable planned tasks (they seek to maximize the ratio of input to planned output), the targets set by public economic policy consume more resources than otherwise required. Thus the ability of the state to collect infor-

---

[22] For a discussion of Gramsci's concept of hegemony in capitalism, see Carnoy (1984).

[23] For an extensive discussion, see Kamiński (1989b) and Kamiński and Sołtan (1989).

mation critically hinges on assuring cooperation of the lower layers of the hierarchy, which cannot be taken for granted.

The inevitable autonomy of actors (enterprises and lower level authorities), in part because of information-processing constraints and the dominance of bargaining as a method of allocating resources, makes the enforcement of a state's preferences impossible.

The process of information gathering and allocation of resources based on bargaining generates tensions that limit the range of feasible public policies and the state's ability to enforce its preferences. Within the ideological parameters set by state socialism, the party has monopolized the domain of public policy initiatives; all special interests have been channeled into forms of association that, except during the periods of political crises, remain controlled by the party (White, Gardner, and Schöpflin 1982). Perfect knowledge combined with a monopoly over policy initiative and the means of policy implementation are crucial for the socialist state to identify the best strategies and enforce its preferences. In its absence, when the state does not act as a coherent body, information indispensable to devise a rational plan of development that will ensure the best use of available resources is strongly curtailed and economic growth performance is impaired.

Thus the subordination and loyalty of the party apparatus to its leadership and the cooperation of lower levels of state administration and party apparatus affect the capacity of the state to identify and enforce preferences. But neither the party nor the public is passive and plastic to the power of leadership. Loyalty of the party and its apparatus as well as public acceptance has to be won by leadership. Some, although limited, level of public acceptance can be obtained through skillful perception management, the distribution of rewards, the use of repression (police controls), or some combination of these techniques.

The failure to strike a "right" balance between the carrot and the stick undermines the state's ability to ensure satisfactory economic performance and political stability. Excessive repression demoralizes the party-state administration. The provision of resources to the local authorities without hierarchical controls on their use depresses allocative efficiency and fosters "dash for growth" strategies, as happened in Poland in the 1970s. In the absence of social and market-type financial checks, there is always a danger that too large a share of resources will be allocated for investment purposes and that they will not be allocated where they would be most efficiently used. Although neither the local nor the central authorities desire to overstress the system, the systemic forces push them in this direction. The only solution to this problem compatible with the institutional design of state socialism is to suppress conflicting interests.

Whether or not this drive on the part of all actors to increase their share of the centrally distributed resources produces a crisis depends upon the ability of central authorities to impose discipline. The lack of discipline may be due to the strength of local authorities, to the militancy of industrial workers, or to the disintegration and demoralization of the party. The history of Gierek's regime in the 1970s, for instance, provides an extreme illustration of the loss of control by the central authorities over the economy. Gierek's regime sought to maintain social stability by indiscriminately allocating investment funds and granting wage increases. The strategy failed because the central authorities did not back these efforts with increased supplies of consumer goods.

Despite growing demoralization and the indifference and cynicism of the party apparatus and society at large, other socialist states have pursued strategies more in line with their economic capabilities and the constraints built into the institutional design of state socialism. These states maintained a degree of control and prevented outbreaks of social unrest for much longer than did Poland. Their "success" was also attributable to social inertia and the sophisticated use of methods of adaptation and social control, backed by a vast network of repressive apparatus and the reliance on extra-legal activities (Schöpflin 1981; White 1986). As a result, they were more successful in suppressing individual interests (Poznański 1986b). Yet they all followed a "path of inefficient economic growth" (Economic Commission for Europe 1986, 135).

The fusion of the state and the economy places other limits. They go beyond limits to information collection and processing to perfect knowledge and the state's capability to enforce its preferences. These limits can be presented in terms of Max Weber's dual concept of formal and substantive economic rationality. Formal economic rationality refers to the "extent of quantitative calculation or accounting which is technically possible and which is actually applied" (Weber 1978, 85). It denotes the most efficient use of resources within a *specific institutional environment and determined objectives*. Substantive rationality involves an assessment of the institutional framework itself in terms of *ultimate values* (Weber 1978, 85). Economic action guided by substantive rationality aims at ultimate values rather than just the efficient use of resources.

Departures from formal economic rationality are common. Unless they feed upon themselves, they do not endanger the viability of a politico-economic order. As Albert Hirschman (1970, 1) noted: "Under any economic, social, or political system, individuals, business firms, and organizations in general are subject to lapses from efficient, rational, law abiding, virtuous, or otherwise functional behavior." The frame of reference for assessing what constitutes a departure from "virtuous" behavior in state socialism is not unambiguously defined. It is not clear which behavior ensures the proper functioning of state socialism. But when the economy is fused with the state, the dominance of political criteria in defining functional behavior flies in the face of the efficient use of resources.

The incompatibility of command planning with economic efficiency, which leads to the economic nonviability of state socialism, was suggested in the 1930s by Ludvig von Mises and Friedrich von Hayek in a great debate on the economic rationality of socialism. Their conclusion, rephrased in terms of Max Weber's dual rationality concept, is that formal economic rationality is lower under command planning than under a market system. In other words, command economies are not viable because they cannot efficiently use economic resources.[24]

Abraham Bergson (1986) later observed that the issue was not whether command planning was viable, but which system, capitalism or socialism, is more efficient in practice. But the crux of the matter is that the absence of a mechanism for correcting deviations from economic efficiency results in their cumulation, which ultimately leads to an economic slowdown or even contraction.

The possibility of a general decay of state socialism is enhanced by the absence of a feedback mechanism for identifying inefficient enterprises, production lines, and capital projects. When prices are determined by the state, not by the interplay of supply and demand, no information is readily available as to what activities have comparative advantage.

At issue, here, is not the redistribution of resources through the state (or more precisely its budget) that results in maintaining inefficient producers, but the lack of information to distinguish between the efficient and the inefficient. As a result, attaining the same objectives requires more and more inputs. The infusion of new technologies, or the activation of reserves (e.g., hidden unemployment in agriculture) inherited from the past, may temporarily defer this trend toward increasing inefficiency. But once the reserves are depleted and access to new technologies becomes difficult—because of, for instance, high indebtedness—the economic performance declines. Thus the fusion of the economy with the state significantly weakens the homeostatic controls that would force an adjustment before it becomes excessively costly, both politically and economically.

Substantive rationality links action to ultimate ends, not just the efficient use of resources. As was argued earlier, the ends that state socialism is *capable of attaining* have nothing to do with microeconomic efficiency. Janos Kornai (1986a) argues that state socialism cannot meet the ultimate test of microeconomic efficiency, because the latter would run against such principles of socialist ethics as solidarity, equal pay for equal work, and job security. This implies that a rejection of these principles, or ultimate ends, would automatically restore both formal and substantive rationality. But this is not so because

---

[24] The reasons, as we have seen, are rooted mainly in the inability of central authorities to enforce their preferences.

the ultimate ends, as exemplified by Kornai's principles of socialist ethics, are *not* externally imposed on the economic system.

To the contrary, the system's behavior is formally rational given its set of substantive ends. Full employment (job security), for instance, is not a policy objective but a result of built-in capacity to generate persistent shortages of services and goods as well as factors of production. Unemployment, even if declared by the authorities to be a policy goal, would not necessarily materialize as long as the economy remains fused with the state. On the other hand, the inevitable violations of economic efficiency adversely affect economic growth performance and, therefore, preclude the realization of the Communist society.

The congruence between systemic outcomes and the need to meet some socially desirable objectives, even at the expense of violating the principles of economic efficiency, is accountable for blocking the changes that would improve economic efficiency. Job security, a hallmark of state socialism, increases social resistance to the rejection of the arrangements that would not automatically ensure full employment. State socialism creates a tacit alliance between the nomenklatura thriving on privileges obtained by directly controlling the economy and a sizable portion of the population willing to sacrifice uncertain extra material gratification for job security. The focus on shortage management combined with its legitimating aspect reduces the organizational capability to cope with economic problems. Any significant change in the rules of the state involvement in the economy threatens to undermine the compliance-generating mechanism based inter alia on patron-client relationships fueled by shortages. The range of corrective actions that the elite can implement without threatening political stability is thus significantly curtailed. By the same token, no mechanism of recuperation is readily available.

Capacity for Redesigning Itself

A cursory examination of the history of economic reforms confirms that the possibilities for change within the confines of state socialism are quite limited. Since the late 1950s, economists and policy makers first in Eastern Europe and later in the Soviet Union have recognized the need to change the arrangements underlying interaction between the state and economy. They have recognized a contradiction between the current system of planning and management and the requirements associated with the transition to an intensive stage of economic growth. Economic reforms have become a recurrent theme on the political agenda. The need for reform has been justified in terms of the necessity to create an organizational environment favorable to modern economic growth. Evidence is ample that they have failed either to put state socialism on a path of intensive growth or to eliminate shortages; capital and labor productivity have been stagnant, and both macro- and microeconomic decisions have been guided by bargaining and the management of shortages (Comisso and Tyson 1986).

A distinction between institutional change that alters the rules governing the interaction between the state and economic actors and economic policy designed to attain economic objectives without altering the rules of the game is relevant to an understanding of the potential for decay inherent in state socialism. Reform, understood as "meaningful change in the operating *principles* of an economic system" (Brus 1988, 65), would fall in the category of institutional change, whereas changes in the number of ministries, tax rates, allocation of resources, exports, and imports, which are exogenous to the economic system, fit into the second category. The question addressed here is the extent to which the state has the capacity to reform itself in order to adapt to a changing environment.

The obstacles to redesigning the state's interaction with the economic actors (i.e., its organizational framework) to meet domestic and external challenges are formidable. They are rooted in the ideology, the nature of power relationships, and the patterns of social relations that have emerged as a result of the removal of the institutions that separate the state from the economy and the society.

The change within state socialism is limited to administrative planning and management procedures, and the range for potential corrective action is rather narrow. Improvements consist of the eradication of some practices that fly in the face of common sense like, for instance, the use of global output as a measure of enterprise performance or the introduction of cost accountability in enterprises. Once the obviously irrational procedures that produce some of the worst distortions are removed, there is very little room for improvement. The "reform proposals" that were published in various countries between the mid-1950s and the 1980s contained, as a rule, the same components, for example, alterations in the performance criteria of enterprises, closer integration of annual and long-term plans, and contractual delivery obligations. Limited implementation was usually followed by a reversal of some of the changes, thus setting a pattern of progression and retrogression.[25] Their recurrence suggests that the pool of available ideas for the improvement of state socialism is narrow and that even these limited measures have never been fully implemented.

One alternative to administrative modifications that has emerged during institutional experimenting is development of a "socialist market." The adjective socialist implies that the market is treated instrumentally to improve the quality of planning and coordination. It is something to be squeezed into an administratively controlled environment. This raises two problems—ideological and technical. Communist ideology assumes progressive demonetization

[25] See, for instance, Knight (1983); Nuti (1987b).

and the disappearance of commodity relations. Use of the instruments and categories of "capitalist" origin, implied in the blueprint for a "socialist market," is an admission of the failure of Communist ideology. It neither provides guidance nor justifies action. Although the categories of market provenance were reluctantly introduced under the pressures of economic inefficiency, the economy has remained fused with the state. Underlying ideological considerations is the realization by the elites that market reforms would substantially alter the existing structures of control, ownership, and exchange.

The technical problem is that the economy cannot be both fused and separated from the state. When a fusion dominates (Kamiński 1989b), even the private sector becomes subsumed by the state. There has been a trend toward replacing directive "physical" commands with financial instruments transplanted from market economies. The market provenance of interest rates, taxes, and other financial indicators used extensively in "reformed" socialist states (e.g., Hungary and Poland) has not resulted in the emergence of the market mechanism or the disappearance of persistent shortages. Attempts at marketization without an overhaul of the hierarchical bureaucratic structure commanding the economy have not improved economic growth performance. As the Polish economist Adam Lipowski (1987, 5) showed, effective "planning is possible only when the addressees of plans relate to each other through genuine markets in which money plays an active role."

The progression and retrogression of Hungarian reforms since 1968 represent an extreme case of a shift to market instruments under state socialism. This experience shows that the deficiencies of an approach seeking to reconcile physical central planning with financial controls of enterprises cannot be overcome. Assessments of the degree to which patterns of behavior of the state and economic actors in Hungary deviate from those typical of "nonreformed" socialist states shed some light on the range of responses available to the socialist state. There seems to be a consensus among Hungarian and Western experts that the Hungarian economy in the 1980s was still subject to the centralizing logic of shortages. Having carefully analyzed developments in the Hungarian economy in the early 1980s, Kornai (1986a, 111) concludes that "the Hungarian system may be still considered a shortage economy to a considerable degree." Hence, changes in the planning and management system have fallen short of removing the political and economic mechanisms of shortage generation.

Kornai (1986a) also shows that the price reforms of the early 1980s intended to link enterprise performance to financial incentives failed. Price-setting rules turned out to be subject to individual negotiations with the state; the rules were neither stable nor impersonal. In spite of changes in the mix of instruments used by the state to enforce its preferences and in discretionary controls and the distribution of formal authority, the mode by which economic activity was steered through secretive bargaining and shortage management has survived.

The replacement of some quantitative directives by financial instruments has not drastically changed the rules of the game. Patterns of behavior are not shaped by impersonal market forces but by negotiations with the authorities. Assessing the Hungarian system, Paul Marer (1987, 244) notes "the authorities and not the market establish and manipulate the regulators by trying to simulate—generally with not a great deal of success, in industry especially— what the market would do if it existed . . . but . . . it is utopian to believe that the operation of a market can be simulated by planners instead of it being allowed to develop." Without institutional changes aimed at eradicating the fusion of the state and the economy, the deficiencies of the approach that seeks to reconcile physical central planning with financial steering of enterprises cannot be overcome.

The need for an adjustment that may require changes in economic policies and institutional arrangements may stem from domestic considerations. Domestically, it arises when the economy falls short of delivering goods and services needed to assure social stability. Repression combined with a safety-net provided by the state and job security may increase social tolerance. As Mieczysław F. Rakowski (1987, 3) observed, while commenting on the dismal conditions of everyday life in Poland in 1987, "If a capitalist society were transplanted into our economic reality, it would quickly start a revolutionary struggle." Thus even when the economy fails to generate desirable surplus, the pressures to correct the situation are either counterproductive (e.g., strikers' demands of higher wages) or extremely weak.

Indeed, the timing of successive waves of debates on economic reform in Eastern Europe has not been shaped by already demonstrated symptoms of deteriorating performance and economic reforms, but it has been determined by such political factors as pressures from Moscow, usually emanating during periods of succession, or leadership change in East European countries. This suggests the absence of a relationship between deteriorating economic performance and the recognition of a need for corrective actions, except when economic deterioration produces political crises. This has often been the case in Poland (see chap. 3). In addition, in contrast to a market economy where deterioration is reflected in an excess of supply over demand, in state socialism economic deterioration is accompanied by growing shortages. The dilemma is that this calls for centralized controls whereas amelioration in the economic performance that results in decreased pressures of excessive demand provides little incentive to take risks associated with economic reforms. Therefore, neither of these conditions is conducive to organizational change.

This absence of pressure from below is not necessarily compensated by actions from the top, especially when adjustment requires an institutional change in the nature of power relations. This amounts to a call for the party-state to reform itself, because the burden is put on those party and state *apparatchiks* (party administration) whose position is likely to be altered. The omnipresence of the state and institutionally built-in politico-economic order favor changes in the policies or in the organization that do not affect those power relations derived internally from the control of goods and services distribution. Therefore, the pressure for adjustment is considerably weakened. As the history of economic reform in Eastern Europe shows, there is no political willingness to assure compatibility between the growing complexity of the economy and the steering mechanism, which should become more sophisticated.

The declining international competitiveness of the economy in socialist states emphasizes the need for adjustment. But even the pressures of external adversity as a substitute for competition (Leibenstein 1966) are not sufficiently strong to evoke an institutional overhaul (at least as long as the economy is not on the verge of collapse, as are those in Hungary and Poland). Because socialist domestic economies are insulated from the world markets and producers cannot respond autonomously to the changing external conditions, the responsibility for identifying problem areas and selecting appropriate responses falls on the state. Assuming away other obstacles to adjustment, time delays are unavoidable in collecting, processing, and transmitting information through bureaucratic channels.

The weak link between domestic and international prices further erodes responsive capacity because of the difficulties involved in identifying and closing inefficient enterprises. State socialism "contradicts the establishment of macroeconomic structures and product structures competitive in the world market," as Hungarian economist András Köves (1985, 111) has succinctly put it. The poor export performance of these economies demonstrates the incompatibility of domestic structures of state socialism with the operation of the world economy (Poznański 1988a; Winiecki 1987a, 30–32). It is striking that even the very high levels of international indebtedness experienced by such countries as Hungary and Poland have failed to overhaul the fusion of the state and the economy (Kornai 1986b; Kamiński 1989b). Although the regimes of state socialism might have a strong motive (e.g., to preserve national security in a potentially hostile world) to adjust their economies to the exigencies of world markets, the reliance on the Soviet umbrella and the ability to insulate the military sector weakened pressures for adjustment that would involve meaningful institutional changes.

The institutional "infrastructure" of state socialism not only leaves little room for adjustment between the demands of the economic sphere and the demands of the state structure but, because economic decisions have been assigned to political processes, it also creates the potential for strong resistance to meaningful changes in the operating principles of the economic system. The range of solutions that would not violate the inner logic of political and economic mechanisms of state socialism is limited; the range of demands on the socialist state is limitless.

CAPACITY FOR EXTERNAL ADJUSTMENT

When confronted with a balance of payments disequilibrium, there are two policy options: to finance it or to adjust to it. Adjustment involves stabilization measures to reduce domestic spending on goods, services, and investment. The reduction in real absorption rates should be combined with measures designed to make the economy more flexible and more efficient. Adjustment may involve continued borrowing, but instead of financing current consumption, the credits are used to restructure the economy. The second option is a "wait and see" approach. The option of financing the disequilibrium postpones implementation of adjustment and austerity measures, which usually are highly unpopular, by borrowing from external sources or by using accumulated international reserves. Except for political instability and economic cost considerations, the kind of economic system, that is, administrative or marketized, has little pertinence for the choice between the "wait and see" and adjustment options.

The state socialist economic system, however, determines policy instruments used to implement the adjustment strategy. In principle, the adjustment strategy involves two types of policy: expenditure-reducing and expenditure-switching. Although both of them aim to cut purchasing power, the expenditure-switching policies are designed to encourage exports and discourage imports through changes in relative prices rather than through direct cuts in the expenditures of households, government, and enterprises. For instance, a devaluation encourages consumers to substitute domestic goods for imports and producers to divert goods from the domestic to the export market. The underlying assumption is that both consumers and suppliers are sensitive to price signals. As a rule this does not apply to producers in state socialism. The absence of markets confines adjustment strategy to expenditure-reducing policies.

CONCLUSION

State socialism has serious institutional flaws especially when assessed against a backdrop of an external environment that requires rapid adaptation. Like many theocratic and authoritarian regimes from the distant past, its capacity to adapt to an environment that rewards flexibility and responsiveness is limited. Fusion of the state limits the scope for experimenting with various methods of organizing interactions between the state and the economy. The state has neither adequate information nor the ability to fully enforce its preferences and elicit the best response. The central authorities have to compromise with local preferences to the point of becoming their prisoners, as actors tend to pursue their own interests even if such action is detrimental to strategies adopted by the state. Their cooperation cannot be taken for granted.

State socialism has evolved in response to changing domestic and international circumstances. With some exceptions (e.g., Romania), state socialist regimes have become gentler and kinder to their populaces. "Bribing" has largely replaced coercion as a source of mass compliance. Because of the increased selectivity in suppression of diverse interests and more sophisticated conflict management skills, the autonomy of the society has increased while a regime's previous aspiration to total control has decreased (Kamiński and Sołtan 1989). The party-state has become more sensitive to popular demands and, therefore, "more" accountable to the ruled. Movement has been away from instrumental/purposive law to universal law, although less lawlessness does not necessarily amount to a rule of law (because soft law constraint still prevails and so does the principle of rule bending). Finally, although the state and the economy have remained fused, the state has withdrawn from direct control over some domains of the economy. Although the principle of variability is in effect, the shift has been away from detailed physical commands to broader financial parameters. The economy remains supply-constrained in spite of the expansion of contractual links.

The evolution has failed to increase the developmental potential of state socialist countries. To the contrary, despite very substantial savings rates, economic growth rates in most socialist countries have fallen since the late 1950s.[26] The survival of state socialism through withdrawal from ideological chains and political aspirations of the ruling elite has occurred at the expense of its declining capacity to generate steadily increasing surplus. Although the implemented measures have assured prolonged periods of political stability, they have only deferred the arrival of a general systemic crisis—the crisis that can be solved only by throwing the institutional design into the dustbin of history.

Various political concessions fueled, for instance, by fears of the repetition of Stalinist terror, which did not spare members of the ruling elite, or by threat of social upheavals have contributed to the erosion of administrative discipline crucial to the functioning of the political economy of state socialism. Mario Nuti (1988, 355) notes: "The need for reform is intimately linked to the systemic difficulties of socialist economies. These difficulties are primarily due to a generalized failure to provide the incentives to operate an otherwise quite perfected planning process. Neither enterprises, nor workers have the incentive to offer the best response." Neither have those at the very top of the party-state hierarchy any incentive to act in line with the broader national interest. The lack of purposiveness pervades the whole society. Because the original purpose of transforming society has been replaced by short-term considera-

---

[26] In attempting to maintain economic growth, state socialist regimes have had to use increasing amounts of labor and capital. The Soviet Union, for instance, now has to expend twice as much capital as it did in the early 1970s to achieve the same increment in national income (Hewett 1985, 288).

tions favoring the status quo, the noninnovative loyal—those instrumental to the achievement of this objective—have been rewarded.

The prolonged periods of visible economic waste as well as the penalty and reward structure that defies a common sense of responsibility and integrity produce societal apathy and indifference. The authorities can dominate the society, but they cannot mobilize it. Without a market environment, or its functional equivalent, providing for autonomous stimuli to innovation and microeconomic efficiency, nothing is left in the institutional design to increase flexibility and productive as well as allocative efficiency. All these factors contribute to the growing cost of sustaining economic development. The only alternative to inevitable economic stagnation and a declining standard of living is the overhaul of state socialism. In this sense, development and diversity are foes of state socialism; they create a trap from which there is no escape.

CHAPTER TWO

The Limited "Reformability" of State Socialism

THE FUSION of the state and the economy accounts for the limited experimentation with various institutional frameworks and, therefore, for the limited repertoire of public policy instruments available to the socialist state. As will be shown, most tools of indirect control are not available to policy makers in state socialism because of the fusion.

Poland's "reform measures" shed light on the limits to institutional redesign under conditions of duress. Poland's experience offers unique insights into the reformability of state socialism. The inconsistencies between institutional framework and policy instruments have been dramatically revealed because of domestic socioeconomic and external economic pressures. Because the radical reform measures have never been contemplated under satisfactory economic performance conditions, the Polish experience is more generally valid for studying the "reform" of other state socialist societies. It shows that the use of financial instruments with market origins when fusion is not eliminated increases shortages and inflation simultaneously. Poland's experience should also warn reformers in other state socialist countries that the Polish path taken from 1981 to 1989 should not be followed.

The major changes in the Polish economic system introduced in the 1980s have affected the repertoire of economic instruments available to the state. They have also affected the behavior patterns of economic actors as the ways to pursue the best use of resources have been modified. Among the major questions to be addressed: Has the use of various instruments of market provenance led to effective decentralization in economic decision making or has it merely replaced "physical" directives with "financial" directives? To what extent have the response patterns of enterprises changed in response to economic reform measures? What is the role of the state budget?

The structure of the analysis in this chapter is as follows. The first part sets the framework for analyzing the reduction in scope of mandatory central planning. The second part reviews reform measures implemented in the 1980s. The next two sections discuss the changes in the role of state budget and the changes in the mix of public economic policy instruments in Poland during the so-called first stage of the implementation of economic reform measures between 1982 and 1986. Finally, the last part compares the scope of a switch from direct to indirect controls in Poland with changes in Hungary and China.

LIMITS TO REFORM IN A NONMARKET ENVIRONMENT: CONCEPTUAL CONSIDERATIONS

By taking as a criterion the dominant allocative mechanisms, two clusters of solutions can be distinguished: the market mechanism and the administrative mechanism. They roughly correspond to capitalism, or market economy, and state socialism, or central planning, respectively. These two mechanisms imply distinctive modes of organizing the interaction between the state and the economy as well as different types of state involvement in the economy. The essence of indirect intervention is to shape relevant components of the decision environment of economic actors by making autonomous self-interested responses (adaptation) congruent with the state's interests. The important feature of indirect control is that it is based mainly on *indirect* intervention subject to relatively stable impersonal rules. This type of intervention contrasts sharply with intervention in an economic system from which the market mechanism has been deliberately removed. The administrative or bureaucratic (Kornai 1986b) mechanism is related to state intervention based on direct controls; its major form of intervention is the "individually addressed" directive.

Taking into account the dominant forms of ownership, four ideal types of economic institutional arrangements can be identified (see table 2.1): market socialism, free enterprise, state socialism, and war capitalism. Although there can be different mixes of public and private ownership, the dominance of an administrative or political mechanism excludes the existence of a mixed economy. The sizable private sector in Poland, for example, still operates in an environment that could be characterized as paternalistic because many of the rules shaping its financial situation are *directly*, on an individual basis, shaped by the state's ad hoc interventions. On the other hand, as long as a market environment exists, it is possible to achieve different mixes of administrative and market mechanisms of allocation.

The history of aborted reform blueprints suggests that three major approaches to modifying the state-owned economic system can be identified. One can be termed the administrative, or organizational approach; the second, a financial approach; and the third, which has been gradually emerging since

TABLE 2.1
Modes of Organizing Economic Activity

	Mechanism of Allocation	
Forms of Ownership	*Market*	*Administration*
Public (state)	Market socialism	State socialism
Private	Free enterprise	War capitalism

the mid-1980s, may be dubbed the³ market-oriented approach. The administrative-organizational approach focuses on the improvement of the administrative mechanism by developing more accurate planning procedures and viable organizational structures. As a rule, it calls for the closer integration of annual and medium-term plans and the incorporation of a larger number of economic actors in the task of setting plan objectives. Its focus is on designing more transparent administrative procedures to enhance the discipline of enterprise management and to clarify the decision authority within a modified organizational environment. Organizational changes have usually comprised a change in the number of functional and branch ministries and their respective responsibilities. This administrative streamlining usually has not been sufficient to move the economy toward decentralization of production and investment authority.

The financial approach focuses on enhancing the discipline of economic actors through replacing directive "physical" commands with financial instruments transplanted from market economies. This approach usually calls for the reduction of the scope and detail of plans. In its extreme form, enterprises are to operate without mandatory plans imposed from top. Instead, central planners tune tax rates, subsidies, and so forth, to elicit maximum effort from enterprises. This approach consists of imposing financial instruments on the existing hierarchical structure. Its implementation does not result in the movement out of the cell "state socialism" as depicted in table 2.1.

Finally, the last approach seeks to dismantle the institutional structure of central planning. Its objective is to create a market environment while retaining the dominant share of state ownership. The creation of a market economy has been a declared policy objective in Hungary and Poland.

The market-oriented change is qualitatively different from the first two. In this respect, many analyses of the economic system under state socialism are misleading. Władysław Jermakowicz (1988), for instance, describes the regulatory system of the economy as a three-dimensional space. The first coordinate (direct regulation) depicts administrative directives expressed in physical or other accounting units. The second coordinate (indirect regulation) corresponds to financial instruments of market provenance or shorter parameters, while the third (market) stands for the degree of competition and autonomy of economic actors. This conceptualization, which suggests the existence of a three-dimensional "reform menu" curve, is erroneous because both administration and market cannot be dominant mechanisms of regulation in an economic system. Instead one may visualize two, two-dimensional "reform menu" curves: one for state socialism depicting various combinations of directives and financial instruments, and the other for market systems depicting various combinations of the state's intervention in markets.

The approaches to economic reforms, except for the administrative-organizational one, assume experimentation with different combinations of financial and physical directives. The changes in the economic system of state socialism implemented thus far can be presented as a downward movement along the "reform" menu curve. The market is not activated for the state-owned sector.

The changes in the mix of directives and financial measures do not amount to a significant qualitative change in the nature of the state's intervention in the economy. As long as financial instruments belong to the realm of direct rather than indirect controls, both the behavioral patterns of economic actors and the dominant mechanism of allocation retain their basic characteristics. The mechanism is based on direct controls. Financial instruments are direct controls if (1) the parameters used in the formulas to assess enterprise performance are subject to direct negotiations between producers and the planning hierarchy; (2) the enterprises are not accountable for losses and profits. In more general terms, no clear-cut institutional line is drawn between the state's authority for direct intervention and its authority to control the external decision environment of the enterprise.

Direct financial controls require a discretionary tax policy and the use of subsidies. To finance subsidies, some products have to be overpriced. As a result, prices do not reflect scarcities and resource productivities. The larger and more widespread the discrepancies between costs and prices, the more active is the role of the state budget in financial intermediation among enterprises. Extensive microeconomic intervention is then a dominant form of government policies. Instead of a reduction of the administrative burden usually associated with indirect controls that absorb fewer administrative resources, the burden may actually increase with the growth in the number of "direct" financial instruments used in a nonmarket environment. Because enterprises are not separate accounting entities fully responsible for profits and losses, the introduction of direct financial controls does not provide extra incentives to respond to financial signals and to honor various contractual obligations. Because no link exists between economic results and enterprise performance, the financial results of enterprises do not reflect changes in productivity. The absence of clearly defined rules for microeconomic intervention contributes to the emergence of bargaining over tax rates and subsidies as a major method of resource allocation. Under these circumstances, indirect tools, such as fiscal and monetary policy, will not provide for a congruence between state economic objectives and enterprise responses. The crux of the matter is that as long as controls are not effected by the price mechanism, the state has little choice but to rely on direct forms of control.

Thus, the existence of bargaining between producers and planners is an indication of the dominance of direct controls. The rules of bargaining are neither stable nor universal. Their addressee is not a situation to be controlled but an economic actor. Crafting rules for each producer or group of producers renders macroeconomic policies ineffective, thus setting the stage for microeconomic intervention. Bargaining also erases the link between the economic performance of the enterprise and its financial results, which necessitates state budget financial intermediation between loss-producing enterprises and those that are excessively profitable, given the state price policy.

The above discussion should not suggest that the change in the mix of instruments does not involve a departure from the traditional mandatory planning mechanism. With the growth in the informational complexity of planning and managing, the degree of autonomy of economic actors has, in most cases, increased as has their sophistication in bargaining for scarce resources. Enterprise management has a greater say in both the choice of output and investment decisions. Typical lines of vertical subordination have been supplemented, but not replaced, by the horizontal lines (contracts among producers), and the number of products subject to rationing has decreased. Direct administrative coercion has been reduced, and economic actors are left with a wider range of options. Nonetheless, unless economic reform measures violate the conditions just mentioned (negotiations of parameters and the lack of full accountability for losses and profits), the tools introduced fall into the set of direct tools of public economic policy in spite of their "market" provenance.

Even if direct controls prevail over indirect controls, central planning authorities' decisions concerning money supply, interest rates, and revenue-raising instruments are likely to have an impact on enterprises and the rules of the "bargaining" game. However, the impact may be individually offset by various compensations in the form of tax reliefs or subsidies. In other words, through changes in the environment within which the planning process occurs, the activation of the indirect tools of public economic policies defines a new decision situation. As long as its components are subject to bargaining, the tools will be "individually" corrected. Under these circumstances, the essence of fiscal policy consists of eliminating the distortions in the financial results of the enterprises caused by the state's actions.

A more complicated case introduces a new principle of tax levying. For instance, calculating the turnover tax at a fixed rate rather than as a difference between sales and cost links retail prices with producer prices. If the prices are not at market clearing levels, this opens a possibility for inflationary pressures. Therefore, if the authorities want to maintain price stability, they will have to "weaken" this link by budgetary subsidies or extra charges on enterprise net revenue. Consequently, a measure designed to make a producer more responsive to consumer demand may turn out to be self-defeating; instead of coupling financial results with economic performance, it calls for a similar or higher level of involvement of the state budget in income redistribution among enterprises. Suppressed inflation exacerbates difficulties associated with the use of fiscal instruments to achieve macroeconomic objectives. As a result, the changes in the use of various fiscal instruments amount to a change in the name of the revenue-raising instrument. Incidentally, this example also suggests that a different mix of policy instruments is not likely to produce significant changes in the behavioral patterns of planners and other economic actors.

Several tests can be used to assess whether an economic system is close to breaking its symbiotic relationship with the state. First, following Kornai's (1980) path-breaking study, one test may check for the existence of shortage-generating mechanisms. Shortages are bred by taut planning, which encourages inventory hoarding and generates income increases without the corresponding growth in productivity. Their common symptom is the absence of full "domestic convertibility" of money, which is just another label for market disequilibria. Equilibrating the economy is a condition for activating the indirect tools of the regulatory structure. Thus, as long as the management of shortages, an equivalent of various forms of direct or indirect rationing, remains one of the major tasks of public economic policy, the economic system remains essentially intact although the mix of directive controls may change.

Second, with the greater role of financial instruments and growing budget "hardness," the significance of prices for the enterprises may increase. Rationing means that consumer access to goods and services depends on demonstrating public desire and need to obtain the required allotment and/or establishing a network of personal contacts with those in charge of rationing. Thus, the degree of bargaining, as illustrated by the extent of individually tailored financial instruments, may be used as a test of the degree to which the economic system has changed.

Third, another set of measures is related to the role of the state budget in the redistribution of incomes among enterprises. The growth of the role of the state budget suggests a centralizing tendency no matter what change has occurred in the mix of physical and financial instruments.[1]

CHANGES IN THE ECONOMIC SYSTEM IN THE 1980s

In the 1980s, the issue of comprehensive economic reform was the subject of an intensive public debate in 1981 and from 1986 to 1988. During the period following the imposition of martial law, the legislative framework of the reform was introduced as well as some innovative measures. The government's effort was not sustained beyond 1984. As Jerzy Kleer (1988) noted, "Although over the last years political elites and the government have been per-

---

[1] Taking into account that a theoretical justification for the use of budgetary provisions and fiscal policy is market failure, the absence of a market economy in state socialism raises several questions. What role does fiscal policy play? What is the rationale for the use of fiscal instruments in a reformed economic system? What are the implications of the increased reliance of the planning hierarchy on financial instruments for the response patterns of enterprises? To what extent do they become profit maximizers? Does the introduction of fiscal instruments without monetization of the economy merely produce a tendency toward "overregulation" of the economic system?

sistently stressing willingness to implement a wide range of economic and social reforms, nonetheless—at least between 1984 and mid-1987—they were not sufficiently determined to implement them.'' Once the crisis was diffused, and the government became again less accountable to the society, the radical components of the reform were dropped.

In spite of the rhetoric to the contrary, reform was derailed. In late 1986, the Five-Year Plan draft together with a package of eleven laws which, if passed, would effectively have put the 1981 Program of Economic reform to rest, triggered an effective protest by reform supporters. The eleven laws were shelved, and a new debate ensued on the future shape of the economic system. The new program was dubbed the second stage of economic reform.

What distinguished the reform blueprints of 1981 and 1988 was a perception among the authorities that a radical change in the rules of the game in the economic sphere was the last resort for overcoming the crisis. Although Gierek was able to contain the 1970–1971 crisis by tapping external resources, this option was not available to policy makers in the 1980s. The depth of the economic crisis, the self-limiting Solidarity revolution, and Solidarity's legacy set a new tone for the debates on economic reform.

The blueprint of the Party-Government Commission for Economic Reform, ''Kierunki reformy gospodarczej'' (The directions of economic reform), formally accepted by the 9th Extraordinary Party Congress in 1981, was a significant departure from the institutional framework of the economic system erected in the late 1940s.[2] It went beyond the earlier blueprints by implicitly linking political changes with changes in the economic system. The government's economic policies were to be brought under the control of the Sejm. In addition, other mechanisms of social participation were to be introduced. Instead of fulfilling planned quotas, enterprises were to become profit/value added maximizers operating in a competitive environment. Thus the program directly challenged the lack of direct accountability of policy makers and the principle of fusion between the government apparatus and the economy. It called for a significant dismantling of central controls and for the establishment of direct industrial democracy. This was by far the most radical blueprint yet proposed even when judged against the most reformed countries of state socialism. Stanisław Gomułka and Jacek Rostowski (1984, 388) noted that if the blueprint were implemented in full, ''the Polish reform would be more radical than the Hungarian, and if bankruptcies were really allowed, it would be more radical even than the Yugoslav reform.''

---

[2] See ''Kierunki reformy gospodarczej-projekt: Projeckt ustaw o przedsiębiorstwach państwowych-o samorządzie przedsiębiorstwa państwowego'' (The directions of economic reform project: The project of laws on state enterprises—on workers' self-management of state enterprises), *Trybuna Ludu* (Warsaw), July 1981. The official blueprint was the least radical among several programs debated in 1981. For a discussion of the programs, see Fallenbuchl (1981b). For a review of Solidarity's program, see Kamiński (1985).

In contrast to earlier discussions of economic reform measures, the program recognized the necessity of major changes not only in planning and management instruments but also in the framework of the party-state involvement in the national economy. At the core of the reform blueprint was the transfer of some powers from the government to society and economic actors. It also called for changes in the institutional tenets of the economic system by introducing strict and transparent rules of economic intervention by the state. Thus, it challenged the rule variability principle.

Direct industrial democracy, strongly reminiscent of the 1956 "October" blueprint, was to be achieved by thorough organizational and financial changes in enterprise regime. As the enterprises were to be self-dependent, self-managed, and self-financed, this may be called the SSS regime. Self-dependence implied emancipation from a central plan imposed from above. The scope of central planning was to be reduced mainly to parameters of indirect controls, budget-financed social infrastructure, and large-scale projects in key economic sectors. Social participation in central planning (i.e., in choosing the objectives and the means to attain them) was also envisioned. Self-management meant granting decision autonomy to workers' councils in enterprises employing more than three hundred workers and directly to workers in smaller enterprises. Self-financing, in turn, denoted less financial support from the government and a link between an enterprise's financial results and its employees' incomes as well as enterprise investment activity. Wages and bonuses were to be directly linked to production and productivity growth, whereas the state would guarantee minimum wages. In consequence, a soft-financial constraint, in Kornai's terminology, was to be replaced by a hard-financial constraint.

The authors of the blueprint understood that the SSS regime would require the restructuring of prices, the introduction of competitive markets and an overhaul of the existing banking system. Prices were to be brought to market clearing levels. Competition was to be encouraged through antimonopoly laws and the exit of inefficient producers, that is, bankruptcy. The issue of entry, symmetrical to exit, was not mentioned, however. To assure access to financing, the banking system was to be reformed by establishing competing commercial banks controlled by the Central Bank.

Finally, the program called for institutional changes designed to streamline the central economic administration, strengthen functional ministries (e.g., Ministry of Finance, trade, etc.) at the expense of branch ministries (e.g., Ministry of Mining), increase the role of representative bodies (regional councils), and eliminate the intermediate administrative layer (*zjednoczenia*).

In spite of its comprehensive approach attacking organizational, financial, and "competition" arrangements, the program was conceptually flawed on three major counts. First, in marked contrast to the 1946-1951 "reform," which completed the Communist takeover in Poland,[3] it paid little attention to the sequence and timing of economic reform implementation. Reform failed to recognize that it is easier to destroy markets, as was the case from 1946 to 1951, than to create them, and that the transition from the "economic dictatorship of the state" to markets would be a difficult feat. The timing was not defined: according to the blueprint, the implementation was to be spread over a period of two to three years beginning on 1 January 1982.

Second, the program was based on the assumption that output growth and its structure would be shaped by administrative central plans rather than by market forces. Competitive markets were to be regulated by central plan. Planning (industrial policy), however, can coexist with analytically tractable markets but only in an economy where planning is designed to correct market failures. In the absence of markets, there are only state failures, and only the state can correct them.

Third, the program envisaged the introduction of "economic coercion," to borrow a phrase used in Polish debates. Economic coercion implies bankruptcies and subjecting enterprises to hard budget constraints. The blueprint failed to recognize that the option of bankruptcy must be accompanied by its symmetrical equivalents—awards for good performance and the possibility of entry to a given sector. In addition, economic coercion could be effective only if the state has confined its standards to economic efficiency. The issue of how to reconcile state preferences, often carried through microeconomic interventions, with the notion of economic efficiency was not tackled by the program.

In addition to the conceptual fallacies of the program, the imposition of martial law significantly altered the social and political environment in which reform was implemented. The objective of martial law—to centralize political controls over society—was not compatible with the idea of direct industrial democracy and social participation.[4] The authorities, however, pledged their commitment to implement the reform. Thus, instead of revoking the laws on state enterprise and self-management enacted on 23 September 1981 by the Sejm, its major provisions were suspended. The thrust of martial law propaganda was to portray Solidarity as a major impediment to the realization of justified demands for change. Reform was to bring about a modicum of legitimacy to the government whose credibility had been badly damaged by its decision to impose martial law and to crush Solidarity.

The combination of conceptual fallacies, martial law, and the government's formal commitment to an "outmoded program" produced what Fallenbuchl (1988, 117) described as a "dual discrepancy." The first discrepancy was between the original program "Kierunki reformy" and legislation enacted by

[3] For more, see Kamiński (1989).

[4] A renowned Polish economist, Jan Mujżel (1982), argued that this incompatibility was a major threat to the economic reform as outlined in "Kierunki." For a comprehensive analysis of political impediments, see Jack Bielasiak (1988).

Sejm, and the second between specific legal acts and their interpretations in the supplementary regulations that were issued by various levels of the central economic administration. As a result, the current economic system differs in many respects not only from the original blueprint but also from the spirit of its legal pillars.

Implementation of the reform began in early 1982. Its legal foundation was two laws enacted by the Sejm on 25 September 1981. One was on the state enterprise and the other on workers' self-management. These two laws were supplemented by nine acts and amendments.[5] Together with the restructuring of productive inputs prices (1 January 1982) and consumer goods price increases (1 February 1982), they codified the terms of the reform (Mieszczan-kowski 1987a). The measures introduced also expanded the menu of public economic policy tools and affected the organizational structure of economic administration.

There were several modifications in the organizational structure. In 1981, the central economic administration was streamlined: the number of branch ministries was reduced from nine to four. This fell short of the reform proposals that called for a single branch ministry, the Ministry of Industry. The measure reduced neither the number of positions in central economic administrations nor the powers of branch ministries over enterprises.

Not all the sectors were equally affected by the new policies. A significant part of the economy was exempted, direct administrative controls were retained over the coal, cement, sugar, power, and meat industries. The list of industries exempted from reform measures was broader than that envisaged in 1981.

In 1982, the intermediate layer of industrial administration (the associations of enterprises—zjednoczenia) was obliterated. Shortly afterwards, a new provision was introduced that compelled the re-creation of some associations and encouraged enterprises to form voluntary associations. As a result, the intermediate level, regarded as obsolete in all reform proposals, survived. Miesz-czankowski (1987a, 4) carefully notes that from the onset "some trends conflicted with the stipulations of the reform." These trends were the outcome of a growing incompatibility between persistent shortages of goods and services and the reform measures that can operate effectively only in an economy where prices clear excess demand.

The consumer goods price increase implemented on 1 February 1982, which was 63 percent higher than the growth in nominal incomes, significantly

[5] This legislative activity by generating interpretations, instructions, etc., raised fears that the inflation of regulations would create a situation in which nobody would be able to master all the details of economic reform. See the discussion "Piąta bitwa o reformę" (The Fifth Battle for the Reform), *Przegląd Techniczny* (Warsaw) no. 3, 1982. Subsequent assessments confirmed these fears, see Jeziorański (1986c).

curtailed excessive demand in spite of a contraction in supply.[6] Between 1982 and 1985, direct rationing was gradually removed. This movement toward a less-shortage-based economy was short lived, however, as excessive demand increased in subsequent years, especially in 1987 and 1988. Similar patterns could be observed in raw materials, intermediate products, and capital goods. Although in 1983—according to a survey of the Consultative Economic Council—only 13 percent of enterprise managers complained about the growth of shortages, the number of complaints increased to 42.5 percent in 1986.[7]

The growing disequilibria indicated that the price reform had fallen short of implementing mechanisms that would effectively eliminate hidden inflation and insulate the economy from the state administration. Enterprises were granted a considerable discretion to set prices in 1982. The introduction of "free" prices subject to direct negotiations between the contracting parties affected between one-third and two-thirds of all products, depending on the industry, of the state-owned sector.[8] But "free" prices were imposed on an unchanged organizational environment with enterprises still subjected to direct state intervention. Contrary to what one might expect, given a high level of suppressed inflation, free prices did not increase faster than the regulated ones. Because of informal bureaucratic pressures to keep inflation under control, and because of fears of retaliation by suppliers whose financial situation would be affected by rising production costs, even contract prices were set below equilibrium levels. Clearly, enterprises did not take advantage of newly acquired freedom to set prices at market-clearing equilibria. Instead they set prices at a cost plus a double profit rate. The reasons were not clear. One may suspect that administrative constraints on the choice of customers, obligatory sales to a central wholesaler, traditional ties enhanced by multiyear sales agreements, as well as likely pressures from the central authorities to keep price increases at a minimum might have played a role. All in all, this was not a profit-maximizing behavior.

Regardless of the enterprises' reluctance to set prices at equilibrium levels, maximum ceilings were put on the growth of contractual prices in 1983, although the true sources of inflationary pressure were a lack of financial discipline, budget deficit, and debt burden whose servicing required running foreign trade surpluses. In 1984, the government changed the procedure of contractual price setting by explicitly linking prices to "justifiable economic cost." As one observer noted, "Contract prices . . . have become a form of

---

[6] Food prices increased by more than 160 percent, while—because of the increases in prices of raw materials and intermediate products—the prices of final consumer goods increased by slightly more than 100 percent.

[7] *Życie Gospodarcze*, no. 44, 1987, 1.

[8] The so-called contract or free prices—negotiated between a supplier and a consumer—were extended over 75 percent of total sales of raw and basic materials and 60 percent of manufactured products.

regulated prices" (Polański 1986, 8). The inflexible cost-plus formula of price setting, because prices were determined by supply rather than demand, prevailed. As a result, all prices were again under some form of central control, either explicit for administrative prices or implicit for contractual and regulated prices.

Prices set at below market-clearing levels, symptomatic of the failure of price reform, ruled out a greater role for financial policies. The implemented reform measures introduced new financial and nonfinancial tools. Nonfinancial tools included government contracts and the obligatory fulfillment of the tasks of "operational programs."[9] The use of "operational programs" was gradually reduced in favor of contracts. Incentives designed to make government contracts more attractive to enterprises included preferential access to scarce hard currency and raw materials. The use of these tools perpetuated administrative rationing and thereby violated the spirit and the letter of the reform.

Changes in the tax system, in the enterprise cash flow, and in investment financing provided central planners with new financial tools or levers. There was a shift to the direct taxation of profits in the socialized sector.[10] On top of a revenue-raising function, the new tax system was to enhance economic efficiency and to enforce the government's preferences. Because of self-imposed limits on the use of nonfinancial directives, the government sought to accomplish economic objectives by using tax rebates, exemptions, and so forth. The promised universality of taxation rules adopted in 1982 was altered already in 1983. The efficiency-enhancing function of the taxation system was thus undermined. The principle of variability of the rules (see chap. 1) fully reestablished itself.

The first victim of these policies was the principle that the rules be stable and transparent. For instance, turnover tax rates that originally were not to be changed more frequently than once a year became fully flexible at the discretion of the Ministry of Finance. Similarly, the rules underlying taxes or levies designed to curb wage increases were subject to volatile changes. From 1980 to 1985, for example, the central authorities used a progressive levy (the so-called PFAZ, which stands for State Fund for Professional Training) on above-norm wage payments to be paid by enterprises. In 1986, the PFAZ was replaced by PPWW (a tax on above-norm payments), which was to eliminate wage increases above gains in labor productivity. They were both frequently modified. Each new version of PPWW (and the rules were often modified several times during one year) became more and more complicated (Brach 1989).

---

[9] For more, see Fallenbuchl (1988).

[10] For a discussion of implemented changes, see Gomulka and Rostowski (1984). Allocative effects and changes in tax burdens of various sectors are discussed in B. Kamiński (1988).

Another victim was tax universality and neutrality. Tax exemptions and rebates started to proliferate in 1983, the second year of the reform implementation. In subsequent years, there was a shift away from tax neutrality. Rates, indices, rebates, definitions of various components of formulae, and so forth, were all subject to negotiation. In comparison to those tax reliefs granted according to predetermined rules (e.g., export incentives), the share of individually negotiated tax reliefs significantly expanded between 1983 and 1985 (Mieszczankowski 1987b). To a degree, this expansion was the outcome of a misplaced search by policy makers for an effective tool to suppress wage increases.

Experiments with various forms of taxes designed to curb the wage growth distorted the objective function of enterprise management and exacerbated fiscal tensions in the system as a whole. For instance, enterprise management was forced by the changes in taxation, and more or less formal pressures, to maximize the value of output sold (Crane 1987) instead of focusing on profit maximization, as the blueprint envisaged. The taxation system became a mess of preferential treatments, tax reliefs and exemptions, and subsidies. As a result, its efficiency-enhancing and revenue-raising functions were eroded.

The economic policies pursued in the 1980s failed to create equilibria and competition. As a result, the SSS enterprise regime was eroded and the regulatory system became extremely complex. It could hardly be otherwise, given a reluctance of the authorities to fully implement price reforms and to demonopolize the economy. In the presence of shortages, enterprise management was not in a position to improve microeconomic efficiency. To encourage managers to do so, the authorities sought to either adjust tax rates or to use direct rewards—preferential access to scarce materials, and penalties. For instance, because enterprise management had little incentive to use its labor force effectively, special levies or taxes designed to curb wage increases were used. But also there were no autonomous forces that would encourage enterprise management to effectively use capital assets, to improve the quality of production, and to increase exports. The authorities, once they abandoned the use of more drastic measures to attain equilibrium and to introduce competition, had to extend a system of selective measures that undermined the reform. Thus the introduction of legislative foundations of the SSS regime into the administrative environment riddled the regulatory system with tensions and incompatibilities.

The most dramatic attempt to remove inconsistencies came in 1986. The government circumvented the procedure of consulting with official trade unions and various semi-official advisory bodies (e.g., the Consultative Economic Council) by submitting directly to the Sejm a package of eleven acts concerning the functioning of the economy. The package would have resulted in full restoration of direct command planning had it been implemented. Because of strong protests, the government was forced to retreat. This incident brought to the fore the realization that the economic reform had been derailed.

In April 1987, the government submitted for public debate the "Tezy w sprawie II etapu reformy gospodarczej (Theses on the second stage of economic reform).[11] The theses were later supplemented by two other official publications: "Tezy w sprawie kształtowania struktur organizacyjnych gospodarki" (Theses on shaping organization structures in the economy) and a program put forward by Poland's national bank to strengthen Polish currency. The programs drew responses from both the official trade unions and Solidarity.[12]

The overall objective of the second stage reform was the introduction of a viable combination of planning and effective "self-regulatory market mechanism," to borrow a term from the government's "Theses on Designing Organizational Structures." Although the same goal was in the 1981 blueprint, the dominant theme, under the pressure of deteriorating political and economic situation, focused on the institutional changes necessary to create conditions for—as it was described in the report of the Polish National Bank—a domestic convertibility of Polish złoty.[13] Conceptually, the second stage did not go significantly beyond the 1981 program. Politically, the most important aspect of the debate was a promise that after several years of inaction the government's commitment would go beyond rhetoric.

The program of the second stage pledged institutional changes compatible with the SSS enterprise regime. The program was in many respects a carbon copy of the 1981 blueprint. It reads like a list of measures that already would have been implemented had the government followed an activist approach like the one pursued in 1982 and 1983. In line with the measures already implemented to extend remonetization of the economy, the program called for the establishment of a competitive banking system.[14] It also called for a more active antimonopoly policy and for an end to the policy of discrimination against the private sector. The central economic administration was to be reorganized and streamlined. Finally, measures were to be introduced to bring effective demand for consumer and productive goods in line with their supplies.

As in the first stage, implementation began in late 1987 with the reorgani-

[11] See *Rzeczpospolita*, Warsaw, 12 April 1987.

[12] For the assessment of economic reform by the Provisional Council and the Provisional Coordinating Commission of Solidarity, see Solidarity Provisional Council (1987) (Gdańsk-Warsaw, April 1987, Mimeograph). The assessment by OPZZ has been presented in "official" Trade Union Confederation (1987).

[13] See also Kaleta (1987).

[14] The program calls for the establishment of nine commercial, self-financing banks: Industrial-Commercial Bank in Cracow; Silesian Bank in Katowice; Deposit-Credit Bank in Lublin; Common Economic Bank in Łódź; Wielkopolski Credit Bank in Poznań; Credit Bank in Gdańsk; Pomorski Credit Bank in Szczecin; Western Bank in Wroclaw; and National Credit Bank in Warsaw.

zation of the central administration. The total number of ministries was reduced from sixteen to eight.[15] The new ministries will focus on developing industrial policies and new institutional mechanisms rather than on day-to-day management. It is too early to gauge the impact of this reorganization. But it is possible to assess the impact of the attempt to restructure prices, enigmatically labeled in Poland as the price-income operation. It is still unclear why the government decided to go ahead with this operation in spite of almost unanimous opposition among professional economists, semi-independent consultative bodies, and official trade unions.[16] The operation was criticized because of fears of violent reaction from society as well as on purely economic grounds. Subordinating the price increases to the reduction of subsidies, it was argued, would do little to eliminate shortages without effective demand management. In addition, the operation would lead to panic buying. This, in turn, would exacerbate disequilibria already strained by the increased exports of consumer goods in 1987. As was anticipated by critics, the operation has backfired and may have jeopardized the whole program. It has so far triggered two waves of workers' strikes and dramatically undermined the government's credibility.

The objective of the price income operation was to reduce subsidies and, consequently, to raise the relative prices of food. The operation failed. As of January 1989, it was clear that the food prices have not increased in relation to manufactured goods' prices, which was the intention of policy makers, and subsidies are not likely to fall. Paradoxically, the price increases in 1988, estimated at 66 percent, would amount to a de facto fulfillment of a radical price variant that was rejected by the Sejm as well as by the population in the 1987 referendum on the second stage of economic reform.

THE SCOPE OF ADMINISTRATIVE ACTION: THE LOGIC OF CENTRALIZING

Because the extent of change in the economic system can be measured by the reduction in the state's involvement in income redistribution, it is particularly

[15] Five branch ministries were replaced by the Ministry of Industry; the Communication, Telecommunication, and Maritime Office ministries were fused into the Ministry of Transportation, Maritime, and Telecommunication; the Ministry of Foreign Trade and the Council of Ministers' Committee of Economic Cooperation with Abroad were replaced by the Ministry of Economic Cooperation with Abroad; the Ministry of Education and the Ministry of Science and Higher Education were merged into the Ministry of National Education; and, finally, the Central Committee of Physical Education and Tourism and the Ministry for Young People were merged into the Committee for Youth and Physical Education. The names of two remaining ministries were changed: the Ministry of Labor, Wages, and Social Problems became the Ministry of Labor and Social Policy; the Ministry of Construction, Regional and Communal Economy became the Ministry of Regional Economy and Construction. See *Trybuna Ludu*, Warsaw, 13 October 1987.

[16] See, for instance, a report of the Consultative Economic Council, strongly critical of the operation, Konsultacyjna Rada Gospodarcza (1987) (hereafter cited as KRG). The program was also strongly criticized during the Polish Economic Association Congress held in Cracow in December 1987.

relevant to assess the role of the state budget. In spite of the rhetoric of the SSS regime calling for less involvement of the state in the direct management of the economy, an analysis of the state budget suggests persistence of a strong centralizing logic. After a brief contraction following the reform measures implemented in 1982–1983, the government's direct involvement in redistributing income among state-owned enterprises has been increasing, thus undermining the very premise of its own blueprint for reform.

The share of national income passing through the state budget is an indication of the extent and the scope of a government's involvement in running the economy. This is an approximate measure of the use of the administrative mechanism to allocate resources in relation to the market mechanism. With some qualifications, which will be explored at some length, the larger a share of the state budget in national income, the larger will be the scope for administrative action.

The reverse does not necessarily hold for two major reasons. First, although an enterprise may be granted financial autonomy and the prices may be set at the level assuring its financial viability, various regulations and the absence of an efficient system of financial intermediation may impede their spending decisions and freedom to invest. For instance, a shift in the sources of financing of investment projects from the state budget to enterprises and banks, although it will reduce the size of budget spending, may amount to a mere substitution of government authority for bank authority.

Second, if prices are not market clearing, then the state is the only institution available to manage the resulting shortages. For these reasons, the assessment of administrative action and of the extent of direct controls cannot be easily derived from some simple measures of the state budget weight in the extraction and the distribution of resources.

The share of national income going through the state budget in Poland increased throughout the 1970s and in the early 1980s. The expansion was particularly fast between 1978 and 1981, during a period of retrenchment in global output that reached its trough in 1982. The ratio of budget expenditure to national income distributed rose from 47.3 percent in 1978 to 67.9 percent in 1981 (see table 2.2). Following a contraction in 1983, it rose in 1984 and

TABLE 2.2

Shares of State Budget Revenue and Expenditure in National Income Distributed (percent)

	1978	1981	1983	1984	1985	1986	1987
Revenue	52.5	61.0[a]	44.4	45.9	47.1	45.8	42.9
Expenditure	47.3	67.9	44.8	46.9	47.5	46.2	43.8

Source: Rocznik statystyczny (1980, 1983, 1988).

[a] Includes a transfer from the National Bank of Poland from budget surpluses accumulated in previous years.

1985 and declined again in 1985. Still, almost half of the national income passed through the state budget.

The persistent sizable proportion of national income distributed through the state budget since 1983 is rather striking given the government's emphasis on the autonomy and self-financing of state-owned enterprise as well as the autonomy of self-budgeting agencies.

Some have argued that the increase in the degree of centralization between 1983 and 1985, approximated by the proportion of national income allocated through the budget, was due to "the resumption of investment, rather than adverse institutional change" (World Bank 1987b, annex 1: 66). This explanation does not seem to be well founded. The contraction in investment outlays came to an end in 1983 when, for the first time since 1978, the volume of investment increased. The annual growth rate of investment volume peaked in 1984. In the next two years, the growth rate (in constant prices) fell from 11.2 percent to 4.1 and 4.6 percent. The largest increase in the ratio of budgetary expenditure to national income took place in 1985, when the investment outlays growth rate was only two percentage points higher than the growth rate of consumption. This difference was 3.6 percent in 1983, 7.5 percent in 1984, and 0.6 percent in 1986. These data suggest that the resumption of investment activity should have had a much greater impact in 1983 and 1984 than in 1985 and 1986, but this did not happen.

Similar conclusions about the insignificant impact of a revival of investment activity on the increased role of the state budget from 1983 to 1985 can be drawn from data on investment outlays by origin. Direct state involvement in investment financing decreased in this period (table 2.3). Although the proportion of centrally planned investment increased in 1985 as compared with 1984, neither the size of the increment (by 0.6 percentage points or a 3.8 percent share's increase) nor its weight account for the faster growth of budgetary expenditure than of national income. From 1985 to 1987, the share of budget expenditure in national income distributed fell more (3.7 percentage points) than the share of government investment outlays in total budget expenditure (2.3 percentage points). Other factors accounted for this increase not the resumption of investment.

The share of investment outlays in total budgetary expenditure stabilized at about 15 percent after almost doubling in size between 1981 and 1983. Interestingly, this 15 percent share was actually larger than the share prior to the economic reform; investment outlays comprised 11 percent of the total budgetary expenditure in 1978. The larger share of investment outlays in the reformed economic system than in the prereform period suggests that the reforms increased the degree of centralization. However, the increase occurred not between 1983 and 1985[17] but earlier. Thus, we have to look at the patterns of state spending for an explanation of the increase in centralization.

[17] This was the period discussed in the World Bank report on Poland (1987b).

While the portion of national income passing through the state budget gives some indication of the scope of administrative intervention, the relationships between revenue-raising instruments and the patterns of public spending provide some clues about the "revealed" preferences in public economic policy making.

Because of the dominance of state and cooperative ownership of capital assets, the bulk of national income is generated in the socialized sector. This sector accounted for between 70 and 80 percent of the state revenues in the 1980s.[18] In the industrial sectors, net income (or "financial accumulation") corrected for the difference between extra losses and extra profits is divided between the state and the enterprise.[19] The ratio of state revenues (after various deductions from financial accumulation) to national income produced can be regarded as an approximation of the extent of the redistribution of purchasing power through the budget.

The magnitude of this ratio indicates that the budget has been extensively used as a tool to redistribute financial claims in Polish industrial sectors.[20]

TABLE 2.3
Investment Outlays by Origin in the Socialized Sector

	1983		1984		1985		1986		1987	
	(zl)	(%)	(zl)	(%)	(zl)	(%)	(zl)	(%)	(zl)	(%)
Government	167[a]	16.9	215	16.4	285	17.0	362	16.5	421	14.1
Local government	154	15.6	179	13.7	223	13.2	295	13.1	388	13.0
Enterprise	505	51.0	712	54.3	922	55.1	1,235	56.4	1,780	59.7
Housing	164	16.6	204	15.6	243	14.5	306	13.6	390	13.1
Total[b]	990	100.0	1,310	100.0	1,673	100.0	2,198	100.0	2,972	100.0

Source: Rocznik statystyczny (1986, 1988).
[a] In billions of złotys.
[b] Total does not include suspended investment projects and investments from social funds.

[18] Income from taxes levied on the households and private sector accounted for 6.5 percent in 1987 and was the fastest growing item in the 1980s. It was 2.4 percent in 1980.

[19] The following definitions are used in Poland:
net income (in Polish terminology, the equivalent of "akumulacja finansowa," literally financial accumulation); = sales − own costs − costs of external inputs; gross profit = net income − turnover taxes + subsidies + price equalization accounts (in Polish terminology, the equivalent of "wynik finansowy," literally financial result); net profit = gross profit − profits tax − PPW tax.

[20] Financial accumulation in the socialized sector accounts for the bulk of budget revenues: its share amounted to 62.5 percent in 1982, 71.1 in 1983, 69 in 1984, 66 in 1985, and 66.7 percent in 1986.

According to one estimate (Wojciechowska and Żytniewski 1987), the budgetary revenue due to various charges on the financial accumulation of enterprises accounted for between 35 and 45 percent of national income produced from 1958 to 1972. It fell to 30–35 percent from 1973 to 1981 and bottomed at 14.1 percent in 1982. During the first stage of economic reform between 1982 and 1986, the ratio rapidly increased to the level attained in the 1970s. Thus there was a return to the "pre-reform" situation.

Another indication of the active role of the state is the ratio of budgetary expenditure in the socialized productive sector to the budgetary revenue from this sector. The closer this ratio is to unity, the larger is the transfer of financial resources effected by the state. The lower the value of this ratio, the more financially independent are the enterprises. The ratio is shaped by several factors. First, it denotes the extent to which before-tax profitable enterprises contribute to financing of the nonprofitable ones and, therefore, the extent to which the state budget serves as a "financial intermediary" between loss-making and profit-making activity. Second, it depends on the degree to which decisions on public spending are concentrated; for instance, in a traditional command system large capital projects have been financed from the state budget. Even in market economies, this ratio is usually larger than zero because of either market failure, necessitating budgetary provision of goods and services (Musgrave 1959), or state subsidies (e.g., to agriculture or some sunset industries in developed Western economies).

The scope of budgetary involvement was considerable. For instance, in the socialized sector the ratio of public spending to budget revenues from this sector exceeded .8 from 1958 to 1965, fell to .4–.5 from 1966 to 1975, and increased again from 1976 to 1985 (Wojciechowska and Żytniewski 1987). The ratio fluctuated in the 1982–1987 period (table 2.4).

The ratios of budgetary expenditure to budgetary revenues in various sectors are given in table 2.5. Between 1982 and 1986, the ratio of budget revenue to budget expenditure in each sector fell except in the agriculture and transport and communication sectors. What is striking is the increase in the allocative function of the state budget in relation to its most important sector, industry. It is also noteworthy that the agriculture and transport and commu-

TABLE 2.4
State Involvement in Redistribution: Ratios of Public Spending in the Socialized Sector to Revenue from the Socialized Sector (percent)

	1958–1965[a]	1966–1975[a]	1976–1980	1982	1983	1984	1985	1986	1987
Ratio	80	40–50	70–80	59	52	56	52	51	54

Sources: Rocznik statystyczny (1986, 1988). [a]Data for 1958–1965 and 1966–1975 were taken from Wojciechowska and Żytniewski (1987).

TABLE 2.5

Relative Contributions/Burdens of Major Subsectors of the Socialized Sector to the State Budget: Ratios of Budget Expenditure to Revenue from a Sector

	1975	1981	1982	1986	1987
Industry	.161	.261	.264	.394	.402
Construction	1.473	1.724	.192	.226	.168
Agriculture	11.500	5.894	3.952	3.630	3.939
Forestry	.053	.348	.077	.154	.099
Transport and Communications	1.357	2.449	3.278	1.686	2.059
Internal Trade	.473	.294	.531	.589	.662
Foreign Trade	3.912	3.194	1.426	.154	.062
Housing and nonmaterial services	24.163	29.857	25.753	42.428	55.034
Total socialized sector	.545	1.055	.587	.506	.543

Source: Rocznik statystyczny (1983, 1988).

nication industries are deficit subsectors: they absorb more budgetary resources than they contribute to the state budget.

The increase in the ratio of agriculture between 1986 and 1987 occurred despite large increases in the prices of agricultural products and a drastic reduction of the ratio from 11.5 in 1975 to 3.9 in 1982. But in 1987, the amount of subsidies returned to the 1982 level. Thus agriculture remained a major drain on the state budget while the manufacturing and consumer durables sectors were major contributors.[21]

A comparison of the ratios for 1975 with those in the 1980s points to an increased involvement of the government in across-the-board redistribution. The pattern of demand for budgetary allocations and the supply of budget revenues by subsectors was similar to the pattern in 1975 with the exception of increased subsidization of the construction and reduced subsidization of the agriculture subsectors. Except for the increase in subsidies to housing, no significant qualitative change occurred between 1982 and 1986. Quantitatively, however, state budget involvement has increased thus pointing to a govern-

---

[21] The food-processing industry and coal industry accounted for 44.4 and 29.7 percent of budgetary subsidies of the socialized industrial sector in 1986, respectively. In some cases, subsidization of prices was very high; for instance, the price paid for milk purchased by state agencies was almost twice as high as its retail price (Albinowski 1987). On the other hand, the price of a Polish color television set was more than two times (2.3) larger than its production cost; about 95 percent of net income was transferred to the state budget (see Życie Gospodarcze [1987], 27).

ment's "revealed preference" to rely on direct budgetary allocations to accomplish public policy objectives.

The growth in the ratio of public spending to revenues from the socialized productive sector has been shaped by budgetary allocations to cover deficits of loss-making enterprises.[22] The budget in state socialist economies has traditionally played an important role in price and profit equalizing. A good indication of the use of the budget as an instrument of pricing policy is a ratio of "objective subsidies," that is, subsidies per unit of output to turnover tax.[23] The turnover tax—a very important instrument of revenue raising that accounts in Poland for about one-third of budgetary revenues—is a one-stage tax paid by the producer or the importer on sales of output. It is only levied on consumer goods sold wholesale. Therefore, the ratio of objective subsidies to turnover tax shows the degree of the state's involvement in transferring surpluses from profit-making to loss-making products.

During the 1980s, two extremes of the ratio of objective subsidies to turnover tax were reached: a maximum in 1981 and a minimum in 1983. As a result of a decline in output, wage increases, and stable prices, the ratio reached a record level in 1981. Because of drastic increases in intermediate products prices (January 1982) and prices of consumer goods (February 1982) and rebounding output, the ratio fell significantly in 1983. However, it has been increasing thereafter. Given a sharp rise in all cost components after the price increases (the price-income operation) in 1988, the decline of this ratio in 1988 was rather unlikely. Again, this indicator points to a growing role of the state budget and to the reluctance of the authorities to reduce discrepancies between prices and costs. It is noteworthy that the ratio was much higher in 1984–1985 than it was in the 1960s and the 1970s.[24]

Thus, the demand for subsidies increased, not faded.[25] Budgetary subsidies

---

[22] Although the enterprises are technically the beneficiaries, about half of subsidies benefit the households directly or indirectly (World Bank 1987b, annex 1:72). However, subsidies also imply that some products are excessively priced; they distort consumer and producer choices. One could, therefore, make a case that subsidies bring a net welfare loss.

[23] The distinction between "objective subsidies," which are linked to products whose prices "for social or economic reasons are set at a low level" and "subjective subsidies," which are used "in order to make the enterprise as a whole profitable" (*Rocznik Statystyczny* 1986, 101) is ambiguous. The main source of ambiguity is the absence of clearly defined and stable rules of subsidies distribution. They are usually based on production cost assessments submitted by enterprise management to the state administration and as such are subject to bargaining.

[24] The proportion of "objective subsidies" in turnover tax levied on industrial enterprise was below 15 percent in the 1960s. It increased to 35 percent from 1971 to 1975 and 55 percent in the late 1970s (Wojciechowska and Żytniewski 1987).

[25] In Polish practice, the category of so-called budgetary subsidies does not exhaust all forms of de facto subsidies from the state budget. In addition to budgetary subsidies, price equalization accounts are managed by branch ministries as a tool of financial means to "high-cost" enterprises and exchange correction accounts. For instance, budgetary subsidies amounted to about 1,850 billion złoty in 1986, out of which subjective subsidies were more than 100 billion, objective

grew faster than the value of the sales of socialized enterprises. According to one estimate, in both 1985 and 1986 each percentage point of the increase in sales required a one and one-half percentage point increase in the subsidies (Misiak 1987). The share of subsidies in current budgetary expenditure reached in 1981 its record level in the 1980s. But in 1986 it fell short of setting a new record level only by one percent (see table 2.6).[26]

The major recipients of subsidies in the industrial sector are the coal industry and food processing (Misiak 1987). In 1981, the food processing industry accounted for 70.3 percent and coal for 25.6 percent of all subsidies—together they absorbed almost 96 percent of all budgetary subsidies (from data in Wojciechowska and Żytniewski 1987). Their joint share fell to 81 percent (coal, 22.6; food, 58.4) in 1982, but thereafter started to increase. They accounted for 86.5 in 1985 and 83.8 percent in 1986.[27]

Wojciechowska (1987, 3), when assessing developments in the planning and management system in 1986, notes the relative growth in budgetary subsidies and, more significantly, the increased role of intermediate layers of administration hierarchy in redistribution of financial resources.[28] The propor-

TABLE 2.6

Share of Subsidies (Socialized Enterprises) in State Budget Current Expenditure and National Income Produced (in percent)

	1981	1982	1983	1984	1985	1986	1987
Budget	45.0	40.1	40.0	39.4	37.4	39.5	42.9
Income	28.5	18.3	15.3	16.0	15.1	15.1	15.4

Source: Rocznik statystyczny (1988, 1985, 1982).

---

subsidies to enterprises were 1,083 billion, and price subsidies were about 650 billion (estimates by Albinowski [1987]). Total subsidies should also include payments from price equalization accounts, which amounted to about 550 billion złoty; its inclusion would yield an amount 29.7 percent higher. Because the management of those accounts also call for administrative action, exacerbated by a lack of stable rules of redistribution, transfers from these accounts should be included in the assessment of the scope of direct state involvement in management of the economy.

[26] The share of subsidies in current budgetary expenditures amounted to 30 percent in 1986, whereas it amounted to 31 percent before the economic reform of the 1980s. According to one source (Albinowski 1987), the share of subsidies in budgetary expenditure was even higher and amounted to 35 percent.

[27] Because of a faster increase of subsidies to coal production, the distribution of subsidies between these industries changed in the 1982–1986 period. The share of coal in the state subsidies rose from 21.6 to 37 percent, whereas the share of food processing in total industrial subsidies fell from 58.4 to 46.7 percent in 1986. The subsidies to the coal industry recorded the largest annual growth rate of 57 percent in 1986, which contrasts with a 12 percent growth in the food processing industry subsidies.

[28] These observations are derived from the survey of managers of state-owned industrial enterprises.

tion of loss-making enterprises increased in the 1984–1987 period. In 1987 and 1988, subsidies to socialized sectors increased faster than budgetary expenditures and revenues. This suggests that the primary concern of the fiscal system remains the redistribution of income in money and in kind mainly within the public sector through the use of direct control instruments.

All the measures reviewed of the state budget's role in the Polish economy point to the growing reliance on direct rather than indirect controls. Mainly because of the growing state budget involvement in the transfer of purchasing power from profitable to loss-making enterprises, there has been a significant increase in the portion of national income redistributed by central authorities. To effect this redistribution, high taxation of the net income of enterprises has been inevitable, and the amounts of earnings retained were highly limited. Simultaneously, the share of subsidies in the value of sales has increased and so have the payments to the budget and to other special funds administered by the units at higher layers of the economic management hierarchy. The implication is that spending decisions have been made by the central government rather than by individual enterprises.

It is unclear whether the reduction of the financial autonomy of enterprises was a declared goal of economic policy. Yet, the behavioral patterns of enterprises were, to a large extent, shaped by the financial policy of the state. In theory, the most important task of financial policy is to use financial and price-setting instruments to ensure the best use of resources. This analysis suggests only that the magnitude of income redistribution significantly increased in the 1980s. The most general explanation that can be inferred from this analysis is that the central planners allowed for growth in the discrepancies between production costs and prices. The resulting inflationary pressures were only marginally reflected in the prices of basic consumption products. A Polish economist observed this was the price "to be paid for maintaining social peace" (Mieszczankowski 1987a). Whatever the reason, the policy clearly favored short-term social objectives over economic efficiency.

RULES OF ALLOCATION: THE RESPONSE PATTERNS OF ECONOMIC ACTORS

The behavioral patterns of enterprises are shaped by the institutional and organizational arrangements within which they operate. The institutional and organizational arrangements also determine the instruments of public economic policy available to the authorities. A change in the institutional and organizational arrangements results in modifying the objective function of enterprise management by making it sensitive to a different set of economic policy tools used by the state.

This analysis will examine the changes that occurred in the behavioral patterns of economic actors and in the instruments of economic policy as a result of the reform measures implemented in the 1980s. The analysis is organized around the following three questions: What changes have occurred in the behavioral patterns of economic actors as revealed in the planning process? What are the determinants of employment, investment, and procurement decisions by enterprises? What changes have occurred in the instruments available to the state to control the economy?

A good point of departure to highlight response patterns is to examine the enterprise behavior revealed in the plan construction process. According to a new planning procedure introduced in the 1980s, a central plan sets general guidelines that serve as a frame of reference for the enterprises. These guidelines also include various measures affecting the profitability of the enterprises. In a traditional central planning system, the essence of the game during plan construction is for the producer to maximize input/output ratios while central authorities seek to minimize them; producers seek to obtain the lowest production assignments and the largest allotments of rationed inputs. In addition, producers seek to maximize their claims on central investment funds. This game is rooted in central authorities' imperfect knowledge of the enterprises' production function and in the practice of setting plan objectives at last's year achieved level, increased by some fraction.

Although central plans are no longer formally binding for enterprises and the planning procedures have been modified, the enterprise behavioral patterns did not change. This is the conclusion drawn from the plan projects of enterprises, which offer clues about the prevailing behavioral patterns of enterprises.[29]

The enterprises outlined their programs after having been acquainted with the Central Annual Plan (CAP) for 1987 and the National Socioeconomic Plan (NSP) for 1986–1990. The comparison of the aggregate of their individual plans with the CAP and the NSP allows us to address the question of whether there was a change in the rules of the bargaining game between planners and enterprises.

The following observations can be made. First, central planners continue to use "taut" plans as an instrument of mobilization. As far as output is concerned, both the CAP and the NSP tend to be much more "taut" than the plans of enterprises. The discrepancies are especially acute in the production of raw materials. The aggregate of enterprise production plans yields an output 9 percent higher in 1990 than in 1985, whereas the goal set in NSP is 14 percent. In addition, there are strong differences in the production mix—the production of some raw materials and intermediate inputs is to increase more according to enterprises' projections, and others less. The deviations of output

---

[29] The plans of two thousand industrial enterprises were retrieved and compared with the Central Annual Plan for 1987 and with the National Socioeconomic Plan for 1986–1990 by Poland's Planning Commission. See "Ankieta" (Survey) *Rzeczpospolita*, 30 July 1987.

derived from enterprises' plans from the CAP amount in some cases to 40 percent.

Second, producers tend to maximize the input/output ratio. Planners would like to see the maximization of the output/input ratio, instead. For example, the demand for raw materials and intermediate products derived from individual plans exceeds the consumption targets set in the CAP and the NSP. According to the enterprises, materials intensity (consumption per unit of output) is to fall in the 1987–1990 period at an average annual rate of 1.2 percent. According to the planners, it is to decrease at an annual rate of between 1.6 and 2 percent. Even larger deviations are projected in energy consumption per unit of output. The NSP projection of a 8.8 to 10.8 percent reduction in energy intensity between 1985 and 1990 is well below the enterprises' target of a 4.1 percent reduction. Enterprises' plans to increase employment also deviate from the central plans. The industrial enterprises project their demand for labor in 1990 to be 4 percent higher than in 1987, whereas the authorities "planned" a zero growth in this period.

Third, by far the largest deviations are in the sphere of investment programs. For instance, the 1987 CAP envisages a 2 to 3.3 percent increase in investment outlays in the socialized sectors of the economy. This stands in stark contrast to the 77 percent increase implied in enterprise plans for 1987. In 1990, the volume of investment according to the NSP is to stand at 120 percent of its level in 1985, whereas if the enterprises have their way it will stand at 232 percent. This difference is mainly due to investment programs of the industrial branches that traditionally have been accorded priority by central planners. For example, machine-building enterprises want to increase investment outlays by 300 percent between 1986 and 1990, electricity-producing enterprises by 224 percent, and chemical enterprises by 280 percent. The major source of investment financing is to be bank credit. To meet the demand, the supply of credit will have to increase sixfold.

Despite the dramatically larger investment outlays anticipated by enterprises, the increase in production capacities in the enterprise plans falls short of the central target by 4 percent. The efficiency of the investment process as perceived by enterprises is thus significantly lower than that assumed in the central planners' projections.

The comparison of enterprise programs with central plans indicates that the behavioral patterns of enterprise management typical for the process of plan construction in the institutional framework of command planning persist. The deviations between actual economic performance and the detailed projections of both state and enterprise plans seem to be a rule rather than an exception.[30]

[30] It is worth recalling that the observation of significant discrepancies between plan and performance supported by the analysis of organizational and institutional constraints to plans coordination prompted some students (Birman 1978; Wilhelm 1979) of Soviet-type economies to question the adequacy of the term "planned economy."

Enterprise management seeks to sanction maximization of input/output ratios and continues to reveal an unsatiable demand for centrally financed investment, which—according to Kornai (1980)—is an important component of the mechanism of shortage generation. As a Polish economic commentator observed, "A road from directive-distributive plan to new methods of planning and management is neither straight nor short" (Misiak 1987).

The reasons for the persistence of systemic drawbacks are rooted in the decision environment of industrial enterprises. The decision environment remains conducive to bargaining relatively unconstrained by objective market criteria or the knowledge and ability to impose the preferences of central planners. The changes introduced have not undermined the dominant role of negotiations in the allocation of resources. A lot can be gained by enterprise management from bargaining with central authorities. The objects of bargaining have changed, however. For instance, in the game over the allocation of an investment fund, the object of bargaining is no longer confined to the allotment of investment funds. Because profits determine the amount of funds available for wage increases and investment, bargaining also includes factors affecting the volume of profits. Viewed from the perspective of investment spending decisions, the increased importance of financial indicators has changed the components in the objective function of enterprise management without significantly altering the mode of interaction between central authorities and enterprises. Although the giftlike character of investment has been reduced, enterprise management has to rely on bureaucratic skills. Profits are shaped less by the efficiency of the use of available resources than by the tax relief and subsidies determined by bargaining.

Employment has also been subjected to a hybridization of regulations. The "new" measures have not removed those behavioral patterns typical for traditional command planning. The administratively set limits on enterprise employment were replaced first by a levy, and then by a linear tax rate on above-norm wage payments.[31] Introduced in 1987, the 500 percent tax rate on payments exceeding 12 percent of the previous year's wage fund amounts to a cap on employment. In addition, the Ministry of Labor, Wage, and Social Security introduced an upper limit on wage rates that survives today under various guises. In practice, the upper wage rate limit and the outlays subject to taxation have remained negotiable. Although many enterprises have sufficiently high profits to afford higher wage rates (Jeziorański 1986c), they are not allowed to exceed the limit because they have insufficient bureaucratic clout. Others cannot afford it, but they can offer wage rates exceeding the upper limit

[31] Above-norm wage taxes replaced the State Fund of Employment Activization tax in 1986. Wage increases exceeded the threshold determined by the product of the rate of growth of output sold and standard coefficient (set at .5); 2,950 enterprises out of the total 6,194 enterprises obtained some form of tax relief (Mieszczankowski 1987a).

if they succeed in convincing central planners that they should be allowed to charge labor into production cost, which is not subject to "wage" taxes.

The combination of financial, negotiable parameters and physical limits has produced regulatory chaos, which has substantially decreased the capacity of the state to control wages and employment.[32] For instance, because of the pressure of persistent shortages, the central authorities allowed an untaxed increase in wage payments if an enterprise increased its output above the level originally anticipated in the enterprise plan. If enterprise plan targets were set at levels below those of the CAP, then a contract was signed with the authorities to provide extra output. The strategy of hiding productive reserves and keeping plan targets at levels that could be exceeded easily has thus retained its viability even under the reformed economic system. It pays to bargain for a lower plan during its construction stage. All in all, the observation that the employment and wage system is "open to all sorts of bargaining and political maneuvering to gain exemptions" (World Bank 1987b, 33) is well founded.

The bargaining regime, in turn, fuels a shortage-generating mechanism. Had there been a genuine labor market where enterprises could compete for a mobile labor force by autonomously setting wage rates, the existing labor market would have been a seller's market. For the marginal product of labor to equal marginal wage rates, wages would have had to increase significantly. Relatively low wages and small wage differentials combined with negotiability of the financial results of an enterprise make the hoarding of labor a reasonable strategy.

Although rationing violated the spirit and the letter of the 1981–1982 blueprint for economic reform, it was still pervasive despite a fall in the proportion of centrally allocated inputs. Some observers have argued that the changes in the amount of central allocation indicate decentralization of decision making.[33] This is not the case, however. The decline did not amount to moving away from command planning. The organizational forms of rationing became more diversified. For instance, the allocation of such products as consumer goods and some agricultural inputs was assigned to local governments. This measure also failed to take into account the "obligatory brokerage" that covered 50 percent of enterprise procurement in the 1983–1984 period and between 40 and 42 percent in 1986. Finally, the use proportion of centrally allocated inputs fell because of such organizational substitutes as contracts

---

[32] For instance, incomes to be taxed were reduced for those enterprises that failed to pay their "wage" taxes in 1985. The tax relief was equal to the unpaid amounts; the payments were spread over a long period at a low interest rate. (Wojciechowska 1987). Consequently, enterprise management that raised wages without paying attention to tax implications was rewarded; these enterprises could increase the nontaxed wage fund more than those who pursued a policy of "wage" tax burden minimization.

[33] This is used by some authors as proof of the movement away from command planning. See, for instance, World Bank 1987b, annex 1:9.

between government and industrial enterprises. As a substitute for market stimuli, the government guaranteed supplies of raw materials and intermediate products in exchange for an enterprise commitment to increase supplies.[34] For those reasons, the decline in the proportion of centrally allocated inputs from 90 percent of all industrial inputs in 1978 to 35 percent in 1987 is meaningless for the assessment of weakening of the fusion between the state and the economy.

The area crucial for enterprise financial performance encompasses the rules concerning price setting, subsidies, and profits. Central planners have not developed a coherent tax/subsidy policy. For instance, neither the subsidy (e.g., the difference between the "object" and the "subject" subsidy) nor the rates and the rules of allocating subsidies have been clearly defined.

The most striking feature of these arrangements was the tendency to compensate enterprises for every effort through the calibration of the prices and financial support or relief. Taxes commanded a very large portion of enterprise resources. Their rates and burden varied from one enterprise to another. The rates were determined on the basis of "cost estimates submitted by an enterprise and are subject to bargaining with an institution granting subsidy."[35] Because rates were highly arbitrary and their levels uncertain, tax liabilities were difficult to predict. So were the tax rebates used as incentives to accomplish various centrally imposed objectives (export promotion, production quality, investment, employment of old age pensioners, etc.). The importance of tax rebates, which are subsidies in disguise, had been growing. For instance, the total amount of rebates in income taxes increased threefold between 1983 and 1985. Although some portion of these tax breaks was granted in accordance with predetermined rules and rates (e.g., tax rebates for exports), the share of individually negotiated tax reliefs significantly expanded from 27.6 percent in 1983 to 34.2 percent in 1985 (Mieszczankowski 1987a). Under these circumstances, the tax system could not be used effectively as a tool to shape economic behavior and improve economic efficiency.

This examination of various spheres within which enterprises operated suggests that all components affecting a "situation" of an enterprise were by and large subject to bargaining with planning authorities. Thus the reform fell short of substantially changing the behavioral patterns of economic actors. Instead of adapting to exogenous financial parameters, enterprises were able to adapt the parameters to their needs. In other words, bureaucratic bargaining rather than the market mechanism shaped the allocation of investment, raw materials, intermediate products, and productive activities. The reform did not produce an institutional environment conducive to the effective use of indirect

[34] As far as consumer goods were concerned, this system included twenty-eight finished consumer goods categories, twenty-one procurement items, and eight categories of spare parts used in domestic appliances (Żychowicz 1987).

[35] See Marek Dąbrowski's comment in *Zarządzanie* 13 (1987):39 quoted in Albinowski (1987).

controls by the state. Instead, as will be shown, the measures introduced exacerbated tensions in the steering system of the economy.

THE INCOMPATIBILITIES BETWEEN DIRECTIVES AND (QUASI-) PARAMETERS

The introduced reform measures changed the mix of public policy tools in favor of the financial instruments, which are theoretically tools of indirect controls. The problem was that they could be used only as tools of direct controls because the reform measures introduced fell well short of decoupling the state from the economy.

Indirect controls cannot function properly unless (1) prices reflect the relative scarcities and productivities of resources; (2) the environment is competitive; (3) enterprises are fully accountable for profits and losses, with bankruptcy as a final penalty and ownership rights unambiguously specified; and (4) there is an efficient system of financial intermediation. The institutional environment of the Polish economy did not satisfy these conditions.[36]

Although it is not clear what indirect controls can accomplish in a nonmarket environment, evidence abounds about what problems they may produce. The case for state intervention is usually made in terms of its ability to correct market failures in order to maximize welfare. The conclusion that can be drawn from the analysis of the Polish experiment with economic reform is that use of market measures in a nonmarket environment brings about the worst of worlds. The "monetization" of central controls produced galloping inflation coexisting with shortages. The absence of competition and markets produced pressures toward increasing the scope of direct microeconomic intervention by the state.

The measures that are both sufficient and necessary to introduce the market have not been "institutionalized" in the state socialist economy. The objective of establishing a link between the economic performance and the financial situation of an enterprise and its efficiency was not realized. The command planning instruments—material balances, central allocation, and "planning from the achieved level"—continued to be used, although increasingly at lower levels of administrative hierarchy. Although enterprise management became more sensitive to prices, interest rates, and taxes, it was increasingly faced with the conflicting signals of the financial indexes and the rigid commands of central planning. However, no matter how badly or how well they fared, their survival was guaranteed. So were the bonuses as long as the ad-

---

[36] Instead, the measures introduced have created an environment conducive to "manual steering." This term used in the Polish discussion of the present economic system captures the essence of the state's involvement in the economy. But manual steering based on the use of financial instruments and administrative coercion (or on the combination of economic and administrative coercion) is not necessarily superior to traditional command planning.

ministration found an enterprise performance satisficing. The satisficing criteria were not clearly defined.

Enterprises did not become profit maximizers, although as a result of the fiscal instruments introduced they became sensitive to financial indicators. There was almost no relationship between "original" profitability, a profitability before tax and subsidy, and after-tax, after-subsidy profitability. Tax reliefs and subsidies were tailored to the specific needs of an enterprise. Further, they changed frequently—one of the major shortcomings of the reform.

Existing circumstances did not allow for the activation of indirect controls (monetary and fiscal policy). Their common denominator is money, used as a vehicle for the allocation of resources. Monetary policy can undermine fiscal policy if the money supply is not controlled. Central planners had to cope with two interrelated problems. First, although there was some progress, the monetization of the economy was rather limited. Bargaining over rationed goods and financial rules was a major mechanism of resource allocation. Because of the various constraints related to shortages, the expansion of credit did not necessarily stimulate the increase of production unless bottlenecks were removed. For similar reasons, any expansion in the total aggregate wage bill was inflationary. The Polish experience in 1985–1986 demonstrated that a more expansionary credit and wage policy produces inflation.

Second, although plans existed for credit expansion and the issue of currency, they were of little relevance in the absence of financial discipline. Government policies allowed for the existence of soft budget constraint, to use Kornai's term. Expenditure above-plan and revenue below-plan easily resulted in budget deficits. Given the erosion of the revenue-raising yield of a tax system caused by unavoidable rebates, exemptions, and reliefs, this was a likely outcome. In contrast to countries with well-developed financial markets where a budget deficit is financed by drawing on the savings, the socialist state's budget is simply financed by printing money. This passive or accommodative monetary policy contributed to the inflationary growth of nominal demand (Crane 1987, 6).

The reform introduced financial links and feedbacks that exacerbated inflationary pressures, given the highly distorted price mechanism. In contrast to conditions under traditional command planning, a rise in production costs *may* affect prices in a reformed system. Prices are not totally exogenous from the point of view of enterprise management. In the absence of competition and the presence of persistent shortages, enterprises can pass the price increases on to their customers. Because an enterprise's freedom in price setting is often limited, the state is under pressure to alter deductions and subsidies to prevent bankruptcies and the subsequent loss of production. The resulting increased role of the state budget in reallocation of incomes is an invitation to new claims. This situation leads to budget deficits and inflation without alleviating shortages, a trademark of state socialism, unless there is a strong government capable of suppressing these demands.

Grzegorz W. Kołodko (1988, 18) argues that a combination of price inflation and shortages, which he aptly calls a shortageflation, is the result of the incomplete operation of the market and, as such, is characteristic of the transition to a "reformed socialist economy." Shortageflation is an inevitable outcome of reform. He notes that shortageflation occurs because "real-life social and economic mechanisms *no longer* permit to fully repress inflation, but do not *yet* permit—mostly for political and social reasons—turning to an open price inflation" (Kołodko 1988, 19). My analysis suggests a slightly different explanation of shortageflation: shortageflation is a symptom of hitting the limits of reformability of the state socialist economic system.

First, shortageflation is the result of changing the mix of public economic policy tools in favor of financial instruments without overhauling the institutional arrangements responsible for shortage generation. But the reform measures in Poland in the 1982–1989 period did not challenge the principle of fusion or, more generally, state socialism. Cezary Józefiak (1987) rightly describes them as "a concept of indirect centralization of the economy . . . which consists of replacing administrative commands by financial parameters shaped not by the market, but by central planning authorities." The loss of control over money supply was, in part, the result of a failure of the reform to solve a systemic problem of misdirected incentives. The reform fell short of providing the incentives to elicit maximum effort from economic actors. It merely complemented (and frequently substituted) administrative orders with financial rewards. The result was a regulatory chaos, a hybrid of subsidies and preferential treatments that would fuel inflation if left unchecked. In short, the persistence of fusion was accountable for shortages, whereas the introduction of financial tools in the economy with no markets contributed to inflation.

Second, in addition to the structural mechanisms of shortage generation (see Kornai [1986a]), there is also a political mechanism exploring money illusion that only indirectly is connected to the transition to a reformed socialist economy. This mechanism was particularly visible during a crisis of state socialism, as in Poland in the 1980s or increasingly in the Soviet Union. It consists of granting wage increases without corresponding increases in productivity and the supply of consumer goods. The authorities accept wage demands to diffuse strikes because they are unable to suppress social discontent or to mediate labor disputes by other means. Because of the introduced economic measures, the prices are somewhat linked to costs of production. The result is open inflation. Yet because of price controls, prices do not clear excessive demand. The increase in the inflationary overhang contributes to the growth of shortages.

The problem is not mitigated by the increase in supplies because there is no mechanism linking shortages with investment decisions.[37] Both shortages and inflation can be exacerbated by excessive investment strategy and other economic policy blunders such as two price-income operations (i.e., increases) in 1982 and 1988.

CONCLUSION

This analysis of the changes in the economic system in Poland in the 1980s demonstrated the limited scope for adjustment within the institutional framework of state socialism. The 1984–1988 period witnessed a significant increase in the intensity of direct intervention instead of a declining direct intervention in the economy. The implemented reform measures changed the mix of public policy tools used to coordinate economic activities and achieve balance between the supply and demand in favor of financial directives. Because of the incompatibility between physical shortage and financial instruments, the introduction of financial tools into economic policy during the first stage of economic reform in Poland made the system of planning and management internally inconsistent and "overregulated." As the authors of the World Bank put it: "The actual Polish system today is a new hybrid" (World Bank 1987b, annex 1:7). This hybrid provided a fertile ground for the bargaining that continued to be the dominant mechanism of allocation.

Disequilibrium prices failed to provide enterprise management with information about relative scarcities. In addition, the absence of any link between financial performance and wages and bonuses as well as the enterprises' monopolistic position did not encourage maximization of capital and labor productivities. The financial performance of enterprises was also of limited value as a guide for the conduct of financial policies by the government. Given the scope of the budget involvement, it became impossible to identify enterprises and sectors that were really profitable. In all, the government was condemned to rely on direct microeconomic interventions carried out by ministries and banks instead of selecting and using financial and price-setting instruments so that the best use of resources would be pursued by enterprises.

The movement along a "reform menu curve" restricted to different combinations of physical directives and quasi-parameters (financial tools) falls short of solving the problem of the lack of incentive to elicit the best response from economic and administrative actors. The change in the mix does not increase the capacity of the state to improve efficiency. Without activating the third dimension of competition and markets, there is no solution to this problem. Because this solution implies going beyond the institutional confines of state socialism, it illustrates the limited scope for reform under state socialism.

[37] As is shown in chapter 3, investment decisions are shaped by the logic of a closed system, that is, priority is assigned to the production of industrial inputs.

CHAPTER THREE

The Logic of a Closed System:
The Vicious Cycle of Decline

THE EAST EUROPEAN economies followed similar paths of development and face similar problems today. They all experience the loss of developmental momentum, deteriorating growth performance, environmental crisis, declining productivity, and decreasing international competitiveness in manufactures, albeit to varying degrees.[1] This is so despite significant differences in their respective political and economic circumstances, in levels of development, endowments in natural resources, size, cultural traditions, etc. Because they all share the same politico-economic order, the explanation of the similarities lies in the institutional framework. The institutional framework, we shall see, leaves little room for diversity in developmental concepts and strategies.

In chapter 2, I argued that the range for institutional adjustment is limited. Institutional innovations without an overhaul of state socialism fall well short of erecting the institutional structures that would assure success in the contemporary international economy. The thesis of chapter 3 is that fusion of the state and the economy creates an institutional environment conducive to inward-oriented development strategies that inexorably lead to a vicious circle of decline. Policy makers are enslaved by the system that allows for a limited range of economic strategies. Moreover, they all deplete developmental potential. The moment of a general crisis may come sooner or later depending on the choice of strategies and on the capacity of a regime to assure social compliance without resorting to excessive economic concessions (see chap. 4). Although many authors put the blame on the system, relatively little research effort has linked development patterns to the institutional framework of state socialism.[2]

The argument developed in this chapter can be summarized as follows: State socialism has a built-in mechanism of shortage generation (or is a supply-constrained economy as compared to a demand-constrained market system). Together with the absence of autonomous activities geared to finding the most

---

[1] See, for instance, Kovës (1985), Marer (1988), and Prybyla (1988).

[2] Exceptions are few. Some authors (Beksiak 1972; Kornai 1972) have related specific features of the economic system to strategies of economic development, and others, e.g., contributions to edited volumes by Comisso and Tyson (1986) and Drewnowski (1982), A. Kaminski (1989), and Poznański (1988b), explored the impact of the institutional framework on selected aspects of political, economic, and social developments.

efficient ways of producing goods and services for both domestic and international markets, this mechanism compels central planners to allocate resources to the sectors whose products alleviate shortages throughout the economy. I shall call this the logic of the closed system. The preference in investment policies is accorded to the production of producer goods. Producers of producer goods obtain a privileged position not because of a lobbying effort but because of the systemic arrangements. Simultaneously, output expansion requires ever-increasing quantities of energy, raw materials, and intermediate products as well as investment goods because of the absence of a link between microeconomic efficiency and rewards. This is a so-called "extensive" path of economic development. The expansion in industrial output inevitably leads to the depletion of the resources necessary to generate growth.

This development pattern is crisis generating. It can be sustained only if the following conditions are met: (1) there is a wide social latitude for economic deterioration; (2) the demand for ever-increasing amounts of productive inputs can be easily met either internally or externally; and (3) new technologies for reducing consumption of resources per unit of output are available.

These conditions have been met to some extent in various state socialist countries, but they constrain economic growth. The reserves of labor as well as an expansion of the domestic resource base (or, in East European countries, access to Soviet natural resources) allowed to meet the rapidly increased demand. They are both finite, however. Technologies mostly imported (or copied) from the West allow for a decreased use of production factors in various industries. All three conditions may be mitigated also by external financing, but international debts have to be serviced (if not repaid). Gierek's strategy of indebted development in the 1970s as well as Jaruzelski's policies of external adjustment, if they deserve this name, provide an extreme illustration of the consequences of incompatibility between institutionally determined developmental patterns and export orientation.

CLOSED SYSTEM LOGIC

The system's structural impact on the choice of economic strategy is conceptualized in terms of closed system logic. The *New Webster's Dictionary* defines logic as "the apparently unavoidable cause and effect relationship of events leading to a particular conclusion." The "cause and effect relationship" is determined by the institutional arrangements of state socialism. The "particular conclusion" is the "extensive" path of economic development that depletes developmental potential and gives producers of producer goods a special position. Their special position is not merely an interest-group role. As long as state socialism exists, it is "unavoidable," that is, the only alternative to inevitable economic stagnation and a declining standard of living is the overhaul of state socialism. In this sense, development presents a challenge to state socialism, it creates a trap from which there is no escape within its own institutions.

As a result of the fusing of the economy with the state, the economic system has become closed to economic transactions (initially also with respect to the movement of ideas and people) and it has become prone to shortage generation. The closure of the economic system has several implications for foreign trade behavior.[3] The approach to foreign trade, typical for state socialism, is probably best summarized by Oskar Lange who wrote: "In socialism the foreign trade is, in principle, determined by import needs. Export is only a means to pay for indispensable imports (Lange 1973, 363). Because export is conceived in terms of wasted resources necessary to secure imports, this may be called the *residual* approach. The attainment of a full autarky is not a feasible task. The result is constant tensions between the import needs of the expanding economy and the export-restricting characteristics of a command planning system. These tensions have been, with varying degrees of intensity, a permanent feature of socialist economic development. They are much more acute in relations with capitalist economies than with state socialist economies.

The residual approach to foreign trade that treats exports only as a necessary sacrifice to pay for indispensable imports is functionally coherent with the organizational framework of state socialism. The institutional monopoly of foreign trade effectively shields economic actors from international markets. Instead of horizontal links based on contractual relations, typical for a market economy, the dominant links are the vertical ones running through Ministry of Foreign Trade and foreign trade organizations (FTOs). The lack of links between domestic costs and prices extends to foreign trade transactions.[4] To compensate for discrepancies between enterprises' production costs and prices is a variety of different exchange rates and an elaborate system of equalization accounts. As a result, enterprises have neither opportunities to learn about international technological requirements and marketing nor incentives to compete and emulate more efficient foreign enterprises. They have few incentives to develop new technologies and products.

The concentration of economic decision-making authority contributes to underspecialization (Winiecki 1987b). Because of the administrative fragmentation of industries and the fact that the bulk of transactions occurs among enterprises subordinated to the same intermediate lever and the same ministry, the capacity of FTOs to base their export strategies on specialization is severely curtailed (Wolf 1990). Central planners display an affinity for "large" foreign trade transactions involving exports of homogenous products or raw

---

[3] On these and related issues, see Pryor (1963), Wiles (1968), and Wolf (1990).

[4] In Poland, for instance, the introduction of the official exchange rate of 1 US dollar to 4 zloty in 1949, which bore no relation whatsoever with domestic costs of exports, broke the link between domestic and international prices. This exchange rate in the form of *złoty dewizowy* (devisa or foreign exchange złoty) was used in the statistics of foreign trade until 1981.

materials simply because they create neither domestic coordination planning problems nor difficulties related to adjustment to changing demand.[5] Raw materials and other technologically simple goods, for instance, account for about 70 percent of Eastern European exports to the nonsocialist world, whereas the share of high technology accounts for about 0.5 percent (Bautina and Wojciechowska 1988).[6]

Although the monopoly of FTOs has been undermined in a number of countries (e.g., enterprises may obtain licenses to conduct foreign trade in Hungary, Poland, the People's Republic of China [PRC], and the Soviet Union), this process has fallen short of creating an institutional environment conducive to effective adjustment by firms to highly diversified and rapidly changing markets for manufactured goods. A number of studies (Poznański 1986a, 1988a; Winiecki 1988) suggest that the international competitiveness of Eastern European economies has declined.

The institutional arrangements governing foreign trade behavior (and generating the residual approach) are not trade creative, but "trade averse" (Brown 1968). In contrast to interactions with the West carried out at the level of firms and subject to market rules, "the administration-by-edict system of economic management that has grown up in each of the socialist countries has been accurately reproduced in relations within CMEA [Council for Mutual Economic Assistance] too" (Grinberg 1988), and so has the closed system logic. Franklin Holzman (1986, 64) noted that CMEA has been "the most restrictive, autarkic trading group in recent history."

Although aversion to dependence on capitalist world markets may be explained by national security concerns or fear of uncertainty of supplies, it would seem that similar considerations should not apply to intra-CMEA relations. One might expect that etatization of foreign trade would favor development of commercial interaction with partners having similar economic systems. Long-term contracts signed with other governments empowered to directly coerce producers' give governments a sense of stability lacking in contracts with states deprived of the authority to intervene directly into foreign trade decisions of enterprises that would foster intra-CMEA trade. The history of CMEA convincingly demonstrates that this sense stability fails to overcome the impediments to intra-CMEA trade. The preference often accorded by policy makers to trade with other state socialist economies has usually backfired because of the competitiveness of their respective economic structures. This has been the outcome of parallel economic development strategies pursued by them not only during the "socialist industrialization" in the 1950s but also during the opening to the West in the 1970s (Marer 1984). As a result, not

[5] For illustrations, see, for instance, Kovës (1985).

[6] Ibid. Between 1980 and 1986, the share of high-tech goods fell from 1.2 percent to 0.6 percent. In the same period, this share in the exports of Third World countries increased from 9.8 to 13.2 percent.

many products have been available for mutual exchanges, and those products that are marketable for hard currency, the so-called hard goods, have been directed usually to international markets rather than to other planned economies.[7]

The similarity between domestic and CMEA arrangements has not produced a rapid expansion of intra-CMEA trade except with the Soviet Union. Because of its ample endowment of natural resources and its imperial political dominance, the only planned economy that has been able to provide hard goods in exchange for soft goods has been the Soviet Union. The dominant feature of intra-CMEA trade has been the growth of integration along the lines of a radial pattern centered around the Soviet Union, the major supplier of energy and raw materials and the consumer of Eastern European manufactures.[8] There has been neither incentive nor opportunity to develop multilateral ties.[9] Even if a supranational central planning system were established, the new agency would have to overcome the tendency of firms to underspecialize in a domestic context triggered by the unreliability of supplies, poor coordination of plans, and shortages.

The closed system logic operates also at a firm's level. It is revealed in a striving to produce whatever is possible locally, so that there will be no need to rely on external supplies. One may thus conclude that a certain "trade aversion" can be traced to domestic institutional arrangements rather than other factors, for example, the often-mentioned Western discrimination against trading with the East.

The fusion of the state with the economy has excluded export orientation (to nonsocialist markets) from the range of policy options available to central planners for three major interrelated systemic (not policy) reasons. First, the absence of markets and the nonconvertibility of domestic currency deprives planners of the information necessary to assess comparative advantages (Wolf 1990). The information system serving command planning, which makes running the domestic economy possible, is too coarse to make sophisticated decisions concerning international specialization and foreign trade (Marer and Montias 1981).

Second, the persistent shortages of inputs, intermediate products, and consumer goods, force central planners to favor development projects that are designed to meet immediate domestic needs. Because the payoffs of export-

[7] The unwritten rule of trade among smaller CMEA members has been to sell whatever was marketable; the so-called "hard goods" are sold to the West and the lower quality "soft goods" are kept for the intra-CMEA trade.

[8] For more on institutional arrangements governing intra-CMEA trade, see Brabant (1973).

[9] The share of the Soviet Union in the trade of Eastern European countries with CMEA-members accounted in the 1981–1985 period for between 76 percent (Bulgaria) and 50 percent (Romania); calculation from German Institute for Economic Research (DIW) data in European Parliamentary Working Documents A 2–187/86. For more see B. Kamiński (1989a).

oriented projects are not known with certainty, pressure is strong to choose investment programs that assign priority to import-substituting projects.

Third, the success of export-oriented strategies in rapidly changing world markets is critically dependent on the ability of economic actors to identify and to respond quickly to business opportunities. But they are impaired by the double insulation and the absence of competitors. State socialist firms are insulated from domestic and foreign consumers. Their autonomy is strictly limited. Even if the state transferred foreign trade decision-making authorities to selected firms, this change would not lead to an export-oriented economy unless principles and rules similar to those that govern world markets were introduced. The institutional characteristics of state socialism limit the capacity to compete effectively in world markets (especially for manufactures) and thus limit the choice of strategies to those that are inward oriented. This has, we shall see, a profound impact on economic performance and the choice of development strategy.

The institutional preference for self-sufficiency did not immediately produce a crisis in the smaller, resource-poor, Eastern European economies because of the access to Soviet resources. The Soviet Union promoted the development of a radial, bilateral pattern through a variety of measures. The Soviet shopping list (Marer 1984) has had a profound impact on the productive structures of Eastern European economies. The relations of CMEA members with the Soviet Union have been based on the complementarity of their respective economic structures mainly because of the imposition of state socialism, although direct Soviet penetration played an important role, especially in the 1950s.[10] Assessing the Stalinist development policy in Poland from 1950 to 1955, Zbigniew Fallenbuchl (1981a, 337) succinctly observed that "as a result of this policy, an industrial structure was created that ignored developments in the outside world, not only in the West but even in other countries of the bloc, except the Soviet import requirements." This observation applies to other Eastern European countries. A number of industrial branches were established in response to Soviet import needs and very often on the basis of Soviet blueprints and technological know-how. In the 1950s, for example, a very large Soviet demand for Polish mining products was an important factor

[10] The case of Poland is illustrative for other Eastern European countries as well. The period following World War II has witnessed a dramatic reorientation of the Polish foreign trade geographical pattern. By the early 1950s, the Soviet Union became the major trading partner; its share in Polish foreign trade increased from a mere 1 percent in the interwar period to 22 percent in 1948, and 32 percent in 1952. Trade with the capitalist world declined dramatically from 93 percent in the 1930s, to 66 percent in 1948, and to 33 percent in 1952. Interestingly, the share of Polish exports to capitalist countries increased between 1946 and 1950 from 40 to 47 percent, and so did the import share—from 22 to 40 percent. The outburst of cold war and Stalinist style socialist industrialization reversed this trend; in the whole postwar period the share of Poland's export to non-Communist countries hovered around 40 percent and exceeded the 50 percent mark only once in 1981, while the import share was higher than 50 percent only from 1974 to 1976.

in the decision to increase investment outlays in extractive industries (Fallen-buchl 1981a).

The Soviet shopping list has traditionally included machine tools, transport equipment (locomotives, freight and railway passenger cars, etc.), and other products of engineering industry. Although with the opening to the West in the 1970s, the Soviet Union's role in technology transfer to its Eastern European partners decreased, it has remained, nonetheless, the most important supplier of raw materials and the single most important outlet for their industrial exports.

One may conclude that the closure of the economy is an unavoidable consequence of fusing the state and the economy. The economic system, deprived of autonomy and merged with the state, assumes to a certain extent such premises of the state as territoriality and a degree of autonomy with respect to the society and to the external world. As Robert Gilpin (1987, 11) thoughtfully observed, "Whereas powerful market forces in the form of trade, money, and foreign investment tend to jump national boundaries, to escape political control, and to integrate societies, the tendency of government is to restrict, to channel, and to make economic activities serve the perceived interests of the state and of powerful groups within it." A reflection of this tendency is the closed system logic that locates economic resources not to the activities that are most productive and profitable but to those, we shall see, that ease domestic physical constraints to growth. An import-substitution strategy and the bias in favor of energy- and capital-intensive production structure are the offspring of the institutional design of state socialism, in particular of the arrangements governing foreign trade.

INSTITUTIONAL RAMIFICATIONS AND DEVELOPMENT

Decisions on the allocation of productive factors, the choice of technologies, the location of economic activities, and the choice of what is to be produced are political or public policy decisions serving the interests of the dominant groups (nomenklatura) within the state. Although, as we have seen in chapter 1, the state has neither perfect knowledge nor perfect ability to enforce its preferences, institutional ramifications of state socialism to a large extent determine preferences in public policy. The main task of the socialist state is the management of shortages (Comisso and Tyson 1986). By the same token, the available resources should be allocated to those activities that contribute to relieving the pressure of shortages, or to the maximization of output, and to removing constraints on economic growth. Because of fusion, the options available to decision makers only marginally include the active use of foreign trade as a tool for shortages management. Sustaining economic growth is a never-ending shortage-generating process in a state socialist economy. In addition, ever-increasing quantities of productive inputs are required to sustain the economic growth.

The economic system under state socialism is not only closed but also growth oriented. In addition to the ideological promise of catching up with the highly developed capitalist economies and the regime's dependence on economic performance for legitimation, the institutional arrangements favor mobilization as the means to elicit a maximum effort from society. Institutionalized mobilization through command planning is a shortage-generating mechanism. This is especially visible in the process of planning and resource allocation.

Construction of plans that set objectives and allocate resources involves participation and the exchange of messages as well as bargaining among all layers of the party state administration. This is not a conflict-free process; to the contrary, conflicting interests are inherent to the process. This is the process during which the state acquires knowledge about itself and the economy that is indispensable to performing its functions of planning and management. The state thus transforms itself into an arena of negotiations among various groups. The bargaining has several important implications for development strategy, typical patterns of cooperation, and conflicts under a traditional economic system, as opposed to a modified system that relies more on financial indicators; it will be briefly discussed.[11] As demonstrated in chapter 2, the nature of bargaining has remained unchanged within a framework of the modified economic system, although the object and actors participating in it have changed.

Central planners seek to impose ambitious tasks, whereas enterprises try to lower them to minimize effort related to their fulfillment, particularly if bonus systems tend to reward overfulfillment of plans, as is usually the case. The rule generally followed in plan construction is to set plan objectives at last year's "achieved" level, increased by some fraction (ratchet effects). It is in the interest of both managers and workers to keep plan targets at levels that can be easily exceeded and to take all possible measures to prevent central planners from discovering the enterprise's production possibility frontiers. Thus, information withholding is a major strategy followed at lower levels.

Because the plan is constructed every year and central planners are aware of the bargaining strategy pursued by producers, there is a strong possibility that with the passage of time central planners would be able to identify the real productive capacities unless there are significant changes in the production functions. This explains inter alia why enterprise management displays such a strong proclivity to invest, to change technology, and to introduce organizational changes as often as possible. Each change removes in time the moment

---

[11] Discussion is based on the author's direct observation of the process of plan construction in Poland in the 1970s. Studies of strategies revealed in the process of plan construction in other countries show remarkable similarities; see, for instance, Birman (1978), Laky (1979), Wilhelm (1979), and Kornai (1986a). The modified economic system introduces financial parameters of market provenance that are shaped not by a market, but directly by central planners.

when central planners finally discover the contours of a true production function. Or, put differently, it introduces "new" information indeterminacy, enhancing the bargaining power of the enterprise. The paradox is that stagnation makes the task of central planning easier because central planners are more likely to overcome information indeterminacy when the productive structure of the economy is stable. There are, however, strong systemic and external pressures to stimulate economic growth. The state's counterstrategy is to develop alternative communication channels, set highly mobilizing targets, and scale down inputs. The essence of the game for producers is to maximize the input/output ratios in defiance of formal economic rationality while central authorities seek to minimize them.

Enterprises seek to obscure central planners' knowledge by obtaining investment funds. The ability of producers to hide their productive reserves and to obtain investment allocation depends on cooperation with the local party apparatus and the local trade union administration. To boost their position in the state hierarchy, local authorities seek to win a share of the investment pie, and, therefore, they support enterprises in their quest for new investment funds. Potentially, those organizations, as components of the socialist state, may provide central planners with communication channels parallel to those of the state economic administration. If the representatives of these organizations identified themselves with central authorities, the producers' bargaining power would be drastically reduced. However, their loyalties may be split between the necessity of gaining a minimal degree of local support and winning the approval of higher layers of the party-state apparatus. The assessment of their performance, and thus career opportunities, is subject not only to economic criteria, such as plan overfulfillment, but also to political criteria. An important component for appraising the performance of the local authorities is the sociopolitical stability of the region under their control. As Renata Siemieńska (1984, 4) observed, "Local authorities are under vertical pressures, resulting from their ties to the central authorities, and under pressures brought to bear by the local community, including the inhabitants forming various pressure groups, local institutions, and agencies of central institutions located in the area under their jurisdiction." Although this assessment relates to empirical research conducted in Poland, similar observations underlie Jerry Hough's (1969) ground-breaking study.

The outcome of these contradictory pressures is what János Kornai (1986a) dubbed a centralized mechanism of shortage generation.[12] Although the mech-

---

[12] According to Kornai (1986a, 23), two mechanisms lead to a "self-generating vicious circle of shortage": centralized and decentralized. In the decentralized mechanism, three interrelated components are responsible for shortage generation. First, shortages breed shortages: uncertainties about product availability are an invitation to excessive inventories. Second, from the point of view of an enterprise, inventories are never excessive. Because of shortages, domestic "convertibility" of money is limited. And if money cannot buy, then it is less valued than products, which almost always can be bartered for other products. Third, there is no mechanism to move

anism, as we have shown, is triggered by the central planners' expansionist drive, the drive is caused not by idiosyncratic features of those in power but is the consequence of the institutional arrangements within which the only available mechanism of resource allocation is bargaining. Because except for taut planning there is no other method to combat inertia inherent in the state socialist economy, a centralized mechanism of shortage generation, an outcome of the bargaining over planned quotas, is fueled by the practice of setting unrealistic goals to elicit maximum effort from economic actors and to overcome informational indeterminacy in plan construction. As a result, plans tend to exceed the actually available resources in some areas, while in the others they remain below the "production frontiers," and bottlenecks proliferate in the economy (enhanced by the multiplier effect). Although shortages in one area tend to be accompanied by slacks in others, the latter are in the form of unutilized productive capacities rather than easily available raw materials and intermediate products.[13] This in turn increases the bargaining position of producers of producer goods in a struggle for investment allocation.

Shortages exert pressures on central planners whose policy actions, designed to reduce their negative impact on economic performance, are by and large restricted to new investment.[14] Thus the pressures to invest come from above. They are exacerbated by the pressures coming from below, from enterprises and local administration. In addition, because the investment projects are cost free, there are no restraints on their investment demand. (This is another area where their interests overlap those of industrial managers.) To maximize their share in the national investment fund, the projected costs of investment projects are underestimated and the benefits are overestimated. Even knowing that excessive investment may produce inflationary pressures and waste, regional authorities will push for further investment because a region's gains far outweigh losses that result from inefficient allocation of capital *because gains are accrued by the region whereas losses are spread over the whole economy*. Thus powerful systemic forces push the economy toward an investment overheat.

THE PRIVILEGED POSITION OF PRODUCERS OF PRODUCER GOODS

The management of shortages, a major task of the socialist state, and the information limitations faced by central planners lead to a very special role for

---

"excessive" inventories from one producer to another simply because money is not fully a medium of exchange. Some possibilities for barter exchange exist, but they are always restricted by a necessity to match demand bilaterally.

[13] This is so because uncertainties in supplies lead to hoarding of productive inputs and factors. As a result, bottlenecks are rarely accompanied by an excess supply of labor or other raw materials and intermediate products.

[14] This is mainly because their capacity to assure more efficient use of resources in firms is institutionally limited. They have neither the policy tools nor sufficient information to do it.

the suppliers of products widely used in economic activities; these products are producer goods, that is, capital equipment, raw materials, and intermediate products. They occupy a very special position in all state socialist states that goes beyond a mere interest-group role, as depicted by Khrushchev's "metal eaters." Their position, in many respects analogous to Lindblom's concept of the privileged position of business in market-oriented politico-economic systems, derives from their relative autonomy vis-à-vis central planners and their strategic economic position.

Because central planners do not have full knowledge about the economy, economic actors (local authorities and enterprises) have a certain degree of autonomy. The experience of all socialist states with running the economy on pure administrative coercion, as under Stalin, demonstrates that coercion is a grossly inefficient method with a strong potential for political destabilization. Although the authorities can formally command the actors to perform, they have to offer benefits (e.g., privileged access to rationed inputs, investment funds, bonuses) to them to overcome the tendency to maximize the input/output ratio rather than output/input ratio.[15]

The necessity to induce economic actors creates the political underpinnings similar to Charles Lindblom's (1977) analysis of a privileged position of business in the government and politics in the "market-oriented" systems. The privileged position of business stems from the linkage between a government's survival and strong economic performance, the constitutional rules (e.g., protecting private property) that prohibit governments from commanding business to undertake certain kinds of activity and from the mobility of capital. The businessman "will not risk capital, reputation, or the solvency of an enterprise in order to undertake an entrepreneurial venture unless the conditions are favorable" (Lindblom 1977, 176). The autonomy of businessmen derives not from their ultimate responsibility for the profitability of their activities but from the limited directive capacity of the socialist state. The leverage that "business" enjoys in state socialism is more limited than in market societies because it has to respond not to market signals (which have been eliminated) but to administrative commands combined with offers of benefits.

The mechanism of resource allocation leads to a privileged position for the representatives of some segments of the economy. Note that the claims on the limited resources are placed on the state by all layers of the party-state administration. Because the position of local leaders in the intraparty personal peck-

[15] Plan quality or, more generally, economic efficiency, depends upon the ability of central planners to overcome local obstruction. This participation by obstruction, as some (A. Kaminski 1989) dubbed it, distorts information flows, enters illicit agreements with other actors, breaks the law, and so forth. The net result is that the state's ability to identify desirable courses of action and to enforce its preferences in the economic sphere decreases, and so does its ability to maintain satisfactory coordination between various economic activities (Wilhelm 1979). Consequently, plans are often a hybrid of lower level obstruction and central level incomplete knowledge.

ing order depends on the socioeconomic status of the region under their jurisdiction, they have a strong interest in appropriating as many resources as
possible for their regions. Faced with the insatiable demand, the central authorities have to make choices concerning the use of resources. Although the
patron-client relationships do play a role in resource rationing, an overall re-
source-distribution pattern favors the "politically" strong enterprises and
regions. They can, on the one hand, avoid excessively tight quotas and, on the
other hand, obtain easier access to investment funds.

Who are those politically strong actors? For Lindblom's market-oriented
system, they are those who contribute to economic prosperity and who can
cause economic distress by withdrawing capital, that is, all capital owners.
For state socialism, the answer is rooted in the state's direct responsibility for
management of shortages.

The rationing through administrative means favors output maximization at
the expense of technological innovation and new product developments. Because there is no link between pricing and scarcity, planners are unable to
make sound economic decisions, and the criteria become highly politicized.
Yet they are not entirely free from economic exigencies. If socially tolerable
economic performance is to be sustained, access to resources has to depend
not only on networks of personal contacts with those in charge of rationing but
on the assessment of the economic consequences of not allocating required
amounts of inputs to an economic actor. This favors investment in those sectors that have the highest potential for causing disturbances in acute shortages.
Faced with shortages of some basic inputs (e.g., energy, machines, and equipment), a natural (i.e., in line with the closed, fused system logic) response of
the central authorities is to expand or develop domestic production. If this is
not feasible for some reason, then the next option would be to seek their supplies from other Communist countries (the Soviet Union).

Therefore, in contrast with Lindblom's market-oriented system where a
privileged position is derived from owning capital, a privileged position in
state socialism is limited to those in charge of selected sectors of the economy.
These sectors include suppliers of products whose reduced availability may
cause disturbances throughout the whole economy, such as energy, raw materials, and intermediate inputs. Thus because of the closed, fused system
logic, these are mainly producers of producer goods who have easier access to
centrally allocated investment.

There is an important analogy between the privileged position of business
in politics of the market-oriented system and in state socialism. The role of the
representatives of the sectors crucial to economic performance is not an interest-group role. They have a privileged position not because they represent
special interest but because they perform functions essential for the survival
of state socialism. A central planner who has to decide whether to allot investment funds to a coal mine or to a factory producing machine tools faces a

question about the economic welfare of the whole population, not about favoring or not favoring a particular interest group. The argument is not that representatives of these sectors do not lobby for resources. All sectors do. The problem is that as long as the economy is subject to the closed system logic, central planners accord priority to the producers of basic inputs whether they lobby for resources or not. As a well-known Polish economist and a Solidarity deputy to the National Assembly Jerzy Osiatyński (1989, 5) observed: "I am not quite sure whether I would not like to defend inefficient producers of steel. Wherever I went during my election campaign I could not but observe that the basic product in short supply is steel. Because of it, we do not have washers, fridges, freezers, etc." With or without lobbying efforts, the producers of basic inputs have a more powerful bargaining position than the producers of other goods.

The closed system logic flies in the face of a popular "theory" that puts the blame for the bias of investment policies in favor of producers of producer goods on, for example, an allegedly all-powerful coal or metal-eaters lobby, as Khrushchev used to call it. Although undoubtedly the careers of a group of people are tied to the expansion of, say, the energy sector, there is nothing distinct about it. Many other groups share common interest in the survival of a sector (e.g., the state agricultural farms lobby). The power enjoyed by the producers of producer goods derives from the uncertainties involved in any attempt to pursue an outward-oriented development strategy within the institutional constraints of state socialism. Although most decision makers now seem to agree that, for example, energy-saving activities would require fewer resources than the construction of new coal mines, the reluctance of the central authorities to rely on this option comes as no surprise. There are no grounds to believe that the central authorities would suddenly succeed in making producers more sensitive to energy consumption. The economic system of state socialism has repeatedly failed to provide incentives to elicit the desired response of economic actors.

The "producer goods" sector has developed at a rate significantly faster than "consumer goods" sectors in state socialist economies. The strategies pursued by socialist states have discriminated against industries producing consumer goods and accorded priority to heavy industry. According to a recent study, the shares of light industries and a food industry in total industrial output declined steadily between 1971 and 1985.[16] Although in the 1981–1985 period the average rate of growth of consumer goods was higher (in particular in Hungary, Poland, and the Soviet Union) than that of producer goods, this was the result of the contraction or stabilization of investment activity as well

[16] See Economic Commission for Europe (1987/88, 240–41). The only exception is Romania where the share increased from 13.8 percent between 1971 and 1975 to 14.7 percent between 1981 and 1985. This, however, may be attributable to a notoriously low reliability of Romanian official statistics as well as different wholesale price relations.

as energy and raw materials constraints affecting the energy-intensive capital goods sector. Moreover, the slight improvement took place against the backdrop of the declining growth of outputs. The consumer goods sector proved to be less crisis prone, because it relies less on energy. Despite the pressures related to debt servicing and consumer demand, the shift was limited and so was its impact on economic efficiency. As the authors of the UN study note, "The slow progress of structural change [thus] acted to reinforce the factors which contributed to the declines in industrial efficiency growth and to the general slowdown in industrial output growth"(Economic Commission for Europe 1987/88, 247).

This "slow progress" (or lack of progress, as I shall demonstrate for Poland) cannot be blamed on the "theory" of industrialization once shared by all Communist regimes and reflected in their development priorities. According to this theory, the faster rate of growth of producer goods output was a necessary condition for industrialization. The assumption that concerns about national security necessitate the expansion of heavy industry did not solely account for the persistent bias in favor of heavy, defense-oriented industries. The main reason was that fusion and closure of the economy undermined (if not totally excluded) the feasibility of other development sequences, such as a simultaneous development of industry and agriculture. Other sequences would require reliance on a supply of producer goods from the outside. But the decoupling of economic actors from domestic consumers made the reliance on outside goods very difficult.

In addition to generating a closed system that is institutionally incapable of integrating with the economies beyond the state's jurisdiction, the producers are unable to improve (or even averse) microeconomic efficiency, i.e., the output/input ratio. Because of the persistent excessive demand, they have little incentive to develop new products and to improve the cost-effectiveness or quality of their products. As a result, the economic development produces a vicious circle: output increases are "based on ever increasing quantities of all available factor inputs—energy, raw and other materials as well as investment goods." (Economic Commission for Europe 1987/88, 242). To maintain economic growth more and more inputs are needed. This, on the one hand, assures a privileged position of the producer goods sector and, as we shall see, depletes the development potential of the economy.

REVEALED INVESTMENT PREFERENCES: POLAND

Planners' preferences, as revealed in the sectoral pattern of investment allocation, have changed over time in Poland. The changes notwithstanding, some common traits have remained invariant. First, the authorities have favored industry that accounted for more than one-third of total investment expenditures since 1950. Under the pressure of faltering economic performance, the share of industry declined rather significantly between 1975 and 1983. The industry was hit by a forced adjustment to both balance of payments and social demands that the authorities were unable to suppress. Nonetheless, the sectors producing factor inputs (energy, raw and other materials, and capital goods) have retained their privileged position. Second, the authorities have discriminated against investments in agriculture (especially the private sector), the consumer-goods sectors, and rural and urban infrastructure.

Within the industrial sector, preference has been accorded to the extractive industries and those sectors producing capital equipment.[17] As the productive structure of the economy evolved, there were some inevitable modifications in the investment patterns. Yet despite the occasional declines in the share of industry and the increase of expenditures on housing and rural/urban infrastructure, mineral extracting, machine-building, and chemical industries were always accorded preferential treatment. As can be seen from table 3.1, the process of political consolidation and normalization after the imposition of martial law in 1981 was no exception, although the share of the so-called nonproductive investment (housing and infrastructure) increased.[18]

Even during the economic duress in the 1980s, the composition of "productive" investment outlays did not change in favor of capital-saving and less energy-intensive sectors. As can be seen from the data in table 3.1, the "four leading sectors" were less affected by cuts than the other industrial sectors. Investment policy followed the logic of a closed system by completely ignoring the challenge of the debt and the necessity of restructuring the antiquated productive structure. Faced with strongly depressed investment funds, the authorities accorded priority to highly capital-intensive projects in energy and resource extraction despite strong criticism (and not just from the opposition). The investment pattern in the 1980s was even more biased in favor of the energy-producing sector than during the Six-Year Plan of Socialist Modernization in 1951–1955, which focused on the development of the energy and resource industrial base.[19] Despite the criticism voiced by the Government's Consultative Council and the Socioeconomic Council of the Sejm, the coal and energy-producing sectors absorbed roughly one-third of total investment expenditures in the socialized sector in the 1980s.[20] This was at the expense

[17] Fuels and energy, metallurgy, chemicals, and engineering have accounted for more than 70 percent of total industrial investment outlays since 1956.

[18] Their share increased from 32 percent in 1980 to 35.1 percent in 1985 and fell to 34.7 percent in 1987 (Rocznik Statstyczny 1983, 1988).

[19] While commenting on a rapid increase of the share of investment in coal-and energy-producing sectors, the authors of a report of the official Consultative Economic Council noted, "Thus in the mid-1980s, we have attained it seems higher shares [of energy and coal industry in total investment] than during the Six-Year Plan (1951–56), which accorded priority to the development of the energy base" (Życie Gospodarcze 2 [1988]: 4).

[20] According to this source, the share of coal industry, which was simultaneously the largest

TABLE 3.1

Investment Structure in Selected Years (percent)

	1956	1960	1970	1975	1982	1983	1984	1985	1986	1987	1986–1990[a]
Industry	41.8	44.7	40.1	45.4	29.1	27.8	28.3	29.0	29.5	29.6	34.5
Fuels and energy[b]	31.5	30.6	26.8	19.4	40.0	36.6	34.9	36.3	36.5	33.6	35.4
Metallurgy[b]	16.0	11.8	13.1	16.9	5.2	5.2	5.9	6.4	6.4	5.9	8.1
Chemicals[b]	14.3	11.6	12.1	9.5	10.1	10.2	10.2	9.5	8.2	7.9	10.1
Engineering[b]	15.1	14.2	19.8	24.3	21.0	23.2	22.9	21.3	22.1	25.2	20.3
Others[b]	23.1	31.8	28.2	29.9	23.7	24.8	26.1	26.5	26.8	27.4	26.7
Agriculture	10.4	8.0	15.4	13.4	18.6	18.4	17.6	16.2	15.5	15.6	17.3
Transport and communications	11.5	11.7	13.0	11.7	6.0	6.0	7.0	7.7	8.0	8.1	7.3
Housing and communal economy	16.9	18.4	17.4	15.9	33.7	34.3	33.2	32.0	31.3	30.6	27.9
Others	19.4	17.2	14.1	13.6	11.6	13.5	13.9	15.1	15.7	16.1	13.0

Sources: *Rocznik statystyczny* (1956–1988) (GUS, Warsaw); Draft Plan (Planning Commission) for 1986–1990, Warsaw 1986.

[a] Plan for 1986–1990. It was revised in 1988; the major cuts will affect fuels and energy.

[b] The share of a sector in investment outlays in industry.

of more efficient energy-saving and export-oriented projects. The latter accounted for a tiny proportion of investment expenditures. Their share of investment was raised from about 2 to 3 percent in the 1982–1987 period to 8 percent in a revised version of the 1986–1990 plan in 1987 (Jeziorański 1988).

In view of the radical change in the economic external circumstances in the 1980s, the self-reproductive capacity of the industrial structure (a symptom of the persistence of systemic limitations of state socialism) was rather astounding. Jan Główczyk (1989) estimated the shares in total output of the three sectors producing (1) inputs for the production of machinery and equipment, (2) inputs for the production of consumption goods, and (3) consumption goods in 1972, 1984, and 1987. Except for a switch toward consumption goods–related sectors in 1984, the structure displayed a remarkable stability: the share of sector 1 was 54.1 in 1972, 50.8 in 1984, and 53.5 in 1987; of sector 2, 18, 19, and 18.1; and of sector 3, 27.9, 30.2, and 28.4.[21] The share of consumer goods in industrial output, about 40 percent, has not changed since 1960.

Changes within the state-owned industry in the 1980s were explicitly inflationary as well as anticonsumer and antiexport oriented. After a contraction in investment activity between 1979 and 1982, investment growth rates signifi-

recipient of subsidies from the state budget, in total investment outlays increased from 7.6 percent from 1971–1975 and 11.1 percent from 1976 to 1980 to 17 percent.

[21] All the shares were calculated in 1984 prices; thus price changes do not distort the picture.

cantly exceeded the rates of growth of the Net Material Product (NMP). Although the investment level was lower in 1988 than in 1978, it was higher than in 1980.[22] The lion's share of investment was in those sectors that did not contribute directly to the increase of the consumer goods supply. More than one-third of total investment was spent on fuels and energy in the 1982–1987 period. With engineering, these two industries received more than 60 percent of the total investment in industry. The increased share of light industry in this period did not contribute to faster growth.[23] Thus with some modifications in favor of energy production and the coal industry, the basic priorities of the investment policy in the 1970s were retained in the 1980s; the victim of cuts in investments were mainly consumer goods sectors.

In their developmental decisions central planners tended to neglect the agricultural, consumer-producing sectors, and investments in rural and housing infrastructure.[24] Except for transitory shifts in favor of agriculture and sectors producing consumption goods following social upheavals (e.g., the mid-1950s), central planners' investment preferences tended to return to the pattern observed in the early 1950s. Central planners displayed a strong bias in favor of heavy industries. Thus, producers of producer goods were able to retain their privileged position.

Although the secretaries at the helm of the PUWP changed, the structure of capital accumulation remained similar to the structures of the past, despite rhetoric to the contrary. Declarations of policy intent were not transformed into policy actions. The policy toward the private agricultural sector provides a good illustration. Gierek's policy of "consumption as an engine of growth," announced in the early 1970s, did not result in giving priority to agriculture. The share of agriculture in total investment expenditure declined from 16.5 percent between 1961 and 1970 to 15.7 percent from 1971 to 1980. A report of the Central Committee at the 9th Extraordinary Party Congress in 1981 declared: "We must radically break with the anti-agrarian nature of the industrialization pursued in the 1970s."[25]

The treatment given by central planners to the consumer goods sector was not much better. The share of consumer-oriented branches declined by about 4 percent in the second half of the 1970s. This trend was not reversed in the 1980s.

The policies also suffered from the ideological bias against the private sector. Despite the promise of equal treatment made in 1957 and repeated at the

[22] In contrast to 1980, domestic savings were not supported by external financing. On the contrary, foreign trade surplus contributed to inflationary pressures.

[23] The share of light industry increased from 3.7 in 1982 to 5.8 percent in 1987, while the share of the food processing industry fell from 12.2 to 11.6 percent.

[24] This ideologically driven disdain for the private sector was particularly acute in Poland where the process of collectivization was not completed.

[25] See "Sprawozdanie Komitetu Centralnego" *Trybuna Ludu*, 15 July 1981, 5.

6th PUWP Congress in December 1971, the bulk of investment expenditures was allotted to the rather inefficient socialized agricultural sector.[26] Peasants had little savings that could be invested because of the artificially low prices of agricultural products. In addition, they had no access to credit. For instance, the private sector that accounted for almost 80 percent of total agricultural output spent 48 percent less on investments than did the socialized sector in 1980.

With a rapid economic deterioration, the political environment became more favorable to the private agricultural sector. As a Polish economist Jerzy Wilkin (1988, 106) noted:

> One of the promises given to the peasants in 1981, i.e. a pledge to allocate 30 percent of investment to the food-producing sector remained, like many others, on paper. The share of these investments has persistently declined. While it amounted to 24.5 percent of total investment outlays in 1982, the proportion amounted to only 20.7 percent in 1987. The share of agricultural investment in the total dropped from 19.1 to 15.7 percent.

The increase in procurement prices in 1981 augmented peasants' incomes. Combined with the contraction government's investments in the state agricultural sector, this increase produced a turnaround. As can be seen in table 3.2, the share of private agriculture exceeded 50 percent in 1982. However, because urban incomes have risen faster than the incomes of private agricultural producers since 1984, peasants "do not have financial resources sufficient to invest or even to finance current production" (Wilkin 1988, 107). The 1988 "price-income" operation further eroded the financial situation of the private agricultural sector.

The built-in bias in state socialism against private agriculture combined with systemic inability to increase the productivity of the socialized sector undercut industrialization. This confirmed William Arthur Lewis's (1954) famous observation that without a simultaneous expansion of the agricultural sector the industrial transformation would never be complete. Although in

TABLE 3.2

The Share of Private Agriculture in Total Agricultural Investment Expenditures (percent)

	1980	1981	1982	1985	1986	1987
Investment	34.2	44.5	51.3	53.2	53.3	53.6

Source: Calculated from *Rocznik statystyczny* (1983, 1988).

[26] For instance, although the private agricultural sector supplied about 80 percent of the agricultural products, it obtained only 30 percent of the centrally rationed productive inputs in the 1970s.

many nonadministratively planned economies market stimuli provided for the emergence of industries serving agricultural sectors, socialist planning failed to do so.

The transportation and communication sectors have been neglected in development programs. The demand for transportation and communication services is derived from the growth of construction and industry in general, and the geographical distribution and specialization of industrial plants in particular. Between 1965 and 1978, the share of transport and communication sectors in GDP increased by 57 percent (Alton 1981). Within the transport sector, the share of rail transport steadily fell while freight transport increased rapidly. In spite of the increased share in GDP, investment funds allocated to this sector lagged behind. As a result, its share in all fixed capital assets declined between 1950 and 1980 to a level that was the lowest among Eastern European economies (Gomułka 1984).

THE DEPLETION OF DEVELOPMENTAL POTENTIAL

The capacity of state socialism to mobilize resources turned out to be a short-lived phenomenon. It was significantly reduced by the mid-1950s, and the initial success of reconstruction and industrialization can be attributed in part to factors unrelated to state socialism. Its shortcomings in economic development have outlived the initial mobilizational qualities. Uncorrected lapses from economic rationality revealed themselves in the "mortgaging the future" development that leads to the accumulation of deferred developmental costs and the reliance on "exogenous reserves"—extensive factors of development and transfers of resources from abroad. Polish economic development involved the depletion of exogenous reserves without putting the economy on a path toward self-sustaining, efficiency-oriented growth.

Identification of patterns of development depends on the selection of variables to serve as major indicators and on the time-period over which the chosen indicators are averaged. To put Poland's economic performance in perspective, five variables have been selected: investment, consumption, gross industrial production, gross agricultural production, and NMP. The rule stipulating that at least three of the selected indicators display at least a three-year period of above-average performance has been adopted to eliminate fluctuations (see table 3.3).

An examination of the time distribution of the above-average, long-term growth performance (1951–1987) of major economic aggregates points to two periods of significant improvement in the overall economic performance: the first occurred between 1951 and 1957; and the second between 1971 and 1977. The first was followed by a prolonged period of economic stagnation (with the exception of gross industrial output, no other variable recorded an above-average performance beyond a period of three years in the 1960s), whereas the

TABLE 3.3
Economic Performance of Selected Variables, 1950–1988

	Periods of Above-average Long-Term Performance		
Gross capital formation	1951–1953	1972–1975	
Consumption	1954–1957	1971–1977	
Industrial output	1951–1961	1967–1976	
Agricultural output	1953–1958	1971–1973	1982–1984
Net material product	1951–1957	1971–1977	

Source: Rocznik statystyczny (1958, 1960, 1965, 1970, 1972, 1975, 1977, 1980, 1982, 1985, 1986, 1988).

second was followed by a dramatic contraction in aggregate economic activity between 1978 and 1982 and a recovery on the edge of stagnation with a contraction in aggregate economic activity in 1989.

One of the important reasons for the initial fast reconstruction and "socialist modernization" was the legacy of capitalism. As a result of the new political order in Europe that emerged following World War II, Poland's territorial boundaries were moved several hundred miles westward.[27] From an economic point of view, this was beneficial. Poland acquired territories that were better developed and endowed with natural resources, which had preserved an almost undestroyed urban infrastructure. On the other hand, the predominantly rural eastern territories were taken over by the Soviet Union. Consequently, in spite of the destruction caused by the war, Poland's economic potential was greater in 1946 than in 1939. Gomułka (1984) estimates that the industrial fixed capital assets per capita increased by about 50 percent because of territorial changes and population decline.

On the other hand, Poland's initial conditions for development were adversely affected by a substantial loss of human capital, especially acute among the intelligentsia. It was estimated that about 80 percent of the engineers, economists, lawyers, teachers, and other professionals were either killed during the war or did not return to Poland.

The rapid reconstruction in the 1940s, shared by all other European countries, did not owe much to a new politico-economic order. The reconstruction of the Polish economy was fully completed by 1949. The production of all major industrial outputs was significantly higher in 1949 than in 1939.[28] The

[27] As a result of this westward territorial shift, its gross area fell from 389.7 to 311.7 thousand square kilometers.

[28] For instance, the production of pig iron (in tons) stood in 1949 at 200 percent of its level in 1939, the output of rolling products at 160 percent, of coal at 205 percent, and of fertilizers (nitric and phosphoric) at 195 percent (calculated from data in Müller [1988, table 1]).

end-of-war enthusiasm and the relative ease in alleviating production bottle-necks that war losses had created played an important role (Jezierski and Petz 1988, 70–71). Yet, these were not the most important factors explaining rapid reconstruction. Because industrial investments were low in the 1940s, the increased share of industrial output in national income from 18.2 percent in 1939 to 28.1 percent in 1949 as well as the increased proportion of urban population (from 27.2 to 36.2), resulted from the acquisition of more industrially developed territories. The much higher increase in industrial output compared to industrial stock of fixed capital assets illustrates that this contributed significantly to the growth performance between 1946 and 1953. Gomułka (1984) estimates that these external reserves accounted for about 85 percent of the increased output in that period. Thus a better initial endowment in productive capacities than in 1939 was responsible for the impressive reconstruction. In addition, it is worth recalling that the reign of state socialism in the economic sphere began in 1950.

Prewar development of infrastructure and easy-to-activate industrial capacities also contributed to the industrial growth in the early 1950s. The economy could capitalize on the urban infrastructure that was built before the war. Investment resources could be put directly to productive uses instead of being used to maintain and expand the railroad network, and so forth. Because infrastructure investments are also highly capital intensive, this was an important factor that facilitated economic growth for a long time. A transient factor was "surplus population."

Another reserve was surplus labor in the agricultural sector. The ability to activate labor "reserves" should be credited to state socialism. As argued earlier, there were two waves of accelerated economic growth, which were followed by periods either of faltering economic growth performance (1959–1970), or crisis and stagnation (1978–). During the first period of economic expansion from 1951 to 1957, the availability of an underemployed agricultural population provided a strong boost to economic growth.

Massive entry of "baby boomers" into the labor force in the 1970s coincided with the second acceleration in economic expansion.[29] Therefore, because periods of economic expansion coincided with an above-average growth in the supply of labor, the industrial employment factor explains a significant portion of the variation in economic growth performance.[30]

---

[29] A cursory examination of the rates of growth of industrial employment reveals a positive relationship with economic growth performance. For instance, taking as a criterion the average annual rates of growth in industrial employment, the following periods can be distinguished: rapid growth in 1951–1957; stagnation in 1958–1960; relatively rapid growth in 1961–1976; contraction and stagnation in 1976–1987.

[30] Most studies of factors contributing to Polish economic growth estimate that purely quantitative growth of capital capacity and labor has accounted for at least 40 percent of the growth of

The increased share of industrial employment and output in the total economy and the inevitable depletion of surplus labor in the agricultural sector meant that economic growth would be hampered unless other untapped reserves of growth became available. Macroeconomic data on Polish economic performance in the 1960s clearly demonstrated that in spite of a relatively rapidly increasing labor force the maintenance of historical growth rates became increasingly costly. The "reserve" of integrating women into the workforce was exploited by the end of the 1960s. The expanding industrial sector and the slow growth in productivity contributed to a rapid growth of employment opportunities for women. Between 1950 and 1982 the share of women in the total workforce increased from 30.6 to 43.3 percent, which meant that all women willing to work were employed. The largest increase occurred in the 1960s when the percentage of women in the total workforce climbed from 33.1 to 39.4 percent.

To maintain positive rates of growth, an increasing share of national income had to be allotted to capital formation. With the disappearance of the agricultural labor surplus and the incorporation of women into the labor force, extensive factors of growth were close to depletion. Only technological and organizational improvements might have triggered increases in the productivity of labor and capital. However, although official declarations pointed out the necessity of moving from the extensive to the intensive stage of economic development, the new stage of growth based on the increased productivity from the activation of internal reserves was not forthcoming.[31]

The economy would have plunged into stagnation in the early 1970s had it not been for access to Western credits. As a Polish economist Aleksander Müller (1987, 7) succinctly notes:

> The Polish Crisis had already made its appearance in December 1970. At that time the economy suffered the breakdown, the economic system had failed and the ruling group collapsed under the pressure of labour protest, despite the use of considerable military force. In the years 1971–75, the economy was *reanimated* through a transfusion of foreign credits.

The sudden improvement in economic performance in the 1970s was only partially due to internal factors. In contrast to the first industrialization drive in the early 1950s, when the activation of the agricultural labor surplus and exploitation of "infrastructural" reserve contributed to an economic leap forward, the second industrialization drive was due mainly to the activation of "reserves" available in the foreign economic sphere. The 1970s also witnessed the entry of postwar "baby boomers" into the labor markets. The ac-

---

the economy, whereas technological progress and higher labor productivity explain the remaining 60 percent (see Nasilowski [1974]; Gomułka [1984]).

[31] For a discussion of extensive and intensive growth, see Wilczynski (1972).

cess to foreign credits allowed an increase in net capital formation that in turn absorbed the available labor force and triggered an economic expansion.

The activation of the "foreign reserve" was made possible by an increase in international liquidity in the early 1970s, the favorable political climate for East-West economic interaction, and Poland's high creditworthiness.[32] Because of the extremely prudent policies of Gomułka, who was often accused of "petty peasant" mentality for his attitude toward foreign credits, the total Polish foreign indebtedness was very low.[33] In conjunction with latent industrial capacities, the increased imports of intermediate products financed by Western credits immediately raised output as well as labor and capital productivity as bottlenecks were removed that in turn activated idle industrial capacities. In addition, favorable weather conditions and a temporary reversal of a traditional antipeasant bias in agricultural policies further boosted overall growth performance.

The reserve of "past mistakes"—as one author called it (Brus 1982, 120)—was depleted by the mid-1970s because the Polish exports did not generate sufficient income to pay for increased imports and to service the rapidly expanding foreign debt.[34] Without substantial increases in labor and capital productivity and drastic cuts in government and private spending, the economy would have headed for a balance-of-payments crisis. An attempt to reduce domestic absorption rates by cutting individual consumption did not succeed because of workers' protests in 1976. Although Poland had access to international credits for another four years, it used them to finance standards of living exceeding its economic capacities rather than for an adjustment of production structure. The result was a crisis; cuts in imports of industrial inputs and capital equipment led to a dramatic contraction in production that further depleted hard currency revenues.

[32] Internationally, two developments were favorable to the activation of this domestically accumulated "reserve of past mistakes." First, the improvement in American-Soviet relations produced a political climate conducive to more intensive East-West interaction in the economic realm. Second, stagflation of Western economies and, associated with it, reduction of attractive investment opportunities contributed to the active interest among international banks to extend credit to the Soviet Union and other Eastern European Countries. This trend was later reinforced by the so-called petrodollar recycling. Other CMEA countries also turned to Western governments and banks for credits, but they did so on a lesser scale.

[33] The total foreign indebtedness, including long-term loans to be paid in the 1990s was about $1.8 billion in 1971. In the 1960s, the aggregate deficit in the balance of trade with the developed West did not exceed $300 million, whereas in 1970 it showed a hefty surplus of $80 million (Machowski and Zwass 1972, 120). It is worth noting that throughout almost the whole period between 1946 and 1971, the Polish economy experienced a net outflow of resources; only in 1957 and 1959 were inflows from abroad higher than outflows (see Fallenbuchl 1984, table 12.4).

[34] The hopes that Western technologies would make the Polish industrial sector competitive in international markets were also shattered; as it turned out, technology transfer could not have brought about a viable export sector because the investment programs included projects that either faced saturated markets or were moving in that direction (for more, see Marer 1981, 63).

Because no other easily tapped "reserve" was available, aside from radical political and economic reforms that would overhaul state socialism, the consumption of internally accumulated reserves (e.g., capital equipment) became unavoidable. The former "foreign reserve" turned into an impediment to economic development. The need to run a positive balance of hard currency trade to service the debt constrained investment outlays.[35] A fall in national income reduced savings.[36]

Capital surpluses were not adequate to replace worn-out machinery and capital equipment. In addition, the investment shortage was exacerbated by policy mistakes. The authorities did not come up with an overall program focused on the improvement of economic efficiency, which would selectively abandon capital investment projects begun in the late 1970s. Ad hoc restrictions were extended only to about 15 percent of the investment projects[37] (*Życie Gospodarcze* 32 [1985]: 7). Because of unchanged amortization rates while prices of capital components were raised after the 1982 price shock, enterprises were starved of resources to replace obsolete capital. As a result, the industrial base has eroded.

The proportion of obsolete equipment was particularly substantial in research- and development-intensive sectors such as electronics (70 percent), synthetics (78 percent), machine tools (71 percent), electrical equipment (80 percent).[38] The average operation time of machinery also increased—from 11 years in 1974 to 15 years in 1985 for machine tools used in engineering. In 1985, more than 66 percent of machine tools had been in operation for at least ten years.[39]

The prospects for halting decapitalization are rather grim. It has been estimated that to freeze the process of decapitalization about Zł 5 billion would have to be spent between 1986 and 1990. Reversal would absorb at least another Zł 5 billion. Because the total investment outlays including the projects already started, infrastructure, education, and so forth, were set at Zł 10 billion in the 1986–1990 period, this expenditure would exceed the present capacities of the economy unless consumption was significantly depressed. The process

[35] The debt crisis led to the outflow of resources of about 25–30 percent of the annual hard currency export in the 1980s. In spite of this significant effort, Poland was not able to pay interest on its outstanding debt. The total of unpaid interest in the 1981–1987 period amounted to $10.2 billion, or a quarter of Poland's total hard currency debt in 1988 (Olechowski and Wojtowicz 1988).

[36] Poland's cuts in industrial machinery imports were among the largest in the indebted countries; only Romania and Argentina implemented similar import austerity measures. Poznański (1988a, 55) estimates that about $4.3 billion in the value of capital stock between 1980 and 1984 was not replaced.

[37] *Życie Gospodarcze*, no. 32 (1985): 7.

[38] Albin Plocica's estimates, published in *Finanse*, no. 1 (1986) and quoted in Baczynski (1986, 4).

[39] Ibid.

could be controlled by increasing the share of modernizing endeavors in total investment outlays, but this has not been the case.[40]

The decapitalization does not bode well for the prospects of a real turnaround in economic growth performance. Worn-out machines are subject to more frequent breakdowns. They consume more energy and intermediate inputs thereby constraining production in other areas. They also contribute to the lower quality of manufactured goods and to the growing technological gap between Poland and the Newly Industrialized Countries (NICs), not to mention the West. Thus, the inability to replace used-up capital is both a symptom and a cause of a precarious and uncertain recovery.

There are multiple signs that the long neglected infrastructure needs upgrading (Gomułka 1984) and that the pollution of the natural environment has reached levels that endanger biological survival of the population. The extremely wasteful if not plunderous use of natural resources and a disregard for the natural environment present other barriers to development. According to the recent report published by the Chemists' Association, annual economic losses in the 1980s directly attributable to environmental pollution reached 20 percent of the GNP.[41] The level of pollution in many industrial areas is a threat to public health. A projection of the historical rates of water consumption indicates that demand will exceed disposable water supplies in the late 1980s (Kozłowski 1983). Although environmentalists' forecasts have a poor predictive record, this projection cannot be disregarded in an economic system deprived of self-regulation and subject to pressures for growth at any price.

In Defiance of Institutional Limits: The Failure of Gierek's Modernization Strategy

Gierek's modernization strategy in the 1970s provides an extreme illustration of defying the institutional limits of state socialism. At first glance, nothing was wrong with the modernization strategy based on imports of capital equipment and technology from the West. Nothing was wrong also with the reliance on external financing in an era when credits were extremely cheap and easy to obtain. Historically, many countries followed this path quite successfully.

Yet Gierek's modernization strategy accelerated the decay of state socialism by bringing about the total crisis—political, economic, demographic, ecological, and so forth. As we shall see in chapter 4, the crisis was not only the result of import-led modernization strategy; it was also caused by the Gierek regime's inability to assure social compliance and stability through noneco-

---

[40] It required the authorities to make hard choices about which industries should be allowed to stay afloat, but because of lack of social support, they were not able to do it. In addition, the economic system in its present form would hardly provide central planners with the information about relative scarcities and comparative advantage that is indispensable to make those choices.

[41] Quoted in *Solidarność News* (Brussels), 133, 1–15 May 1989, 4.

nomic measures. This resulted in a significant shift in the composition of Western imports in favor of consumer goods.[42] The "wait and see" strategy that was pursued until 1981 contributed to the rapid increase of the debt burden between 1976 and 1981 without adding anything to the export capability of the Polish economy. The opening was only to imports; it was not accompanied by the changes in the economic system to make firms responsive to the stimuli of international markets.

From the point of view of the present discussion, it is irrelevant which factor, import-led growth or excessive consumption, contributed more to the crisis. The crux of the matter is that both factors were the product of the institutional arrangements and that an import-led growth strategy could not be successful without abolishing the fusion principle and closed system logic. The absence of effective constraints on bargaining resulted in a "centrally planned anarchy" in the investment sphere. Thus, the institutional arrangements were detrimental to the economy's capacity to compete effectively in world markets for manufactured products.

The major assumptions of import-led strategy were incompatible with what was institutionally feasible. Gierek's modernization strategy was flawed on several counts. First, it did not include institutional changes that would provoke the best response from economic actors. The dominant view of the new policy among the ideologues was that wage increases would provide a strong motivation to increase productivity. A simultaneous expansion of consumption and investment would thus guarantee rapid growth in productivity; economic growth would be consumption led.[43] The basic flaw was the lack of reasons to suppose that increased wages would indeed boost labor productivity unless the rewards were unambiguously linked to an improved performance beneficial to the economy as a whole. There was nothing, however, in the existing design of the economic system to ensure that this condition be met. Gierek clearly drew on his earlier experience running Silesia where he had succeeded in combining production and consumption expansion but at the expense of other regions.[44] On the national level, the strategy could be repeated only by drawing on external resources.

[42] The CC debt was already at the level that would make its management painful for society in the mid-1970s. See appendix B.

[43] At its outset, the strategy was extremely risky. There was uncertainty whether consumption "downpayment" would be turned into higher labor productivity growth and whether new technologies would be quickly absorbed and spilled over the economy. The strategy also critically hinged on the continuation of favorable conditions in world markets. No one took into account that the simultaneous expansion of investment, consumption, and international borrowing left the authorities with little room for maneuvering to absorb possible adverse developments.

[44] The Katowice voivodship, encompassing most of Silesia, during Gierek's rule as voivodship first party secretary was envied by other regions. The region was called "Polish Katanga," a reference to the province in the Congo that sought secession from the central government because of its riches.

Second, the strategy designers realized that any growth in labor productivity was conditioned on both work intensity and on technology. This was to be accomplished through the increased imports of Western know-how and capital equipment. The Gomułka regime policy of keeping hard currency imports in line with hard currency export revenues was to be discarded. Thus the development was to be import led until a viable export sector was established. Yet the economic system remained both fused and closed.

Third, the relaxation of controls over the economy distinguished the policies of Gierek's regime from other state socialist countries. Gierek seemed to believe that a major obstacle to economic growth was rooted in laws that defied economic rationality and in the shortages of inputs caused by Gomułka's excessively deflationary policies (Bozyk 1983). He failed to grasp that all these constraints were "substitutes" for decentralization, competition, and economic discipline. In the absence of markets, less coercive methods of governance than those of the Gomułka regime produced a "centrally planned anarchy."

Fourth, the success of Gierek's strategy of indebted development hinged on the development of an internationally competitive industrial sector. Yet no significant changes have been introduced in the institutional system, which, as was argued earlier, was incapable of competing effectively in the international markets for manufactured goods. Although credits were used to modernize industry and to sustain production,[45] they failed to improve industrial competitiveness.[46] In other words, the closed system logic turned out to be incompatible with the increased imports from the West.

The blame for the lack of focus on export promotion in investment policy (convincingly demonstrated by several authors, e.g., Brada and Montias [1984]; Bozyk [1983]), could be put not only on flawed policies but above all on the institutional limitations of state socialism. The incompatibility between levels of consumption that the economic system could sustain and the new demands on the system's capacity to export was one of the main direct causes of the economic crisis.

The conditions accountable for the "Polish economic miracle" of the early 1970s quickly evaporated. The limits to growth emerged once the previously idle industrial capacities—activated thanks to increased imports—were used while the new ones were delayed because of growing imbalances in the econ-

[45] From 1971 to 1976, capital equipment imports accounted for 35 percent of Poland's hard currency expenditures (Szeliga 1982, 19). In addition, current production required more and more Western industrial inputs.

[46] Poznański (1988a) shows that importations of Western equipment and know how contributed to the increase in Poland's competitiveness as measured in unit values for manufactures but "the improvements did not last beyond 1979" (p. 49). However, such measures as the share of high-processed manufactures or unit values are also influenced by the foreign trade deficit. If it is financed mostly by external borrowing, as in Poland, exports do not include less profitable items.

omy. By the end of the decade, it became clear that the consumption- and import-led strategy had led Poland into a debt trap.[47]

The Polish debt crisis cannot be satisfactorily explained in terms of exogenous developments, such as the world recession in the early 1980s, the oil shocks, skyrocketing interest rates in the international financial markets, natural disasters, or increased protectionism in the market economies of the West. External developments may have caused additional pressures, but they can hardly be held responsible for the scope of the crisis. The reasons were rooted in the impossibility of pursuing an outward-oriented strategy within the institutional framework of state socialism. Because the institutional changes implemented by Gierek did not alter the principle of fusion and the closed system logic, the collapse of the strategy illustrated the consequences of defying institutional limitations.

The Polish economic crisis was homemade, although some exogenous developments contributed to it. International developments were, however, less important than in the cases of other state socialist countries. For instance, Poland's terms of trade with the Soviet Union, its major trading partner and supplier of oil and other raw materials, deteriorated following changes introduced in 1975 in the formula for intra-CMEA foreign-trade prices.[48] But the decline was the smallest among Eastern European economies.[49] Rapidly increasing costs of debt servicing and growing competition in the increasingly protected Western markets adversely affected the Polish balance of payments position.[50] This certainly contributed to a decreased debt-servicing capacity, which had already eroded in the mid-1970s, that is, prior to the second oil and interest rate shocks.[51]

Although the subsequent crisis was also the result of foreign borrowing to finance excessive consumption (see chap. 4), its seeds were also planted by a systemic failure to curb the appetite for investment and to institute a two-way opening of the economy. The sudden availability of resources significantly eased constraints on the allocation of investment and eventually exceeded the country's investment absorptive capacity.[52] The prevailing sense of an abun-

[47] For more, see appendix B.

[48] These changes provided for annual adjustments based on moving averages of world prices, instead of the earlier system of adjustments every five years. Because of the moving average, however, increases in the oil prices charged by the Soviet Union did not keep pace with world prices.

[49] Between 1978 and 1983, they fell by 13 percent, which was less than the decline in other Eastern European countries (see Marer 1988, 32). The decline was also the smallest between 1974 and 1976 (Kohn and Lang 1977).

[50] For an excellent analysis of a relative decline of competitiveness of Eastern European exports on Western markets, see Poznański (1986a).

[51] For a detailed analysis of the sustainability of the Polish debt, see appendix B.

[52] This was the result of the so-called Large Economic Organizations (WOG) reform. For more, see Fallenbuchl (1981a) Jerma Kowicz (1988).

dance of capital was triggered by a sudden relaxation of the heavy-handed discipline of Gomułka, which sharpened the appetites of all economic actors. The changes in the economic system increased the monopolization of the economy and the bargaining power of industrial enterprises and thus undermined the ability of central planners to administer the economy in accordance with the five-year plan.[53] With easy access to capital, economic actors "hiked themselves onto the plan." Once they were in the plan, their requirements were stepped up and annual investment plans were perpetually overfulfilled.[54]

Although the propensity to invest was probably strongest at the lower levels of economic administration, the "top" central planners were not innocent. In fact, two major capital investment projects of the 1970s, the Katowice Steel Mill and the Northern Port Refinery in Gdańsk, were started "outside of the investment plan," thus destroying whatever was left of the original national investment program for the 1972–1975 period. Incidentally, these projects illustrate the bias of the central authorities in favor of producer goods sectors.

The state's loss of directive capacity over investment expansion was not the only problem, although it was accountable for growing shortages throughout the economy. The investment strategy suffered from four other weaknesses. First, it failed to encourage intersectoral specialization. Jósef Brada and John M. Montias (1984, 405) ascribe "the apparent failure of specialization . . . to the scattering of investment associated with excessive egalitarianism in allocating investments among enterprises." The lack of concentration of investment activity was accountable inter alia for the lengthening of the gestation period, exacerbated by the inadequate capacity of the construction industry.

Second, a dramatic increase in imports from the West did not lead to the formulation of a proexport investment strategy focused on a few branches of the economy or to a significant redesign of the organizational structure of foreign trade. Although the so-called Large Economic Organizations (in Polish WOGi) established in the 1970s, were more closely integrated with the FTOs and were to be allowed to retain a portion of hard currency earnings, these provisions of the reform either were not fully implemented or were suspended because of the balance-of-payments constraint. These changes, together with a limited linking of some prices to the world prices, probably helped to reduce the insulation of producers from world markets. This was not congruent, however, with the extent of the opening to Western imports, and, more significantly, it was not accompanied by a concentration of resources on proexport endeavors.

[53] The 1971–1975 plan was soon in shambles, particularly hard currency imports, which exceeded the plan by more than 71 percent, and investment outlays, which were higher by 54 percent.

[54] From 1971 to 1975, for example, the total sum of investment planned by the various ministries exceeded by 15.2 percent the guidelines set in the central plans; in 1976, the figure was a spectacular 25.8 percent.

The persistence of shortages, exacerbated by investment expansion, provided little incentive to central planners eventually to cut out inefficient production lines and specialize in export production. Brada and Montias (1984, 392–93) argue that the priority status of export-oriented sectors was lowered because of military demands to expand the machine-building industry. The increased investment outlays in the military industrial complex reduced the resources available to other traditional recipients, such as the energy-producing sector.

Third, the rapid expansion of energy-intensive industries (e.g., metallurgy and heavy engineering) coincided with neglect in the fuels and energy-producing sectors. Planners tended to give preference to large-scale energy-intensive projects such as the prefabricated house industry or to the expansion of cement and nitrogen fertilizer production. Despite warnings from experts that the energy production sector was underinvested, maintenance was neglected, and its capital equipment, increasingly outdated and worn-out, was subject to growing breakdown rates. Some authors (Gomułka 1981) argued that the supply of energy had already become a constraint by 1973–1975.[55]

Fourth, the bias against the private agriculture sector provided another limit to economic growth by exacerbating disequilibria. The Gierek period was no exception to the traditional pattern of agricultural policy vacillation between ideological orthodoxy and pragmatism.[56] Gierek's initially pragmatic policies brought about a very impressive growth of agricultural output; during the years 1972 and 1973 the growth rate was 8.4 and 7.3 percent, respectively. However, once the PUWP's political controls were consolidated, the policy changed and began to favor the socialized sector and threaten private farmers with the prospects of forced collectivization. As a result, agricultural production stopped growing. In addition, the high priority given to increasing meat production in the mid-1970s resulted in grain imports for both food consumption and animal feeding. These imports were an extra drain on the already overstretched balance of payments.

THE FAILURE OF ADJUSTMENT IN THE 1980s: THE TRAP OF THE CLOSED SYSTEM LOGIC

The economic policies pursued by the Jaruzelski regime after the imposition of martial law in 1981 brought about, as we have seen, an accelerated deple-

[55] An indirect indication that energy had become a major macroeconomic constraint was given by the fact that outputs of energy-intensive products such as cement and nitrogen fertilizer were the first to be drastically reduced; in 1979 their outputs were 10 percent lower than in 1977. Because increasing amounts of coal were needed for export, electric power plants often experienced shortages and cut electricity supplies mainly for industrial users. Hence problems of the external balance of payments spilled over into other sectors of the economy.

[56] For an extensive discussion of the vicissitudes of Polish agricultural policies in the 1970s, see Korboński (1981).

tion of developmental potential, an increased Convertible Currency (CC) debt, a deteriorating quality of life, triple-digit inflation, and increased shortages. This situation was not simply the result of policy blunders; mainly, the regime, faced with domestic political constraints, had very little room to maneuver.[57] Once it rejected the Ceaucescu approach to "solving" the debt crisis through massive repression and by imposing extreme hardships on the population, nothing short of overhauling state socialism would reverse the deterioration.[58] The analysis of "adjustment" in the 1980s illustrates the systemic limits on interaction with world markets under the conditions of extreme external financial stress.

The credit squeeze that followed the imposition of martial law forced the authorities to abandon the previous pattern of postponing adjustment through external borrowing.[59] Although CC imports were adjusted downward beginning in 1977 (the peak volume of imports was in 1976), a surplus in the CC balance of trade was not achieved until 1982. Between 1982 and 1988, the CC surplus increased in 1983 and 1984, when it reached its record level of about $1.5 billion. Subsequently, the surplus declined steadily to $941 million in 1988.

The surplus emerged not as a result of an export expansion but from the suppression of imports. More significantly, the improvement in the CC balance of trade had little to do with exports generated from industrial capacities built during the so-called second industrialization drive. They were *the result of a combination of more extensive exploitation of nonrenewable natural resources and of austerity measures that reduced domestic absorption of agricultural products.* Initially, the improvement occurred in those areas that remained highly responsive to centralized administrative measures. Later other sectors improved thanks to a belatedly introduced, more flexible exchange rate policy and a better-designed reward system.

The dominant pattern of response to the necessity of generating CC trade surpluses can be described as "coal-food" with a slight shift toward "miscellaneous manufactures" from 1986 to 1988. Agriculture and food processing played a crucial role in generating a surplus in the nonsocialist balance of trade. In 1982, cuts in the imports of Western grain by 95 percent and food

[57] For the analysis of political constraints, see chapter 5.

[58] As revealed in chapter 2, the reform measures introduced in the 1980s represented the "maximum" level of coopting market instruments without destroying state socialism.

[59] After the imposition of martial law, the only source of new money was credit lines arranged earlier. But they also evaporated: between end-1980 and mid-1982 the number of credit lines available in Western commercial banks decreased by $2.7 billion (Organization for Economic Cooperation and Development *Financial Capital Markets*, Paris, March, 84, 1983). By mid-1984 medium- and long-term credits available to Poland dried up. Between 1981 and 1983 Poland did not obtain international medium- and long-term credits either through publicized bank credits or bond issues. The only source of new credits was a revolving trade facility linked to interest payments on commercial debt.

and live animals by 55 percent were made possible by compression of domestic consumption and favorable weather conditions.[60] Agricultural imports were cut twice as much as the average suppression of CC imports. Food-related imports dropped from $1,103 million in 1981 to $754 million in 1982. The cut accounted for 47 percent of the total decline in Western imports (Kamiński 1987, 169). Agricultural and food imports, which accounted for more than 40 percent of CC imports in 1980 (in current prices), dropped to 24 percent in 1984, while the agricultural share alone fell from 25 to 11 percent.[61] Although Poland remained a net importer of agricultural products in the 1980s, the magnitude of the agriculture-related import contribution to the swing from a CC foreign trade deficit to surplus was the largest among industries and sectors.[62] It is noteworthy that the food-processing industry was a net CC exporter throughout most of the 1980s.

As had frequently occurred, coal turned out to be the major source of export revenues after the imposition of martial law. The imposition of military rules and discipline on coal miners combined with longer working hours increased output (Fallenbuchl 1983). During the first year of martial law, the volume of output increased by 16 percent and the volume of coal exports increased by 88 percent. The trend remained in 1983 as exports increased by 23.8 percent and exceeded the 1981 volume by 44 percent (*Mały Rocznik Statystyczny* 1984, 239). Coal with other nonrenewable natural resources like gas, coke, copper, silver, and sulphur accounted for about one-third of nonsocialist exports in 1982. Their share remained at this level until 1985, when it was 32 percent, and fell to 25 percent in 1986 and 23 percent in 1987.[63] Net CC exports (minus CC imports) of fuels and the energy sector alone accounted for between 78

[60] Favorable weather accounted in large part for several successive years of high harvests from 1982 to 1985, which permitted lower cuts in food consumption that accounted in Poland for more than 50 percent of personal expenditure. Value added of the agriculture sector increased at an average annual growth rate of 7.6 percent from 1982 to 1984 as compared with an average annual growth rate of 2.2 percent industrial value added, which grew at a 2.2 percent rate between 1982 and 1984.

[61] Polish purchases of food and live animals (Standard International Trade Classification [SITC.0]) from the United States, financed mostly by the Commodity Credit Corporation, fell from $531 million in 1981 to $120 million in 1982 and were at $130 million in 1984 (from the UN Trade Data System).

[62] In order of decreasing contribution to the improvement in hard currency balance of trade measured as the absolute change in sectoral trade balance in 1984 as compared with 1981, the following list can be drawn: (1) agriculture (+ $964 million); (2) food processing (+ $677 million); (3) fuels and energy (+ $500 million); and (4) construction (+ $16 million). Author's calculation from the data in *Mały Rocznik statystyczny* 1985, converted from złotys at the official exchange rates.

[63] In the 1985–1987 period, coal accounted on average for 15 percent of CC exports in current prices, gas coke for 0.5 percent, copper for 4 percent, silver for 1.8 percent, and sulphur for 4 percent. Their total share in this period amounted to 25 percent. (Calculated from *Rocznik statystyczny handlu zagranicznego* [1988]).

percent (1985) and 52 percent (1987) of the CC trade surplus in the 1982–1988 period.[64]

Although exports of resources continued to be important CC net earners, wood and paper and light industry increased their contributions to CC trade surpluses in the 1985–1987 period.[65] The loss in surplus because of reduced coal exports was more than offset by the gains of underinvested light industry, which responded positively to more realistic exchange rates and other incentives such as retained CC accounts. The victim of the increased net CC exports, especially of the light industry, was the domestic consumer goods markets. In 1987 and throughout most of 1988, many consumer goods were diverted to CC markets at the expense of domestic market supplies.[66]

Ironically, the sectors that brought about improvement in Poland's balance of trade were not those that attracted the bulk of investment in the 1970s. The failure of the import-led growth strategy was illustrated by a rapid decline in machinery and equipment, whose share did not make any significant gains in the 1980s. In volume, it dropped from 32.1 percent in 1981 to 19.8 percent in 1984. That this drop came as a surprise to planners is demonstrated by the fact that exports of this sector were 27.6 percent below planned targets for 1984 (Gruzewski 1985). With the exception of 1986, the volume of engineering industry CC exports increased at rates lower than total CC exports. By generating sizable soft currency exports, which on average accounted for more than 60 percent of socialist exports in the 1980s, the engineering industry indirectly contributed by supporting imports of fuels and energy that otherwise would have had to be purchased with convertible currency.

The absence of changes in the commodity composition of exports reflected the basic structural and systemic weaknesses of the Polish economy. The composition of exports to both the developed and developing world countries did not undergo any significant change. Exports remained dominated by commodities characterized by relatively high resource intensiveness and a low degree of industrial processing, such as mining, agriculture, or the food industry. As can be seen from table 3.4, the nonsocialist exports of raw materials and low-processed goods (i.e., food, raw materials, and the mineral fuels line total), accounted for roughly the same proportion of overall exports in 1987 as in 1982. The slight decline of 4.5 percentage points in Western exports was offset by a 5 percentage point increase in the Third World's share. The share of the low-processed commodity group in total nonsocialist exports was 40.8 percent in 1987 and 40.0 percent in 1982. There was no turnaround in 1988.

---

[64] In 1982, the ratio was 58.9 percent.

[65] The deficit of Zł 11 billion in 1985 turned into a surplus of Zł 63 billion in 1987, accounting for 18.3 of the CC surplus (derived from *Rocznik statystyczny handlu zagranicznego* [1988]).

[66] Consequently, shortages and inflation increased and thereby contributed to the outburst of strikes in 1988.

TABLE 3.4

Composition of Exports to Socialist Countries, the Developed West, and the Third World (SITC Classification in Percent, Current Prices)

	1978			1982			1985			1987		
	(1)[a]	(2)[b]	(3)[c]	(1)	(2)	(3)	(1)	(2)	(3)	(1)	(2)	(3)
A[d]	3.1	16.6	10.5	2.4	14.1	2.9	3.3	17.0	4.8	3.5	20.2	4.0
B	2.1	9.3	4.0	3.0	9.8	7.2	3.5	12.7	10.5	2.9	9.1	10.1
C	11.1	25.9	9.2	11.2	25.5	8.0	9.7	26.8	10.5	7.8	15.6	9.1
Total	16.3	51.8	23.7	16.6	49.4	18.1	16.5	56.5	25.8	14.2	44.9	23.1
D	6.2	3.5	6.6	5.6	4.3	2.9	6.6	6.0	3.8	7.4	7.0	7.1
E	54.0	18.2	38.1	57.6	19.3	49.3	57.0	10.1	44.8	52.2	14.9	21.2
F	23.4	25.9	31.6	20.1	27.0	30.0	20.1	27.4	25.7	26.2	31.7	48.5

Source: Calculated from *Rocznik statystyczny handlu zagranicznego* (1980, 1984, 1988).

Note: Beginning in 1986, construction exports have been classified as "other industrial commodities," which previously were included in the "Machines and transport equipment" category. Because of rounding, the totals for columns may not yield 100.

[a] (1)—Socialist economies.

[b] (2)—Developed West economies.

[c] (3)—Third World economies.

[d] A—Food, beverages, tobacco; B—Raw materials; C—Mineral fuels; TOT—sum of A, B, and C; D—Chemicals; E—Machines and transport equipment; F—Other industrial commodities.

As the authors from the Institute of World Economy at the Central School of Planning and Statistics noted:

> There was some improvement in foreign trade in 1988 as compared with 1987. The growth of exports and imports accelerated. Some noteworthy achievements included a twofold increase in revenues from exports of licenses as well as a reduction, albeit limited, in direct financing of imports by the state. On the other hand, clearly the most disadvantageous was the absence of change in the commodity composition of exports to countries from the Second Payment Area [convertible currency transactions] (*Gospodarka Światowa*, 1989, 84)

As the changes in the structure of production and the commodity composition of exports were limited, the adjustment process was more of the "expenditure-reducing" rather than the "expenditure-switching" type. The factors that contributed to a swing from deficits to surpluses in hard currency trade included a drastic reduction in personal consumption in 1982, a shift of consumer goods (e.g., durables) from domestic to international markets from 1987 to 1988, deep cuts in imports of agriculture-related products and of machinery and equipment, expansion of mining output, increases in agricultural production, and longer working hours (combined with military discipline in extractive industries).

Their positive impact on the CC trade surplus was not sustainable over a longer period. The authorities were unable to curb personal consumption after martial law because of political stability considerations. The two waves of strikes in 1988, caused among other things by the fall in availability of consumer goods, were a warning that a redirection of those goods to CC markets to compensate for a growing shortage of coal was a politically risky strategy. Because of constraints on coal output[67] and growing domestic demand, fueled by the persistently high-energy intensity of the productive structure, coal exports could not increase indefinitely. Cuts in imports of grains and animal feeds contributed to a contraction in the number of cattle and pigs, thereby depriving the economy of possible hard currency earnings. In addition, the export potential of manufactured goods decreased as a result of declining competitiveness from the significant curtailment of Western equipment imports. This pattern of adjustment turned out to be shortsighted and left Poland in a worse situation to cope with economic problems than that immediately after the imposition of martial law.

Myopic as it was, there was, nevertheless, some internal logic in this pattern of adjustment. The expansion of exports of raw materials and of low-processed products that are relatively homogenous, simple, and easy to sell in international markets was the least risky way to obtain a CC surplus. For one thing, its success did not hinge upon the introduction of reform measures that would make enterprise management responsive to the international economy.[68] The dominance of fuels and energy as well as energy-intensive products in CC exports combined with the legacy of already started capital investment projects in the 1970s automatically led to the investment policy that assigned priority to fuels and energy sectors and absorbed more than one-third of the investment outlays from 1982 to 1987. The industries, such as fuels and energy, metallurgy, and chemicals, which accounted for 38 percent of CC exports in 1987, are highly energy-intensive. Their share in total consumption of energy by socialized industrial sectors amounted to 70 percent in 1987. Because of the high capital outlays required to increase the output of fuels and energy and the rapidly expanding costs of coal extraction, this was a shortsighted strategy that rapidly depleted the developmental potential of the Polish economy.

If the Polish economy is to avoid another economic crisis, exports of man-

[67] The maximum technically feasible growth of coal production from 1986 to 1990 was estimated to be at 2 percent (see *Rzeczpospolita*, October 20–21, 1984).

[68] Exports of coal, for example, can be handled more or less efficiently by a bureaucratic FTO, whereas machinery exports require some more sophisticated marketing skills and their quality is strongly affected by the economic system itself.

ufactured goods will have to provide a growing share of hard currency revenues. In addition to reforms that would eliminate some of the most obvious drawbacks of the command planning system, both agriculture and industry will remain major stumbling blocks unless they are modernized. Aging capital stock needs an infusion of new capital equipment that can hardly be procured in CMEA countries (Olechowski 1982). But without Western imports the technological gap will grow and make exports to both CMEA and Western countries increasingly difficult.

Thus, the dilemma facing the authorities is how to increase hard currency export earnings indispensable to service the debt while simultaneously increasing imports of the Western investment goods necessary to reduce the technological gap, which, in turn, will hinder increases in manufactured exports. There is no solution to this dilemma as long as Poland remains in the grip of state socialism.

CONCLUSION

The institutional arrangements encourage crises-generating actions while at the same time blocking recuperative actions. Development under state socialism unavoidably leads to the exploitation of growth factors without simultaneously creating reserves that could be tapped in the future. Poland is obviously an extreme example.

The same forces that ultimately lead to a general crisis of state socialism have been operating in other state socialist countries, however. At a micro level, for instance, the complaints of coal miners striking in the Soviet Union in 1989 about gross wastes and excessive exploitation of mines had a familiar ring; they read like a list of demands of Polish coal miners during strikes in 1980. At a macro level, even though other state socialist countries have not registered an economic slump similar to Poland's, this was not so because of institutional arrangements better suited to handle domestic and external economics. The other regimes were slightly less prone to corruption and, more significantly, less pressed by their respective populations to legitimize their rule by the increased consumption. But the same pressures that brought about the Polish crisis are increasingly catching up with them.

The institutional arrangements block the changes that would remedy the situation in many levels. First, the monopoly over collective action by the party state is an invitation to ignore symptoms of a crisis. For instance, the ecological crisis endemic to all state socialist countries did not erupt in the 1980s; it had been in the making for a long time. Yet voices of concern were simply suppressed. Those economists who were, for example, critical of the Gierek regime policies were removed from any position of influence. Every Communist regime tended to minimize the scope and extent of the problems that should be addressed and a response, if there was one, came belatedly.

Second, the policy actions available to decision makers exacerbated (or deferred) a crisis rather than coped with it. Because of the specter of shortages and a limited capacity to compete effectively in world markets for manufactured products, producers of producer goods tend to obtain a lion's share of investment. Because these are usually energy-and material-intensive as well as highly polluting sectors, and, on the other hand, there are no mechanisms to reduce excessive consumption of industrial inputs, a vicious circle of decline is generated. It may be somewhat weakened by imported technologies, but it cannot be avoided.

CHAPTER FOUR

Crisis Management: The Trap of Negative Legitimation

IN THE ABSENCE of political mechanisms to deal with private and group interests, the socialist state has simply to impose its will to assure social compliance and stability. The instrumental use of law reduces the base for legitimation of state socialism. In the extreme case, it can assure obedience only by terror and massive repression. If this option is not acceptable (or not available) to the authorities, political and social stability becomes critically dependent on granting economic concessions to the populace. The development of state socialism in Poland demonstrates a link between economic performance and political upheavals and provides evidence of the devastating effects of ensuring compliance through economic concessions.

The actions undertaken to ensure political stability and compliance (countercrisis management) have comprised either giving back some individual freedoms and autonomy or making limited economic concessions to the consumers. The reconciliation with the limited capacity to control all domains of public life, forced upon the authorities by social pressures, has contributed to the erosion of state socialism as the state's capacity to suppress individual and group interests has declined. In a similar vein, economic concessions have been counterproductive because they violate the logic of a closed system.[1]

NEGATIVE LEGITIMATION AND THE POTENTIAL FOR UPHEAVALS

A politico-economic order is legitimate in the perception of the populace if members of the population acquiesce to the existing distribution of power and privileges. It is legitimate if they accept the existing order not solely because they fear the use of force by the state. The order is legitimate if the acquiescence comes also from the fear of shame or guilt that results from violating internalized values and norms. As Mark Kelman (1987, 263) notes, "*Acquiescence* is contrasted sharply with *obedience*, which could presumably be grounded in a purely self-interested fear of the force of those who both control and get the benefits of the state's exercise of power."

A politico-economic order can be legitimated by law, religion, tradition, or

[1] As discussed in chapter 3, this logic gives producers of producer goods a privileged position. As developments in Poland and recently in the Soviet Union have shown, workers employed in this sector may be in a position to veto the authorities' decisions.

a charismatic leader. Legitimation by law is a unique feature of the Western political evolution—the development that was recognized by Marxist writers. The Italian Marxist Antonio Gramsci (1971, 260), for instance, wrote that "the revolution which the bourgeois class has brought into the conception of law, and hence into the function of the State implies inter alia belief in the rule of law enforced by the state, consists especially in the will to conform [hence ethicity of the law and of the state]." There is no room for conformity to the law within the institutional framework of state socialism.

By rejecting this conception of the law, state socialism has rejected the law as a source of legitimation. As I have argued elsewhere:

> Soviet courts under Stalin were adorned with posters proclaiming: "Law is what is good for the Party." They expressed well the antilaw bias of totalitarian communism. It was a system in which the discretional intervention by the party and state, including extensive reliance on repression and terror, replaced the rule of law. (Kamiński and Sołtan 1989, 375)

Clearly the rejection of the law could not be complete, because this would make governing through bureaucratic organizations impossible. Bureaucratic law, as opposed to autonomous law, had to be retained.[2] The "designers" of state socialism have assigned a very instrumentalist role to the law. Lawmakers have become servile followers of the party, whereas the privileged remain outside the reach of the legal order.

A legal order subject to the whims of the authorities is unlikely to infuse values and norms shared by the population. To be accepted by the populace, the legal system has to be autonomous, and basic legal norms should reflect actual shared values.

But the establishment of an autonomous legal system is not possible within the confines of state socialism. There is little room for legal legitimation when the autonomy of neither the society nor the economy is institutionally recognized. As I argued in chapter 1, state socialism is task- not rule-oriented. In a politico-economic order that rejects the market and democracy, rule-oriented behavior would be dysfunctional; it would produce social and economic chaos. The rejection of the market accounts for the exercise of economic control based on the rules variability principle. Law implies well-defined rules applying to all actors and not only those actors targeted by the state. But not only economic actors are subject to "soft-law" constraints. Although the state administration operates through formal bureaucratic procedures, these are circumvented whenever the need arises. The system of curbing administration through the ad hoc intervention of the party apparatus (the rule-bending principle) favors informal procedures (Kamiński, 1989). Finally, the lack of ac-

---

[2] Bureaucratic law is an instrument of authority, whereas autonomous law—guaranteed by an independent judiciary—controls and limits authority.

countability of rulers does not provide them with incentives to conform to the legal order.

The absence of ideological, cultural, and moral hegemony pushes the socialist state towards greater reliance on coercion than in societies where there is harmony between the values professed by the political system (ideology) and those dominant in the society. Social compliance or stability is based on apathy and passive acceptance as well as on coercion. However, the capacity of the state to suppress (or to neutralize) sources of independent values is crucial to preventing the crisis.

The state socialist politico-economic order can thus only be legitimated by a charismatic leader, religion, or Communist ideology.[3] But the supply of charismatic leaders is limited, and the ultimate test of the ideology is living up to its promises. As long as state socialism can demonstrate its superiority over other politico-economic systems, its claims are justified. Large segments of the populace will then accept the existing distribution of power and perquisites because the system works. Some may not like the state's excessive interference in private life and suppression of liberty, but they may see these conditions as the price for better living. They may also be comforted by the thought that their granddaughters and grandsons will live in a harmonious and abundant society. Then the system's capacity to deliver becomes decisive in assuring a spontaneous support for its institutions.

Having renounced religious and traditional values, the legitimation of state socialism has become intertwined with its capacity to generate economic performance (preferably better than average). Thus the system's economic performance has become a crucial condition of its legitimacy (White 1985). Post-Stalinist Communist authorities have sought "to strike a bargain with their citizenry. If the people agreed to remain politically passive, the tacit understanding went, they could anticipate better economic conditions" (Nagorski 1990a, 90).

The promises of a Communist revolution of material abundance and conflict-free society have turned out to be impossible to fulfill. The atrocities committed in its name quickly lose their justification. The enthusiasm of the few was replaced by the apathy of many. As George Kennan, then American Ambassador in Moscow, perceptively noted in his letter to the State Department in 1952:

[3] The line of argument is similar to Pakulski's (1986) analysis of the sources of legitimacy in Soviet-style societies. He examines four types of legitimacy: legal-rational, charismatic, goal-rational, and traditional. Emergence of each of these types requires fulfilling a different set of conditions that are usually not met in Soviet-type societies, as Pakulski convincingly shows. Because one may also doubt whether charismatic, traditional, or goal-rational legitimacy commonly occur in other industrialized societies, legal-rationality seems to be the single most important type of legitimacy for contrasting state socialism with capitalism.

Thirty years ago people were violently for it [communism] or against it, because all of them felt Soviet power as something springing from human action, and affecting their own lives in ways that raised issues of great immediacy and importance with respect to their own behavior. Today most of them do not have this feeling. Their attitude toward it is one of increasing apathy and detachment, combined with acceptance—acceptance sometimes resigned, sometimes vaguely approving, sometimes unthinkingly enthusiastic. In general, I think it fair to say that the enthusiasm varies in reverse relationship to the thoughtfulness of the person and to his immediate personal experience with the most terrible sides of Soviet power—such things as the experiences of collectivization, recollection of the purges, or personal unhappiness as a victim of the harshness of the bureaucracy. (Kennan 1989, 153)

The letter was written at a time when many believed that suppressed freedom would be rewarded by economic and material gains in the near future. More than thirty years later, even many Communist leaders question this claim of superiority. Yet passive acceptance has endured for so many decades. The reasons are not only rooted in the repressive power of the socialist state but also in the unique set of relationships that have developed between the rulers and the ruled—a set of relationships that is best captured by the concept of negative legitimation.

The social approval of the regime is not a condition sine qua non of compliance to authoritative directives. There are other reasons. An individual living under state socialism is almost completely dependent upon the state—the state is the main employer, the provider of services and the final arbiter of what is wrong and what is right. Individuals fear the repressive might of the socialist state. But other motives push people toward accommodation with the regime and, thus, ensure the stability of the social order. The most important motives include the sense of security that comes from overfull employment and special welfare provisions, the sense of the irreversibility of the political order, the sense of quietude that comes from the conviction that everything has a predetermined place within the society, the fear of the unknown, and the awareness of the existence of a powerful state terror apparatus backed by the Soviet Union.

Additionally, the socialist state has skillfully implemented various forms of pseudoparticipation, such as the "transmission belt" mass organizations that link the state to its citizens and serve to channel discontent and control dissent. In all socialist countries, a great number of associations have been created to represent various interests. When the socialist state operates normally, these associations remain under strict control of the party apparatus. They are engaged, more or less actively, in symbolic activities designed to support current policies of the regime. But during political crises the role of some of those organizations increases.

These various forms of pseudoparticipation, including voting in nonelections, provide the state with additional channels of communication, although they are a poor substitute for the contribution of democracy to political stability.[4] This sphere of appearances is a pillar maintaining political arrangements of state socialism. The use of pseudoparticipation as a part of political impression management is one of the reasons that socialist states are superior to various authoritarian or fascist regimes in stability and longevity.

But these are hardly conditions that would produce a zeal for following the directives of the state. Rather they create conditions conducive to a *negative legitimation*.[5] This consists of the rejection of the monopoly of power of the Communist party combined with *passive* acceptance often derived from the perception that alternatives are absent and the Soviet military might be employed to support the state. As Vaclav Havel declared, "All of us have become accustomed to the totalitarian system, accepted it as an inalterable face and thereby kept it running."[6] The legitimation is negative because the elite's rule is not normatively validated and because its acceptance is based on a combination of negative incentives and rewards for loyalty. The line between passive acceptance and active rejection is thin at best. As a result, when the authority trembles, the whole politico-economic order is in danger.

This often involuntary and usually passive acceptance has been sufficient to maintain cohesion of the society and ensure the system's reproduction. The uniformity of social action and prolonged periods of stability has clearly demonstrated it. This quasi legitimation is based on the rejection of noncompliance by the ruled. In Soviet-type societies the social contract deprives the society of some autonomy and natural rights in return for the economic security and social action programs provided by the state. Thus economic performance is crucial to the survival of state socialism.

Social compliance also depends upon the assessment of consequences of insubordination as measured against expected payoffs from the act of noncompliance. The capacity to organize collective action is limited. If the costs of insubordination are low and expectations are high, the potential for political instability increases (Pakulski 1986). This potential leads to upheavals when cleavages occur within the ruling elites, as in Czechoslovakia (1968), Hungary (1956), and Poland (1956, 1970, and 1980).

Occasional breakdowns in social compliance directly threaten the survival of the state socialist politico-economic order. Khrushchev's de-Stalinization

[4] Nuti (1982) claims, for example, that the abolition of workers' councils was a factor contributing to the eruption of strikes in Poland in 1980.

[5] The concept of negative legitimation parallels in many respects Jan Pakulski's (1986, 48) concept of conditional tolerance defined as "social perception of relative costs of (in)subordination." It seems, however, that obedience is not grounded solely in a self-interested fear of the repressive power of the state. There is also a certain amount of acquiescence not driven by immediate benefits.

[6] Havel, Vaclav, New Year's Day Address, *New York Times*, 2 January 1990.

campaign, an important component of the succession struggle after Stalin's death, contributed to the upheavals in Poland and Hungary in 1956. The Soviet intervention in Hungary and fear of the intervention in Poland showed the limited legitimacy of state socialism in those countries. Prague Spring was a delayed response to de-Stalinization. Although Communist reformers were in control of political developments, their dynamics might have led to the elimination of the basic principles of state socialism had Moscow not intervened in August 1968. A few countries (Bulgaria and Romania) were spared upheavals until the fall of 1989. Until the summer of 1989, there was no major crisis of authority in East Germany, except for a wave of strikes in 1953 put down by the Soviet Army.

Except for the cyclical inability of the Polish authorities to prevent social upheavals, a remarkable stability existed in the Soviet bloc between 1968 and 1988. Other Communist governments managed to avoid confrontation with their populations and appeared to be firmly in control. The level of open repression declined. Such favorable developments in the international political economy as detente increased access to Western financial markets, and the availability of Western technology increased living standards until the early 1980s. In return, the people remained politically passive. The regimes of state socialism adjusted their political structures and became tolerable to their respective populations. The system was neither loved nor respected, but it was passively accepted. As the results of limited free elections in Eastern Europe have recently shown, this legitimation was precarious. The majority gave a noconfidence vote to the party-state, when they had the opportunity to express their views for the first time. Thus under the appearance of control and order there was a potential for instability; a wall of dynamite as George Konrad (1984, 31) put it.

CRISIS MANAGEMENT: IN SEARCH OF LEGITIMATION

Crisis management in state socialism is referred to as the normalization. The term "normalization" is ambiguous.[7] In its broadest sense, it denotes a sequence of policy actions designed to restore the central controls of the state party apparatus over the society. The objective of normalization is to assure governability within the institutional perimeters of state socialism. This goal is predicated upon the state's capacity to suppress individual and group aspirations. It also defies a common understanding of this term superbly illustrated

[7] To cope with this ambiguity, some authors distinguish between consolidation and normalization. Jiri Valenta (1984, 105), for example, defines consolidation as the reestablishment of central controls, whereas normalization amounts to "long-term policies encouraged by the Soviets and developed under specific national conditions over a period spanning a decade or more." What distinguishes those policies, except for the Soviet tutelage, is not clear. Others (e.g., Bielasiak [1988] and Brus [1988]) simply describe it as a restoration of monolithic controls.

by a Prague graffito referring to the post-1968 normalization campaign: "They tried to normalize us, but we were normal all the time" (quoted in Nagorski [1990a, 96]). By "Communist" definition, normalization is a response to the outburst of freedoms temporarily leading to social autonomy and to calls for reforms that would limit the socialist state's power over society.

Yet normalization does not necessarily amount to a full restoration of the system before the "period of freedom." The upheavals were the result of tensions along several dimensions of the state's policy toward society. Policies pursued during normalization seek to ease some of these tensions. Therefore, some modifications in style and substance of governing usually take place. Normalization slows down the process of evolution but does not necessarily arrest it. As a result, it is difficult to unequivocally identify the conclusion of normalization. Some authors suggest that normalization ends when people give up their aspirations for change.[8] However, aspirations may persist, but the willingness to carry them out may be missing. For the purpose of this discussion, the situation becomes "normalized" when the authorities no longer have to resort to overt repression on a massive scale to assure governability and social compliance.

Upheavals shape the rulers as well as the ruled. They also affect various components underlying their relationship. Each crisis weakened the official ideology as it became increasingly clear that the existing arrangements had failed to produce satisfactory political and economic outcomes. Each crisis was triggered by the inability of the state to contain outbursts of dissatisfaction. As a rule, each crisis was followed by three phases: a short period of liberalization, the recentralization of political controls (the so-called consolidation and normalization), and a period of illusory stability that would end in yet another political and economic crisis. This pattern has repeated itself only in Poland, thus giving rise to a cycle.

Before the 1980–1981 revolution, neither the notion of crisis nor that of the cycle were officially used.[9] The term was reserved for capitalism because— according to the official ideological stand—the introduction of social ownership and of central planning had put an end to social contradictions and cyclical development. The successive crises were referred to as the "events" (in Polish, *wydarzenia*) identified by the month (i.e., October, March, December) when they occurred. These events tended to be discussed in terms of policy blunders rather than of inherent drawbacks in the political order. The crisis was officially recognized as a result of the ideological transformation triggered

[8] For instance, Ost (1985, 77) argues that "normalization in a state socialist country occurs when people believe that the will to change things is lacking."

[9] The notions of crises and cycle were reserved to describe allegedly inevitable outcomes of capitalist contradictions between the social character of production and the private appropriation of surplus value.

by developments during the Solidarity period in Poland and Gorbachev's new approach,

There were four major crises in the history of state socialism in Poland: the 1956 October upheaval, the 1970 December workers' riots, the 1980 summer workers' strikes, and the two waves of strikes in 1988 that led to the Solidarity participation in government. Some authors (e.g., Karpiński 1982) add to this list the revolt of students and intellectuals in March 1968 and the workers' riots against price increases in June 1976. Although these rebellions had a profound impact on the course of developments during the 1970 and the 1980 crises,[10] they did not produce cleavages within the ruling elite that would result in the change of leadership nor did they represent a head-to-head confrontation between society and the authorities.

Poland so far has experienced three periods of normalization: the first in the late 1950s and the early 1960s, the second in the early 1970s, and the third in the 1980s. Each of them had specific traits. The options open to the authorities following each successive upheaval have been narrowing. None of them has succeeded in restoring a degree of control over public life comparable to the phase preceding the liberalization period. Each weakened the pillars of state socialism; this is especially true for the normalization that followed the emergence of Solidarity.

Each normalization marked a regression in political freedoms in comparison to the preceding period of upheaval. Yet each normalization brought about a less repressive regime. The restoration of the leading role of the party was accompanied by a decline in ideology and in the state's directive capacity. Each time, the price of state socialism continuity was the loss of control over some domains of public life. Gomułka had to accept coexistence with the Polish church, which directly challenged the party's monopoly over social values. Gierek was not able to quell the opposition institutionalized in the Committee for Defense of Workers (KOR) or to destroy the underground publication circuit that directly challenged the party's monopoly over information. Jaruzelski was forced to tacitly accept the role of the church as the mediator between his regime and the society writ large.[11] In fact, the political dynamic of General Jaruzelski's normalization was shaped by the regime's inability to reconcile political and economic demands of the population and

[10] Neutrality, if not hostility, of workers during the 1968 confrontation between intelligentsia and Gomułka accounted inter alia for the indifference of intellectuals and students in December 1970. The response of some intellectuals and students to workers' repression by Gierek's regime following the riots in Radom laid the groundwork for subsequent solidarity between workers and intelligentsia in the summer of 1980.

[11] He was forced to allow for direct power sharing with non-Communist organizations. This possibility, discussed in the Polish mass media since the first wave of strikes in April/May 1988 (see, for instance, Modzelewski [1988]; Bugaj [1988]; and Passent [1988]) has become a reality with the emergence of the cabinet led by Solidarity.

Western creditors with the institutional constraints of state socialism. As a result, the regime had to allow for greater liberalization by 1988 than even during the first Solidarity period in 1980–1981, and, finally, in 1990 it gave up power.

The differences in normalization patterns stem from the unique circumstances that preceded them. These circumstances in turn reflected varying public perceptions of the viability and reformability of state socialism. The normalization orchestrated by Gomułka, which followed the period of liberalization from 1955 to 1958, was predicated on the reformability of state socialism. In contrast, the demands voiced solely by workers, which Edward Gierek had to satisfy to contain labor unrest, concerned the improvement of living standards. Given the legacy of Gomułka's deflationary policies and the regime's access to Western financing, they could have been met. The first Solidarity period was a combination of an unprecedented economic and political crisis. General Jaruzelski's war symbolized the nonreformability and economic nonviability of state socialism, whereas Gomułka embodied the popular hope of the reformability of state socialism. The promise of the latter was "likeable socialism," as Włodzimierz Brus (1988, 72) has called it; the promise of the former was austerity.

The normalization that followed the brief period of de-Stalinization from 1955 to 1958 was masterminded by the most popular Communist leader in Poland's history. Gomułka gradually withdrew freedoms gained during the so-called Polish October of which he had become a symbol.[12] It diverged significantly from the normalization in the 1980s, which restored some freedoms that were aborted by the martial law decree.

Thanks to Gomułka, state socialism survived almost intact, but his regime did not. Gomułka's reign ended abruptly with the Gdańsk and Szczecin workers' riots in December 1970. The December 1970 upheaval marked the first time that the army was used by the "workers' state" to crush a workers' strike. There was no need to resort to martial law, because the crisis was quickly diffused by the change in leadership, economic concessions to the population, and the promise of comprehensive reforms. It was succeeded by the rationalization of economic controls. In contrast to the late 1950s, when the economic reform was abandoned, a program was devised and implemented in some areas of the economy. The objective was to deconcentrate decision making in order to improve central controls. The objective was not achieved; instead, the reform produced the "state of centrally planned anarchy" (Bozyk 1983).

---

[12] It is interesting to note that many ideas first articulated in the 1950s survived in social consciousness. The unfulfilled promise of Polish October, the idea of industrial democracy (workers' self-management) gained prominence again during the Solidarity period. The program of economic reform adopted in 1981 drew heavily on the 1956 unimplemented recommendations. For more, see Brus (1988).

The ascension to power of Gierek was not followed by an eruption of political freedoms; the political legacy of the Gomułka regime remained. In 1970, Gierek faced hostile workers and a frustrated intelligentsia still resentful of the workers' indifference to the crackdown on the universities that followed the revolt of intellectuals and students in March 1968. The "December events" of 1970 were a workers' revolt. As Brus (1988, 72) succinctly noted: "The events of 1970 marked a new powerful dimension . . . : the articulated interests and attitudes of the industrial working class." However, the articulation of interests was politically less explicit than in 1956.

The intelligentsia, politically marginalized as a result of post-March 1968 purges, remained passive during the unprecedented confrontation between the industrial proletariat and the authorities. There were no radical political demands. Social stability was achieved thanks to a substantial improvement in living standards. The pressure from below was effectively terminated when price increases introduced in December 1970 were canceled in March 1971. The access to Western credits, which allowed removal of the barriers choking economic performance under Gomułka's prudent policy of not borrowing, contributed to the regime's legitimacy.

The circumstances of normalization in the 1980s embraced the worst features of the earlier crises for the Communist authorities, both politically and economically as well as domestically and externally. In fact, none of the previous normalizations had occurred under such adverse political and economic conditions. Further, General Jaruzelski, unlike Gomułka, lacked political charisma. In contrast to Gierek, he could not tap external economic resources to support his normalization strategy. His regime was isolated in the West and ignored by the East.

Jaruzelski's team never enjoyed the level of public support available to Gomułka's. Jaruzelski's regime also lacked the credibility available to Gierek because of his "economic miracle" in Silesia. Whereas Gierek could exploit the rifts between the intelligentsia and workers—a legacy of the ill-fated students' and intellectuals' revolt in 1968—Jaruzelski had to deal with a population united in its deep skepticism toward the viability and legitimacy of state socialism. The military regime could not rely on the economic carrot because of accumulated external debt and the legacy of past blunders in other areas of public economic policy. None of the previous normalizations had been preceded by such an outburst of political activity outside the institutional structure of the regime. Although one may argue that Solidarity's ideology was socialistic, it was socialistic in the Western not the Soviet sense. As such, it constituted a threat to state socialism.

None of the previous normalizations had been carried out under such adverse international circumstances. Gomułka and his policies were viewed in the West as the first real opportunity to implement a policy that promoted diversification within the Soviet bloc. Therefore, Gomułka obtained a grain loan and most-favored-nation status for Poland from the United States. On the other hand, Moscow, after ruling out intervention, also provided some assistance to help him normalize the situation. Gierek presided over an unprecedented inflow of resources from the West, whereas Jaruzelski oversaw the largest outflow of resources in Poland's postwar history.

The circumstances of the Polish crisis in the 1980s produced a different path of normalization than that experienced in post–1956 Hungary or post–1968 Czechoslovakia. The differences were rooted in the conditions preceding the respective interventions, be it domestic (Poland) or "fraternal" (the Soviet Union in Hungary and selected Warsaw Pact armies led by the Soviets in Czechoslovakia). The challenge of Solidarity was more than a synthesis of the Hungarian and Czechoslovak defiances. Unlike in Hungary, the opposition was organized and aware of the limits of Soviet tolerance. Nor was the process of democratization controlled from above, as it was during the Prague Spring. It did not trigger a widespread reformist movement within the Communist party—a major characteristic of the Prague Spring.[13] In Poland, the liberalization was forced upon the authorities by Solidarity, a force external to the existing institutional arrangements. As in Hungary, Solidarity's rebellion against the regime mobilized the masses. The Hungarian revolt lasted, however, a few weeks, whereas the Solidarity-led upheaval lasted sixteen months. The Hungarians had little time to consolidate their organizational forms.

The unique trait of the Solidarity challenge was that for the first time in state socialism the working class was able to organize itself nationwide. Solidarity was a political movement disguised as a trade union. Although the other rare crises have given rise to spontaneously established strike committees and workers' councils, these organizations never encompassed such a huge proportion of the population. The differences do not end here.

Unlike the Hungarian or Czechoslovak case, the revolution was crushed not by external intervention but by a domestic force. The domestic solution did not trigger a massive massacre, like the Soviet intervention in Hungary. Neither did it produce the dissolution of the party (Hungary) nor massive purges of supporters of change from the Communist party (Czechoslovakia), although many Solidarity activists lost their jobs as a result of "verifications."[14]

In contrast to both Czechoslovakia and Hungary, the coup was not followed by a change in the political leadership; consequently, General Jaruzelski was spared the need to consolidate his power at the central and local levels of the state-party hierarchy. The process of regime consolidation that followed the

[13] Because of the memories of the Prague Spring, attempts to revive the PUWP were opposed not only by the party officials but also by the opposition. For more, see app. A.

[14] During the first weeks of martial law a "verification of cadres" was conducted in a number of institutions. Solidarity members were requested to sign a loyalty pledge containing a clause stating that they were giving up their membership in the union. For the text of the declaration of loyalty, see *Poland Watch* 1 (1982): 89–90.

invasions in Hungary and Czechoslovakia began in Poland during the Solidarity period and ended once Solidarity had been deprived of the capacity to organize effective protests. Factional infighting in the PUWP ended with the crushing of the horizontal movement, which had called for a radical reform of the party, and the triumph of Jaruzelski's team at the 9th Extraordinary Party Congress, held in July 1981. Unlike Czechoslovakia, the PUWP did not offer any channels for articulating reformist ideas. Those who sought change joined Solidarity. Those who were scared of Solidarity closed ranks behind General Jaruzelski. The imposition of martial law combined with subsequent verification of cadres in the state administration and mass media marked the final stage of this process.

The repression that followed the imposition of martial law was limited and short-lived. In Czechoslovakia, repression has persisted, although with some occasional relaxations. It lasted a few years in Hungary. The strategy for building a national alliance in Poland had some similarities with the strategy pursued by Kádár after the 1962 amnesty for political prisoners. They were both based on the idea of co-opting non-Communist groups. As a result, the political system evolved and became more flexible, although it retained distinctive features of state socialism. In contrast, Husak's normalization in Czechoslovakia blocked evolution. The political system remained rigid and inflexible like its predecessor under Novotny.

Seeking to "normalize" the situation, the Polish authorities resorted to measures similar to those employed in Hungary. These measures included a general amnesty for political prisoners (in Poland five years after the imposition of martial law and in Hungary six years after the Soviet invasion); the relaxation of censorship; a limited multiple-candidate competition for elected offices; the acceptance of the limited autonomy and greater social responsibilities of trade unions; the relaxation of direct central controls over the economy; and the active search for reconciliation with the respective diaspora in the West. Within different time spans, both Kádár and Jaruzelski "relaxed" political systems and brought an end to terror.

Notwithstanding similarities, there were significant differences between Kádár's and Jaruzelski's normalizations. These differences stemmed from distinctive international and domestic circumstances. What Kádár was able to achieve in the 1960s through the cautious pursuit of policies designed to round the edges of the system was not possible for General Jaruzelski, even if he genuinely wanted to emulate Kadarization. The normalizations took place during different phases in the evolution of state socialism; Kádár's occurred at its stage of vitality fueled by Soviet political and technological successes, whereas Jaruzelski's took place during a period of growing recognition by the elites in the Communist world of inherent limitations of state socialism. Kádár was successful in modifying the political system to make it more tolerable to the people and still acceptable to the party-state apparatus. Judging by the rhetoric of the Rakowski government (1988–1989), the economic arrangements were regarded as less and less bearable by officialdom.[15]

The option of "goulash" communism, as Khrushchev called Kadarization, was not available to Jaruzelski without enacting a complete overhaul of command planning and obtaining substantial foreign assistance. In Hungary, the shift from "dash for growth" policies to a strategy of balanced growth brought a significant improvement in living standards in the 1960s and the 1970s. The deeply entrenched structural problems troubling the Polish economy left little room for any improvement in living standards. To the contrary, even radical economic reform would have been accompanied by a period of austerity. The absence of radical reform perhaps allowed smaller cuts in personal consumption but at the expense of future productivity and economic growth. The solutions that made the Hungarian economy viable in the 1970s were too conservative to cope with the depth of the Polish crisis.

In all, the periodic breakdowns in social compliance have been a trademark of Poland's state socialism.[16] In contrast to other Eastern European countries, Polish Communists were able to contain crises by resorting to domestic means. They felt compelled to impose martial law to contain Solidarity in 1981, but this did not involve a direct external military intervention. The repression was milder. There was, however, an economic price for the change in weights of the negative legitimation formula.

LEGITIMATION AND THE POLITICO-ECONOMIC CYCLE IN POLAND

There is no clear-cut relationship between fluctuations of economic growth rates and increased social tensions. Social expectations are not shaped only by economic performance. Moreover, there is always a time lag between changing social expectations and the actual availability of goods and services.

To identify the link between pulsations in the economy and politics, one may use, as a first approximation, the rate of net investment and its share in Net Material Product (NMP). Some authors claim (Báuer 1978) that the cycles are the outcome of the periodic increases and decreases in investment tensions. The changes in net investment rate are a major indicator of the economic cycle. The excessive investment rates lead to increased shortages in the economy and a decline in capital and labor productivity. Investment programs that exceed a country's economic possibilities spill over the whole economy and neg-

---

[15] See, for instance, an interview with Mieczyslaw Wilczek, then minister of industry, who commented on the project of a new law on entrepreneurship (that would dramatically extend freedom to establish private firms): "This a return to the Polish road to economic affluence from the aftermath of World War II, which we left for roadless tracts of Stalinist economy" (*Polityka*, no. 48 [1988]: 4).

[16] China is a possible exception. Yet it should be borne in mind that the Cultural Revolution was instigated and controlled from above.

atively affect the overall situation. Because these programs favor the producers of capital goods, they contribute to the increased shortages of consumer goods and growing societal dissatisfaction (see chap. 3). As a Polish economist Jan Rutkowski (1988, 140) notes: "The economic potential increases, but this does not result in the expansion of individual consumption. This systemic pressure to increase socially unproductive capital assets hits only one limit—the limit of social resistance."

Indeed, investment rates have been sensitive to changes in social tensions. When the tensions are relatively weak, the authorities submit to the investment pressures of economic actors. Some authors (Kornai 1980, 212) argue that the "upswing lasts until the process hits 'tolerance limits' and other constraints." According to a study (Grosfeld 1987) covering the 1956–1981 period, Polish planners have responded to changes in the growth of real personal consumption (proxied by real wages) by manipulating investment rates.

Moskwa and Kearney (1984), using the rate of net investment as a criterion of a cycle, identified four cycles distinguished by four turning points, defined as local maxima of the rate of investment. Each cycle contains an upswing and a downswing. By expanding the time horizon of their analysis, which covered the period between 1949 and 1981, to the 1982–1988 period, five turning points and four cycles can be identified.

The share of investment in NMP reached local peaks in the following years: 1953, 1962, 1969, 1974, and 1988. Local minima obtained in 1957, 1964, 1971, and 1982. However, the decline in the rate of investment was so small in 1964 that it fell within the range of statistical error. In fact, the variations in the 1960s were smoother with contractions in investment activity less pronounced than either in the 1950s or the late 1970s. Therefore, between 1949 and 1982, there were three rather than four full cycles: 1949–1957, 1958–1971, 1972–1982.[17] The year 1983 marks the beginning of the fourth cycle, which completed its upswing in 1988.

The juxtaposition of "investment cycles" with political upheavals yields some interesting insights. First, all cycles ended with a political crisis. Although there were symptoms of economic stagnation in the 1960s, the 1968 crisis was limited to a rebellion of students and intellectuals. The workers' protest against price increases in 1976 took place before the trough in the economic cycle was reached. These crises did not result in a change of leadership in the Communist party.

Second, crises and changes in PUWP leadership occurred one year before the end of a cycle. Thus, once a regime consolidated its grip over the society (roughly a year or so after new First Secretary was selected), resources would

---

[17] According to the 1986–1990 plan, the share of net capital formation was to increase. But the "contract," signed between the governmental coalition and Solidarity opposition in April 1989, promised a reduction in the share.

be reallocated from consumption to investment. The emergence of Solidarity altered the pattern slightly. The Jaruzelski regime, established in 1981, reversed the trend toward declining net investment rates in 1983—that is, a year late in comparison to both Gomułka's and Gierek's. But the Jaruzelski regime's countdown started with the imposition of martial law in December 1981, when personnel changes in the leadership of the PUWP were no longer effective for dealing with the crisis.

A more comprehensive attempt undertaken by two Polish authors, Eysymontt and Maciejewski (1985), sheds interesting light on the link between upheavals and economic development. In their analysis of the Polish upheavals, they developed a set of measures describing the satisfaction of economic and social needs of the population. The list includes such variables as share of the private consumption in total consumption, the ratio of marriages to newly built dwellings, and the previous year growth rates in the final agricultural output, real wage index. Their analysis extends over the 1955–1980 period. In terms of the variables identified, the worst situations, or bottom turning points, were in 1956 and 1980. They thus coincided with two major confrontations between the populace and the authorities. They also coincided with cleavages within the ruling elite that eventually led to the changes in the leadership of the PUWP. The best situation was in the 1971–1975 period. Other "good" periods were 1957–1958, 1964–1966, and 1978–1979. It is worth noting that the deterioration in 1980 was much less pronounced than in 1956.

Interestingly, although the 1956 October crisis had economic underpinnings, as demonstrated by workers' riots in Poznań (June 1956), its dynamic was shaped more by the winds of destalinization blowing from Moscow.[18] In contrast, the political dynamic of the 1980–1981 upheaval was shaped by the deteriorating economic situation and the legacy of Gierek's political and economic strategies; their major legacy, as we shall see, was the veto power of the populace (mainly of workers) over some economic decisions (mainly wages and prices).

THE WORKERS' VETO POWER AND THE CRISIS

The management of upheavals in Poland produced a privileged position for the workers. In the market-oriented politico-economic systems, workers work because their livelihoods depend on it (Lindblom 1977, 176). Therefore, they

---

[18] Gomułka's rise to power was mainly the result of the stalemate between party hard-liners and reformers and of his social credibility thanks to several years spent in a Communist jail. Gomułka, who in 1956 was probably the most popular Communist leader in Poland's postwar history, symbolized something different for various social groups. For the general populace, he symbolized a promise of de-sovietization. For devoted Communists, he represented a promise of socialism with a human face. For the party apparatchiks, he was one of them and symbolized a promise of their survival.

do not qualify for a privileged position similar to that of business. The bargaining position of workers vis-à-vis the socialist state (the main employer) is potentially stronger. There is a permanent shortage of products and inputs including labor. Fear of firings and layoffs is less acute and the link between effort and pay less transparent. Workers work with special inducement from the state. This inducement may be administrative or economic depending on whether workers are able to organize themselves. If the state is not capable of imposing administrative discipline, it has to use a mix of administrative and economic rewards and penalties. The workers have veto power when they are capable of organizing strikes in response to government policy actions. They demonstrated this power effectively for the first time in December 1970, when in response to the price increases strikes erupted in northern Poland.

One of the legacies of October was a more or less permanent shift away from massive repression as a means to assure social compliance. Gomułka gradually lost the political capital that he had in 1956, as some freedoms previously bestowed were withdrawn and promises of social and economic reforms remained unfulfilled. Those channels for upward professional, social, and political mobility that remained open and increased standards of living associated with the process of urbanization gave some segments of the populace a stake in state socialism. Nonetheless, the price for maintaining some modicum of legitimacy was an expansion of cultural contacts with the West and uneasy coexistence with the Catholic church, reluctant acceptance of the private sector in agriculture, and some sensitivity to population standards of living.[19] Yet, when the workers went on strike in response to an arrogant decision to raise food prices just before Christmas in 1970, Gomułka turned to the army to quell the riots. Gomułka was then replaced at the helm of the PUWP by Edward Gierek.

The post-December normalization had an interesting feature when compared with the first one following the industrialization drive of the 1950s. The investment drive coincided with the increase of consumption.[20] Faced with hostile workers and an intelligentsia still frustrated by the crackdown on universities, Gierek sought to contain the crisis through a rapid expansion in personal consumption and the promise of substantial economic and administrative reform. As Brus (1982, 92–93) observed, "This time—unlike the economic

[19] The sensitivity to standards of living was, however, strongly limited by an overall unimpressive economic growth performance. Developmental strategy favored capital-intensive industries, leaving insufficient savings to be used in consumer-oriented sectors. Consumers were a "victim" of this strategy; real wages, in the 1958–1970 period, recorded a modest increase of less than 2 percent per annum, which was the lowest growth rate among Eastern European economies.

[20] Unlike the investment drive in the early 1950s, skyrocketing investment rates were accompanied by simultaneous rapid gains in personal consumption. Real wages increased between 1971 and 1976 by about 39 percent; the average annual rate of growth of 6.6 percent contrasted sharply with an average of less than 2 percent from 1958 to 1970. The comparative losses in consumption standard in relation to other Eastern European economies were recovered in this period.

policy switch in the mid-1950's—the gains in consumption were not to be achieved at the expense of investment; the planners learned the lesson of an abrupt cancellation of a development programme (among other things inducing a persisting cyclical movement) and on the whole preferred rather to extrapolate past trends with even a slight increase in the share of investment in national income.''

The initial economic success was due to the activation of unused productive capacities, the legacy of Gomułka's prudent economic policies, and extensive borrowing abroad (see chap. 3). Social stability was bought with a consumption spree, financed from abroad to a significant degree. This, however, could not last long.

The link between personal consumption and the regime's means of ensuring social stability came to the fore in 1976 when the authorities sought to redress domestic disequilibria through the "price-income operation," a buzzword for austerity measures. Faced with a wave of strikes, the authorities had to back down on the measures, already adopted by the Sejm, to increase food prices. Although the participants in the strikes were later prosecuted, Gierek clearly feared triggering a fullfledged confrontation. Instead he resorted to foreign credits to sustain personal consumption above the levels that the Polish economy could actually support.[21] About 34 percent of all credits drawn between 1977 and 1980 were used to finance purchases of agricultural products (25 percent) and other consumption products (9 percent).[22] Financing the current consumption through foreign credits could not prevent the economic situation from deteriorating.

Nothing could have improved Poland's external economic position short of drastic cuts in individual consumption and a successful export drive. Export drive was rather unlikely given the institutional constraints of the economic system. The regime was clearly paralyzed by the fear of a popular response against austerity measures. The awareness of the authorities that their only source of legitimation was "nested in meat" shaped economic policies throughout the 1970s and the early 1980s. The combination of poor agricultural performance and the government's fear that a sharp decline in food supplies would undermine political stability forced imports of agricultural products from the West and thus exacerbated Poland's already strained balance of payments. Between 1975 and 1981, agricultural trade deficits accounted for 41 percent of total debt increment.[23]

This strategy of containing social dissatisfaction through wage concessions

[21] For more, see appendix B.

[22] Computed from the data in Szeliga (1982). From 1971 to 1976, this group accounted for 26 percent of all credits. Agricultural trade deficits accounted for 26 and 38 percent of the increase in hard currency debt in 1977 and 1978, respectively (Boyd 1988, 35).

[23] During this period, the debt increased by $19.5 billion while Poland's cumulative agriculture-related trade deficit amounted to $8 billion (Boyd 1988, 35).

combined with the absence of any attempt to redress external and internal disequilibria contributed to the disorganization of the economy. Inflationary pressures, suppressed until 1982, were due inter alia to the excessive reliance on the "money-illusion effect" as a mechanism to reduce growing criticism of the regime. The authorities' indifference to the impact of increases in wages on the already ailing economy was startling, although it was consistent with policies that were pursued throughout the decade.[24] However, the "accounting" realities of the economy can be defied only up to a point. The augmented purchasing power of the population could not be fully converted into increased consumption because of rapidly growing shortages of consumer goods. In 1981, the market for consumer goods disintegrated.[25] Thus, the policy makers chose to ignore the link between wages, labor productivity, and the supply of consumer goods. Neither the Solidarity period nor the post-Solidarity era (1982–1989) was an exception to the rule.

Another attempt to reduce consumption through price increases triggered the workers' veto—a wave of strikes that encompassed whole industries in 1980. Attempts to buy social peace through lavish wage increases failed to pacify the populace.[26] Because of cleavages within the ruling elite, Gierek did not resort to force to quell the strikes.[27] He was ousted from the position of First Secretary, and Solidarity, which directly challenged legitimation of Communist rule, was established.

The emergence of Solidarity was a direct result of rapidly deteriorating economic conditions accompanied by a growing conviction, shared by an increasing number of people, that only deep changes in the political structures could help eliminate the cyclic pattern of crises.

Except for the Solidarity period (when the party-state struggled for its survival) and the martial law period (when personal consumption was drastically cut), there was a tendency to shield personal consumption from the burden of

[24] According to the official data, real wages increased at the following rates: 1978—(−)2.7 percent; 1979—(+)2.0; 1980—(+)4.0; 1981—(+)2.4. Official data tend to underestimate the cost of living index, which does not take into account scarcities of consumer goods forcing consumers to purchase needed products at gray or black market prices and thus "blow up" real wage growth.

[25] The collapse of a consumer goods "market" was manifested in long lines and forced savings. On a per capita basis, the latter increased almost fivefold in 1981 as compared with 1980. The real personal consumption dropped in 1981 by about 4 percent (author's calculations from *Rocznik statystyczny* 1983:102).

[26] Attempting to curb strikes, the authorities readily accepted demands for wage increases, usually within a range of 5 to 10 percent. As information quickly spread from factory to factory, the demands and strikes also spread and obtained similar results.

[27] Deprived of political and economic resources, the Gierek regime had two options during the turbulent summer of 1980: either to use brute force against the rebelling workers or to devolve political power, that is, to accept far-reaching political reforms. Before 13 December 1981 the government was able to do neither and a spontaneous political liberalization (often called a self-limiting revolution) followed without precedent in Poland's postwar history.

economic crisis. The period between 1978 and 1981 witnessed the largest contraction in aggregate economic activity in postwar history[28] with one important exception—the growth rates of most aggregates were negative whereas consumption from personal incomes recorded positive growth rates until 1981.[29] The crisis did not trigger unemployment. Except for a drastic cut in personal consumption during martial law in 1982, individual consumption increased until 1988.[30] Thus, most of the adjustment was absorbed by a drastic reduction of investment activity while the major pillars of negative legitimacy (i.e., tenured jobs and consumption) were sheltered.

Yet the protection of individual consumption was undermined by the faltering economy. In fact, all components of the standard of living dramatically deteriorated.[31] After a brief period (1983–1986) of increased availability of some goods and services, lines in front of the shops lengthened. According to official statistics, real wages fell by 20 percent from their peak level in 1980 to 1987. The per capita consumption of basic consumption goods did not catch up with 1980 levels (Fallenbuchl 1989). The availability of housing also declined; the average waiting period was about twenty-seven years in the mid-1980s. In addition, the ill-conceived price-income operation in 1988, whose objective was to reduce subsidies of basic consumption goods, backfired by activating an inflationary spiral.

The concurrence between the growing inability to reverse a decline in the standards of living and the authorities' sudden change of the policy toward the opposition was clear-cut. The deteriorating economic situation combined with an attempt to introduce austerity measures (i.e., the price-income operation) was responsible for the waves of strikes in 1988. Initially, the authorities sought to contain the strikes in April/May 1988 by relying on wage increases. The second wave of strikes in August/September was a clear indication that social tolerance was wearing thin. Simultaneously, the reserves to continue buying social compliance through wage increases were depleted. Radicaliza-

[28] The volume of NMP fell by 24 percent, the industrial production dropped by 23 percent, and construction declined by 50 percent.

[29] The growth rates of consumption from personal incomes were as follows: 1979—3.2 percent; 1980—2.3 percent; 1981—(−)4.1 percent; 1982—(−)14.6 percent. These contrasted rather favorably with the rates of net fixed capital formation: 1979—(−)15.4; 1980—(−)25.4 percent; 1981—(−)24.2 percent; 1982—(−)19.9 percent (derived from *Rocznik statstyczny* 1983, 1988).

[30] Between 1982 and 1988 the consumption from personal income increased by 23 percent. It was 5.3 percent higher in 1987 than in 1978. The personal consumption per capita was, however, 2.2 percent less than in 1978. Net capital formation stood at 51.1 percent of its peak level obtained in 1978. The crux of the matter is that the authorities sought to protect consumption at the expense of development expenditures.

[31] According to Western estimates, the average annual rates of per capita standard of living rates fell by 0.4 percent from 1980 to 1985. They declined by 0.3 and 0.9 percent in 1986 and 1987 (*Money Income of the Population and Standard of Living in Eastern Europe, 1970–1987*, New York: L. W. International Financial Research OP-103, 1988, quoted in Fallenbuchl 1989, 44).

tion of workers was caused by the falling purchasing power of their incomes and the growing certainty that their standard of living would not increase in the foreseeable future. The major component of negative legitimacy—that things would not get substantially worse—was thus undermined. To restore governability while ensuring economic viability, the authorities had to look for other means to legitimatize their rule. One solution was the agreement between the government and the Solidarity opposition (see chap. 7).

CONCLUSION

No single factor explains the pattern of recurrent instabilities in Poland. The institutional arrangements alone have not been responsible for this pattern. State socialism has also been alien to political traditions of such other Central European countries as Czechoslovakia and Hungary. And the socialist state aspired everywhere to total hegemony (Kamiński and Sołtan 1988). But it has failed to establish a new moral and intellectual order that would express the aspirations of its respective populations.

The failure of the Communist authorities to infuse new values and norms that would be internalized by the majority of society makes the political order extremely vulnerable to immediate economic developments.[32] Under these circumstances, deterioration in economic performance directly threatens the state socialist political order. However, these were factors common in other Central European countries with state socialism. Before the Communist take-over, the state was not all-encompassing there as it was in Russia or China. Most Central European societies were relatively autonomous from the state. The key question is Why were other East European regimes more resistant to catastrophic inputs of deterioration in economic performance than in Poland?

The answer to this query lies with concessions that were made during the 1956 upheaval to preserve state socialism without Soviet military intervention. The recognition of the church and the preservation of private agriculture, a traditional base of the church, have irreversibly changed the nature of Com-munist rule in Poland.[33] It remained "dominant" but less "leading"; it could crush but could hardly mobilize a society. The ideological monopoly was bro-ken. Communist ideology has never been able to compete with the church as a source of social values. As Andrzej Korboński (1988, 47) noted, "in Poland it may be said that the partial surrender of power and authority by the party took place about thirty years ago with the release of the Primate of the Polish Catholic Church from prison." The church has become a major voice of the society, a supporter of opposition activities and a chief mediator between the

[32] As we saw in chapter 1, this vulnerability also has been exacerbated by an ideological prom-ise of economic abundance.

[33] Because of its historic position as a defender of Poland's sovereignty, the position of cathol-icism was much stronger than in other Central European countries.

authorities and society during periods of upheavals. Thus the "price" for the Soviet nonintervention in 1956 was a tacit acceptance of alternative sources of social values by the authorities.

The Communist regime can probably survive, even if it does not have an ideological monopoly and even if it does not resort to massive repression, but only if the system offers upward mobility and higher consumption. After all, the Polish workers declared the state socialist order illegitimate in 1980–1981 after only two consecutive years of contraction in the economy.[34] On the other hand, however, concerns for political stability contributed to the economic decline. Political authorities had postponed introducing austerity measures in the 1970s for fear of encouraging political upheaval.

The struggle for the legitimation of state socialism through economic measures has broader implications. The lesson can be drawn that economic legitimation in a closed system inevitably leads to an economic decline and a total collapse of authority of the party-state. Other state socialist regimes today face similar crises of authority. Although the authority of the Communist party finally collapsed in Poland, and the only way to avoid anarchy (it remains to be seen whether it will be avoided) was to accept a power-sharing agreement with Solidarity, the process continues in other socialist countries. Commenting on the Soviet developments in the summer of 1989, Peter Reddaway (1989, B.1) notes, "The political system has started on what seems an irreversible process of breakdown." It remains to be seen whether this will be indeed the case. Despite the enormous differences between Polish and Soviet circumstances, it is tempting to note that the Soviet instantaneous concessions to miners striking in 1989 are strongly reminiscent of actions taken by the Polish authorities during the turbulent summer of 1980.

[34] The erosion started earlier and was linked with the economic performance. Korboński (1988, 53) notes that a decline "caused the upheaval in 1980–1981, during which the Polish working class declared the communist system illegitimate, hoping against hope to replace it with something of its own creation."

CHAPTER FIVE

Determinants of Normalization: Why Has It Failed to "Normalize" State Socialism in Poland?

AN EXAMINATION of the developments in the 1980–1988 period addresses the factors accountable for the uniqueness of the normalization in Poland. The normalization failed to normalize state socialism. Instead it led to the establishment of the first non-Communist cabinet in the Communist bloc. The failure to normalize was the combined effect of social, economic, and political factors that constrained the state's space to maneuver.

The capacity of policy makers to shape outcomes is constrained by domestic and external factors. The actual path of political development is determined by their ability to cope with the constraints and exploit the opportunities. Forces push in conflicting directions.

The political developments that followed the imposition of martial law were shaped by the legacy of the sixteen-month Solidarity period of unprecedented freedoms, the shock of martial law, the persistence of economic crisis, the Soviet involvement in "conflict management," and, to a much lesser degree, by the economic vulnerability of Poland and other CMEA countries to the West. Their unique character can be explained by a combination of these five constraints and their changes over time. By and large, the dominant constraint relates to the social and ideological damage inflicted upon state socialism by Solidarity. Conceptually, it is the most difficult to grasp. Another important constraint relates to the inability of the authorities to revive the economy.

THE SHOCK OF MARTIAL LAW: GOVERNMENT ASSETS TURN INTO LIABILITIES?

In spite of government's success in crushing the organizational structure of the union, the Solidarity period has continued to haunt the regime during normalization. As the developments after the imposition of martial law amply demonstrated, the struggle between the regime and Solidarity was not a zero-sum game. The elimination of Solidarity from official politics did not automatically boost the government's popularity for two reasons. First, as it turned out, Solidarity had many faces. On the one hand, it functioned as a political organization with its own political agenda, cleavages between various groups, and an anarchic democratic decision-making process. As such, people gauged Solidarity in terms of its ability to extract concessions from the regime and improve the plight of its members.

On the other hand, Solidarity embodied aspirations to human dignity, genuine sovereignty, and freedom. It embodied the opposition to the dominant mode of exercising political power. This opposition went hand in hand with the "considerable sympathy for such traditionally par excellence socialist values as solidarity, egalitarianism, broadly interpreted participation and even self-management," as Kowalik (1986, 34) aptly noted.[1] Because Solidarity in its symbolism was a socialist movement, the authorities were somewhat forced to embrace Solidarity's reforms, but without Solidarity itself.[2] But, on the other hand, they also resorted to a mode of governance that Solidarity challenged with full societal approval. The resulting vacuum could not be filled by the authorities. The authorities inspired obedience but not a following.

Second, the mere necessity of resorting to as drastic a measure as martial law amounted to a public acknowledgment of the total bankruptcy of the regime. According to the official ideology, the socialist state was a workers' state; it was supposed to represent and impose over the whole society (dictatorship of the proletariat) the very interests of the industrial proletariat that the regime had chosen to suppress by introducing martial law. As a consequence, Communist ideology lost its effectiveness in rallying PUWP members, not to mention a broader public. Crushing Solidarity allowed the authorities to regain control over some patterns of social action. It suppressed societal autonomy, but not its sources—that is, individual perceptions and opinions. The price was a total loss of control over values and attitudes.[3]

The necessity of acknowledging that Solidarity was a legitimate movement was an extra invitation to assess the government's actions in reference to the Solidarity period. The official line was that Solidarity had been driven away from its legitimate goals by a group of "anti-socialist elements." The measures that János Kádár used to legitimize his party's rule during the Hungarian normalization would not produce desirable results in Poland because they fell short of the liberalization experienced and envisaged during the Solidarity period. To fulfill these expectations, the authorities would have to reverse the

[1] A good example of the dominant socialist perspective is the utopian program, "Self-government Report," adopted by the Solidarity Congress in September 1981.

[2] In social perception, this, however, was regarded as just another Communist attempt to expropriate society's symbols. The program also could not work because the coup d'état created a political environment subject to different political logic than the one prevailing during the Solidarity period.

[3] The gulf between individuals' actions and their values and attitudes stemming from the recognition that they have to live within the bounds of state socialism in spite of rejecting its ideology, has been emphasized by Solidarity experts in their report *Pięć lat po Sierpniu* (Five years after August). The authors refer to the gap between the "symbolic sphere" and "sphere of action."

situation created by martial law. The alternative, a radical departure from the past that rejected both state socialism and Solidarity, was not envisaged. The only other source of legitimation—improved living standards—was unavailable because of the authorities' inability to turn the economy around. What was left, aside from the "Talleyrand's bayonets," was to maintain and propagate the conviction that any other alternative would be economically and politically more costly. But advocating a lesser evil is hardly a way to trigger enthusiastic support.

The amazing ease with which the authorities succeeded in crushing Solidarity turned out to be a mixed blessing for the authorities. Assessing the long-term effects of the military coup d'état, Aleksander Smolar (1988, 5) succinctly noted, "The shock was enormous and several myths lodged in Polish hearts were shattered; the myth of the national consensus vis-à-vis the communist power; the myth of the united defense of freedom under threat; the myth of the general strike as the ultimate weapon." The failure to act according to the self-image that Poles had of themselves produced a persistent sense of humiliation (Kalabiński 1984, 68–69).

Because of mild measures instituted during martial law, the fear quickly vanished while the humiliation persisted. This was the result of the society's perception being forcefully transformed from a subject to object of politics. "Under such circumstances," Kalabiński (1984, 68) concludes, "the humiliation could not be forgotten nor readily forgiven." Thus, the factors that facilitated the smooth introduction of martial law and, therefore, could be regarded as government assets became liabilities when the authorities later sought to assure social cooperation and acceptance. Put differently, the factor responsible for the success of the military operation remained a persistent source of weakness during normalization.

The authorities' determination to avoid bloody confrontation, which was shared by the church hierarchy,[4] enabled cooperation with the Catholic church conditional on the pursuit of dialogue between the state authorities and representatives of society. Consequently, this was another factor that helped reinforce an adjustment based on avoidance of confrontation. Mild repressions produced the soft tyranny, which in turn induced a "soft collaboration," to borrow a phrase from the 1983 underground publication.[5] The opposition became a minority, albeit a very large minority by pre-Solidarity standards. The majority of the population withdrew from the public forum. There was no

---

[4] The Sunday morning sermon delivered by the Polish primate, Archbishop Józef Glemp on the day martial law was imposed was on the Polish television evening broadcast. Glemp warned against resisting martial law. He said, "Opposition to the decisions of the authorities under martial law could cause violent coercion, including bloodshed, because the authorities have the armed forces at their disposal" (quoted in Walendowski 1982, 54).

[5] Janusz Stachniewicz, "Krajobraz polityczny" (The political landscape), *Niepodległość* 19/20 (September/October 1983), as quoted in Smolar (1988, 6).

visible popular support for the government, yet the government could extract a minimum level of obedience to ensure an acceptable level of governability. This allowed the government to achieve the twin goals of eliminating Solidarity from the public forum and of restoring a modicum of effectiveness to governance without relying solely on the visible forms of repression.

The paradox of martial law was that instead of energizing the policy makers and their supporters to implement measures congruent with the depth of the political and economic crisis, it produced paralysis. In spite of the promise expressed in the slogan, "The winter is yours, the spring will be ours," the opposition was not able to launch a general strike or large street demonstrations that would directly threaten the authorities. Similarly, despite the government's promise to continue the reforms proposed during the Solidarity period, the measures implemented fell short of eliciting public support. Radical changes were needed that would show the government's determination to break with the past. There was no sense of urgency in either the economic or political realms. The changes instituted, although considerable if assessed against the background of the 1970s, were insufficient to reverse the tendency toward apathy and indifference. Put differently, the negative shock of martial law was not neutralized by positive shocks of radical changes.

The paradox of the Polish normalization was that although the government regained a modicum of control, this was at the expense of its ability to assure social cooperation and acceptance. The price for an almost bloodless military coup d'état was social apathy. The price for the strategy of normalization was the loss of government credibility.

THE LEGACY OF SOLIDARITY

Another group of constraints relates to the legacy of the Solidarity period or, more broadly, to "peculiarities in Poland's road to socialism," as experienced in the 1980s. The short-lived Solidarity period witnessed a blow to the pillars of official ideology to which policies under state socialism have been traditionally subjugated. Presented in terms allegedly designed to ensure the dominance of workers' interests, the pillars of state socialism have included: rejection of a market; rejection of law in favor of discretional intervention by the party-state; rejection of human freedoms and democracy; and rejection of the freedom of information.

The evolution of the Communist regime in Poland since the mid-1950s might be described in terms of a more or less gradual erosion of these pillars. Various economic reforms were, by and large, designed to undo the "demonetization" of the economy caused by the introduction of a Stalinist model of economic system development. Various political changes consisted of limiting overt repression and selectively observing the law. The treaty signed with the Church in 1950, followed by a series of unsuccessful attempts to eliminate religion, eventually led to the uneasy coexistence of two value systems embodied in the PUWP and the Catholic church. The authorities have had to recognize limits to their aspirations to total control. Finally, the 1970s witnessed the inability of the authorities to suppress effectively interest groups that contributed to the collapse of the economy (Poznański 1986b).

The striking aspect of the political situation in the 1980s was the dramatic acceleration in the decomposition of Marxist-Leninist ideology. Solidarity, a unique phenomenon in Eastern Europe, has confirmed the astuteness of an apparent incompatibility of Communist political culture and Polish, Western-oriented, political and cultural tradition.

Four domestic factors were critically important for strategy selection and the subsequent dynamic of political process: the government's commitment to selective continuity; the incomplete breakdown of the ideological foundations of state socialism; the fall of the PUWP; and the emergence of the church as the institutionally acknowledged mediator of conflicts between the authorities and the broadly conceived opposition. The combination of these four factors has shaped the course of Polish normalization.

The party-state officials recognized that workers who went on strike in the summer of 1980 had a genuine right to be dissatisfied. As Stanisław Ciosek, then minister for trade union affairs, put it during a Sejm debate on new trade union law on 29 September 1982, "We did not sign an agreement [the Gdańsk Agreement] with a degenerated Solidarity, but with a working class."[6] The interpretation that Solidarity leaders were the villains seeking to capitalize on justifiable workers' discontent to overthrow the Communist government has remained the official interpretation of the Solidarity period. Yet, the authorities would argue that the workers had a right to be dissatisfied because of Gierek's ill-conceived policies not because of the inherent inefficiencies of the state socialist economic system.

The 9th Extraordinary Party Congress acknowledged the policy blunders made in the 1970s and called for limited institutional changes that would prevent the repetition of the crisis cycle. Although theoretically the Leninist party line—because of "democratic centralism"—might be changed instantly, the officials who implemented martial law were the same ones who were elected to the Central Committee and Politburo at the 1981 Party Congress. The use of the Polish army and militia to crush Solidarity would be more difficult, if not impossible, if the imposition of martial law were accompanied by a change in political leadership. Jaruzelski symbolized continuity, and an important component of this continuity was the recognition that those societal demands that did not challenge directly the Communist rule were warranted. Thus, the rhetoric of normalization included a claim that only the authorities were the

---

[6] Quoted in Strzelecka (1985, 60).

genuine inheritors of the Solidarity legacy. It also promised to observe the spirit if not the letter of the Gdańsk Agreement.

Solidarity reforms without Solidarity became the motto of the normalization strategy. The imposition of martial law was under the guise of continuing the reform effort, which, allegedly, was threatened by Solidarity radicals who, as the official propaganda claimed, had seized control of the movement.

However, the commitment to continuity without Solidarity conflicted with the logic of martial law and normalization. The former promised societal emancipation and government's accountability to society, whereas the latter was designed to crush those aspirations. Although this conflict had little to do with the decision to impose martial law, it considerably influenced the political dynamics of the normalization process. It invalidated, for example, the social and political assumptions concerning the environment that were implicit in the 1981 reform blueprint. The centralization of political controls over the society claimed was hardly compatible with the ideas of direct industrial democracy and social participation in public economic policy decisionmaking suggested in the reform proposals.[7] Instead of revising these foundations of the reform that were clearly incompatible with the political reality of martial law (e.g., workers' self-management), some of the provisions were enacted but distorted by operational regulations or simply not observed. Piecemeal implementation led to the emergence of internal tensions in the planning and management system that made the task of central control even more complex than before.

The second domestic factor of critical importance for the assessment of normalization relates to the scope of change in public attitudes and the decomposition of Communist ideology that occurred in 1980-1981. The public "striptease" of the institutions of state socialism lasted for sixteen months.[8] This was too short a time to undo the damage done by years of Communist antipolitical education and to develop a concept of an alternative political order. This period was sufficient for the population at large to reject the ideological claims of the PUWP. In this sense, the breakdown of the ideological underpinnings of state socialism was far from complete on the eve of the imposition of martial law.

The studies of public opinion, "Poles 1980 and 1981," conducted by sociologists from the Polish Academy of Sciences confirm this observation.[9] The

---

[7] For more, see Mujzel (1982) and Bielasiak (1988).

[8] This was much longer than Czechoslovakia's seven months of the Prague Spring or the thirteen days of freedom in Hungary.

[9] I refer here to the public opinion polls conducted by a group of sociologists from the Polish Academy of Sciences in 1980 and 1981. Some results were published in Władysław Adamski, Ireneusz Białecki, Krzysztof Jasiewicz, Lena Kolarska, Andrzej Mokrzyszewski, Andrzej Rychard, and Joanna Sikorska, *Polacy 80: Wyniki badań ankietowych* (Poles 80: The results of survey), Polish Academy of Sciences, Institute of Philosophy and Sociology (Warsaw, 1981). The results of the poll conducted immediately before the imposition of martial law were discussed

results suggest that although the majority was fed up with the leading role of the party, they were unable to formulate a political alternative. As Jan Powiorski (1983, 127) observed: "They [the Poles of November 1981] certainly favored a democratization of the system, and a significant extension of the limits of pluralism. These pious hopes, however, were not finally articulated in the language of concrete political stipulations. New elections, yes, but new political parties, no." [10]

Although the "Poles of 1980 and 1981" had their misgivings about a multiparty system, they unequivocally supported all measures that extended human rights and subjected the state to "social control." In these areas, societal demands to curtail totalitarian controls were more assertive. For instance, four out of the twenty-one points of the Gdańsk Agreement signed by Lech Wałęsa and government representatives in August 1980 dealt, directly or indirectly, with the issue of freedom of speech. [11] The government agreed to subject its rule over mass media and publications to public scrutiny and legal procedures. On 1 October 1981 the censorship law that significantly reduced the scope of censors' activities and granted the right of appeal was passed by the Sejm. [12]

Indirectly, the calls to curtail state control over society was manifested in demands for a greater role of the Catholic church in public life, which leads us to the third set of constraining factors. One of the items of the Gdańsk Agreement, which was promptly fulfilled, called for regular radio broadcasts of Sunday masses. More than three-fourths of respondents to the survey "Poles of 1980," independently of party membership, voiced support for "the increased role of [the] church in public life." [13]

The dramatically expanded role and visibility of the church did not have a negative impact on public attitudes toward this institution. The number of supporters of an expanded role for the church fell only slightly from 80.7 in the fall of 1980 to 77.4 percent in November 1981. [14] In the same period, however, the number of those supporting limitation of the church's involvement to purely religious matters dropped from 48.8 to 29.8 percent. It would seem,

---

by Jan Powiorski in the underground journal *Krytyka* (Warsaw) no. 13/14 (1982), and the English translation by Maya Latynski in *Poland Watch* (Washington, D.C.), no. 3 (1983).

[10] Although this may be one of the factors accountable for the sparse resistance to the imposition of martial law, the mass rejection of state socialism was not a good prognostication for the legitimacy of the government that imposed martial law to restore central control over the society.

[11] Notably, point 3 demanded a respect "to observe freedom of speech and the printed word, that is, not to repress independent publications and to make the mass media available to representatives of all regions." For an English translation of the Gdańsk Agreement, see Ascherson (1981, 290).

[12] For an excellent discussion, see Hauser (1984, 53–91).

[13] It should be noted that support tended to decline with the level of education. Although 90 percent of those with primary educations supported it, only 66 percent of the college educated expressed their support. See Adamski et al., *Polacy 1980*, pp. 113, 114.

[14] All data for 1981 from Powiorski (1983).

therefore, that in spite of the emergence of Solidarity as an advocate of societal interests, a role traditionally reserved in Poland to the church, its right to take a political stand was not imputed in public perception.

Symmetrically, opposition was growing to a greater role for the PUWP. The developments in 1981 did not increase the popularity of the PUWP. Not surprisingly, the notion of "strengthening the role of the party in governance" was more popular among PUWP members, yet almost 39 percent of them were against it. However, 67 percent of both members of non-Communist parties and non-PUWP members expressed their opposition to the role of the party.[15] Although in 1980, 55.7 percent of respondents either tended to (28.9 percent) or definitely rejected (26.8 percent) the strengthening of the PUWP's role in government, a year later, the figure rose to 57.4 percent; 27.2 percent tended to reject and 30.2 percent definitely rejected it (Powiorski 1983, 123).

The majority that repelled state socialism based on the leading role of the PUWP was by no means a homogenous group. Although all members of this group seemed to agree that the existing political order was fundamentally flawed, a significant proportion of them rejected its alternative—the multi-party system. For instance, only 25 percent of the respondents answered "yes" to the question, "Do you believe that a political party should emerge out of Solidarity, and exist alongside the labor union?," whereas 71 percent answered "no."[16] Thus, about half of the majority unsympathetic to state socialism refused to consider the change that would overhaul the monocentric system, and only 17 percent contemplated active resistance.

That the authorities were aware of the loss of appeal of socialism was best illustrated by a careful avoidance of any reference to socialism in the official statements and press publications during martial law. Instead the decision for martial law was officially justified as a means to prevent a collapse of the Polish state and a loss of independence. Thus any pretense at ideological legitimation was dismissed.

Dismissed also was the idea of normalization based on the mobilization of the PUWP. The lack of discipline alluded to in the Kubiak report did not disappear in 1980–1981 but, on the contrary, the Solidarity period witnessed a disintegration of the party. A so-called horizontal movement within the party that directly challenged the Leninist principle of democratic centralism was quickly contained because of a combination of party apparatus conservatism, Solidarity's deeply rooted mistrust of the party, and the lesson drawn from the

[15] Ibid., table 5, p. 115.

[16] According to the 1981 survey, 20.4 percent supported the PUWP's increased role in government, 24.5 percent agreed with the statement that either Poland needs a centralized political authority (13.7 percent) or a decentralized government (10.8 percent), both under the leadership of the PUWP, and 71 percent were against the founding of new political parties (Powiorski 1983, 102–39). More recent public opinion surveys show that 25 percent support the existing version of state socialism (Morawski 1988, 94).

Warsaw Pact (excluding Romania) intervention in Czechoslovakia. The fear of a reinvocation of the Brezhnev Doctrine produced an unusual coalition between party conservatives and the opposition.[17] However, a repetition of the Prague Spring scenario based on the public rallying around the "progressives" in the party was unlikely because the party was in disarray.

This was not manifested in the decline in the number of party members, however. For instance, although the number of candidates dropped by 41 percent from 292 thousand in 1980 to 172 thousand in 1981, its membership fell only by 13 percent, from 3.1 million in 1980 to 2.7 million in 1981. The PUWP members still accounted for about 11 percent of the population above the age of nineteen.[18] Although this may not compare favorably with the proportion of the adult population belonging to Solidarity (about 40 percent), it was not a tiny minority.

Thus the riddle was not in numbers. The problem was that the PUWP lost its sense of purposefulness. So the majority of people lost confidence in the PUWP's ability to govern and provide leadership and guidance. Often a double membership in Solidarity and the party was a symptom of the perceived end of ideology as a legitimizing and mobilizing factor and, consequently, of the decomposition of state socialism. The decision to impose martial law reflected this decomposition. As Adam Michnik succinctly noted: "The principal reason for the December 13 coup was not the radicalism of Solidarity but the weakness of the base of the PUWP. Solidarity's misfortune lay in its political power and military weakness; the nomenklatura situation was the reverse."[19]

Contrary to an often-held view, the conspicuous absence of active resistance to the imposition of martial law and the amazing ease with which a 10 million member movement was crushed cannot be solely explained by organizational features of Solidarity, i.e., democracy, openness, transparency, and strong commitment to nonviolence.[20] Neither can it be explained by a well-planned military operation nor by the government's advantage due to the shock of martial law. The abilities of the authorities to paralyze channels of communication within the Solidarity organization cannot be held responsible for a lack of mass response. Had there been a deeply entrenched conviction shared by a majority of people that resistance would bring about a solution, they would have re-

---

[17] In an open letter to party members, Jan Józef Lipski, one of the KOR leaders, made an appeal not to reform the PUWP. See Smolar (1988, 5).

[18] See *Rocznik statystyczny* 1983 (Statistical yearbook 1983), Central Statistical Office (Warsaw, 1984).

[19] See Michnik *Takie czasy. Rzecz o kompromisie* (These times. A piece on compromise) (London: Aneks, 1986). Quoted in Smolar (1988, 5).

[20] Note that according to the estimate of the underground Solidarity, fifty people were killed during the "state of war." Taking into account Solidarity's membership, the price for crushing the movement in terms of human lives was not high.

sponded with active resistance. The destruction of the communication network would have been irrelevant because people sharing the same convictions respond to the same stimuli in a similar fashion. The crux of the matter was that a careful assessment of the costs of insubordination prevailed over a spontaneous response to the soldiers and tanks that suddenly appeared in the streets on Sunday night, 13 December 1981. Therefore, one has to look for an explanation of the success of the military operation elsewhere.

On the eve of martial law, power elites united by the threat of Solidarity could not rely on the party to regain its hegemonic position. They could count, however, not only on repressive apparatus but also on the indifference of a considerable proportion of the population that exited from the polity. The growing perception of the impossibility of cooperation between Solidarity and the government and the radicalization on both sides was accompanied by retrenchment. The initial Solidarity period, characterized by a belief in the effectiveness of participation, was followed by one in which a growing number of people became convinced it had no influence on political outcomes. This conviction that participation was not effective became a hallmark of the normalization process in Poland.

The growing societal apathy was the result of a rapidly declining belief in the reformability of state socialism as well as of the fear that a continued confrontation between the government and Solidarity might put an end to Poland's "sovereign" existence.[21] A symptom of the growth of passivity, revealed in the public opinion surveys, was the increase in the proportion of answers indicating lack of opinion. In 1980, for instance, the share of respondents who refused to take a stand on the issue never exceeded a few percent of the population; in 1981 this share increased to between 13 and 19 percent. The rapid expansion of the silent minority was, as Jan Powiorski (1983, 130) noted, "the most interesting observation" that could be derived from those surveys. It suggests that a substantial proportion of Solidarity supporters were politically neutralized even before the imposition of martial law.

An examination of social circumstances preceding the military coup d'état indicates that indifferent and active supporters of the regime accounted for a larger share of population than was commonly assumed. An elite, united in its fears of Solidarity, together with its supporters accounted for roughly 20 percent of the adult population.[22] Combined with a politically apathetic silent

[21] In 1980, 47.6 percent of respondents expressed concerns about the sovereignty of Poland; this proportion increased to 52.6 percent on the eve of martial law (Powiorski 1983, 126). Needless to say, the intention of this question was to gauge fears of Soviet intervention.

[22] This conclusion can be drawn from an examination of the results of public surveys. For instance, 20.4 percent supported the PUWP's increased role in government, and 24.5 percent agreed with the following statements: first, that Poland needs a centralized political authority (13.7 percent) led by the PUWP; second, that Poland needs a decentralized government but under the leadership of the PUWP (10.8 percent) (see Adamski et al., *Polacy 1980*, pp. 102–39; Po-

minority (13–19 percent), these two groups accounted for between 33 and 39 percent of the population. The government was, perhaps, in the minority, but this was not a tiny minority. Because only 17 percent contemplated active resistance against forces of order, the military government did not face a majority willing to resort to violence.

Moreover, the remaining two-thirds who rejected state socialism were by no means a homogenous group. Although all members of the group seemed to agree that the existing political order was fundamentally flawed, a significant proportion rejected its alternative. Only 25 percent of them, for example, responded positively to the alternative of a multiparty system, while 71 percent answered negatively.[23] In other words, about half of the majority unsympathetic to the regime refused to consider a change that would overhaul the monocentric system, the fundamental pillar of state socialism. In addition, public opinion polls also indicated a decline in the popular appeal of Solidarity, although its hold over the population was still formidable. However, the group of ardent supporters declined by the end of 1981 by almost 50 percent.[24]

Thus the power of Solidarity, not as a symbol of societal aspirations and dreams—the measure that Adam Michnik erroneously used in the assessment of Solidarity's strength—but as measured by the proportion of the population willing to risk their lives for its survival was much more limited. In fact, the proportion willing to take that risk was more than offset by the indifference of the "two-thirds" and by the fears of Solidarity among regime supporters, factors both skillfully exploited by the government. The cyclical pattern of confrontation—compromise—provocation—confrontation accompanied by a deterioration in consumer good supplies was an important component of the government's strategy to neutralize Solidarity. If the government's objectives included wearing out and polarizing the society, then, judging ex post by the smooth introduction of martial law and by Solidarity's aborted attempts to organize strikes in the second half of 1981, the authorities were quite successful. As a result, the political and social circumstances prevailing in the Fall of 1981 facilitated the decision to impose martial law.

Yet, as was argued earlier, the imposition of martial law to crush Solidarity created a set of new constraints on normalization, ones that dramatically changed the components of the political equation. The rise of societal political expectations during Solidarity undermined the authorities' attempt to practice

---

wiorski [1983]). In addition, 71 percent of respondents were against establishing new political parties. More recent public opinion surveys show that about 25 percent support the existing version of state socialism (Morawski 1988, 94).

[23] The question was "Do you believe that a political party should emerge out of Solidarity and exist alongside the labor union?" (Powiorski 1983, 125).

[24] The proportion of those "definitely supporting" Solidarity fell from 57.9 in 1980 to 33.2 percent in November 1981, whereas those "rather supporting" increased from 31.2 to 37.7 percent. Thus the share of supporters fell from 89.1 to 70.9 percent.

"give and take" politics. The authorities gave without getting anything in return. Various liberalizing measures that would elicit positive social response under the "normal" set of circumstances have gone largely unnoticed. Successive amnesties, for example, were lauded, but not rewarded.[25] The dominant attitude was that there should be no political prisoners. Put differently, kidnappers were not to be rewarded for releasing their victims. Had it been a new government condemning the imposition of martial law and promising a far-reaching political reform, the situation would have been different.

THE ECONOMIC DIMENSION

The economic crisis was a mixed blessing for the Polish authorities. The government's failure to improve economic growth performance figured predominantly among factors that accounted for the ease in crushing Solidarity in December 1981. A dramatic increase in shortages of consumer goods throughout 1981 worked against Solidarity as fatigued and disgruntled consumers became increasingly willing to trade political freedoms for the availability of food staples. Yet slow recovery and the decline of living standards for a considerable proportion of wage earners did not help the authorities gain legitimacy. As shown by two waves of strikes in 1988, the ailing economy remained a threat to political stability. In contrast to the Gierek regime, the postmartial law authorities had a very short economic carrot with which to win support of the population. As a result, having failed to revive the economy, the authorities were under strong pressure to turn to political measures that often conflicted with the traditional concept of normalization.

A rapid deterioration of the economic situation in 1981 inevitably reduced support for Solidarity. The supplies of consumer goods, in particular of food staples, fell and did not keep up with the increase in effective demand. Although the government was charged with deliberately allowing the disintegration of the consumer supply system throughout 1981, there is no firm evidence—except that the improvement in 1982 would suggest prior stockpiling—that the government actually withheld the consumer goods supplies. However, it abstained from taking any action that would ease disequilibria. Persistent physical shortages of consumer goods and lengthening lines produced fatigue and eroded self-discipline, which was a major strength of Solidarity. The hopes of improvements in the economic situation, among other factors, produced ambivalence toward martial law.

On the other hand, although the disintegration of consumer markets might have reduced social resistance to the imposition of martial law, the economic crisis itself presented a formidable challenge to the authorities. Without a sig-

[25] Rakowski (1988, 36) complains that the church did not make a single concession for the release of political prisoners. It is not clear, however, what kind of concession the church should have made except for praising the government's decision, which it did.

nificant reduction of effective demand and suppressed domestic absorption, which are always politically unpopular measures, the shortening of lines and restoration of some semblance of order in consumer markets was not possible. Austerity was an inevitable price for reckless international borrowing in the 1970s. It had an important implication for the choice of normalization strategy. Consumption as a vehicle to gain a modicum of legitimacy, which was so carelessly exploited by Gierek following the 1970 workers' unrest, was not open to Jaruzelski. With or without repudiation of hard currency debt, a significant cut in living standards was inevitable.

Therefore, in the 1980s it was no longer a question of sharing benefits of economic growth but of sharing the costs of economic crisis. Every group tried to shove off its costs upon another. The use of economic rewards was restricted to alterations in the distribution of costs of crisis in favor of the groups regarded as strategic to the survival of the state. In their choice of normalization strategy, the authorities had to account for a limited use of the "economic" carrot, which—according to some authors (White 1986)—remains the main, or even the only, source of legitimation for Eastern European regimes.

However, thanks to an almost 20 percent cut in real personal incomes in 1982, resulting from consumer goods price increases, the increases in global output in subsequent years generated extra resources that allowed increased individual consumption. The authorities rejected the Ceaucescu strategy based on drastic austerity measures. Instead, incomes were allowed to increase. In spite of a severe economic crisis and limited resources, they attempted to legitimize the new rule through economic rewards. For example, the impact of draconian price increases in early 1982 was first watered down by the government's decision to pay compensations. Combined with a failure to improve economic efficiency, it only fueled inflation. It also deferred the solution to the Polish crisis and increased the social and economic costs of putting the economy on the path of resource-efficient development.

The available data do not reveal various "hidden" perquisites and are not sufficiently disaggregated to assess rewards accorded to the regime's strategic support groups—the militia, secret service, army, and higher echelons of central administration. There are indications that their privileged position was enhanced in the 1980s. For instance, the shares of expenditure on national defense and on public administration (including administration of justice, public prosecution, and internal security) increased from 4.8 and 4.3 percent of the total current budgetary expenditure in 1980 to 6.4 and 9.1 percent in 1986.[26]

There is statistical evidence that the authorities sought to minimize the economic burden of those who might directly threaten political stability. This group included workers from large industrial plants. They were among the

[26] Derived from *Rocznik statystyczny* 1987, Central Statistical Office (Warsaw), p. 512.

natural constituency of Solidarity. Those who had to bear a disproportionate burden of the crisis were mainly employees of small industrial plants rather than those from the large plants who could organize highly visible and economically costly strikes.[27] In addition, the income policy was largely predicated on a "money illusion" approach in which personal income increases tended to exceed increases in the supply of consumer goods. In other words, the government sought to buy stability by writing bad checks. This approach contributed to double digit inflation between 1983 and 1988.

The largest increases of wages in state-owned industries occurred in coal mining, iron metallurgy, and engineering.[28] In 1986, an average wage in these sectors, for example, was respectively 117 percent, 42 percent, and 4 percent higher than the average wages in the socialized (state- and cooperative-owned) sector.[29] In contrast, those employed in light industry, the chemical industry, the paper industry, and forestry experienced a decline in real incomes in 1986. By and large, the most substantial increase in wages was in those sectors that already had the largest average wages.

Wage differentials among various industrial sectors increased independently of the changes in enterprise profits and labor productivity.[30] In an official statement, the executive committee of the official trade union (OPZZ) complained that the growing dispersion of wages in various industries "unfortunately, bears often no relation to their economic performance."[31] Instead, a cursory examination of data published annually since 1983 in the June edition of *Zarządzanie* monthly magazine in its list of the five hundred largest industrial corporations seems to indicate that wages were related to the size of the industrial enterprises.[32] The list does not include coal mines, which on average had the highest wages. By and large, top wage earners worked in the

---

[27] For instance, it is rather telling that in 1983, in spite of a 2 percent increase in average real wages, real wages of about 45–50 percent of those employed declined. Information from the Polish Statistical Office, quoted in *Tygodnik Powszechny* (Cracow) (12 February 1984).

[28] See data in *Życie Gospodarcze* 50 (1986).

[29] See *Związkowiec* (Warsaw) (14 July 1987).

[30] This was confirmed by various empirical studies. For instance, Baczko (1987) calculated the correlation coefficient between wage rates and labor productivity measured as a ratio of net production sold without subsidies. The correlation of +.312 suggests a weak relationship between wages and productivity.

[31] Ibid.

[32] For instance, the average wage rates for each one hundred largest enterprises generated the same ranking according to the size of enterprises as those in 1984, and almost the same in 1986, except for the fifth one hundred that had an average wage rate slightly higher than the fourth one-hundred (23.3 thousand zlotys as compared with 23.4). Among the top ten enterprises ranked according to the highest average wage rate in 1986 were (1) Lubin Copper Company; (2) Batory Steelworks in Chorzów; (3) Bumar-Labedy in Gliwice; (4) Repair Facilities of the Extractive Industry at Zabrze; (5) Warsaw Steelworks; (6) Florian Steelworks at Swietochlowice; (7) Northern Shipyard at Gdańsk; (8) Metallurgy Engineering Plant at Trzebinia; (9) Lenin Steelworks at Cracow; (10) Repair Shipyard at Gdynia. Derived from data in *Zarządzanie* 6 (1987), pp. 46–63.

large plants of sunset industries and were mostly involved in producing energy-intensive, low-processed goods.

This distribution of economic rewards in state-owned industry does not simply reflect political considerations. It also reflects economic considerations, another indication of the failure to change the logic of an economic mechanism. The products of coal and copper mines, steel works, and so forth, are the inputs to many industrial processes. They are also easily exportable to hard currency markets. Because the reform failed to introduce measures that would reduce energy- and material-intensity and enhance the quality of manufactured output, energy, and raw materials, basic input-producing sectors have been accorded priority in investment programs and income policies. Therefore, in addition to political factors, those sectors have also derived their bargaining strength from insatiable domestic demand for their products and the potential cost of disruptions in supply to the whole economy.

Another sector in which incomes increased was the private nonagricultural sector.[33] The decision to offer the private sector a little breathing space was prompted by purely economic considerations. The official approach remained highly ambivalent. On the one hand, this sector was allowed to expand, and, on the other hand, it was persistently subjected to various forms of administrative harassment.

An acute shortage of housing has direct political implications. Given the present rate of housing construction, an average twenty-five-year-old Pole will move to his or her own apartment at the age of about fifty-five. According to a number of observers, the acute perception of the absence of economic opportunities has been responsible for the radicalization of young people observed during the strikes in August 1988.

Thus, according the priority to the short-term political goal of ensuring the survival of the state socialist institutional arrangements resulted in the increased developmental costs. It is bound to have negative consequences for future living standards and political stability. The authorities, by substituting meaningful political reforms for economic concessions, have eroded the long-term viability of the Polish economy. Two Polish economists have recently warned the government against the continuation of this policy.

> We do not question burning individual consumption needs and the possibility of finding ad hoc measures to meet them. Yet it would be a catastrophe if under the pressure of a threat of social instabilities triggered by declining current consumption, the consolidation [the name of the economic program prepared by the Rakowski government]—which should lay the groundwork for a sustained economic growth—was exchanged for short-term stabilization, superficial in nature and pernicious in consequences.(Bobek and Zienkowski 1988, 6)

[33] For a discussion of inconsistencies in state policies towards the private sector, see Pawlas (1987).

The slow recovery and deteriorating quality of life undermined public belief in the economic viability of state socialism but did not shatter it yet. The official assessment—as expressed in the resolutions of the 9th PUWP Congress, held in July 1981—linked the Polish crisis to the blunders of Gierek's economic policy.[34] In marked contrast, Solidarity was more sensitive to systemic impact. Solidarity's "Network" Reform Program was based on an implicit premise that the political and economic framework bore the brunt of responsibility for the collapse of the economy (Kamiński 1985, 26–29). The so-called Kubiak report commissioned in 1981 by the politburo of the PUWP and completed after the imposition of martial law, pointed to the breakdown of party discipline as well as to structural or institutional factors to account for the eruption of the Polish crisis.

Yet neither the government nor network program views went beyond the boundaries of broadly defined state socialism. Both envisaged a paternalistic state and the dominance of essentially administrative mechanisms of running the economy. Although the network program directly challenged nomenklatura and the leading role of the PUWP, it fell short of designing institutional changes that would introduce the market mechanism and a multiparty system. Its vision of the economy composed of independent, worker-governed enterprises was reminiscent of nineteenth century French utopian socialism. Clearly, this was not a design compatible with the requirements of a modern economy. Yet it explicitly recognized the systemic roots of the Polish economic predicament. The official program promised some abdication of the state from "total" controls, decision autonomy to self-managed enterprises, and social participation in central planning. It was based on the assumption, however, that basic prerogatives of the state would remain unchanged.

Slow recovery and stagnating personal incomes in 1986 and 1987 affected the public perception of the economic viability of state socialism. The view about the inherent conflict between the requirements of economic efficiency and the organizing principles of state socialism has become more and more accepted among Polish economists especially since the 1987 debate on the second stage of economic reform.[35] For instance, in an influential report the

[34] An appeal issued by the 9th Congress of PUWP argued that the blame for the current economic, social, and political crisis was to be put "not so much on the socialist system . . . as on the former Party and State leaders who betrayed its ideals" (see Radio Free Europe Background Research and Development Report (RFE-RAD)/Chron 3 [1982], 93). As though to emphasize this point, Edward Gierek and his closest collaborators were detained after the imposition of martial law.

[35] For instance, a Polish economist (Lipowski 1987), by demonstrating the incompatibility between state planning and market processes, calls for a complete marketization of the Polish economy. Many authors (e.g., Bobek and Zienkowski [1988]) call for de-etatization of the economy. Others (e.g., Kaleta [1987]) argue for remonetization. The latter view is shared by the report of the Polish National Bank ("Program" 1987), which calls for the creation of conditions for domestic convertibility of Polish złoty, that is, remonetization.

Committee for the Review of Organizational Structures of the Government-Party Commission, after enumerating the organizational changes necessary to diversify organizational structures, the priority of economic over bureaucratic considerations, the direct link between producers and international markets, and so forth, concludes; "These tendencies [i.e., recommended changes] are not a feature of our political system, but they stem from the character of contemporary productive forces in the changing world economy."[36] This implicit recognition of the incompatibility between modernization, economic efficiency, and the existing institutional arrangements has not been translated into policy action. The program of the "second stage of economic reform" adopted in 1987 fell short of overhauling the administrative mechanism to stimulate and coordinate economic activity. As Polish economist Marek Dąbrowski (1988) noted, the implementation of the program revealed "hostility toward the market mechanism." This suggests that the Communist authorities failed to understand that nothing short of excluding the state from the economy could infuse economic viability.

Poor economic performance has deeply affected the course of normalization. Rapid recovery would have strengthened state socialism. The improvement in the economic situation in mid-1983 coincided with the derailment of economic reform, which had been implemented with some vigor in 1982 (see app. A). Sustained recovery would have pacified the population and undermined the opposition. The authorities would not have been under pressure to co-opt various social groups through political concessions and cooperation with the church. The economic situation deteriorated. As Prime Minister Mieczysław F. Rakowski observed in an unpublished report: "If a capitalist society were subjected to our everyday existence, it would probably quickly rise to revolutionary struggle. . . . The society does not strike, does not demonstrate in the streets, does not organize marches of the hungry, and hence it is not so bad . . . One should be reminded, however, that some day social indifference can disappear."[37] The waves of strikes in 1988 partly vindicated this observation.

The lingering economic crisis has directly influenced the process of normalization. It has been accountable for its uniqueness. The attempts to resort to the traditional measures of state socialism have only aggravated the economic situation and have contributed to persistent social tension. The economic crisis forced the authorities to experiment with new political and economic measures. Had the economy revived, social stability could have been bought with another consumption spree, as in the Gierek normalization.

The intellectual barrier to accepting the economic nonviability of state so-

[36] See "Tezy w sprawie kształtowania struktur organizacyjnych gospodarki" (1987, 1).

[37] Rakowski (1987, 3, 17). Report prepared between 6 June and 10 October 1987 for General Jaruzelski. In March 1988, it was leaked and circulated in Warsaw and other parts of Poland.

cialism was strengthened by formidable political obstacles to the transition from the "economic dictatorship of the state" to a market economy. The challenge was that the removal of the institutional impediments to the economic efficiency would undermine economic security that had been the hallmark of state socialism. Because this would require ending the symbiosis between state and business, the privileged position of the state administration and party apparatus would be eroded. The credibility of the government and of the idea of reform was undermined by previous reform measures, which were generally associated with a "decline in real incomes," as vice-chairman of the official trade unions Mr. Martyniuk put it.[38] The authorities had to gain credibility and social acceptance in order to overcome economic paralysis.

THE SOVIET INVOLVEMENT

Although the Gdańsk Agreement initially caught the Soviet leaders off guard, the Soviet Union played a very active and visible role in the management of the Polish crisis. Because Solidarity challenged the ability of the PUWP to control political and economic processes, it was regarded as a threat to the very pillars of the Soviet control over Poland, that is, democratic centralism and party supremacy. Yet, because of the astounding rapidity of the emergence of Solidarity and because of international constraints the Soviets' room for maneuver was significantly circumscribed.

The crisis in Poland erupted at the most inopportune moment for the Soviet Union. Because of its global reach strategy, which it pursued vehemently in the 1970s, the Soviet Union was both economically and militarily overextended. The invasion of Afghanistan in December 1979, envisioned as a quick military solution to political turmoil, turned into a long-term military commitment. Contrary to Soviet expectations, it brought about a rapid deterioration in relations with the United States. However, the American sanctions, grain embargo, and boycott of Olympic Games in Moscow, also produced tensions between Western Europe and the U.S. Hoping to exploit the rift within NATO, Kremlin leaders wanted to avoid the deterioration of their relations with Western European governments, which would be inevitable if direct military intervention were used in Poland. Simultaneously, its giant Communist neighbor, China, launched a modernization drive based on Western cooperation. Direct Soviet intervention in Poland would have restored the weakened Western unity and might have induced the West to actively play the China card.[39] Therefore, its room for maneuvering was rather limited.

In addition to the international cost of direct intervention, the Soviet leader-

[38] Interview for Polish Radio, Warsaw, 13 January 1988.

[39] Reportedly, a document purposely leaked by the Carter administration listed providing China with sensitive military technologies as one measure that the U.S. government would undertake in response to Soviet military intervention in Poland (Brzeziński 1983).

ship had to account for the likely military cost. In view of historical experience and strong anti-Soviet feelings among Poles, an absence of violent resistance to a Soviet invasion could not be taken for granted. Therefore, the combination of both external and "Polish" factors was in favor of perpetuating the Soviet grip through finding a domestic solution to the "Polish disease." Military intervention was probably retained as a last resort measure, however.

The Soviet global goal was to restore traditional mechanisms of control in subordinated Communist countries.[40] Because the dominance was achieved through the control of the PUWP leadership (in turn, committed to nomenklatura and the democratic centralism principle), Soviet crisis management focused on obstructing cooperation between Solidarity and the PUWP. As Andrzej Korboński (1984, 82) succinctly noted, "The Soviets adopted a strategy as straightforward in purpose as it was manipulative in tactics: never permit the Polish party to strike a genuine compromise with Solidarity; disrupt even temporary lulls that might allow the union to consolidate its legal and political status; and ultimately force the Poles themselves to end the threat to one-party rule."

To be effective, the Soviet leadership had to use public channels of communication. First, Soviet military preparations for invasion (December 1980) and joint military maneuvers (March/April 1981) were widely publicized by Western mass media; the apparent objective was to remind Poles of the Brezhnev doctrine. Second, visits by the Soviet officials were usually followed by criticisism of Solidarity and the PUWP leadership's inability to control the situation. The PUWP was accused of the greatest heresy, that is, revisionism, while Solidarity was accused of fermenting "antisovietism" and "antisocialism." These criticisms emerged from press denunciations, *Tass* communiques, and official warnings issued by the Soviet Communist party.[41]

The Soviet involvement, designed to prevent a genuine compromise between the authorities and Solidarity, has been responsible for what Korboński (1984, 82) called a cycle of confrontation-compromise-provocation-confrontation. The cycle had a different impact on political developments at each occurrence. Initially, a sequence of provocation, confrontation, and compromise contributed to a rapid expansion of Solidarity membership in the fall of 1980. Its repetitions wore down the population. The cycle contributed to a growing disenchantment of considerable segments of population with both the PUWP and Solidarity leadership. Another consequence was the increased polarization of society and the radicalization of Solidarity activists. Within the PUWP, this pattern enhanced the position of those who were opposed to any

---

[40] For an analysis of the mechanisms through which the Soviet Union effects its control over Warsaw Pact countries, see Dawisha (1988, 76–80)

[41] The most blatant example was the famous June 5 "open" letter of the Soviet Central Committee addressed to the Polish Central Committee. For the full text of the letter, see the *New York Times*, 11 June 1981.

meaningful reform of the Communist party such as the changes recommended by the so-called horizontal movement.[42] In all, each cycle reduced the political base of those among the authorities and Solidarity leaders who were in favor of striking a social compact. In this sense, in each cycle there was increasingly more room for confrontation than for cooperation. The logical, although not inevitable conclusion of this cyclical pattern, was the imposition of martial law, which was the least politically costly solution of the Solidarity challenge for the Soviet Union.

The imposition of martial law put an end to high visibility of the Soviet involvement in Poland. Before the December 13 military coup d'état, not all Soviet actions were publicized, however. There is ample evidence that the Kremlin was involved in its preparation, precipitation, and execution.[43] After the coup d'état, there was a return to the usual pattern of bilateral Soviet-Warsaw Pact member interaction.

However, the Soviets had many reasons to be less than satisfied with the normalization. The progress toward political conciliation, economic reconstruction, and restoration of the state central controls was remarkably slow. Although the leaders in the Kremlin might have found some consolation in crushing the legal Solidarity and the seizure of direct control by generals—whose appointments had been traditionally very carefully scrutinized by Moscow and, therefore, could be relied upon—Brezhnev as well as his two quick successors, Yuri Andropov and Konstantin Chernenko, carefully evaded publicly supporting General Jaruzelski. Only a few articles published in the Soviet press critically assessed the Polish situation or occasionally directly attacked some members of Jaruzelski's inner circle. These publications suggest that there were differences between the Soviet and Polish leadership about what specific measures should be implemented to attain a commonly shared global goal of restoring central controls over the society. On the other hand, given the partial paralysis of the Soviet leadership due to Andropov's illness, it would seem that the Jaruzelski regime had considerable discretion.

The ascension to power of Mikhail Gorbachev significantly increased Soviet appreciation for the complexity of the Polish situation. For one, Gorbachev's "discovery" of the Soviet crisis and his assertion of the ills of state socialism somewhat curtailed the stigma against Poland as a crisis-ridden

---

[42] The implementation of its program, which called for a democratization and replacement of vertical command party structure by horizontal links among local party organizations, would deal a mortal blow to Leninist democratic centralism.

[43] According to Western intelligence sources, a wholly independent communication network was established around Poland, and there was a significant buildup of supplies at Soviet military bases located in Poland in April 1981. Marshal Kulikov visited Warsaw just two days before the imposition of martial law. Finally, an eyewitness account "Wojna z narodem" (War against the NABA) of Col. Ryszard J. Kukliński, who was involved in the planning of the military operation, was published in *Kultura* (Paris), no. 4 (1987). This account sheds unique light on the vast scope of the Soviet involvement.

society. General Jaruzelski was again accorded the position of the "first behind General Secretary," traditionally reserved for First Secretaries of the PUWP in intrabloc hierarchy. The search for new institutional arrangements that would revive stagnant centrally planned economies became legitimized blocwide, if not directly encouraged by Gorbachev's rhetoric of restructuring. As spokesman for the Polish government Jerzy Urban stated in 1987, the Soviet policies gave a "new foundation to Poland's own experiments."[44] Thus, the traditional Soviet constraint under the guise of revisionism was drastically relaxed.

Gorbachev's "new thinking" had two effects from the perspective of normalization in Poland from 1986 to 1988. First, it made obsolete the earlier used argument that "had it not been for Moscow's resistance we would have moved ahead with reforms." The blame for the slow pace of reforms could no longer be put on exogenous constraints. Blaming the Soviets for "domestic" inaction was no longer a credible explanation (Michnik 1989). Glasnost and perestroyka undermined the position of the so-called hard liners, if indeed they had been a threat to Jaruzelski, who seemed to have been firmly in control of the PUWP throughout the whole normalization period.

Second, various innovative measures that significantly changed Poland's political landscape (e.g., glasnost, the reliance on nationalism to assure the regime's stability, the explicit recognition of the church as a main Polish institution) ceased to be viewed by Moscow as signs of revisionism. Even such breakthrough decisions as, for instance, ending the jamming of broadcasts by Radio Free Europe (since January 1988) preceded similar Soviet moves.

The end of the 1980s witnessed a dramatic change in the Soviet approach to its Central European "junior" allies. Although Gorbachev probably did not anticipate the abolition of state socialism, his actions to maintain stability by opening a window of opportunity to change the status quo effectively set the stage for the collapse of Communist regimes. Gorbachev rejected the option of saving state socialism with Soviet tanks. Moreover, his famous telephone call to Prime Minister Rakowski in July 1969 persuading him to observe the results of elections won by Solidarity and not to obstruct the establishment of a first non-Communist government amounted to granting Poland independence.

Although Gorbachev's new thinking legitimized the search for previously unthinkable solutions to Poland's problem, an interaction with the Soviet economy was a stumbling block to radical restructuring of the economic system and investment programs for two reasons. First, because of the antiquated structure of the Soviet economy, its import demand was mainly for the products of traditional "smokestack" industries. This demand combined with do-

[44] Polish News Agency (PAP), 16 February 1987, quoted in Dawisha (1988, 179).

mestic pressures to invest in traditional industries created an extra constraint to a shift to sunrise sectors.

Second, persistent shortages typical for the Soviet economy decreased incentives to stricter product quality requirements. A significant proportion of products, the so-called soft goods, which could be sold to the Soviet Union or other CMEA countries, were not marketable in the West. Thus the Soviet economic connection, important as it had been for the provision of oil and other raw materials, provided few incentives to implement economic reform measures and effective external debt management.

VULNERABILITY TO THE WEST

Fears of severing economic relations with the West affected the choice of measures designed to bring about stabilization. Although these fears did not prevent the authorities from imposing martial law, they played a role in the decision not to follow the Husak variant of normalization after the invasion of Czechoslovakia in August 1968. Both the Husák and the Jaruzelski regimes pursued the same objective, but the means were different. Poland's vulnerability to the West was to some extent accountable for the choice of means.

The goal of General Jaruzelski was to crush Solidarity and to restore central controls over society, that is, to attain normalization and ensure governability within the institutional arrangements of state socialism while minimizing visible forms of repressions. The economic vulnerability to the West was among factors that prompted the authorities to avoid a full-fledged confrontation.

Some publications (e.g., Olechowski [1982]) indirectly suggest that the option to repudiate the international debt was considered by Polish officials.[45] The government rejected this option, however. Although there is no hard evidence that would indicate pressures from other Warsaw Pact governments, Poland's cooperative behavior vis-à-vis its Western creditors was in the interest of both the Soviet Union and other Eastern European regimes. Poland's repudiation might have led to more economically painful sanctions extending over a wider range of commercial and financial relations of the Soviet Union and its junior partners in Eastern Europe than the symbolic ones that had been imposed by the West in response to martial law. It might have led to a Western credit embargo and to a collapse of East-West economic relations.

Taking into account that other Warsaw Pact countries were considerably less indebted than Poland, they would certainly lose more than they would

---

[45] This article carefully examines the costs and benefits of repudiating Poland's hard currency debt. It concludes that costs would significantly exceed benefits. Taking into account the timing (March 1982) and the publication *(Polityka)*, one may infer that this was a response to the views favoring the repudiation option.

gain from a Western credit embargo.[46] This should not suggest that Western economic leverage could have prevented the imposition of martial law. Rather, because of the substantial cost of severing economic interaction with the West, the Polish government and its Warsaw Pact partners shared an interest in minimizing the negative impact of martial law and in "normalization" of their already strained relations with the West.[47]

The actions taken by the Bank for International Settlements (Basel, Switzerland) in 1982 to prevent a collapse of the Hungarian National Bank and by the West German government to stop the run on the East German Foreign Trade Bank (Delamaide 1984) both triggered by uncertainties over the future of East-West relations in the aftermath of the imposition of martial law would be problematic, if the "state of war" spawned massive bloodshed in Poland.

Western governments had a considerable stake in preventing Poland from defaulting because of the size of the Polish debt and because of the fears that its repudiation would produce a domino reaction among other sovereign debtors. In fact, the West *did* assist, albeit indirectly, the military regime. Taking advantage of the Western governments' decision to suspend negotiations over the rescheduling of the official portion of its debt, the Polish government stopped servicing its official debt. It gave a much needed breathing space and allowed a shift of scarce hard currency earnings to service commercial debt. Because the official debt accounted for about 50 percent of the total, this was a form of assistance, as some Polish officials publicly acknowledged (Bobrowski 1987).

Western policy makers realized that cutting off financial relations with Poland would leave them with little leverage. This was clearly one of the resaons that the U.S. government after a lot of deliberation decided against declaring Poland formally in default.[48] In retrospect, this turned out to be a wise decision that eventually paved the way for a very effective two-track policy.

The two-track approach of Western governments' policies toward Poland, that is, supporting the opposition while simultaneously opening the channels of communications with the government, was a boost to the opposition. As Rakowski (1988, 41) bitterly observed: "Visits upon the invitation of the Polish government have been linked with the talks with Glemp or other church dignitaries and provocatively visible meetings with representatives of the opposition. They have become, whether we like it or not, a new component of

---

[46] The best measure of overall indebtedness is the ratio of convertible currency net debt to convertible currency exports. These ratios in 1980 were below 1.00 for Bulgaria (.91), Czechoslovakia (.81), and USSR (.33); below 2.00 for the German Democratic Republic (1.97), Hungary (1.44), and Romania (1.39). Poland had a ratio of 3.27. See Kamiński (1987, 85).

[47] In addition, there was a political cost. Détente has been an important source of legitimation for East European regimes, as Dawisha (1988, 116) noted.

[48] The issue whether to announce Poland's default formally was given serious consideration by the Reagan administration in early 1982. For an in-depth account, see Cohen (1986, 177–205).

the political situation in Poland.'' The practice of meeting the opposition leaders established by Western politicians paying official visits to Poland vindicated the existence of a 1981 triangle consisting of the authorities, the church, and the opposition. It also served as a reminder that Western financial assistance was conditional upon social compact and trade union pluralism.

Although neither the church nor the opposition owed their strong position in Polish polity to Western support, various forms of Western assistance carried out through the church and opposition had more than symbolic significance. The assistance included not only food and medicine but also money, which enabled victims of oppression to survive and helped the underground publishing movement.

Although Poland's diplomatic relations with the U.S. and other Western countries were ''normalized'' by 1984, the absence of a political-economic consensus in Poland as well as slow progress in economic reform implementation remained a major stumbling bloc until the conclusion of the round table negotiations and the legalization of Solidarity in April 1989. The American policy of a ''step-by-step'' reengagement with Poland, as John Hardt and Jean Boon (1987) have depicted it, made the lifting of the sanctions and Western assistance in economic recovery conditional upon the progress in liberalization. For instance, the unconditional amnesty announced by the Polish government in 1986 (see app. A) was followed by the U.S. government lifting the embargo on Poland's application to join the International Monetary Fund (IMF) and to restore Most Favored Nation (MFN) status. It is conceivable that a linkage between domestic policy actions and Western concessions (i.e., selective lifting of sanctions) might have tipped the balance in favor of those in the government who supported political liberalization.

Linking access to Western financial institutions with radical political and economic reform was not a sufficiently strong incentive to overcome forces blocking the change under a Communist government. The economic ''carrot'' that these organizations might offer was not consummated until the Solidarity-led government was established in August 1989.[49] No agreement on the IMF-financed adjustment program was reached. Frequent visits of the IMF and World Bank experts between 1986 and 1989 produced several studies on various aspects of the Polish economy.[50] They enhanced the IMF and World Bank expertise and contributed to a better conceptual grasp by the Polish officials of what should be done to improve economic performance. This new channel

[49] Except for a minor loan of $15 million to HORTEX Cooperative, no programs comparable to those in Hungary were negotiated with the World Bank or the International Monetary Fund before a Solidarity-led cabinet was established in August 1989.

[50] The best known is the World Bank report, *Poland: Reform, Adjustment and Growth*, released on 17 August 1988. Other World Bank studies focused on foreign trade, energy, and steel.

that Poland's membership created ensuring some Western influence over public economic policy was activated after the Communist regime collapsed.[51]

In all, the assessment of the Western impact on normalization defies a straightforward answer. There was little sensitivity to Western public opinion when the regime's survival was at stake. Fears of Western sanctions played no role when the decision to impose martial law was made. The full amnesty was announced only when the opposition was in disarray.[52] Poland's debt did not offer the West a powerful instrument to shape policy outcome in Poland, although vague promises of assistance accelerated the introduction of liberalizing measures.

CONCLUSION

Political developments following the imposition of martial law can hardly be described in terms of normalization. Normalization compatible with the logic of state socialism involves the restoration of the state's capacity to suppress individual and group interest. The relative autonomy of society, characteristic of the period of upheaval, is shattered. The state in turn regains its relative autonomy. Dissenting voices are silenced. People are terrorized. They are scared to express their opinions. The authorities are firmly in control. The system of monolithic controls is restored, and state socialism becomes normalized.

Except for a very brief couple of months after the imposition of martial law, the actual normalization deviated from the classic pattern. The authorities failed to suppress the relative autonomy of society, although it was curtailed. Dissenting voices were not silenced. On the contrary, the authorities had to concede their defeat by loosening their grip over state-controlled mass media. Thus, except for the restoration of political stability and some governability, nothing was reminiscent of "classic" normalization. On the contrary, the decomposition of state socialism progressed dramatically in the 1980s.

The unusual normalization has been the product of incompatibility between the institutional arrangements of state socialism and economic and political changes. As the developments in the 1980s amply showed, the modifications introduced in political and economic management have fallen short of improving the state's capacity to deal with societal expectations and to improve economic performance. As a result, the political measures introduced, although quite radical by the standard of the 1970s, have not elicited much public en-

[51] It was instrumental for the Mazowiecki Solidarity-led government to launch a stabilization program in January 1990.

[52] According to many observers, the opposition was in crisis from 1986 to 1988 (e.g., Smolar [1988]). Adam Michnik (1990, 23) wrote that the "government's mechanism of repression was weakening, but so were the underground structures that Solidarity had built."

thusiasm. Although they have been quite effective in containing the opposition, they have failed to overcome the economic and political stalemate.

Multiple constraints stemming from a combination of domestic and external factors shaped political dynamics in Poland between the 1980 summer wave of labor unrest and the Solidarity-led government in 1989. Domestic factors were responsible for self-imposed limits on the dynamics of political process during the Solidarity period. The developments after the imposition of martial law were characterized by a similar sense of the limited scope for maneuvering.

Paradoxically, neither the government, ideologically shattered by the inability to regain control without resorting to a state of war, nor Solidarity, organizationally destroyed by its inability to respond by launching a general strike, could claim victory (before 1989). The absence of resistance justified mild repressions. This created an illusion of restoring governability, which in turn deprived the authorities of the sense of urgency to look for long-term solutions to the Polish malaise. The sequence of self-limiting revolution followed by a combination of self-limiting resistance and self-limiting repression also produced self-limiting reforms. This sequence assured political stability but at the expense of a persistent stalemate between the government and the opposition. The crux of the matter is that the opposition was not able to directly challenge the government, while the latter was unable to fully suppress it.

Repression, self-limiting as it was, did not ensure the state's capacity to suppress the society's autonomy. The failure to revive the economy further eroded this capacity because a fast economic recovery would have boosted the popularity of the government thereby undermining the opposition and lessening the West's leverage. Instead the government had to reconcile itself with considerable political pluralism.

But no institutional changes were introduced into state socialism to accommodate varied interests. To assure a modicum of governability, the state had to rely on the institutions that were outside its political structure—mainly the Catholic church. Even the organizations internal to state socialism, such as the "official" Trade Union Confederation (OPZZ) and popular front organizations (Patriotic Movement of National Rebirth [PRON]), obtained some autonomy although not much respect. Contrary to expectations, they did not become traditional transmission belts of the state's policies.[53] Under the pressure of public opinion, they sought an independent position, which occasionally helped the government to undermine the opposition.[54] The active search

[53] For a similar observation, see Smolar (1988) and Rakowski (1987).

[54] Various statements issued by the OPZZ clearly illustrate this point. A statement in March 1987 protesting the government's economic policies drew the following response from one of the officials: "This was a protest against the fundamental principles of socio-economic strategy adopted by the 10th Party Congress, confirmed by the Sejm and its trade union deputies. . . .

for the church's cooperation and acceptance of various forms of independent collective action were symptoms of the decline of state socialism. In the next chapter, I shall turn to the questions What were the other symptoms? and What implications did they have for the disintegration of the politico-economic order?

'Our' trade unions threatened to launch a general strike!? They did so because they rightly sensed the attitudes of the masses. Basically, we should be happy that the OPZZ channeled the social discontent rather than the opposition'' (Rakowski 1987, 19–20).

CHAPTER SIX

The Institutional Decomposition of State Socialism: The Syndrome of Withdrawal

> It is not the nation which has broken down, but the state that is out
> of order and in need of repair.
>
> —Edmund Osmańczyk

A COMMON SYMPTOM of changes that occurred in the 1980s in Poland is withdrawal. Two major tendencies have set the pace of the erosion of the organizing principles of state socialism: a spontaneous withdrawal of large segments of the society from political and economic spheres directly controlled by officialdom and a reluctant withdrawal of the socialist state from the pretense of directly controlling various spheres of social, political, and economic life. Because they represent two sides of the same coin and often reinforce each other, I shall refer to them as the syndrome of withdrawal or exit.

The syndrome of withdrawal is the result of a response to a cumulative process of economic deterioration. As Albert Hirschman (1970) has convincingly shown, exit is one of the responses to a decline in firms, organizations, and states. When individuals express their rejection of the politico-economic system by refusing to participate in it, the mechanism is analogous to consumers' decisions to express their dissatisfaction with a firm through exit.

Hirschman does not include in his analysis the withdrawal or exit of the state. The reason for the state's withdrawal is its inability to improve economic performance and ensure social compliance. Because the socialist state is omnipresent by institutional design, the implications of its exit are far-reaching; they affect the very foundations of the political order.

The theme that I emphasized in chapter 5 was constraints that had shaped the post–martial law normalization strategy. Because of domestic and international circumstances, the option of Ceaucescu-style massive repression and coercion was not available. The option pursued was the accelerated withdrawal or exit of the state from the aspiration to control everything, especially when the economic recovery began to crumble in the mid-1980s.

Although the evolution of state socialism could be characterized as a reluctant reconciliation of the authorities with the impossibility of controlling all

Edmund Osmańczyk in a speech delivered at the Sejm debate on the law of trade unions on 8 October 1982.

domains of public life, the process acquired some new characteristics in the 1980s. First, the withdrawal was the result of a deliberate policy action designed to enhance the regime's legitimacy and to ensure more effective control over selected domains of public life. Second, the scope and pace of its withdrawal had no precedent in the history of state socialism, except for short periods of upheavals (e.g., the 1956 Hungarian uprising or the 1968 Prague Spring). Third, withdrawal was also an expression by the authorities of their dissatisfaction with the existing politico-economic order.

WITHDRAWAL: CONCEPTUAL CONSIDERATIONS

The Nobel laureate in economics Kenneth Arrow (1963, 947) once observed that "when the market fails to achieve an optimal state, society will, to some extent at least, recognize the gap, and non-market social institutions will arise attempting to bridge it." In the nonmarket economy, the burden to revive the economy is on the state. In an attempt to control the political impact of the inability to infuse economic vitality, the Polish government sought to "de-etatize" some spheres of political and economic activity. Although the response to the government's policy was increased societal indifference, the possibility cannot be excluded that market institutions will arise to overcome the economic crisis. In the late 1980s, the combination of political liberalization and the state economy's rigidities has increased incompatibilities between the existing institutional framework and emerging "autonomous" political institutions.

The analysis of Poland's 1982–1988 normalization from the perspective of withdrawal has some broader implications, as similar developments of state socialism occur in other countries. Notwithstanding the differences, the processes underway in Hungary or in the Soviet Union can be analyzed also as accelerated withdrawal. The case of Poland shows that the withdrawal designed to reverse the decline of state socialism speeds up its decline. Withdrawal limited by continued adherence to the principle of fusion—the reluctance to "liberate" the economy from the administrative grip and to allow markets to develop—only exacerbates internal tensions and contributes to a demise of state socialism. This form of crisis management cannot be successful without scrapping at least the principle of fusion (if not the principle of one-party rule).

The socialist state owed its sturdy survival in Poland to self-imposed limitations (and to the Soviet Union). I shall argue that survival was made possible by creating opportunities for limited withdrawal and for larger responsiveness to expressions of dissatisfaction voiced by the strong. The strong who stayed within the direct reach of state socialism tend to obtain preferential treatment. The growing wage differential between those employed in large industrial plants and in the small ones illustrates this phenomenon. But the competent and strong have also been allowed to exit or to operate outside the direct reach of the socialist state. Total escape excluding emigration, however, was not possible. The weak have remained exploited by the incompetent and lazy. The society has been penalized by an overall poor economic performance for which—under the existing institutional arrangements—the state bears the ultimate responsibility.

The normalization in the 1980s brought about palliatives of the recuperation mechanisms characteristic of modern societies. As discussed in chapter 2, the changes in the economy have fallen short of anything resembling the homeostatic controls characteristic of the market mechanism of allocation, although economic actors have become more sensitive to profits consideration. As a result, economic activity has remained highly politicized. The changes in polity have fallen short of instituting a political mechanism of choice and accountability. The state socialism remains state socialism because it has retained its major institutional traits.

The withdrawal of the state is a form of escape from its own predicament, the catastrophe of its own making. This escape has economic and political components that lead to more or less limited economic and political pluralism. Political and economic spheres become more diversified and open. When the discussed components are measurable, their interpretation raises a number of questions. Does the fall, for instance, in the number of centrally allocated tasks indicate the state's withdrawal from day-to-day management of state-owned enterprises, as one study has suggested?[1] Is the increased openness of mass media, for example, an indicator of pluralism?

The withdrawal of the state from the economy can take several forms that range from privatization of the economy to loosening the ties that bind state-owned enterprises to their owners. Privatization may involve closing down all state-owned enterprises, a highly unlikely option when the state owns most capital assets, sale to the private sector, and promotion of private production. So far, the Polish government has not disposed of some of its assets by selling them. However, it loosened its formal hold over the economy by opening some activities to the private sector. The share of the private sector in total output, for instance, increased in the 1980s. Yet the private sector remained subject to cumbersome controls from the local state administration (Kamiński 1989c), although a new law on "undertaking economic activity," enacted in December 1988, held the promise that the state's paternalism would be significantly curtailed (see app. A). Thus, the state "withdrew" from taking risk in starting the business, but it retained a considerable degree of direct control, incomparably higher than in market economies where the state's intervention

[1] See World Bank (1987b).

is subject to general rather than individually crafted rules, although exceptions account for natural monopolies, externalities, and imperfect information.

Another form is the retention of state ownership while allowing for the operation of markets. This form entails granting significant autonomy to state-owned enterprises. The state then gives up its prerogatives to directly control entry, prices, conduct of business, and so forth, except for some cases related to market imperfections. The vertical subordination of state-owned enterprises is then partly replaced by horizontal links based on contractual relationships, interdependence between buyers and sellers, and responsiveness to price signals.

Both in privatization and the delegation of decision authority, the litmus test of the withdrawal is the degree to which direct microeconomic ad hoc intervention has been replaced by indirect macroeconomic controls.[2] In other words, the state shapes the decision environment of enterprise management, direct intervention is not a rule but an exception.

Political components of withdrawal are more difficult to analyze and interpret. In general terms, they boil down to the state's tacit acceptance and coexistence with the organizations representing alternative values and the opening of opportunities for independent collective action. As in withdrawal from the economy, the state's concessions are based on the recognition by the authorities of the impossibility of imposing total control on the society. Attempts to do so would produce economic inefficiencies and political instabilities. The withdrawal from the polity consists, for example, of seeking modus vivendi with the Catholic church and the opposition. Its other expression is allowing the establishment of associations that would not be "transmission belts" of the state.

The ultimate stage of the withdrawal involves the creation of a competitive political system with autonomous law guaranteed by independent courts. This would amount to the death of the socialist state. In-between, however, the degree of withdrawal can be assessed by the extent to which the dialogue with non-state-controlled institutions shapes political outcomes and the degree to which the foundations for a pluralist society have been established. As will be shown, various political and economic measures implemented as a part of "normalization" strategy have resulted in the withdrawal of the socialist state from some spheres of political and economic life.

The other side of the withdrawal syndrome is exit from the state, that is, from the socialist system. The exit from the system is an escape to the family life and alternative society (as various forms of "underground public" life were called in Poland), to the private sector, or to the West. The symptoms of escape range from alcoholism, expansion of a parallel economy, or a de-

---

[2] Microeconomic controls include: direct shaping of wages in enterprises; price setting; allocation of capital to various sectors; and setting tax rates on individual basis. See chapter 2.

creased participation in various forms of official political activity. Because the whole population cannot leave the boundaries of the state, withdrawal can never be complete. Because the majority of those who stay have to live in an environment dominated by the state, withdrawal is limited to some areas. Excluding emigration as a symptom of dissatisfaction with the existing political and economic arrangements, withdrawal consists of staying as far away from the state as possible.

The degree of exit by individuals from the state is determined by the extent to which the state has actually withdrawn. The two are complementary because to keep individual options to withdraw from becoming too costly, the state has to make room for activity outside its direct control. The expansion of the private sector, for instance, is determined by policy action of the state, and so is the scope of the shadow economy. Similarly, liberalized regulations concerning foreign currency accounts held by Polish residents have allowed an escape from domestic currency.[3] The use of foreign currencies as a unit of account, a medium of exchange, and a store of value by the population is the result of the state's loss of control over the money supply. As such, this is not a deliberate withdrawal of the state but the admission of a failure that has been left uncorrected.[4]

Exit from the state is also determined by the consequences of withdrawal. The socialist state is in a position to influence the cost of withdrawal. Namely, it can impose cost on exit from its political core, in particular the PUWP. It can create legal obstacles to emigration. It can impose various extra costs on those who want to move to the private sector. Various forms of harassment imposed upon those who give up membership in the PUWP may effectively discourage others from taking this action. Repression of the opposition, in turn, works in favor of silent exit from politics. The inevitable outcome of harassment and repression is societal apathy and indifference. This allows the state to dominate but not to mobilize the society.

There are two exits from state "politics": one that leads to silence, and another that leads either to a "quasi-official" or an "underground" opposition. The first option implies indifference stemming from the conviction that nothing can repair state socialism. The "underground" option, although sharing the conviction that state socialism cannot be repaired, implies active struggle against the state outside of the "quasi-official" political arena. The difference between the quasi-official and the underground opposition is not clear-cut. It boils down to a difference in assessment of the effectiveness of promoting change through political means, which, in turn, is a function of the state's willingness to coexist with the opposition.

[3] The escape from the złoty was spurred by inflation and negative interest rates on savings accounts denominated in Polish złoty.

[4] As Gilpin (1987, 122) has observed, paper money is political money. The escape from the zloty is a reflection of the greater confidence people have in other governments' policies.

Withdrawal from the state's political core, primarily from the PUWP, is rooted in the conviction that the system's functioning cannot be improved from within; it is not reformable. Hirschman's (1970, 33) observation that "the voice option is the only way in which dissatisfied customers or members can react whenever the exit option is not available" is only partially applicable to the circumstances characteristic of state socialism. The alternative to withdrawal may be an active expression of dissatisfaction, but it may also be indifference. A member may decide to "hang on" despite the deeply entrenched conviction that opportunities to improve the system are absent.

This is more likely to happen if there is a price to be paid for withdrawal. The cost of withdrawal from the Communist party has tended to decline. Under Stalin, withdrawal amounted to treason. The price to be paid was often one's life, the Gulag, or both. This was well captured by Stalin's maxim: "whoever is not with us is against us." Kádár's modification of this maxim to "whoever is not against us is with us," adhered to in his policy since the mid-1960s lowered the penalty for exit. In Poland, the cost of withdrawal from the PUWP has also significantly declined since the late 1970s.

The declining cost of exit accompanied by a suppression of dissenting voices deprives the party of those who are alert, sensitive, and innovative. The Hungarian uprising, Polish October, and Prague Spring, the events that preceded the periods when the exit option was extremely costly, were led by people convinced that "voice [from within the party] will-be effective," to borrow a phrase from Hirschman (1970, 37). Those who became involved were the most innovative. They were also those who were most penalized. The Polish upheaval from 1980 to 1981, on the other hand, rested on the assumption that only pressure from outside of the state can actually force it to introduce changes. The Polish authorities have tacitly accepted this assumption. Over the last decade, their strategy has been to make this option available in order to get rid of those criticizing the party leadership for its failings. This in turn has further reinforced the conviction that voice is futile.

The futility of voice from within the state does not automatically strengthen the opposition; even the cost of joining the opposition declines because of limited repression. The success of the opposition is critically dependent on its responsiveness to the voice of its members and its ability to convince possible constituencies that it has a viable program of change. If either of those two conditions is not met, the opposition is weak. Because it is deprived of the repressive apparatus, it is weaker than the socialist state even though the strong and competent withdraw from it.

The withdrawal syndrome is a reflection of a crisis of state socialism. In view of the deteriorating economic and political situation, withdrawal is the only possible response unless the situation can be remedied by internal modifications. The state itself cannot simply withdraw if political stability is to be maintained and economic viability restored. The withdrawal must be orderly, and the institutions that would replace the state's direct command structure with indirect controls and effective conflict mediation have to be introduced. I will now turn to the question of the extent of withdrawal and its institutional expression.

SYMPTOMS OF THE WITHDRAWAL SYNDROME

Withdrawal of individuals from state socialism can be either complete (emigration) or partial based on the minimization of involvement by individuals in socialism's core political institutions, political parties, and "ritualistic" mass organizations. Leaving aside emigration, the withdrawal can be from the polity and the economy. The "escape" from the latter can be either to the private sector or to the shadow economy, both of which depend on the state's policies. Withdrawal from the former can be either to the opposition or to private life. It is reflected in a decision to leave (or not to join) core political institutions, or in the refusal to participate in political rituals, for example, referendums or elections. Because the many strands of the opposition have taken different views on reformability of the system, withdrawal to the opposition may be predicated on differing assessments of the methods to achieve political and economic change.

"Complete" Withdrawal: Emigration

A striking feature of the normalization in Poland has been the creation of opportunities for withdrawal in all of its forms. This has included total withdrawal, or emigration. Although the authorities encouraged the emigration of its most ardent foes immediately after the imposition of martial law, the overall approach could be characterized as benign neglect. In 1982, there were pressures on interned Solidarity activists to take a one-way passport; some accepted, but most rejected the option of "forced" freedom. The leaders of KOR and Solidarity were offered the option of temporary exile in exchange for dropping the charges against them (see app. A). In 1985, a Solidarity activist was not allowed to pass the border at the Warsaw airport although he was a Polish citizen.[5] Leaving aside those instances, the new policy consisted of shifting responsibility to immigration authorities of Western countries. In Hirschman's terms, this could be characterized as a policy of lowering the cost of exit without, however, providing direct incentives to withdraw.

[5] Seweryn Blumsztajn was in France negotiating with trade unions on behalf of Solidarity when martial law was imposed. He stayed in France, where he became actively involved in various activities in support of Solidarity. On 5 February 1985 he returned to Warsaw. He was not allowed to enter Poland on the grounds that his passport was used for a purpose other than it was issued. According to this interpretation, he either should have returned to Poland in 1981 or he should have applied for a different passport. He was forcibly sent back to Paris. See *Poland Watch*, no. 7 (1985): 36–37.

The incentives were rooted in political and economic paralysis for which the government bore its share of responsibility. Leaving aside a drastic fall in standards of living, the group that was particularly negatively affected were college graduates, especially medical doctors, scientists, and engineers. In fact, the existing income structure penalizes higher education. For example, in the 1960s the ratio of salaries of university graduates to the average wage was about 1.8; it fell to 0.79 in 1984.[6]

The crushing of Solidarity and persistent economic crisis have turned out to be a strong incentive to seek a complete withdrawal. The true scope of this phenomenon is perhaps less evident in the number of emigrants than in its composition and public attitudes. According to the official statistics, the outflow in the quinquennial 1981–1985 period was smaller than in the 1976–1980 period, the period before the economic crisis.[7] The official statistics report the number of those who acquired emigration status before leaving Poland. They do not take into account those who left without formally applying for emigration. The total number of those who stayed abroad in the 1980s is put around 750,000. It is estimated that every year about 250,000 people extend their stay abroad over the declared period.[8] It is not clear how many of them will return.

There are grounds to believe that the average emigrant from Poland was young and well educated. Between 1981 and 1988 (as of 30 June 1988), for example, 4,524 physicians left Poland (Łazowski and Machowski 1988, 17). Taking into account that this total amounted to about 6 percent of Polish physicians in 1987, this number was quite significant. This constituted a significant loss of human capital; about 18 percent of those physicians were described by Łazowski and Machowski (1988) as very young.

I do not have access to data for other professional groups. Available data suggest a considerable outflow of people with university diplomas. According to government spokesman Jerzy Urban, out of 177,500 who emigrated between 1983 and 1987, 21,500 were university graduates.[9] According to another source, 76,300 university graduates left Poland in the period 1980–1987.[10] An indication of the scope of withdrawal may be illustrated by comparing this number with the total number of graduates between 1980 and 1987. The total for this period was 543,200; the number of emigrants was equivalent to 14 percent of the total.[11]

[6] See *Polish Perspectives* (Warsaw) no. 4 (1988): 70.

[7] From 1981 to 1985, 120,000 people left Poland as compared with 142,000 from 1976 to 1980. *Rocznik statystyczny* (1988, 155).

[8] This figure amounted to 1.1 percent of the economically active population (in the age bracket 18–65) in 1987.

[9] *Polish Perspectives* 4(1988): 70.

[10] *Życie Gospodarcze*, no. 3(1989): 3.

[11] Calculated from data in *Rocznik statystyczny* (1988, 1985, 1984). Needless to say, a considerable percentage of emigrants obtained their university diplomas in the 1970s or even in the 1960s.

Various appeals urging young people not to emigrate that came from such diverse sources as the government and the Catholic church demonstrate that emigration was recognized as an important economic and social problem. This is symptomatic of the loss of belief in the reformability of state socialism and of the grim economic perspectives.

According to a public opinion poll by the Center for Studying Public Opinion, in 1987 about 70 percent of Poland's young people indicated that they would like to leave Poland either temporarily or for good. This attitude was reportedly shared by their parents. In another study by the Polish Academy of Sciences, in January 1988 about 64 percent responding to the question "What future would you choose for your child?" suggested a temporary "exit" and 9 percent, emigration.[12] Thus a syndrome of withdrawal in its extreme form seems to have encompassed considerable segments of the society.

The effects of withdrawal are difficult to gauge. As a rule, because of the risks associated with starting a new life in a foreign country, those who decide to emigrate are not only well educated but also have some entrepreneurial spirit. Had their exit been a stimulant to introduce innovative changes that would encourage them to stay, its impact would have been beneficial. There are no reasons to believe that this was the case. Therefore, the loss of skilled workers and professionals may be much less significant than their numbers might suggest. From the point of view of political stability, an open border policy encourages exit not efforts to fight for change. Therefore, if the primary preoccupation of the authorities is to ensure political stability, then emigration brings some tangible political benefits. There are some economic benefits as well because of unrequited transfers from those who work abroad. Because there are grounds to believe that human capital in Poland has not been optimally used, from the point of view of immediate political and economic interests, liberal emigration policies have been advantageous to the socialist state.

Withdrawal from Political Institutions

The syndrome of withdrawal has affected the core political institutions of the party-state. Membership in political parties and social organizations serves as one measurable indicator of the scope of withdrawal. Membership fell substantially between 1980 and 1986. The total membership in social organizations fell by almost 20 percent and in political parties by about 25 percent. Although the Peasant's and Democratic parties increased their membership, as measured against the size of the adult population their respective proportions remained stable; the membership in the ruling Communist party shrank by about 31 percent.

[12] Quoted in Łazowski and Machowski (1988, 17).

Although in the 1985–1987 period the party membership slightly increased,[13] this trend was reversed during the first three quarters in 1988 when the number of those withdrawing exceeded the number of newly admitted members and candidates (Henzler 1988, 6). As can be seen from table 6.1, in comparison with 1980, the party lost more than one million members by 1987.

Demographic changes did not account for this decline (see table 2). In contrast to the "nonleading" parties that retained their holds over approximately the same proportions of the adult population, the share of Communist party members in the population eligible for membership (that is, 18 years old or more), fell from 12 percent in 1980 to 8 percent in 1986. In 1987, more than half (53.5 percent) of the PUWP members were more than 50 years old![14] The "aging" of the party is mainly attributable to a dramatic decline in the popularity of PUWP membership among young people. Although in the late 1970s about 5 percent of the population between 18 and 24 years old held party cards, their share fell to 2 percent in 1982 and 0.6 percent in 1986.[15] Moreover, the proportion of college students in this age group was minuscule; only about nine hundred college students were party members out of 23 thousand members in the 18 to 24 year age bracket. Only about 1.5 percent of college students belonged to the PUWP, and in every fourth college not *a single* student was in this organization in 1988.[16] Thus, in the coming years the per-

TABLE 6.1
Changes in the Number of PUWP Members in the 1980s (thousands)

	1980	1981	1982	1983	1984	1985	1986	1987
Membership (thousands)	3,092	2,691	2,327	2,186	2,117	2,115	2,129	2,149
1980 = 100	100	87	75	71	68	68	69	70
previous year = 100	—	87	86	94	97	100	101	101

Source: Rocznik statystyczny (various issues).

[13] It increased by 1.6 percent from 2,115,000 in 1985 to 2,149,000 in 1987 (*Rocznik statystyczny* [1988, 33]).

[14] See *Rocznik statystyczny* (1988, 35). Until 1984, the official statistical yearbook contained a category "retired PUWP members" with the latest information for 1982. It disappeared from the 1985, 1986, and 1987 editions. It returned in 1988 with the data for 1970 and a note that retired PUWP members were included in appropriate categories by trade and profession. There is little doubt that this was the most rapidly expanding category. Between 1970 and 1982, its share increased from 4.4 percent to 14.8 percent. In 1970, retired party members accounted for 2.9 percent of all the retired and for 8 percent in 1982.

[15] Calculated from *Rocznik statystyczny* (1981, 1987).

[16] In December 1987, 879 college students were members of PUWP: 58 at the University of Warsaw, out of 16,500; in Cracow with a student population of 35,000 only 34 were party cardholding students. In the late 1970s, about five thousand students each year joined the PUWP (*Gazeta Wyborcza*, 15 May 1989).

TABLE 6.2

Membership in Political Parties and Selected Social Organizations

	1980	1986	Index[a]
Polish United Workers' Party			
Membership (thousands)	3,092	2,129	68.8
As percentage of population above age 17	12.1	8.1	66.7
Share of members age 18–29 in total membership	23.4	6.9	29.5
As percentage of the population age 18–29	8.8	2.1	23.9
Above 29 in the population	10.7	10.1	94.4
United Peasants' Party			
Membership (thousands)	479	498	103.9
As percentage of population above age 17	1.9	1.9	100.0
Share of members age 18–29 in total membership	20.1	21.4	106.4
Democratic Party			
Membership (thousands)	114	118	103.5
As percentage of population above age 17	0.4	0.4	100.0
Share of members age 18–29 in total[b]	—	—	—
Total Membership			
Polish United Workers, United Peasants, and Democratic Party			
Membership (thousands)	3,684	2,745	74.5
Share of members in population above age 17	14.4	10.4	72.2
Union of Socialist Youth of Poland			
Membership (thousands)	1,993	1,504	75.5
As percentage of population age 16–24	36.2	32.4	89.6

Source: *Rocznik statystyczny* (1981–1988).

[a] Index: 1980 = 100.

[b] Statistics on the age structure of the Democratic Party's membership provide information for the 18–35 age bracket, but not for the 18–29 bracket. The share of members aged 18–35 in total was 30.2 percent in 1980 and 26.7 percent in 1986. Thus the share stood at 88.4 percent of its level in 1986.

centage of university graduates in the total PUWP membership will fall dramatically. The PUWP's loss of appeal to younger generations is one of the most telling indicators of the decomposition of Communist ideology in Poland.

The PUWP membership distribution is highly uneven among the regions and the sectors of the economy (Henzler 1988). In some regions the proportion of party members is well above the average (Słupsk voivodship, 11 percent) and in some it is below (Nowy Sącz voivodship, 5 percent).[17] The data quoted by Henzler (1988) suggest a larger proportion of party members among those employed in large heavy industry plants than among those working in consumer products industries. There is significant variation within the sectors, however. In 1987, about 36 percent of the employees of the coal mine "Sosnowiec," for instance, were party members, whereas in the "First May" only 11.5 percent. In a cotton textile plant in Łomża about 8.4 percent of the total workforce was in the PUWP, whereas in the one in Zduńska Wola 30.4 percent.

The PUWP has not only become old but it has also been losing its "worker" character, as expressed by workers' share in total membership. Their share fell from 46 percent in 1978 to 38 percent in 1986.[18] Since 1972 there have been fewer party members among the workers; their proportion among workers employed in the "socialized" sector fell from 16.7 percent in 1978 to 12.2 percent in 1982 and to 10.6 percent in 1986.[19]

The ideological claim of the "workers' and peasants' alliance" as a foundation of state socialism in Poland was hardly supported by the composition of the ruling Communist party (Staar 1988, 164–67). In 1986, peasants and workers did not account for the majority of PUWP membership; their combined share (peasants, 9.4 percent) declined from 55.4 percent in 1978 to 47 percent (peasants, 9 percent) in 1986. The exit of peasants from the PUWP was thus less pronounced than that of the workers.[20]

The largest group in the PUWP were white collar workers, accounting for 52 percent of the membership and 25 percent of all white collar workers. The majority were public administration employees or executives in the state-owned sector. The largest proportion of party members was among the re-

[17] The variation cannot be explained by differences between their economies. In both cases, industrial investment accounts for about 16 percent; they have similar industrial branch structures with consumer products and machine building contributing between 54 (Słupsk) and 58 (Nowy Sącz) of total industrial output in 1987 (see data in *Rocznik statystyczny* [1988, lix]).

[18] Given the change in classification criteria (the disappearance of the retired from 1986 data), it is not clear what percentage of workers had retired. One may suspect that the inclusion of retirees as a separate category would lower the workers' share.

[19] Author's calculations from *Rocznik statystyczny* (1980, 1982, 1988).

[20] In 1970, 4.6 percent of those working in private agriculture and cooperatives were in the party. Their share fell only slightly to 4.2 percent in 1986 (calculated from data in *Rocznik statystyczny* [1980, 1987]).

gime's strategic support groups. On average, every second employee of the state administration held the PUWP card (Henzler 1988, 6). One may suspect that the proportion was even higher among employees of the Ministry of Justice or Ministry of Internal Affairs than in public health administration. The penalty of exiting from the party for this group was the loss of executive position. As a result, the proportion of party members among white collar workers has probably remained unchanged. According to one estimate, in 1989 about seven hundred thousand (about one-third of the total membership) party members were retired bureaucrats and former managers of state companies, whereas another nine hundred thousand still worked for the state.[21] Thus, the PUWP became a party of retired and current nomenklatura.

In the 1980s, the PUWP changed the combination of voice, exit, and loyalty. The cost of exit for those who did not occupy executive positions in the state administration and the economic system fell significantly.[22] The decrease in membership demonstrated the declining belief in the possibility of internal reform. This weakened chances for reform as the more potentially activist individuals either opted not to join the PUWP or to withdraw from it. This move was illustrated by a significant decline of the share of young and educated people in the PUWP. Yet, because 8.1 percent of the adult population belonged to the PUWP, this was still a mass organization.

Withdrawal is preferred to voice if there is no belief in influencing policies and in the reformability of the organization (see Hirschman [1970, 33–59]). The availability of the exit option weakened "proreform" voice within the PUWP by driving out the most dissatisfied and nonconformist members. The review of party membership after the imposition of martial law probably accounted for much of the almost 20 percent decline in the membership between the end of 1981 and of 1982. Those who left, voluntarily or involuntarily, were opposed to the military solution of the "Solidarity problem." In addition, the existence of alternatives to the PUWP did not contribute to the activation of voice and attraction of those who would be instrumental in activating reforms.[23]

Most of those who remained in the PUWP did so because of fears of the loss of power and influence rather than because of any conviction that a reform

[21] As estimated by Wojciech Lamentowicz, a Solidarity advisor, quoted in John Tagliabue, "Pressures Rising for Polish Party," *New York Times*, 18 June 1989.

[22] The cost of dropping party membership, very high in the 1950s and the 1960s, already declined in the 1970s. For example, contrary to expectations, one of Gierek's advisors, who in protest against the government's policies left the party, was allowed to retain his job at one of the Warsaw colleges. The expectation was that he would be offered a position in a noneducational research institution and prohibited from teaching courses at his college.

[23] Contrary to earlier expectations, the organizations established after martial law (e.g., official labor unions, Patriotic Movement of National Rebirth (PRON), the consensus group or Jaruzelski's Consultative Council) have offered some possibilities for autonomous activity affecting policy outcomes.

of state socialism could be achieved "from within." To the contrary, most of those who stayed did so because they were against any reform that would end the party's direct control over the economy.[24] Those advocating reforms and dialogue with the opposition, for example, were usually opposed by a significant number of party members, particularly within the party apparatus.[25]

Yet, many probably remained out of conviction that given the proximity of the Soviet Union the only way to restore the system's vitality was through the PUWP. They believed in the reformability of state socialism and in their own ability to influence the party's policies. Given the hierarchical structure of the PUWP and obstacles that would have to be overcome to attain the position of influence, this belief could scarcely lure new members, however.

"Ideological" loyalty considerations, which according to Hirschman (1970) may prevent deterioration from becoming cumulative, could play a role in the decision to stay only under one condition. Namely, they would have to believe that the retreat from the struggle for communism was only temporary. Or, to paraphrase Rakowski (1988, 46), if this retreat involved only "getting rid of the old skin and putting on the new one." Given the large scope of the retreat from ideological pretenses, the authorities would have a difficult time in convincing an "orthodox Communist" that this was only a tactical move.

In its search for identity, the PUWP appropriated many of the symbols of national history. The party was active in commemorating the 70th anniversary of Poland's independence. Marshal Piłsudski's portrait was officially popularized on postal stamps.[26] Yet this was the same party that was brought to power by the Red Army twenty-four years after the 1920 Battle of Warsaw won by Piłsudzki's soldiers. The victory prevented them from seizing power then. The party officials were busy laying flowers under such monuments as the "Poznań 1956" or "Gdańsk 1970 and 1981," which were built to commemorate "the state's aggression against the people," as Grudzińska-Gros (1983, 21) aptly observed. Yet this party retained its organizational features. Under those circumstances little room was left for loyalty stemming from ideological considerations.

Unfortunately, there have been no published—to my knowledge—studies

---

[24] Rakowski (1988, 50) succinctly noted that the factors accountable "for the position of the party . . . in the society have been rooted primarily in the economic sphere. In fact, the party, or more appropriately, its leading organs have administered productive means and have been in control over their uses."

[25] For instance, Stanisław Ciosek was elected to the Politburo during the 10th Central Committee, held in Warsaw in December 1988, by one of the lowest number of votes (143 out of 212). Reportedly, this was because of his participation in the government-opposition talks (Henzler 1988, 6).

[26] To maintain "ideological equilibrium," the authorities issued in the same series a portrait of Julian Marchlewski. The irony was that Marchlewski organized a provisional government that would have replaced Piłsudski's government had the Red Army won the Battle of Warsaw in August 1920.

on how the role of party apparatus in governing the country has been affected by Solidarity, martial law, and political and economic reform measures introduced in the 1980s. There are, however, some grounds to argue that the state administration has been strenghtened vis-à-vis the party apparatus (Mieszczankowski 1987b; Sobczak 1987). In a similar vein, a Polish sociologist Antoni Kaminski (1989, 99) notes: "The party influence has been waning to the advantage of other sectors of the system." Discussing the positions of various groups vis-à-vis the issue of reforms in Poland, Crane (1988, 18) notes that "it is difficult to find an area where the Polish United Workers' Party (PUWP) has left a significant mark on the theoretical foundations of the reform." Thus these observations suggest that the relative weight of the PUWP apparatus has declined because of a shift in the power distribution in favor of central administration at the expense of local party apparatus. This failure would further discourage potential activists from joining the PUWP.

A renaissance of the ideological appeal of Marxism-Leninism seems rather unlikely. The ideological decomposition of the PUWP dates back not to the emergence of Solidarity but to an earlier period. Its beginnings can be traced to a de-Stalinization campaign of the mid-1950s that culminated in the October events of 1956. Although party discipline was again tightened in the 1960s, promotion considerations increasingly replaced ideological appeal. Under the Gierek regime in the 1970s, whatever was left of ideological pretenses gradually disappeared. The emergence of Solidarity and the decision to impose martial law dealt the party a very serious blow.

Political developments during normalization did little to enhance the image of the PUWP, although the authorities used sophisticated techniques of social engineering (see Poznański [1988b, 22–23]). The suppression of discontent was selective. In stark contrast to their predecessor, the authorities tended, for instance, to paint a pessimistic view of the economic situation to lower societal expectations.[27] Discontent, that is, the opposition, was tolerated. Permissiveness and a gloomy vision of the future bode ill for the party's ideological attractiveness. But there was a price for it. The revival of PUWP as an efficient, ideologically dominant organization rigidly following the leadership's political and ideological orders became impossible (if it was possible at all). Instead the political developments made the party a kind of trade union that protected the interests of the rulers.

Withdrawal from "Rituals"

Two specific elements of the political culture of state socialism have been the development of party-controlled mass social organizations and the insistence

[27] Planned outputs were set at low levels. Poland is the only socialist country where planned targets were exceeded in the 1980s, including inflation, which was usually higher than "planned."

on mass participation in elections. Both forms are highly ritualistic. The purpose of membership in the Society for Polish-Soviet Friendship, for instance, has been to demonstrate the pro-Soviet attitudes of Poles, whereas mass participation in elections has been regarded as proof of the PUWP's legitimacy.

Interestingly, the decline in PUWP membership was accompanied by declining membership in various mass ritualistic organizations and withdrawal from other state-sponsored rituals. Even though the decrease in membership in various civil and quasi-professional associations was considerably smaller than in the political parties, it was quite significant (see table 6.3). However, its political implication remains obscure. Three mass organizations were most affected by a decline in membership: the Polish Red Cross (a 20-percent reduction); the Society for Polish-Soviet Friendship (a 43-percent contraction); and the Union of Polish Scouts (a 35-percent decline). These three organizations are among the largest social organizations. They together claimed 44 percent and 35 percent of the total membership in social and professional organizations in 1980 and 1986. It should be noted that their size has thrived on

TABLE 6.3
Membership in Social and Professional Organizations

	1980	1986	Index[a]
Social and Professional Organizations[b]			
Membership (thousands)	28,910	24,395	84.4
As percentage of population above age 6[c]	92.6	74.2	80.1
Social and Professional Organizations[d]			
Membership (thousands)	16,278	15,843	97.3
As percentage of population above age 17	62.3	60.1	96.5
Official Trade Unions[e]			
Membership (thousands)	5,044[f]	5,681	112.6
As percentage of population above age 17	19.4	21.5	111.5
As percentage of employment in nonprivate sector	40.9	45.4	111.1

Source: Rocznik statystyczny.
[a] Index: 1986; 1980 = 100.
[b] Not all organizations are included. The list does not embrace trade unions and scientific associations.
[c] A low age limit was chosen because the Polish Scouts Organization and the Polish Red Cross were included.
[d] Excludes the Polish Red Cross, Polish-Soviet Friendship, and Polish Scouts.
[e] Includes member and nonmember organizations of the Polish Trade Agreement.
[f] Membership in 1984.

the compulsory membership of elementary and high school students. One may suspect that the reductions have occurred because of the unwillingness or inability of the authorities to use coercive measures to secure mass participation. Yet it is symptomatic of the syndrome of withdrawal that the authorities avoided the old methods of eliciting artificial forms of mass pseudo-participation.

The only exception to the general tendency toward diminishing membership in social organizations are the official trade unions. Although unionization is still significantly lower than in the 1970s, when almost 100 percent of employees of the state-owned sector were trade union members, the 11-percent change of share over two years was quite impressive. Access to various material rewards that unions offer was probably not the sole factor responsible for the increase. Another factor was the transformation of trade unions themselves. Forced to compete with delegalized Solidarity, the new unions declined to become transmission belt organizations that traditionally filled the space between the state and society. Some authors claim (Wiatr 1988) that the new trade unions have become part of the intrasystem opposition, or the opposition accepting the existing order.

One illustration of withdrawal from rituals of state socialism was an increase in the number of people refusing to vote. The days when turnout was 98–99 percent are long gone. Depending on whether the opposition's or the government's estimates are taken into account, on average, between 25 and 40 percent of eligible voters decided not to participate in the elections to People's Councils (1984), Sejm (1985), and the referendum on economic reform (1987).

Low turnouts tended to be hailed as victories by the opposition, which as a rule called for election boycotts. They were not, however, acknowledged as defeats by the government, which found consolation that in Western democracies turnouts were similar.[28] Had the game between the opposition and the state been zero-sum, an increase in absenteeism from 1–2 percent to 25–40 percent would have fully justified the opposition's claim. Undoubtedly, the levels of turnout in the 1980s demonstrated that the state was no longer capable of mobilizing people to vote in spite of using its various apparatuses to force them to go to the polls. In more general terms, the state was no longer able to impose sanctions in order to raise the cost of withdrawal.

On the other hand, those who chose not to cast ballots were not necessarily ardent opponents of state socialism. Various sociological surveys conducted in Poland indicated that a significant proportion ranging between 20 and 35 percent of the population refused to participate in politics.[29] They suggest that

---

[28] In response to questions from Western correspondents, the government spokesman observed, "We are convinced that our results will not differ from what you can observe in your own countries." See *Rzeczpospolita*, 19 June 1984.

[29] For instance, about 25 percent of the population is of the opinion that state socialism cannot

a significant proportion of those who abstained withdrew from political rituals but did not necessarily support the opposition. Some decided that the voice option was not available, whereas the cost of withdrawal was perceived as negligible.

WITHDRAWAL FROM THE "OFFICIAL" ECONOMY

The weight of the private sector, the shadow unofficial economy, and the substitution of convertible currencies for domestic złotys provide measures of withdrawal from the "official" economy.

Private Sector

The expansion of the private nonagricultural sector was very impressive in the 1980s. Its share in national income produced increased 1.5-fold, from 6 percent in 1980 to 9 percent in 1987. Employment in the private nonagricultural sector increased from 622,000 in 1980 to 1,111,000 in 1987. Between 1985 and 1987, the total employment increased by 97,500, while the employment in the private nonagricultural sector increased 153,500. There was a significant shift in favor of the private nonagricultural sector at the expense of private agriculture in which employment fell by 102,100 and of cooperative-and state-owned sectors in which it increased by 56,000.

TABLE 6.4

Changes in the Position of Private Agricultural and Nonagricultural Sectors

	1970	1980	1982	1986	1987
Share of employment in					
Agriculture in total employment	35.0	24.5	26.7	24.7	24.4
Non-agricultural private sector in total	2.6	3.5	4.1	5.8	6.2
Private sector in total	37.6	28.0	30.8	30.5	30.6
Share of national income produced in					
Private agriculture	13.5	11.5	12.8	10.2	8.2
Private nonagriculture	5.5	6.0	7.3	8.0	9.0
Private sector	19.0	17.5	20.1	18.2	17.2

Source: Rocznik statystyczny (1983, 1988).

be reformed "from within" (Morawski 1988, 98). According to the supplement by Krzysztof Jasiewicz to Raport z badania Polacy 1984. Dynamika konfliktu i konsensunsu (A Report from the Poles 1984 Survey. The Dynamics of Conflict and Consensus), a silent minority accounted for 32.7 percent of the respondents in 1985 (as opposed to 21.1 percent in 1984), opponents of state socialism for 15.7 percent (22.7 percent), and others for 51.6 percent (56.1 percent) (quoted in Smolar [1988, 9]).

New employment opportunities created by the development of private business varied among sectors of the economy. As can be seen from the data in table 6.5, the fastest increase occurred in transportation and construction. In the latter, one in five workers was employed by private firms. Private ownership dominance in agriculture only slightly increased.

The growth of foreign enterprises (owned mostly by foreign citizens of Polish extraction) contributed to the expansion of employment opportunities in the nonstate sector. Between 1981 and 1987, employment in foreign enterprises increased from 3,300 to 68,000. Workers in foreign-owned enterprises were concentrated in the industrial and construction sectors where they accounted in 1987 for 9.6 and 3.8 percent of total "private" employment, respectively. These workers were an important source of state budget revenue.[30] Foreign enterprises were usually larger than the firms owned by Polish nationals. On average, a foreign firm employed about 93 people in 1987, whereas a "domestically owned" firm employed only 2.05.[31]

Private "domestic" firms are on average small because of a continued dom-

TABLE 6.5
Employment in Selected Sectors of the Economy and Shares in Total Employment in a Sector

Sectors	1980		1987	
	Employment (thousands)	Shares Total Employment (%)	Employment (thousands)	Shares Total Employment (%)
Industry	271.7	5	515.3	10
Agriculture	4,004.1	78	3,850.0	79
Construction	102.4	8	240.5	18
Transportation	10.8	1	28.3	3
Trade	45.7	4	83.1	6
Other	118.2	5	243.8	9
Memorandum[a] Foreign enterprises	3.5	5	68.4	5

Source: Calculated from data in Rocznik statystyczny (1989).

[a] Data for 1981 and 1987. In percent, the share of employment in foreign firms in the total employment of the private nonagricultural sector.

[30] In 1986, their share in state budget revenue from the private nonagricultural sector was 15 percent, while their sales accounted for 13 percent of the sector, and investment for about 10 percent (calculated from data in Zarządzanie (Warsaw), no. 12 (1987) and Rocznik statystyczny [1988]).

[31] Based on data from Rocznik statystyczny (1989).

inance of handicrafts in private sector employment. A significant percentage of those working in the private sector are owners, co-owners, and their family members. They often use state sector employees on short-term contracts. (Therefore, the total number of people involved in the private sector may be larger than the official data indicate.) New firms, leaving aside foreign enterprises, are usually founded by young people, and they tend to be much larger.[32] Most specialize in services that do not need large capital equipment. Labor productivity is significantly higher than in the state sector; so are wages and incomes, although the differential between the state and private sector declined in 1988 (see Bielecki and Majewski [1988]).

The cooperative provides another alternative to working directly for the state. For various legal and practical reasons (easier access to scarce inputs), this kind of ownership is often preferred to the private form. When the government's approach became much less rigid in the 1980s, many new cooperatives emerged.

Various publications and interviews suggest that although economic motives for the formation of cooperatives predominated in the 1984–1988 period, other reasons contributed. On the basis of interviews with founders of new enterprises in Gdańsk voivodship, Bielecki and Majewski (1988) distinguished between three categories.[33] The first category related to those enterprises that were established by members of Solidarity and of the Autonomous Students' Association. They "could not or did not want to work in state-owned enterprises. Their objectives included: to become independent from the party and administrative apparatus; to provide assistance to imprisoned friends; to establish an independent environment; and to provide material assistance to colleagues (Bielecki and Majewski 1988, 4).

The second category encompassed enterprises established by former activists of official trade unions and party apparatus. The main reason for their exit from officialdom was dissatisfaction with political and trade union activity as well as with incomes.

The last category comprises enterprises founded by those who have not been previously involved in political activity. Their major motive has been unhappiness with professional opportunities offered by their state employers. The authors of the study were not able to assess whether political motives dominated over the economic ones or vice versa.

An interesting finding of this study is that the majority of those who were previously involved in politics had gradually withdrawn from any political activity, whether in officialdom or in opposition. In this respect, whether they

[32] A study conducted in Gdańsk voivodship suggests that firms specializing in consulting usually employ 10–30 employees; new construction firms between 30 and 100, and firms selling computer equipment between 10 and 30 (Bielecki and Majewski 1988).

[33] Their study covered a relatively short period between 1985 and 1987. It was also restricted to the northern part of Poland. Nonetheless, their findings seem to be valid for the whole country.

had formerly been party-state apparatus or Solidarity activists made no difference. They all became entirely preoccupied with their new jobs and making money. Thus, an exit to the private sector has often amounted to an exit from politics.

The exit from the state's direct reach cannot be complete because of the persistence of paternalistic arrangements that pervade relationships between the state administration and the private sector. Crisis created more favorable conditions for the expansion of the private sector in general and of foreign firms in particular. But it did not result in the emergence of a strong private sector. Neither was it accompanied by the emergence of a new logic behind the relationship between the state and the economy. The state retained its direct grip on private economic activity through a complex system of authoritative controls.[34]

Because existing regulations tend to give a local administration considerable discretion in determining the tax burden of a private firm, obtaining good cooperative relations with the state administration is important. Private firms, in marked contrast to state enterprises, are probably subject to Kornai's "hard-budget" constraint, but are not subject to "hard" law. Law tends to be "soft," albeit selectively applied. As a result, the state-private economy interface remains institutionalized in a manner that makes the private sector totally dependent on the state's whims. Relationships between the state and private sector are client-patron or, more generally, paternalistic.

Will the new Solidarity-led government bring about a shift from authoritative to more market-oriented controls of the private sector? It is too early to make any definitive judgments. The existing law restricts the discretion of local authorities to set new tax rates. In a similar vein, the new law on foreign enterprises and joint ventures enacted by the Sejm in December 1988 was also liberalized. Because many excellent laws (e.g., on environmental protection) have not been implemented in Poland in the past, it remains to be seen whether the new government will free private entrepreneurship from the state's paternalism.

Second Economy

A common motive that pushes people to undertake activity in the second economy is escape from the state's fiscal reach. Although the desire not to pay taxes is common for both market and nonmarket economies, the persistent structural mismatch between supply and demand, low wages, and "entry" restrictions offers unique opportunities for tax evasion in socialist economies.

---

[34] Polish "entrepreneurs" often complain that had it not been because of excessive and unpredictable state interventions its expansion might have been faster and more beneficial to the national economy. See for instance, an interview with Stanisław Szewczyk, owner of a foreign firm, Top Mart Co., published in *Zarządzanie* (December 1987).

The structural mismatch results in shortages of goods and services and in relaxed labor discipline in the state sector. Low wages encourage people to seek extra incomes outside their main jobs. In addition, administrative restrictions and tax rates subject to whims of local authorities provide strong incentives to participate in the shadow economy.

The second economy did not emerge in Poland in the 1980s. There is evidence, however, that its scope significantly increased. In fact, the second economy flourished during the crisis. The growing disequilibria and a sharp decline in living standards in comparison with the 1970s contributed to a rapid expansion of the second economy. Barriers to entry in the private sector that specialized in providing services, which were at last removed in 1989, discouraged individuals from starting official businesses.[35]

All estimates of the scope of the second economy are subject to some margin of error. One study estimated that in 1986 between 10 and 22 percent of personal incomes were derived from the second economy, depending on the method used to estimate.[36] Kierczyński and Girski (quoted in Morąg [1988, 1]) estimated this share at between 17.2 and 24.7 percent. Although it is impossible to assess which of these estimates is correct, in comparison with estimates for the 1970s the size of the second economy at least tripled. In the 1970s, the share of "second economy" incomes in total personal income did not exceed 5 percent.

The bulk of activities in the shadow economy consisted of taking advantage of price differences between rigid state-controlled prices and market prices or between domestic and international prices. Its expansion corrupted many employees of the state sector. For instance, those having access to highly desirable products at below market clearing prices, like employees of some trade organizations, could easily obtain some extra income. Kierczyński and Girski (quoted in Morąg [1988, 13]) estimated that unofficial income derived from "domestic trade" accounted for 20 percent of total unofficial incomes in 1986.

These incomes were only second to the incomes from unofficial "foreign-related" activity. These revenues were mainly derived from unofficial imports; their ratio to official imports increased from 2.3 percent in 1981 to 4.4 percent in 1986 (Józef Misala, quoted in Morąg [1988, 13]). According to Kierczyński and Girski (Morąg 1988), the incomes "related to the contacts abroad" accounted for about 35 percent of all unofficial incomes in 1986. Their share in personal incomes increased between 1982 and 1986. It was 11.3 percent in 1986, much higher than in 1982 when it amounted to 6.2 percent,

---

[35] These barriers were comparable to those existing in guilds under feudalism.

[36] According to an unpublished study by Marek Bednarski, Ryszard Kokoszczyński, and Jerzy Stopyra summarized in *Wiadomości Bankowe* (Warsaw) 2 (7 November 1988).

but it was significantly lower than (17.7 percent) in 1981 (Józef Misala, quoted in Morąg [1988, 13]).

In some areas, particularly services, the supply was dominated by various forms of unofficial activity. The second sector accounted for between 27 and 76 percent of total supplies of services provided by private and state-owned firms in the repairs of cars, TV sets, household appliances, and so forth, in 1987.

The existence of the second economy has mitigated political stability. It has reduced the costs of economic crisis for those who had appropriate skills and entrepreneurial spirit. By offering opportunities for extra income, it has weakened the potential for instabilities that might be triggered by significantly reduced incomes. In a similar vein, private imports have weakened the impact of drastic cuts in imports from Western economies on availability of consumer goods. Because too much money has been spent on too few goods, the extra supplies contributed to political stability.

Escape from the Zloty

Debasing the value of a currency always triggers an escape from the currency. Under state socialism in Poland, the zloty has never been fully convertible domestically, nor, for that matter, has it been convertible internationally. In spite of an absence of full domestic convertibility (reflected in shortages), the Polish złoty performed the major functions that money usually plays by serving as an acceptable and predictable unit of account, a medium of exchange, and store of value.

A combination of inflation and negative real interest rates significantly eroded the złoty's capacity to fulfill these functions in the 1980s. Each of the price-income operations, that is, massive price increases with some income compensations, substantially reduced the purchasing power of savings held by the population. In addition, nominal interest rates did not keep pace with inflation in the 1980s. As a result of the 1982 price-income operation (see app. A), real interest rates for deposits held by households and the private sector fell to $(-)46.2$ percent. They increased in 1983 and 1984 to $(-)11$ and $(-)6$ percent, respectively, and then they fell again, reaching the 1982 level in 1988.

The persistence of negative interest rates produced a "hidden" redistribution of income. On the one hand, those who had access to credits were heavily subsidized. This "rent-receiving" group included homeowners who paid mortgages at the official rate (usually 3 percent), newlyweds entitled to credits for furniture and appliances (provided they could be purchased), some private firms able to obtain credits, and state-owned enterprises. On the other hand, those who kept their savings in złotys subsidized banks and savings institutions, which meant the state budget. Negative real interest rates encouraged the demand for credit and discouraged savings in złotys.

As can be seen from data in table 6.6, which shows hypothetical interest payments calculated at zero real interest rates, the overall balance of the population's losses in savings due to negative real interest rates and the gains on consumer credits was in favor of the state budget (Kowalski 1988). This "inflation tax" revenue was quite substantial and was increasing. Compared to the state budget's revenue, it grew from less than 1 percent in 1984 to 3 percent in 1987.

The largest gains accrued to state-owned enterprises. In 1987, this interest subsidy amounted to almost one-fourth of the total budget expenditure to subsidize state-owned enterprises. In other words, the state budget subsidies would have been 72 percent larger in 1987 if the interest rate had been equal to the growth rate of inflation.

The combination of negative real interest rates and the state's policy to attract deposits in foreign currency produced a double currency system in Poland. Some authors argue that with złoty being driven out by Eurodollars Poland heads toward a single currency, Eurodollar, economy. As Kowalski (1988, 1) noted: "A question that should be addressed is whether we are not becoming a single currency economy; at any rate, our bank of issue encounters a growing competition from abroad." Indeed the increased number of transactions has been carried out in Western currencies, mainly in dollars. Automobiles and real estate have been sold almost exclusively for convertible currencies.

Many individuals converted złoty savings into foreign currency savings to

TABLE 6.6
Effects of Negative Real Interest Rates. The Difference between Interest Payments Calculated at Inflation Rates and at Actual Interest Rates (in Billion Złotys)

	1984	1985	1986	1987
Personal savings (a)	33	46	92	234
Consumer credits (b)	16	20	30	58
State-owned enterprises (c)	291	328	525	1,823
State's "hidden" revenue (a − b)	17	26	62	176
as percentage of state budget revenue	.5	.6	1.3	3.0
State's "hidden" subsidy to state-owned enterprises as percentage of budgetary expenditure on state-owned enterprises	21	20	27	72

Sources: Kowalski (1988); *Rocznik statystyczny* (1988).

protect their savings from inflation. As a result, foreign currency denominated personal savings exceeded savings in Polish złoty by early 1987. As can be seen from table 6.7, they were higher than złoty savings by 50 percent at the end of 1987.

The availability of alternatives to the złoty and the significant rents derived by some from negative real interest rates reduced social pressures to terminate the policy of złoty depreciation. High-income groups could convert złotys into hard currency. Those who derived "second economy" incomes from "contacts with abroad" benefited from high exchange rates inflated by limited availability of some products and services as well as by the escape from savings in złotys.[37] Some inefficient state enterprises could show profits and thereby obtain higher wages thanks to "hidden" subsidies on credits obtained from the state. This policy helped to keep social discontent in a tolerable range by allowing the most active to obtain rents, although the long-term economic costs of this choice are likely to be very high. The policy of złoty and personal savings depreciation exacerbated the lack of confidence in the government and undermined economic reforms.[38]

WITHDRAWAL OF THE STATE: QUASI-PLURALISM

Except for a short period in the early 1950s, the socialist state in Poland has never been a unitary, all-controlling actor. The closest it came to homogeneity and total control was during the Stalin era. Although the successive regimes of Gomułka and Gierek refused to reduce the scope of state power, both its domain and scope were hindered by the growing inability to control everything

TABLE 6.7

Personal Savings in Złotys and Foreign Currencies (Calculated at Black-market Exchange Rates in Billions of Złotys)

	1983	1984	1985	1986	1987
Savings held in Polish złotys (a)	1,850	1,237	1,667	1,891	2,482
Savings held in foreign currencies (b)	474	589	961	1,789	3,699
Ratio b:a	.26	.47	.58	.95	1.49

Source: Kowalski (1988, 1).

[37] Tadeusz Kierczyński and Zbigniew Girski, quoted in Morąg (1988, 1). The increasing losses related to savings in złotys increased demand for convertible currencies and, thereby, their shadow exchange rates.

[38] Negative real interest rates undermined, for instance, provisions of the economic reform related to self-financing.

from the top. As a result, state power was reduced. The Jaruzelski regime did not reverse this process. On the contrary, a number of policy actions, or often inactions, accelerated the process of state withdrawal.

Given the ambiguity of the power concept, it is scarcely surprising that no universally acceptable set of measures would allow analysts to gauge the extent of state withdrawal. Withdrawal of the socialist state amounts to the reduction in scope and/or domain of control by the state. It can be indirectly measured by the dents in the state's monopoly of information, the release of control over collective action, and the increased accountability of the authorities to society.

The reduced domain is the result of the development of power relationships and shared interests and personal affinities outside the direct reach of the state. Even within the theoretical confines of state socialism, inevitably a societal autonomy and diversity of individual interests seem to have developed. This progress toward a pluralistic political life gained momentum with the founding of Solidarity, and the imposition of martial law did not halt it. The expansion of sophisticated, self-aware public life invariably conflicts with the power aspirations of the state.

Under the social pressures released by the Solidarity turmoil, martial law, and the persistent economic crisis, the authorities had to reconcile the decreased scope and domain of their power. The political system had become increasingly open. The underlying reason was the end of the intellectual hegemony of official Communist ideology. Although earlier, for example, the contending political ideas of liberalism and neoconservatism were easily ridiculed (Staniszkis 1984), in the 1980s hardly anybody even within the ruling elite looked to Marxism-Leninism for solutions to Poland's crisis. Instead, views that prior to the Solidarity period had been labeled "anti-socialist" became part of the official political currency.[39]

The authorities presided over final disintegration of the monopoly of information. The vitality of the underground publication movement, which flourished in spite of state repression, prompted the authorities to liberalize the official mass media. Exception for some aspects of Soviet-Polish relations, censorship interventions became limited.

Allowing for a greater freedom of expression was part of the strategy designed to bring about normalization and political stabilization in the aftermath of martial law. Glasnost became a device used to broaden the political base of the regime and to undermine the opposition. With hindsight, it had failed to achieve these goals.

State monopoly over collective action, another domain of state controls,

---

[39] These views had limited impact on economic policies. The policies carried out by the Messner government suggested the discrepancy between official declarations and promises of linking, for instance, economic reforms with political changes with actual policies that clearly followed "an old track."

was challenged in the 1980s. The state's policy toward spontaneous social initiatives provides a measure of the progress toward democratic pluralism. The posture toward associations reveals the nature of the state and political regime.

Even before the roundtable negotiations between the government coalition and the Solidarity opposition in 1989, the official posture evolved from an initial open hostility to limited reconciliation with the legalization of even outright political clubs. The draft of a bill on associations was prepared by lawyers who represented the state administration and church. The bill was not enacted before the fall of the Rakowski government.

Nonetheless, several associations were established in response to autonomous social initiatives. Their number significantly increased from 80 in 1986 to 179 in 1987 to 80 by September 1988. Simultaneously, the number of rejections by the state administration fell from 74 associations in 1986 to 32 in 1987.[40] Quite frequently, the authorities created enormous bureaucratic hurdles before finally giving their consent.

The reasons underlying rejections defied common sense and demonstrated the state's reluctance to give up control. For instance, the authorities refused to permit a group of citizens to establish an association for housing reform, arguing that "the state is able to satisfy all housing needs" (Król 1987, 8). In a country where the average waiting time to move to a new apartment is about thirty years (and rising), this was not a very convincing argument. On similar grounds, it is also difficult to explain the refusal to a petition to establish an association to organize day care centers for the elderly (Olszewska 1988). These examples show that totalitarian aspirations were hard to uproot.

Most newly established associations addressed marginal, albeit significant, social, cultural, and other public needs. Some of them directly challenged the ideological underpinnings of the socialist state. For instance, the statutes of the Kraków Business Association, established in 1987, praised the virtues of the market economy and rejected administrative forms of state central planning.[41] Its registration was rather an unusual recognition of a divergent point of view and even ideology by the socialist state.

The state did not withdraw without a struggle from its aspiration to monopolize collective action. For instance, when faced with a petition to establish the Warsaw Business Association in the fall of 1987, it sought to dilute the association's significance by taking the initiative in establishing organizations

[40] See *Polityka* (Warsaw) 42 (1988): 4.

[41] The objective of both the Cracow and Warsaw business associations is to protect the private sector from the arbitrariness of local authorities, to provide legal assistance and information on market opportunities, and to create an environment favorable to private entrepreneurship. Interview with the founder of the Warsaw Business Association, A. Paszyński, "Philosophy of Business Association Is the Philosophy of Marketplace," *Tygodnik Polski* (Cracow) 8 November 1987.

addressing similar needs. In December 1987, the Socioeconomic Council of the Seym founded the Association for Encouragement of Economic Initiative and the "official" Trade Union Confederation established the Polish Association of Economic Initiatives, "Promotor." They both announced their support for economic reform and offered legal and administrative assistance to those whose innovative ideas encounter bureaucratic hurdles to their statutory objective.

The timing of their creation coincided with the spontaneous social initiatives of those who had been involved in the private sector. This raised suspicion that their real goal was to justify the decision not to register "free-market" business associations. Because both were created by the state, this looked like another attempt to control the change from above.[42]

Although institutional withdrawal of the state was most visible in social and political realms, the institutional innovations implemented fell short of providing a public forum for interest mediation and political representation.[43] Examples abound. The authorities became sensitive to public opinion, but public participation in political and economic decision-making processes remained limited. Although the role of mass media as vox populi increased, its impact was limited to public economic policies.[44] Although "independent" official trade unions were consulted on various economic policy measures (e.g., on price increases), the consultations became in public perception nothing more than ritual.[45] Attempts to independently raise the issue and to rally support for its solution was regarded as direct threats to the regime unless policy actions had been initiated by the state.

More significantly, the implemented institutional changes fell well short of founding democratic mechanisms that guaranteed the authorities' accountability to society. Democratic pluralism makes government pay for its mistakes, but under state socialism—as a French writer notes—"the people pay for government's mistakes" (Revel 1978, 28). In all, while totalitarian control became "leaky," the withdrawal of the party-state precipitated by the problems

---

[42] It is noteworthy that the Association for Encouragement of Economic Initiatives was sponsored by Mieczysław Rakowski, then vice-chairman of Seym and party secretary in charge of propaganda. Yet, this was the Rakowski government that a year later gave its seal of approval to the registration of the Warsaw Business Association as well as to similar organizations in other parts of Poland.

[43] The "roundtable" discussions between the government and Solidarity have marked the first step in this direction.

[44] The most notable example was the decisive role that the press played in overhauling the 1987 plan submitted by the government for approval by the Sejm.

[45] Rightly or wrongly, there was a suspicion that the government inflated proposed price increases to leave room for conceding to the pressures of the official trade unions, which as a rule suggested lower price increases. Whether this was indeed the case is impossible to demonstrate given the secrecy cloaking the government decision-making processes.

encountered in regaining central controls did not transcend the gulf dividing authoritarian regimes from pluralist democracies.[46]

The decomposition of ideology and of the PUWP forced the authorities to seek the church's cooperation in restoring its linkages with society and its international legitimacy.[47] This occurred despite the official assessment of Prime Minister Mieczysław F. Rakowski (1987, 35) that the church "using patriotic and national phraseology, represents an exceptionally conservative and anti-communist strand." The low degree of repression allowed the opposition to rebuild some of its institutions and compete with the authorities for public support. Although, as many authors claimed (e.g., Smolar [1988]), the opposition was divided (probably the unavoidable result of greater openness), it was strong and numerous in comparison with other Communist societies.[48] Even before the elections in 1989, the opposition was a de facto accepted component of the Polish political landscape.

The authorities did not dare to challenge an important legacy of Solidarity, the officially recognized role of the Catholic church as a mediator between the regime and society writ large. The banning of Solidarity in 1982 shifted the focal point in domestic politics back to the church (Rachwald 1987). The church again became a chief spokesman for society and the only institution that could provide the link between the opposition, the silent majority, and the government. To effectively perform this function, the church had to strike a balance between the different claims of these three actors. This task was not simple, as numerous criticisms of Glemp's policy amply demonstrated.[49]

The church skillfully exploited openings created by societal attitudes and the government's policies. It officially condemned the imposition of martial law, although in very guarded terms, but it simultaneously urged people not to resist because "opposition to the decisions of the authorities under martial law could cause violent coercion, including bloodshed."[50] The church persis-

[46] For the reasons discussed, in spite of greater sensitivity of the authorities to contending views and their wary coexistence with non-Communist organizations, a declaration by the Polish Communist party daily *Trybuna Ludu* (18 October 1986) that "the Polish society is pluralistic" was premature. The state's self-imposed restraint in response to social and economic pressures did not amount to a genuinely pluralistic political system.

[47] The authorities, for example, agreed to the visit of John Paul II with the expectation that it would provide proof to the international community, which ostracized General Jaruzelski for his decision to impose martial law, of the conciliation between the authorities and society.

[48] It should be noted, however, that the notion "crisis" can be used only if the period 1981–1984 is taken as a reference. The opposition encompassed much larger segments of the population and its activities had much more visibility than in any period of Communist rule in Poland.

[49] The editorial board of *Kultura*, a powerful émigré monthly published in Paris by the Polish Literature Institute, has directly criticized Glemp's policy. See *Zeszyty Historyczne* 64 (1983). Given the authority of the church among Poles, this was a highly unusual posture.

[50] Sermon delivered by the Polish Primate, Archbishop Józef Glemp on Sunday, 13 December 1981 (the day martial law was imposed). Quoted from Walendowski (1982, 54–55). In the evening, the sermon was carried on Polish television.

tently called for nonviolence and dialogue with the authorities, which was in line with the posture taken by the silent majority and had been a hallmark of Solidarity during its legal existence in 1980–1981. In doing so, the church demonstrated the ability to read popular mood much better than those Solidarity leaders who promised in December 1981 that "Winter is theirs, spring will be ours." It frequently criticized the opposition,[51] while aiding prisoners and their families. The church also provided shelter for underground independent activity.[52]

The government's policy of manipulating rather than suppressing dissenting voices increased the political weight of the church. The church provided the only channel through which the government could influence activities of the opposition. Although underground publications provided the opposition with outlets for publicly expressing their views on political developments, it was only through the church that these views could be discussed with the authorities. Thus, the church provided an obfuscated institutional platform for quasi-pluralism.

The source of the church's political strength was the absence of democracy and legality. As a Polish underground author writing under the pen name of David Warszawski (1984, 88) succinctly noted, "The history of the PPR [Polish People's Republic] has shown that the Church can flourish in a situation where these conditions are not fulfilled." Indeed, for want of political arrangements that would fill the void caused by the state's limited withdrawal from some political domains, the government often relied on church offices to mediate conflicts between the authorities and various segments of the society.[53]

The considerable tolerance of opposition activities and the government's tacit withdrawal from the aspiration to directly control all domains of public life, weakened the opposition. The developments after the 1986 amnesty demonstrated that many conflicting political currents coexisted under the label of Solidarity (Brumberg 1987; Smolar 1988). The absence of consensus on how to get rid of state socialism contributed to fragmentation of the opposition.[54]

[51] The most extreme example of Glemp's attitude toward underground Solidarity is his interview for the Brazilian newspaper *O Estado de São Paulo* on 2 March 1984. He protrayed some underground leaders as Trotskyites and Communists.

[52] The simultaneous pursuit of seemingly conflicting objectives was facilitated by the diversity of political attitudes within the church hierarchy. A significant proportion of the church hierarchy, in particular younger priests symbolized by Father Popiełuszko, did not accept the official dissociation of the church from Solidarity. To the contrary, some of them became key figures of the independent movement. Their activities were not suppressed by church leaders, however.

[53] The most recent example was a wave of strikes in April/May and August in 1988. The church was invited to mediate between the authorities and strikers. This is clearly an illustration of the fundamental incompatibility between political realities (the Polish quasi-pluralism) and institutional arrangements devoid of mechanisms to mediate between conflicting societal demand.

[54] In his thorough study of the opposition, Aleksander Smolar (1988) distinguished four major currents. First, the church-oriented opposition, initiated and sponsored by the church, included

Neither the government nor various strands of the opposition had a quick solution to Poland's economic plight. Neither did they agree upon a long-term program. The opposition, and in 1988 and 1989 the Communist government as well, blamed state socialism for the crisis. However, rallying public support around the notion that "the system" bears responsibility had its drawbacks. The recognition of what had become common wisdom was not a substitute for a program. In the absence of a political program for change, the public was not confronted with the choice. Uncertainty was not conducive to risking a confrontation with the authorities, as scanty participation in a wave of strikes in August 1988 demonstrated.

The withdrawal of the state and the availability of the option to withdraw for individuals accounted, in addition to the economic crisis, for the political demobilization of large segments of the population. Political apathy weakened both the government and the opposition. It enabled the government to maintain political stability, but at the expense of its ability to mobilize the society. It weakened the opposition because many of its potential activists either emigrated or exited to the private sector.

Conclusion

The pressures of adversity accelerate the process of decay of state socialism. The evolution of state socialism has been characterized by the search for substitutes for the market mechanism, the rule of law, and the institutional form of effective interest mediation. During the decay of state socialism, exit of the state and from the state undermines the capacity of the political system to assure stability and to provide a decent economic performance. As long as there is one political party and bargaining in the economic system is not subjected to universal rules of efficiency, the state is deprived of internal mecha-

---

the Primate's Social Council, Light and Live Movement, Councils of the Ministers of the Working People, Clubs of the Catholic Intelligentsia, and so forth. Second, the realistic opposition sought change by exploiting openings created by the state's policy of limited withdrawal. It included Res Publica group, Young Poland Movement, and new antipoliticians who sought the dominance of the free-enterprise system. The third strand, which Smolar calls a legitimist opposition, represented all forms of opposition "perceived by its adherents as the continuation of legal Solidarity" (Smolar 1988, 11). Although its major constituency has probably remained industrial proletariat, the role of intellectuals has been growing. Its symbol was Lech Wałęsa, albeit some groups within this strand had on some occasions challenged his leadership (e.g., Andrzej Gwiazda, a former vice-chairman of Solidarity, together with other activists have established a dissident working group, National Commission of Solidarity, in January 1989). Finally, the fourth group, this of political radicals, advocated confrontational action. The oldest and best-known is the Confederation for Independent Poland, which was founded in 1979 by Leszek Moczulski. Others have been Solidarity's offspring like Fighting Solidarity founded in 1982 by a Wroclaw Solidarity activist, Kornel Makowiecki.

nisms to restore discipline and to bring back economic performance to a satisfactory level.[55]

The changes in the balance between exit, voice, and loyalty cannot bring about self-recuperation within the institutional framework of state socialism. The withdrawal or exit of the state creates an institutional vacuum that somehow has to be filled.[56] When voice is either suppressed or simply ignored by the authorities, the only reaction to a deterioration in performance is exit or withdrawal. Freedom of speech without free elections and a political alternative to the Communist party can provide a vent for social dissatisfaction but only for a short time. If voice makes no difference, people become indifferent, and loyalty to the state disappears. Yet, the authorities cannot afford to completely ignore voice without jeopardizing political stability. In a politico-economic system in which labor discipline is imposed by the state, not by the market, this results in an unwillingness to work and low productivity at all layers of the economic system.

Withdrawal of the socialist state lays the groundwork for two possible responses. The authorities can get out of the institutional cul-de-sac either by returning to the original institutional design or by overhauling the political and/or economic structures of state socialism. The scenario of reaction cannot be dismissed, although it seems rather unlikely. Reaction is politically and economically dysfunctional, and it has little ideological appeal. The scenario would only accelerate the process of economic decline, and it could trigger a revolution. Thus we are left with the scenario of system eradication, a problem I shall turn to in the next chapter.

[55] The alternative to coercion and repressive suppression of local interests turned out to be not applicable for the reasons extensively discussed in chapter 5.

[56] The vacuum created by the state's withdrawal from those domains, which would not directly threaten its survival, was filled by the institutions that had acquired important status: the church and the opposition.

CHAPTER SEVEN

Beyond State Socialism

> The truth is that our efforts have always been wasted, that our work
> is badly renumerated, that nothing goes as it should. This is the re-
> sult of a bad system and of lack of freedom. On our shoulders we
> still feel the breath of Stalinism. This must not go on. It all must
> change so that life in this country can become normal; so that Poles
> feel citizens in their own country; so that youth not run away from
> their homeland, farmers not abandon their fields and workers not
> feel just hired hands.
>
> —Lech Wałęsa

State socialism, which is neither feared nor respected, is doomed to disinte-
grate. It derives its élan vital from the mobilization of society through repression, ideological appeal, and the lust for power exacerbated by the absence of
direct political accountability. Societal immunity to repression and the decomposition of ideology leaves only raw power and the determination to cling to
it.

Given the Marxian origins of the ideology of state socialism, it is ironic that
Marx's laws of motion have turned out to be more applicable to a formation
that emerged as a result of the Soviet Communist Revolution than to capitalism. State socialism rather than capitalism is torn apart by contradictions between productive forces and relations of production and between the base and
the superstructure. The developments in Poland in the 1980s showed that tinkering with the margins without addressing the institutional core is doomed to
failure. The lesson that can be drawn is that the *only way out* is to reconstruct
the institutions that Marx criticized so thoroughly in his writings.

The objective of political changes implemented in the post-martial law period—discussed in chapter 6 and in appendix A—was to maintain social stability and to elicit better effort from society in tackling economic problems.
The changes in the economic system were to create conditions for improved
economic performance. Neither economic nor political objectives were met
by 1988. The semblance of political stability was achieved at the expense of
social apathy and indifference. Poland's economy failed to generate surpluses
sufficient to reverse a decline in growth potential since 1978. No resources

From Lech Wałęsa's opening speech at the roundtable negotiations, *Solidarność News* (Brussels), no. 127, 1–15 February 1989.

were available to prevent the pollution and degradation of the natural environment, the increase in international indebtedness, and the shrinkage of the industrial base due to decapitalization. As a result, another crisis was bound to
erupt.[1]

The paradox of the policies pursued in the 1980s and designed to restore
legitimacy and to revive the economy was that they only introduced new
stresses into the system. These failures were the result of two fundamental
incompatibilities of Poland's political economy as they surfaced in the second
half of the 1980s. The first incompatibility was between latent pluralism and
the unchanged institutional core of the political system. The second was between the administrative environment and economic policy tools of market
provenance.[2] The first could be solved by creating politics, that is, the recognition of conflicting interests in the institutional design, and the second, by
creating economics, that is, a market economy.

Thus the solution amounts to an effective dismantling of state socialism.
There is no *third way* to liberate society from the devastating grip of an institutional design based on the unity of powers (rejection of the principle of separation of powers) and the principle of fusion of the state and economy (rejection of the market). The thrust of this analysis, vindicated by the developments
in Poland in the 1980s and more recently in other countries under state socialism, is that it is impossible to combine the totalitarianism, no matter how
eroded it is, of state socialism with Western "bourgeois democracy." Once
the fusion principle is removed, there is no third way but many different ways
of organizing a viable politico-economic system. As I argued elsewhere, a
" 'Third Way' of socialist development does exist, but only within the logical
framework of demand-constrained [i.e., market] economies" (Kamiński
1987, 95).

THE POLITICAL ECONOMY OF IMPOTENCE

The failure of policies pursued in the 1980s was reflected in the inability of
the state to restore its directive capacity within the organizing principles of

---

[1] The economic situation deteriorated in 1988, displaying many characteristics similar to those
in the period preceding the contraction in 1979. The growing disequilibria in consumer product
markets and overheated investment activity were symptoms of economic crisis. Polish economist
Jan Główczyk (1989, 6) notes that the "investment tensions are similar to those experienced in
the second half of the 1970s." Indeed, there was ample evidence in indicators measuring the
effectiveness and efficiency of investment programs that the country's investment absorptive capacity was exceeded in 1987. Despite these problems, investment policies were not corrected in
1988. As a result, industrial output fell in 1989.

[2] The roundtable agreement between the government coalition and the Solidarity opposition,
signed in April 1989, addressed the first incompatibility and laid the political groundwork for
solving the second.

state socialism.[3] The Communist authorities were not capable of implementing economic reform and reviving the economy. The economic reform measures did not erode the principles of fusion and of rule variability. The economic system became a caricature of both a centrally planned and market economy. The strategy of legitimation through withdrawal (see chap. 6) backfired and exacerbated tensions in the political system. With the decomposition of ideology and of the party apparatus, rules were bent to promote private interests instead of the public interest.

The persistent crisis was an outcome of two fundamental incompatibilities in Poland's political economy in the mid-1980s: (1) a tolerance of diversity and of the political opposition with a simultaneous rejection of reforms that would make pluralism politically meaningful; and (2) an introduction of economic reform measures congruent with the market economy but not with the state socialist economy. Although opinions and values alien to communism were not suppressed by the authorities, they were not allowed to find their expression in competitive politics. The institution of market that would make reforms economically meaningful was not rebuilt.[4] As a result, Poland's state socialism became a parody of both totalitarianism and democracy as well as of both central planning and a market.

The tolerance of diversity was the outcome of failure to revive the economy by using mechanisms available to state socialism. The deteriorating economy undermined one of two hallmarks of state socialism. The certainty of modest improvement in living standards was replaced by the certainty of a lower quality of life for a sizable segment of the populace. Thus full employment, another hallmark of state socialism and the underlying component of negative legitimacy, has lost its social attractiveness. The reduced economic rewards, despite concessive wage policies, triggered a change in the official policies toward seeking legitimation by granting political concessions to the population. Because of the institutional incompatibility between pluralism and the one-party political system, this strategy furthered the disintegration of state socialism.

The rejection by the authorities of any serious structural rearrangements in the political system was responsible for the apathy and retrenchment of a considerable segment of the society from the polity. Unparalleled official tolerance for free speech, modifications of electoral laws, and the existence of self-management institutions was not accompanied by the emergence of a political mechanism that would translate these voices into political actions. Greater freedom to publish dissenting views on various political and economic issues merely engendered frustration. As Polish columnist Ewa Szumańska (1988, 8) succinctly noted, ''Before, if something was finally published, this was a

[3] See chapter 2.
[4] See chapter 2.

sign that a green light was lit, and . . . this would result in policy action. Now there is a storm, a euphoria of words, with no consequences at all.''

The combination of tolerated diversity and the absence of mechanisms that would make this diversity meaningful provided the authorities with dominance but not leadership. Arthur Rachwald (1987, 372) observed that the resulting indifference facilitated political survival of the regime at the expense of its ability to mobilize society and, therefore, to solve economic and political crises.

The refusal to open the political system eroded the regime's ability to govern. Unable, and unwilling, to suppress various forms of dissent by repression, the government was a party to conflicts rather than a mediator. The government had to resort to the offices of the church whenever confronted with the opposition of the populace. This exacerbated conflicts and made them more difficult to manage. A Polish Communist commentator argued in favor of incorporating the opposition into the political system: "Tensions will be milder and easier to prevent in a context of broader consensus than one of continuing divisions and barricades of distrust and non-communication" (Wiatr 1988, 13).

But the crux of the matter is that pluralism cannot find its multiple expressions unless there are at least two political parties and free elections. Until the beginning of the negotiations with the Solidarity opposition in 1988, the authorities did not contemplate the introduction of a multiparty system. Instead they adhered to the rule that "the people pay for government's mistakes" (Revel 1978, 28).

The failure to develop an institutional expression of tolerated pluralism backfired by limiting the state's capacity to introduce anticrisis policies and reforms. Thus the failure undermined political stability. The political stability, achieved mainly as a result of abdication by the state from the attempt to control everything, initially turned out to be an effective way to defuse opposition. It did not last long, though.[5] Because no politically viable framework for sharing the burden of economic crisis was created, the regime's flexible approach of seeking to co-opt various social groups exacerbated tensions. This was revealed by two waves of labor unrest in 1988.

The imposition of "alien" political arrangements on state socialism exacerbated internal systemic tensions. Instead of passivity and social compliance based on tacit acceptance of state socialism (the principle of negative legitimacy), the political reform called for active participation in the political process. Secrecy and bargaining, a trademark of resource allocation under state socialism, was hardly compatible with the promised freedom of press and full disclosure of economic information. Despite changes that made the state more

---

[5] Before the outbreak of strikes in 1988, the opposition was in crisis, as Michnik (1990) and Smolar (1988) convincingly demonstrated.

accountable to the public, the symbiotic relationship between the state and the economy that shaped the politics of state socialism still persisted. This relationship not only has produced a supply constrained economy in which allocation of resources is not determined by the purchasing power of participants but by bureaucratic clout, but has accounted for a complex social fabric based on the hierarchy of patron-client relationships that thrive on political access to many goods and services.

The failure of reform was responsible for the continued captivity of public economic policy to the logic of the closed system and of the state being held hostage by narrow interest groups. After significant cuts in individual consumption in 1982, the government paid for social peace with wage increases. The policies attempted to minimize the economic burden of those who might directly threaten political stability rather than to reward those who would contribute to increased efficiency. Even the Executive Committee of the "official" Trade Union Confederation admitted that the growing disparity in wages in various industries "unfortunately, often bears no relation to their economic performance."[6] Those who bore a disproportionate cost of the crisis were mainly employees of small industrial plants rather than the large enterprises that could organize highly visible and economically costly strikes. This apparent vulnerability to the demands of an industrial "proletariat," demonstrated by the government's readiness to grant wage increases to striking workers who did not demand political concessions, combined with the political indifference of the majority of society contributed to shortageflation and to the chaos in the economy.[7]

The government's readiness to accede to wage demands, although they put the whole reform in jeopardy, illustrated its inability to suppress group interests. More importantly, it indicated that reforms fell short of introducing effective political mechanisms of conflict mediation. The state, which is not directly accountable to the society for its mistakes, cannot act as a mediator among competing interests. The government's repetitive assertions, for instance, that the strikes in 1988 were but a labor dispute between enterprise management and workers could not be taken seriously. After all, the state maintained monopoly over political and economic processes. It also had the power to introduce the so-called "price-income operation," which was an immediate cause of the unrest in 1988.

The tolerated political diversity fused with the state socialist economic system widened the breach between the demands placed on the economy and its capacity to satisfy them. Given the system's "double" logic of import substitution and a bias against production of consumer goods, it is scarcely surprising that economic policies were seized by two inconsistencies. The first incon-

---

[6] See Życie Gospodarcze (Warsaw) 50 (1987): 1.

[7] This term denotes the phenomenon of coexistence between inflation and shortages.

sistency was between investment programs favoring resources and the capital goods-producing sector and liberal wage policies. The latter was the outcome of a desperate search for a modicum of legitimacy because of fears of political instability. Yet these concessions to social pressures did not result in reorientation of investment policies. Despite consumer-oriented rhetoric, about one-third of investment was absorbed by the energy-producing sector and coal mining in the 1980s.

The second inconsistency was between the need of running trade surpluses to service the foreign debt and the antiexport bias of investment programs. As I have argued throughout this book, systemic arrangements of state socialism favor import-substitution strategies. Reforms have not addressed this systemic preference, although some measures introduced in the 1986–1988 period proved to be quite powerful for stimulating exports. Yet investment activity remained insensitive to world markets. Only a tiny fraction of investment was allotted to export-promoting projects. No reform has been implemented to simultaneously ensure long-term sustainable growth and the country's debt servicing. The approach to debt management has been dominated by a series of ad hoc stabilization measures, which were not sustainable over a prolonged period. Because of mutual linkages between the government's responses to creditors and consumers' pressures, the net result of these twin inconsistencies was a rapid economic deterioration.[8]

The second systemic incompatibility, which remained unsolved in the 1980s, was between the introduction of reform measures congruent with a market economy without, however, the creation of a market that would make those measures economically meaningful.[9] Although enterprise management became more autonomous, the greater autonomy was not accompanied by the emergence of an institutional environment that would elicit the best response from economic actors or coordinate their activities. The decision environment

[8] The investment programs, focusing on nonconsumer products, increased the demand for consumer goods without contributing to their supply. Except for cuts in standards of living, the only option to ease demand for consumer goods was to import them from abroad. Because of accumulated debt, however, Poland had to run foreign trade surpluses. In addition, with a depletion of the export growth potential of coal and other natural resources (e.g., copper, sulphur) and the introduction of export-stimulating measures, the consumer goods-producing industries expanded their exports to Western markets. This in turn reduced their domestic availability. However, in another concession to legitimacy and political stability in the face of growing consumer pressures, the authorities increased imports of consumer products at the expense of capital equipment. The change in the commodity composition of imports from the West in favor of individual consumption was quite significant. For instance, the value of these imports increased in 1988 by 33 percent whereas those for production and investment uses grew by 24.5 and 9.0 percent, respectively. The share of investment imports in total CC imports dropped to 10 percent in 1988. As the authors of the report of the Warsaw-based Institute of World Economy noted, this "will probably be the largest impediment to sustain this year's [1988] expansion in exports to the West in the future" (*Gospodarka swiatowa*, p. 84).

[9] For an extensive discussion, see chapter 5.

remained devoid of contractual relationships, interdependence between buyers and sellers and of autonomous economic agents responding to price signals. But in the absence of a market, there is no substitute for direct controls and rule variability. Further, the introduction of financial indicators undermined administrative controls, because nothing can compel producers to respond to commands in the absence of administrative discipline.

The legislation enacted on the state enterprise and workers' self-management in September 1981 as well as other new laws, which were to provide a basis for the reform, amounted to by far the most radical and comprehensive attempt to change the rules underlying the state's involvement in the economy. Yet they were too limited and misguided to eradicate the principle of fusion of the state and economy. At best, they proved that transplanting control tools from the market system may only produce an inefficient hybrid.

The shift from direct physical commands to direct commands in their financial disguise also partly accounted for shortageflation. It demonstrated that a modified centrally planned economy is deprived of a mechanism for setting prices at market-clearing levels, which thereby leads to the politically explosive coexistence of inflation with shortages. Despite a promise of marketization and competition, the introduced organizational changes in fact reduced competition by increasing the size of corporations. In defiance of the enacted antitrust legislation, the degree of monopolization increased. Hence no mechanism has been established that would compel enterprise management to respond to price increases by reducing costs. Instead, because of a monopolistic position, price increases were passed on to consumers. Under those circumstances, the government's attempts to reduce excessive demand through price increases could only set in motion a price-income inflationary spiral exacerbated by excessive investment, budget deficits, and foreign trade surpluses.[10]

The failure to find an institutional solution to the two incompatibilities of Poland's political economy in the 1980s was glaringly revealed in the labor unrest in 1988. The persistent inadequacy of surpluses generated by the economy to prevent pollution and degradation of the natural environment, the increase in international indebtedness, the shrinkage in the industrial base from decapitalization, and the decline in quality of life for large segments of the population have been visible testimony of the system's nonviability. They brought increasing frustration to the populace. Although the two waves of strikes in 1988 were limited to a small number of factories,[11] they revealed the

[10] In the first quarter of 1989 the prices of consumer goods and services (as compared with their level in the first quarter of the previous year) increased by 74 percent. They increased by 43.2 percent in 1988 and 18.8 percent in the first quarter of 1987. The 1989 Central Annual Plan assumed a price increase of 19.2 percent. According to official predictions, prices were expected to increase in 1989 by about 100 percent. They actually increased by 354 percent.

[11] In 1980, for instance, more than seven hundred enterprises comprised the Interenterprise Strike Committee, whereas during August 1988 only five enterprises proved active (from an in-

growing militancy of workers and the frustration of the populace. They were a warning that with a short carrot and a broken stick social compliance might be impossible to maintain. Because consumption was the main, if not the only, source of legitimation the economic failure eroded governing capability. This produced a vicious circle of impotence: without improved economic performance the state was unable to mobilize the population, and without mobilization no economic improvement was possible.

In all, despite a considerable relaxation of authoritarian political procedures, which considerably weakened the hegemony of the party-state over major institutional systems, neither the state's legitimacy nor its directive capacity increased. This was hardly surprising because the system was deprived of mechanisms that would provide effective conflict mediation congruent with pluralism and economic efficiency congruent with the autonomy of economic actors. Until 1989, no attempt was made to establish a pluralist system endowed with democratic mechanisms that guaranteed the authorities' accountability to the society. Except for rhetoric, not much has been done to untangle the state and economy in spite of the acceptance by the state of the diversity and multiplicity of forms of economic activity. In other words, the monetization of the economy without a market and pluralism without democracy have produced a situation of *systemic impotence*. A way out of structural impotence is either to establish democracy and a market economy or to rebuild a totalitarian system and command economy.

Although the Rakowski cabinet appointed in the fall of 1988 was clearly committed to a market-oriented reform, it lacked the political credibility to introduce measures that would inevitably bring about unemployment and a decrease in the standard of living. The transformation of the economic system called for a strong government capable of suppressing discontent and various group interests. Under political circumstances at home and in the Soviet Union, the option of overt oppression (or of another martial law) was not available to Rakowski. The Rakowski government was thus hardly in a position to steer the transition to a market economy. Without legitimacy and credibility of the authorities, the problem of structural impotence could not be solved.

IN SEARCH OF A SOLUTION: THE ROUNDTABLE ACCORDS

The roundtable negotiations between the government coalition and Solidarity opposition, successfully concluded on 7 April 1989 and limited free elections (4 June 1989) have created an opportunity for an institutional solution to the systemic incompatibility between "underground" pluralism and official "ho-

terview with Jacek Merkel, member of the National Executive Commission of Niezalezny Samorządny Związel Zawadowy (NSZZ) (Independent Self-governing Trade Union), Solidarność, in *Solidarność News*, no. 132, 16–30 April 1989.)

mogeneity." Its provisions calling for a transition from disintegrating totalitarianism to democracy, albeit still restricted, were a first step toward introducing accountability of the government to the people. By ending the seven-year-old ban on Solidarity, which regained the right to legal existence on 17 April 1989, and creating a new system of government including a powerful presidency and a two-chamber legislature, the agreement introduced important institutional changes that paved the way for the emergence of a non-Communist government.

The Solidarity-Government Accords were more specific on political issues, whereas the grand issue of a change in the economic system was barely touched upon. The economic component of the agreement focused on distributive and welfare problems. It is hardly surprising that the references to the most pressing issues, such as debt management, inflation, and economic efficiency, were rather sparse and general. The conceptual underpinning of roundtable negotiations stemmed from the conviction shared by both negotiating parties that a new economic order, as a market-oriented economic reform was referred to in the Accords, could not be implemented without the political support of the majority of society. The Accords attested to the Communist authorities' belief that political support for economic restructuring would not be forthcoming without opening the political system.

The final communiqué of the roundtable negotiations contains three major parts, or standpoints: on political reforms, on socioeconomic policy and systemic reforms, and on trade union pluralism. In addition, eleven annexes covering a very wide range of various issue-areas discussed within the so-called sub-roundtables are an integral component of the Accords.[12] The discussions between the government coalition and Solidarity opposition encompassed all domains of public life in Poland. Although the agenda was dominated by such issues as indexation of wages, the degree of marketization of the economy, and the timing and scope of industrial democracy, the agreements concerning the reform of the political system will have the greatest impact on the future of Poland.

What made the accord a truly historic event was not its economic provisions, which were criticized by many experts, but the acceptance by the authorities of the premise that without political reform no radical restructuring of the economy would be possible. In other words, they rejected an authori-

[12] The annexes contain: (1) minutes from the meetings of the commission on law and judiciary reform and (2) the commission on mass media; (3) the final statement of the commission on territorial self-management; (4) minutes of the commission on associations; (5) recommendations of the commission on education, science, and technological progress, (6) the commission on youth, and (7) the commission on housing; (8) standpoint on the social problems of agriculture and other documents of the commission on agriculture; (9) minutes from the meetings of the commission on mining; (10) the final statements of the commission on public health care and (11) the commission on natural environment.

tarian mode of introducing the reform in rather an amazing political turn-around.[13] Democracy was to be implemented not for its own sake but as a "productive input" and effective mode of governance. The part on political reform was truly revolutionary, as it directly attacked *all* political underpinnings of state socialism.[14] It promised to make government accountable for its mistakes to the ballot and to remove the state from direct involvement in the economy. The Accords stressed the evolutionary rather than revolutionary character of the transition to parliamentary democracy.[15]

The reform of the state envisages the emergence of a constitutional order based on the division of power among three branches of the government, which at least initially favors the executive branch. The reform includes the establishment of a National Judiciary Council, a bicameral National Assembly consisting of the Sejm and Senate and the powerful office of president. A National Judiciary Council, consisting of judges designated by a joint assembly of the Supreme Court, Supreme Administrative Court, and common courts, will assure independence for courts and judges. The National Judiciary Council will recommend candidates for judges to be appointed by the president. The independence of the courts is to be backed by the constitutionally guaranteed irremovability of judges.

The Senate will have legislative initiative and will control observance of human rights and socio economic programs. If the Senate opposes a law enacted by the Sejm, then it will have to be passed by at least two-thirds of the votes in the Sejm. The president will be elected by a majority of votes at a joint session of the Senate and Sejm for a term of six years, thus exceeding the four-year-terms of deputies and senators. The president's veto may be overridden by a two-thirds majority in the Sejm. Executive orders, except actions concerning foreign policy and national security, have to be countersigned by the prime minister. The president is empowered to introduce martial law for three months; its extension, which is limited to three months, requires the consent of both the Senate and Sejm.

Restrictions on free elections guaranteeing the government coalition control in the Sejm and the office of president were to ensure a smooth devolution of power held by the Communist party. Free elections, which were held on 4

---

[13] The Rakowski government adopted a more aggressive posture toward economic liberalization and a more confrontational stance toward the opposition. The delay to the start of roundtable negotiations as well as the announced measures concerning the restructuring of Polish industry indicated that liberalization was not to be extended to the political sphere. By earmarking the Gdańsk shipyard for closing, Prime Minister Rakowski chose confrontation rather than cooperation. This amounted to the rejection of a social anticrisis pact, to borrow a term coined by Lech Wałęsa's advisor Professor Bronisław Geremek.

[14] It is rather noteworthy that the adjective "socialist" cannot be found in the Accords of the Roundtable.

[15] It states that "indispensable reforms of the state should be an outcome of evolution unfolding in accordance with raison d'état" *Dokumenty* (1989, 4).

June 1989, were restricted to the Senate (100 seats) and to 35 percent of the seats (161) in the Sejm, but "the next elections in four year's time must be free or none at all," as Solidarity cochairman of the table on political reform put it (Geremek 1989).

The agreement also addressed the economic underpinnings of state socialism. The policy measures designed to change the institutional environment have been divided into four groups dealing with self-management, property rights, competition, and appointment of managers. The first group marks a return to the ideas voiced by Solidarity in 1981. It contains a set of provisions that would make the institutional framework conducive to the development of industrial democracy. An interesting provision, which may mark the emergence of corporatist structure, concerns the establishment of a nationwide union of self-management activists legally empowered to assess the blueprints of legal acts concerning economic policy and reform.[16] Workers' councils are also to be established in private enterprises employing more than one hundred employees.[17]

The second group contains measures designed to encourage diversity in ownership and privatization. The measures not only call for constitutional guarantees of permanence of various types of ownership and equal treatment of private, cooperative, and state-owned sectors, more significantly, they also seek to assure social control over management of state-owned assets and stop the appropriation of state-owned capital assets by the party-state apparatus.[18] Founding organs are to be replaced by the end of 1990 by a National Capital Assets Fund, whose board will be appointed by parliament, thus providing for some degree of supervision by elected officials.[19] The rules concerning the sale of state-owned enterprises or a majority of their stocks to the public are specified by a new National Assembly. If those rules do not apply, the final decision rests with employers of an affected enterprise.

The third group of measures concerns demonopolization and a significant reduction in the scope and rules underlying the state's administrative action in the economy. The rationing, administrative involvement in price-, exchange rate-, and interest rate-setting as well as government contracts are to be phased out before 1991.

[16] The government project, rejected by the Solidarity opposition, called in addition for the establishment of regional (voivodship) and national chambers representing enterprises (both workers' councils and enterprise directors).

[17] Foreign enterprises are excluded unless their managers consent.

[18] The phenomenon was extensively reported and discussed before the Accords in underground publications and now in the Solidarity-controlled press. It consists of transforming state-owned enterprises into joint stock companies with preferential allotment of stocks to the party-state apparatus, that is, nomenklatura. See, for instance, Dariusz Fikus (1989).

[19] The agreement notes that the government coalition would like to postpone the decision of whether the fund should be outside the executive branch of the government, a solution recommended by the Solidarity opposition, or not until further analysis.

The fourth group, not a well-disguised Solidarity attempt to eradicate no-menklatura in the state-owned sector, contains a set of principles that are to shape personnel decisions in an enterprise. The inclusion of this issue in a set of systemic measures of the new economic order is rather surprising. No-menklatura has been a tool of the PUWP's control over the economy. But unless the administrative economic system is overhauled, enterprises are better off with directors who thanks to their networks in the state administration can negotiate tax rates or secure supplies of rationed goods. The only economic argument in favor of including this issue in the system reform package is resistance to the reform by directors of state-owned enterprises. But one could easily identify other more powerful groups opposed to marketization, for example, workers employed in large obsolete plants.

Although the measures recognize that demonopolization and de-etatization of the economy are a necessary condition for competition and market-clearing prices, they are wanting on several accounts. First, the measures listed in the Accords do not amount to a program. Instead they are a declaration of intent. Neither linkages among measures nor timing of their implementation is identified. As such, they offer no guidelines on how to create a new economic order.

Second, the measures and their discussion do not consistently address the issue of what changes have to be made in the decision environment of enterprises to assure their autonomy from the state. Neither a competitive environment nor the abolition of nomenklatura is sufficient for a meaningful autonomy of economic actors. Other necessary conditions, such as an efficient system of financial intermediation, unambiguously specified ownership rights, and bankruptcy, are not mentioned.

Third, it is also surprising that the anachronic tax system existing in Poland has not been tackled. By international standards, there is an excessive burden on corporate sectors, both private and public, at the expense of taxes on personal incomes, and tax rates are subject to negotiations. Taxes are a very powerful tool of indirect control by the state. The state deprived of it is usually tempted to resort to direct controls. In addition, the inequalities in incomes, which substantially increased in the 1980s, are in part caused by the corrupted system of tax levying and collecting. Therefore, the establishment of a modern tax system is a prerequisite to transition to a market economy.

Fourth, the systemic measures completely ignore or even conflict with recommended economic policy actions presented in the chapters on the standard of living and equilibrating the economy. There is a conspicuous absence of guidelines on how to control prices, combat inflation, increase the supply of consumer goods, cope with the international debt, and simultaneously marketize the economy. Indexation of wages, promised to a tune of 80 percent of quarterly increases in cost of living, in a supply-constrained economy is likely to fuel inflation and, therefore, make the introduction of market clearing prices impossible. In addition, a failure to extend indexation to exchange and interest rates creates yet another impediment to marketization by increasing chances for price distortions.[20]

Because the program calls for reducing budgetary expenditures even though its realization would increase budgetary expenditures, some Polish economists argue that it promises more than the economy can deliver.[21] As Wacław Wilczyński summed up, "For the sake of socio-political realism, we maintain economic fiction."[22] These new claims on economic resources may delay reform because the organizational transition is likely to require some extra resources, for example, to tackle bankruptcies and labor displacement, a likely result of restructuring and marketization.

The agreements were the expression of a consensus among the authorities and the opposition leaders that the only way to confront the crisis was by first opening the political system to overcome resistance to radical economic reform. Thus the Accords suggest a sequence of democracy followed by market modernization. A sequence adopted in the Accords implicitly assumes that low credibility of the government has been responsible for its "reformatory" impotence. In addition, an underlying assumption is that antireform forces can be handled by the democratic political process stripping power from those who are opposed to reform. But these assumptions have never been confronted with a transition program to a market economy because no such program has ever been designed.

The validity of the hypothesis about political reform as a prerequisite to economic reform remains to be tested, although the military crackdown of the prodemocracy movement in China seems to vindicate it. The persistent stalemate of reform, after initial promising actions by former Prime Minister Mieczysław Rakowski and his apparent determination to proceed with reform without Solidarity's explicit approval, also suggests that political change should precede economic reform. There is, however, no historic precedent for a transition from state socialism to a market economy, leaving aside the not very encouraging case of Yugoslavia, which demonstrated that an effort to find a "third way" is a recipe for decades of stagnation and confusion.

Thus, the answer to the question Which sequence is more likely to assure

[20] Although an economic argument can be made in favor of indexation, it is based on the characteristics of the economic system that the Accords want to overhaul. Because the economic system in Poland resembles in many respects an unconstrained bargaining regime (Kamiński and Sołtan 1988) indexation provides a constraint, admittedly a weak one, on wage demands. As long as wage discipline is not imposed by the market, the indexation is a better solution than its absence. In this sense, indexation may impair marketization.

[21] For instance, Kleer (1989) estimated that the fulfillment of 235 tasks spread over a period of three years would cost about Zł 5 trillion, more than $1.5 billion and Tr350 million, even after deducting benefits from conversion of military production for consumption uses or cutting investment programs in coal mining and energy.

[22] See his intervention in the discussion "Czas przeobrazeń" (The time of transformation), Życie Gospodarcze 18 (1989).

the transition to democracy and markets? necessarily involves an intellectual speculation. It critically hinges upon identifying the social groups that are likely to be most negatively affected by it and their ability to influence the process. The most opposed will be those who will lose rents obtained thanks to the existing economic system. However, the roundtable agreements, in rather an unexpected twist of the developments triggered by a double humiliation of Communists in the elections,[23] set the stage for the removal of Communists from power. Communists deprived of their source of power, traditionally derived not from the ballot—as the result of limited free elections unambiguously showed—but from control of the economy and the state repressive apparatus[24] are no longer a factor.

Yet, the program of new institution building, adjustment, and recovery will involve industrial and agricultural restructuring that calls for austerity measures. Given the degree of politicization of economic issues handled under state socialism not by market but by bureaucracy, there are two dangers. First, implicit in democracy, the mechanism of conflict mediation can strip the reform blueprint of all its meaningful components. The pressure coming from diverse constituencies may simply paralyze government.

Second, as long as financial profitability of a state-owned enterprise is not determined by a market, industrial restructuring decisions are likely to trigger more vehement response than in Western democracies where the verdicts of a market can be disputed, but only if improved competitiveness is likely. These redistributive issues combined with a deteriorating economic situation and shortageflation may crowd out, as they did during the roundtable negotiations, the issue of economic reform. They may also deplete the moral capital of Solidarity and trigger polarization.[25]

The crux of the matter is that a combination of democracy with the state-run economy may turn out to be a recipe for protracted conflict. In other words, it remains to be seen whether the assumption that a change in the system of government is a necessary precondition for economic reform is sound.

THE CHALLENGE OF THE FUSION PRINCIPLE: AUTONOMIZATION OF THE ECONOMIC SYSTEM

The direct subordination of the economy to the state is a defining characteristic that accounts for the unique logic of the political economy of state socialism.

[23] Communists were humiliated: first because the national list, where candidates run unopposed, failed to obtain 50 percent of the vote, and second, because all Communist candidates except two were rejected during the first round of the elections.

[24] As a recently elected Solidarity candidate to the Sejm, Wiktor Kulerski, put it during his visit to Washington in June 1989, "They have tanks, and we have votes."

[25] After all, 38 percent who chose not to participate in the first free elections in Poland's postwar history, limited as they were, "may swell to an angry and not so silent majority" (Brumberg 1989a, A-23).

Unless the fusion principle is overhauled, shortages and rationing creating an all encompassing pattern of patron-client relationships will tend to resurface no matter how liberalized the political system becomes. As Usher (1974) demonstrated, the increased direct involvement of the state in resource distribution in Western societies is a threat to political stability and undermines democracy. The solution lies in the introduction of market-clearing prices and "autonomization" of the economic system; the former marks the move from a supply-constrained (soft law and budget constraint) economy to a demand-constrained economic system and the latter to the independence of economic actors subject to hard law and budget constraint.[26]

Solving the institutional incompatibility between democracy and an administrative economic system and between the introduced innovations of market provenance and a nonmarket environment, on the other hand, is crucial to the stability of transition.[27] Unless the economic system becomes competitive and autonomous from the state, an "anticommunist" government risks losing its credibility by becoming entangled in the administrative economic game. It risks becoming involved, for instance, in bargaining over investment allocation and rationing, and thereby jeopardizes political stability. Without abolishing fusion of the economy and state, the transition to democracy will not materialize.

The key to the autonomization of the economic system is to deprive the state of the authority to directly intervene in the decisions of economic actors. The role of the state should be reduced to shaping the decision environment of economic actors, that is, economic regulatory structures. In Western market economies, this objective is accomplished by the dominance of the private sector; thanks to the mobility of capital and constitutional guarantees, this sector has considerable autonomy and can force the state to respect the requirements of economic efficiency. In state socialist economies, the lack of autonomy is largely responsible for the absence of a link between the firm's economic performance and the manager's pecuniary gains. Its absence has

---

[26] This should not imply that the state should play no role in the economy. In nonstate socialist politico-economic systems, there is a great diversity in the extent of the state's involvement in the economy. There is, however, one rule—the state must not directly intervene in decisions made by enterprise management. The term "autonomization" thus denotes the weakest condition for getting rid of the fusion principle.

[27] It is noteworthy that the economic provisions of the Accords, contained in chapter 5 titled "New Economic Order" of the Standpoint on Socioeconomic Policy and System Reform, indicate that the view is shared by both the authorities and the opposition. The new order as envisaged in the Accords is to be based on self-management, nondiscrimination on the basis of ownership, competition, and market, and selection of enterprise managers on the basis of "professional competence." This is clearly a substantially different order than the one characterized by the fusion principle. Conceptually, it recognizes the necessity of eliminating soft law and soft budget, manifestations of the state socialist economic order.

detrimental effects on economic efficiency and accounts for the poor economic performance of state socialism (Nuti 1988, 36).

The autonomization of the economic system sets the groundwork for a smoother transition to a private economy. It offers more time for altering fundamental values such as respect for law and for property rights, a respect that was destroyed by the Communists, and by creating an institution with a sectorwide perspective, it guarantees that competitive markets will be established.

However, one of the legacies of state socialism is the dominance of the state-owned sector, which, for instance, accounts for about 5 percent of the total industrial output in Poland. Even had it expanded at an annual growth rate of about 25 percent, and assuming zero-growth of the state sector, it would take about ten years for the private nonagricultural sector to exceed the 50 percent mark. Thus, the state-owned sector has to be privatized to speed up the move toward a market economy.

Privatization presents formidable problems not only under a state socialist economy but also in countries with well-developed markets, as numerous studies of the privatization effort in the 1980s show.[28] In addition, there are no reasons to believe that selling ownership rights and cutting the size of the state's involvement activities would improve economic performance. A simple transfer of the property rights of existing enterprises from the state to the general public is unlikely to improve the efficiency of the economy. The industrial structure of the state socialist economy is highly concentrated as a result of a persistent effort by state and enterprise bureaucrats to simplify administrative management and a bias of investment policies in favor of large capital projects. The share of large enterprises in various industries is incomparably higher than in Western developed economies. There is very little room for competition. Consequently, privatization will only result in the replacement of the "economic dictatorship" of a Communist state by the dictatorship of privately held monopolies.

Under state socialism in this stage of decay, large industrial enterprises are capable of pursuing their private interests; they are *de facto privatized*. As was argued in chapter 2, their ability to negotiate tax rates and financial targets, to obtain priority allotments of spare parts and materials higher wages, and so forth, contributed to a sluggish overall economic performance. The ability of the state to control them has been rather limited. Although private owners will have perhaps a better understanding of business practices, they are not likely to resist the temptation to line their pockets with monopoly rents. Thus once those giants are privatized, the state will have to step in to protect consumers against monopolies. Because such pathologies of monopolies as gross incom-

[28] See contributions to Vernon (1988).

petence, padded payrolls, and outright looting of enterprises will not disappear, privatization will not contribute to the increase in efficiency.

Thus, the first step toward breaking the symbiosis of the state and economy, that is, the eradication of the fusion principle, is creating conditions for competition. This in turn requires a deconcentration and demonopolization of the economy that should precede the privatization of large enterprises. The privatization of enterprises capable of exercising monopolistic control is a poor substitute for competitive markets. Decentralization and demonopolization is a necessary condition for competition. Only then the removal of direct (or informal) controls over prices, exchange rates, and the banking sector will enhance microeconomic efficiency.

State-owned enterprises are not inefficient because they are owned by the state. As Raymond Vernon (1988, 4) noted: "Where governments have been reasonably competent and responsible, and where comparisons between private and state-owned enterprises have been possible, the technical performance of state-owned enterprises has not appeared much different from that of private enterprises. . . . A public enterprise is not a perennial wastrel." The inefficiencies of state-owned enterprises stem from their size and monopoly power. The underlying reason is that they are subject to political controls and tend to be abused for narrow political interests. The task is to separate the economy from the state—that is, politics from microeconomics, *not* from macroeconomics.

During the transition period, a significant proportion of enterprises will remain state owned. As long as they operate as profit maximizers, a market for managers will emerge. Then, managers will have incentives to maximize profits even if there is no market for ownership rights. Otherwise, they may be fired, and poor records of past performance will make it difficult for them to find new managerial positions. As long as the state acts like main shareholders in the West, state enterprises will behave like private enterprises.

Although historically constitutionally guaranteed private ownership was a wall shielding the economy from the state, and although privatization should be a long-term goal of a post-Communist government, the eradication of the fusion principle can be accomplished through a variety of ways. The independence of the economy from the government without changes in ownership can be ensured by subjecting the state's intervention in the economy to the rule of law.[29] The problem lies in the design of control structures that would compel

[29] For instance, as an interim institutional solution, a special board staffed by professionals appointed for long, but nonrenewable, terms should be established. The board would not be a part of the government. Its members could be elected by the National Assembly upon recommendation by professional bodies. It would exercise control over state-owned industry like shareholders do in the West. In addition, the rules of intervention would be formally and unambiguously specified. The existence of a special board would prevent the government from attempting to use state-owned corporations to garner popular support, for vote seeking, and so forth. Enterprise manage-

the state to run its enterprises on business principles. The state would have to refrain from doing certain things; it would have to induce rather than command business to perform.

The emergence of a single variant to combat the fusion principle is rather unlikely. Instead there will be many solutions including the labor-managed system, the quasi-private (joint stock companies) and private sector systems and, both domestic and foreign systems. Some authors (e.g., Kowalik [1989]; Poznański [1988b]) warn that marketization may lead to a "corrupt" market system in which entry to the areas with highest rents is controlled by the state. Some symptoms of a "corrupt" market were present in Poland in the 1980s, as was argued in chapter 6.[30] However, the new laws on undertaking economic activity and political reforms, including independent local governments, will reduce the scope for bureaucratically derived rents from privatization. Democratization of the political system will create pressures towards the rule of law, that is, clearly defined rules of interaction between the state and the private and quasi-private sector.

CONCLUSION

The transition to a new political and economic order stemming from the declining era of the directive capacity of the socialist state is and will continue to be difficult. The process is probably irreversible. The popular conviction that state socialism as a system is responsible for stagnation and popular discontent makes its return unlikely. This was the threat of an approaching economic crisis and new opportunities offered by political restructuring that triggered change in the state socialist world.

A litmus test for the completion of the transition is the emergence of an order with an autonomous economic system based on competition. There is no third way to organize a modern society. In fact, there are *hundreds of different ways* to accomplish this goal. The state may be more or less interventionist. It may be less or more involved in redistributive activities and the provision of a social safety net. No matter what its involvement may be, it will, however, have to create an environment conducive to competition, technological innovation, and economic growth. The great lesson that can be drawn from the unfortunate experience with state socialism is that an institutional design of a politico-economic order that would be able to survive in a rapidly changing world should observe the autonomy of the economic system and society.

---

ment would be doubly shielded by legal proscriptions and by an industrial board independent from politics. The conviction of board members that a market is superior, quite justified in view of the dismal experience with command planning, would provide extra protection against political abuses.

[30] See also Kamiński (1989c).

Stages of the "Post–Martial Law" Normalization: A Bird's Eye View of Major Political Developments

THE RISE of Solidarity from a small workers' union numbering a few thousand in the summer of 1980 to a nationwide organization cutting across traditional trade divisions and encompassing almost all employees of the "socialized" sector was closely followed by world public opinion. With the decline of visible forms of protest after the military seized control of the country, the developments in Poland lost their "photogenic" attraction. Yet, in many respects, the less visible developments following the imposition of martial law transformed the Polish political system. The changes that took place between 13 December 1981 and the emergence of a Solidarity-led government in August 1989 were cumulatively even more radical than those that had taken place during the so-called Solidarity period in 1980 and 1981.

For the purpose of this discussion, three stages of the political developments in Poland following the imposition of martial law in December 1981 can be distinguished. The first stage covers the "state of war" period, that is, the period between the imposition of martial law on 13 December 1981 and its formal lifting announced by the Military Council of National Salvation (WRON) on 22 July 1983. The second stage, which I call the "illusion of stabilization," extends from the lifting of martial law to the announcement of the unconditional release of all political prisoners on 15 September 1986. This announcement, which came as a surprise to observers both in Poland and abroad, marked the beginning of the third stage, which may be called "toward breaking the deadlock."

Although each stage can be demarcated by a visible policy action, the actual boundaries are not so clear. In fact, there was considerable consistency in the process of normalization. At all stages of political development, the authorities opted for a relatively flexible strategy that rejected both the Kádár and Husak approach of overpowering society through massive repression. In the first stage, policies focused on destroying the mode of interaction between the authorities and society that had evolved during the Solidarity period and on erecting barriers to the reemergence of Solidarity. Later, the strategy consisted of flexibly adapting the means appropriate to the scope of resistance.

PHASE 1: THE STATE OF WAR (1981–1983)

The imposition of martial law was presented as the only option available to the authorities to prevent the total disintegration of the state. Its fundamental objective allegedly was to ensure Poland's existence as an independent state. The only alternative to the government's action, according to the official interpretation spread through various informal channels, was Soviet intervention and the loss of independence. The imposition of martial law was justified as the lesser evil—a domestic solution to homemade problems as opposed to one externally imposed. The restoration of monolithic controls was portrayed as a necessary and indispensable means to implement the political and economic changes demanded in 1981. The changes supported by the military regime were, not surprisingly, devoid of those components that directly threatened the state's political monopoly.

The imposition of martial law on 13 December 1981 caught Solidarity off-guard. Even before martial law was formally imposed almost all of its leaders were imprisoned. The measures implemented by the martial law decree transferred all powers to the Military Council of National Salvation (WRON). Martial law deprived the population of the means to communicate and to relocate. All public communication channels were transferred to the military. Telephone links both within Poland and with other countries were cut and regional television and radio broadcasts were suspended; only the national channels remained active.[1] In addition, the movement of people was severely restricted. To prevent the use of cars, the sale of gasoline was banned. Regional and local Solidarity headquarters were immediately seized by the army. As a result, Solidarity was deprived of its leaders and its communication channels. Finally, unusually harsh weather severely restricted the possibility of launching sit-in strikes.

The main provisions of the decree of martial law passed by the Council of State on 12 December 1981 included:

1. the internment of anyone over the age of 17 for the duration of martial law if they presented a threat to state security
2. the suspension of all organizations whose activities threatened the security of the state
3. the suspension of the right to strike
4. the ban on wearing "specific badges and uniforms"
5. the requirement for prior permission from the appropriate authorities for all publishing, printing, and dissemination of information in any form
6. the requirement for prior permission to hold public meetings
7. the imposition of curfews, bans on travels, limits on all postal and telecommunication services, censorship of the mail and telephone conversations.

The most visible example of the weakness of Solidarity in the face of the government's "state of war" was its failure to launch a general strike. The

---

[1] Except for two dailies, the official organ of the PUWP, *Trybuna Ludu*, and the army's organ, *Żołnierz Wolności*, the publication of all other newspapers was suspended. Jurisdiction over the militarized sectors of the administration and the economy was transferred to military courts.

general strike was regarded as the ultimate weapon that could bring the regime to its knees. However, due to the massive presence of the army, cold weather, and an information and communication blockade, a general strike was not possible. The military coup d'état did not trigger either massive bloodshed or massive resistance. Except for some pockets of heroic defiance, the majority of the people accepted the state of war with resignation and passivity.[2] According to an underground estimate, the total number of deaths attributable to the state of war were fifty.[3] Given the estimated ten million members of Solidarity and the scope of the military operation, this was not a large number.

The government tailored the use of repressive measures to the challenge that it faced. Large demonstrations in May and August 1982 were contained with the massive use of riot police.[4] Many participants were arrested and dismissed from work. The ineffectiveness of the demonstrations dealt a final blow to the hopes expressed in a Solidarity slogan: "The winter is yours, but the spring will be ours." The penalties imposed by the government significantly raised the cost of insubordination. The opposition was forced to reassess the utility of overt actions. It adopted a new strategy of creating an "underground society," which consisted of removing as large a public domain as possible from the government's control.

Because of the limited resistance and correspondingly limited and mild repression, the initial shock and fear quickly subsided, which facilitated the reconstruction of the opposition. Because the strike as a form of social protest was eliminated by martial law, the opposition focused on finding other means to keep the pressure on the authorities. They included largely symbolic gestures, such as occasional underground radio broadcasts,[5] street demonstrations, and a boycott of the official media.[6] Street demonstrations, usually organized on the anniversaries of historically important events, did not draw large crowds. They peaked in summer 1982; subsequently their frequency and

[2] An exception was a strike in the Wujek coal mine that led to the death of nine workers. Although appeals for a general strike were not successful, there were several strikes (mainly in Silesia) that lasted for more than ten days. For a detailed account of strikes in response to the imposition of martial law, see Cave (1982).

[3] The number of deaths was estimated on the basis of the data compiled by the Helsinki Committee in Poland and supplemented by the Solidarity Regional Executive Committee in Warsaw. The list was originally published in *Uncensored Poland*, no. 15, 1984, and reprinted in *Poland Watch* (Washington, D.C.) no. 6 (1984): 22–30.

[4] The most violent manifestations were in Lublin in August 1982. Two people were killed.

[5] The first eight-minute broadcast on 12 April 1982 urged people to express their solidarity against martial law by switching off lights for 15 minutes at 9 o'clock the next evening.

[6] Examples abound. Inhabitants of a small town, Świdnik, drew national attention by their ingenious demonstration of contempt for the official mass media in February 1982. They used to take a walk during the evening television world news, crowding the main street. The authorities responded by turning off the electricity and water. The "walk action" was subsequently carried out in several other towns. Another example of a highly visible protest was an actors' refusal to work for Polish television.

popularity gradually fell. Given Solidarity's inability to launch a general strike and organize massive defiance, these forms of protests were not a real threat to the regime. They helped to boost the morale of the society, which had been deeply humiliated by its inability to react decisively against the imposition of martial law.

Greater significance may be attached to the development of measures that would create the autonomy of society and keep the ideals of Solidarity alive. Informal associations and institutions proliferated.[7] The most visible and effective way to preserve autonomy was an independent publishing circuit that directly challenged the state monopoly on information. The expansion of underground publishing was enormous. According to some estimates (Cave and Sosnowska 1982, 64; Smolar 1988, 27), between one thousand and seventeen hundred publications appeared regularly across the country since the imposition of martial law. The scope and dynamism of underground publishing activity was such that security forces, although they tried hard, could not contain it. This dealt a final blow to the state's aspiration to totally control information. Underground publications established an effective barrier against the state's ideological penetration of society. In the realm of symbols and ideas, the authorities were clearly defeated.

With the disappearance of legal Solidarity, the church again assumed its role as a protector of independent social activity and a speaker for national issues. However, the church skillfully avoided taking sides in the conflict. By retaining its commitment to national values and the oppressed while refusing to condemn forcefully those who imposed martial law, it became a mediator between the people and the authorities.

The church followed a two-track policy. On the one hand, its appeals to avoid violent resistance that could spawn bloodshed found a receptive audience among the authorities. It is noteworthy that Poland's Primate Józef Glemp's Sunday sermon was broadcast almost immediately after General Jaruzelski's speech announcing the imposition of martial law on Polish television on its evening news, December 13. Throughout 1982, Primate Glemp on numerous occasions called for a dialogue between the authorities and the people while he opposed demonstrations organized by underground Solidarity. For example, he vehemently opposed the demonstrations scheduled on 10 November 1982 to protest the formal banning of Solidarity.[8] The church became

---

[7] The dissolved Association of Polish Journalists and the Union of Polish Writers continued their activities. Several bodies with the objective to promote independent education were established. These included: People's Universities, Christian People's Universities, the Council of National Education, the Group of Independent Teaching, and the Social Committee of Learning. See Smolar (1988, 23–26).

[8] They actually showed the underground Solidarity's inability to draw social support for its actions. Whether the small number of participants was because of the primate's appeal or because of growing indifference is not clear.

actively involved in activities designed to prevent civil war and put an end to the state of cold war between the authorities and society. These goals were undoubtedly shared with the administrators of martial law. The primate firmly refused to commit the church to work toward reestablishing the Solidarity trade union.[9] Glemp also urged film and theater actors to end a boycott of the official mass media. Finally, the church shared the government's opposition to Western sanctions imposed in response to martial law.

The church, however, condemned the state of war. The church sought to soften martial law, to restore basic human freedoms, and to defend the prosecuted by using its vast organizational capabilities. It was the only institution, aside from the Polish state, whose informational and organizational structure was left intact by martial law. These autonomous organizational capabilities were crucially important for the opposition. They contributed significantly to its survival. Dioceses assumed new multiple responsibilities. They became information centers monitoring repressions and aid centers that provided food and medicine to the needy. They were also legal centers that intermediated in the provision of legal assistance to the prosecuted. They served as cultural and political centers providing shelter for many independent activities. The church also guaranteed that aid coming from the West did not wind up in the government's hands, as was reportedly the case with aid sent through the Polish Red Cross, which was reportedly controlled by the Ministry of Internal Affairs.[10] The government grudgingly disregarded the church's multiple activities because it was the only channel of communication with society. The church weakened the blows of martial law and contributed decisively to the survival of independent social activity.

Faced with limited resistance, the government quickly shifted its attention to economic problems exacerbated by martial law.[11] To restore some semblance of order in consumer goods markets, effective 1 February 1982 prices were raised by 101.5 percent. Despite the 65 percent increase in nominal personal incomes, real personal incomes fell by almost 20 percent. Although the curtailed purchasing power of the population reduced the lines in front of stores, equilibrium was not achieved.

Anxious to demonstrate its commitment to the economic reform program adopted by the 9th PUWP Congress, as well as to justify martial law, the authorities proceeded to implement a legal foundation of the reform, which began with the two laws on state enterprise and on workers' self-management enacted by the Sejm on 25 September 1981. The first half of 1982 witnessed feverish legal activity; altogether, seventeen bills were enacted by the Sejm, whereas the Council of Ministers passed about one hundred bills that set new

[9] Józef Glemp's remarks at the meeting with Warsaw clergy on 7 December 1982. See *Zeszyty Historyczne* (Paris) 64 (1983): 207–10.

[10] See *Solidarność Biuletyn Informacyjny* (Paris) 10: 12–13.

[11] For an assessment of economic costs of the Polish war, see Fallenbuchl (1984).

rules for planning and management. With the benefit of hindsight, one may argue that this was the most innovative period in the search for new solutions.

However, because of a conflict between the decentralizing logic of reform and the unitary, centralizing logic of military rule, this search was conceptually misguided. The measures introduced eroded some components of the command system, but not enough to assure its elimination. In spite of significant changes, the old system reasserted itself under the new guise of reform measures. The authorities wasted a unique opportunity to exploit the powers amassed under martial law.

Although the measures to activate the private sector fell short of effectively ending unequal treatment of this sector, the law enacted by the Sejm on 6 July 1982 offered incentives for foreigners to establish small enterprises in Poland. These foreign firms—called Polonia firms because their owners were mainly foreigners of Polish descent—eased shortages of some consumer goods. However, the authorities imposed strict limitations on their expansion.

As compared with the economically disastrous performance in 1982, there was a marked improvement in living standards and availability of consumer products beginning in 1983. The increased political stability prompted the government to enact new union laws dismantling Solidarity (October 1982) and to release Solidarity's Chairman Lech Wałęsa from jail (November 1982). These actions set the stage for lifting martial law on 21 July 1983 on the eve of Poland's Communist holiday.

PHASE 2: THE "ILLUSION OF STABILIZATION" (1983–1986)

Three important features depicted this phase: first, the changes in the Polish legal system designed to make the special powers granted by the decree of martial law permanent; second, the tilt in government policies toward national conciliation; and third, the derailment of economic reform.

The months preceding and immediately following the lifting of martial law witnessed a flurry of legislative activity. The legislative package submitted to the Sejm sanctioned the practices of martial law. It encompassed such diverse proposals as the law extending the authority of the Ministry of Internal Affairs, censorship, higher education, constitutional amendments, amendments to the penal code, and special regulations designed for a period of overcoming the socioeconomic crisis.[12] Because of the opposition of the church, not all proposals submitted were enacted before martial law was lifted. Some proposals were withdrawn, whereas others were reworded.

The common denominator of the laws enacted throughout 1983 was that they formally restricted civil freedoms and extended the authority of the state. For example, the amendments to the penal code drastically limited freedom of association and of demonstration. The jurisdiction of military courts, whose

---

[12] For a detailed analysis, see Cave (1983), Hauser (1984), and Strzelecka (1985).

procedures could be closed to the public and whose sentences could not be appealed to the Supreme Court, was extended to civilian cases like terrorism, conspiracy against the state, sabotage, subversion, physical assault, and the "dissemination of information detrimental to the interest of the Polish state" (Cave 1983, 10). Needless to say, the qualifications as to what constituted an action in one of those categories rested with the judicial system subordinated to the state.

By granting the National Defense Committee absolute powers during peacetime, the amendments to the constitution legalized the involvement of the military in civilian life. One of the amendments distinguished between "a state of war" and "a state of emergency"—the former was to be imposed in response to an external threat whereas the latter would be in response to an internal threat. The National Defense Committee would replace the government after either the imposition of martial law or the declaration of a state of emergency. A "state of emergency" could be imposed by the chairman of the Council of State. The proclamation of a "state of war" required a decision of the Council of State. As a result, the previous legal "inconvenience" responsible for the illegality of the decision to introduce martial law was removed.[13]

The other amendments were an exercise in political tokenism. They concerned the replacement of the now defunct Front of National Unity with the Patriotic Movement of National Rebirth (PRON). This was to be a new vehicle of "national unity." Other amendments added a statement about realization of workers' aspirations to the list of objectives of the Polish Peoples' Republic and ensured the permanence of private agriculture.

The law on the Ministry of Internal Affairs was designed to strengthen the security apparatus of the state. It sanctioned the independence of the security service from the police and removed legal limitations on the invasion of privacy for "particularly dangerous political opponents." The criteria for delineating what amounts to a politically dangerous act were not specified. The law was erroneously characterized by the Polish Helsinki Committee as "the legal expression of the process begun on 13 December 1981 consisting of a constant increase in the importance of the police element."[14] The law amounted to a de facto legalization of actions practiced with fluctuating intensity since the Communist takeover in Poland. The security forces have always played a focal role under state socialism.

The "special regulations" were to apply only during the period of socio-economic crisis. The deadline for overcoming the crisis was optimistically set

[13] Prior to the amendments, the Council of State, when the Sejm was not in session, and the Sejm had authority to impose martial law. On December 12, when the Council of State introduced martial law, the Sejm was in session. Therefore, the decision was illegal.

[14] *Analiza prawna sytuacji po zniesieniu stanu wojennego* (Legal analysis of the after–martial law situation), Polish Helsinki Committee, in *Kultura Niezalezna*, no. 8, quoted in Cave (1983, 3).

for the end of 1985. The regulations that linked economic recovery with social stability curtailed the rights of workers' self-management and the autonomy of universities and creative associations and imposed restrictions on labor mobility.

These acts were portrayed by the authorities as a sign of commitment to the Gdańsk Agreements of August 1980. The authorities' claims can be, however, dismissed as sheer propaganda. The new laws were a sign of realization by the authorities that the political and legal system had to be remodeled if it was to cope with new realities in the political situation in the 1980s. In a sense, these laws were a testimony to growing weaknesses of the socialist state.[15] The level of overt repression in socialist states has never been shaped by existing laws. In fact, Stalinist repressions occurred under the aegis of the constitution that guaranteed human rights as they were stipulated in the UN Universal Declaration of Human Rights. As Jadwiga Staniszkis (1984) noted, the weakening of the PUWP grip over society in the 1970s was accompanied by legislative action designed to legalize the leading role of the Communist party. By sanctioning the existent situation, the new laws bridged the gap between actual practices and legal regulations.

The lifting of martial law marked the beginning of a search by the authorities for a modus vivendi with society. It was based on the recognition that containment of the most pressing societal demands had weakened the state's capacity to govern. This recognition stemmed from the official diagnosis that the appeal of underground Solidarity was declining and political polarization of society was decreasing.

The shift toward accommodation with society was also propelled by the regime's search for domestic legitimacy through improved relations with the West.[16] Although each anniversary or party conference was preceded by an increased intensity in police raids and detention, the shift consisted of a series of amnesties for political prisoners, the dropping of indictments against the KOR, more relaxed policies toward the opposition, and the rather surprising approach to the Popiełuszko case.

The second phase of normalization was marked by three amnesties, each of which curtailed the conditions for the release of political prisoners. The first amnesty for political prisoners in 1983, which coincided with the announcement terminating martial law, was limited. Except for women and males under

[15] A symptom of the authorities' weakness was an astounding, even by Communist standards, disregard for legal procedures concerning the submission of proposals. The authorities clearly did not believe that the Sejm would act like a rubber stamp. For an eyewitness account, see Strzelecka (1985).

[16] After the 1984 amnesty for political prisoners, the U.S. government allowed the resumption of Polish-American scientific exchanges and regularly scheduled flights to the U.S. by the Polish airline, LOT. Following the 1986 unconditional amnesty, all the remaining American sanctions were lifted (cf. Hardt and Boone 1987).

age 21 who were unconditionally released, the amnesty included only those who were sentenced to less than three years in prison and were not charged under section 19 of the penal code with crimes against the essential political interests of the Polish People's Republic. Therefore, the amnesty did not include the KOR and Solidarity leaders. Even for those who fell under the provisions of the amnesty, the amnesty was conditional on their good behavior until the end of 1985 (i.e., until the special regulations were to be abrogated). The amnesty also had provisions promising that no proceedings would be taken against those in hiding who reported to the authorities by 31 October 1983. As a result, the 1983 amnesty neither significantly reduced the number of political prisoners nor put an end to political trials. Given its limited scope, it neither triggered a wave of popular support for General Jaruzelski nor damaged his regime in the eyes of the party-state apparatus or the Kremlin.

The second amnesty was announced on 21 July 1984 on the eve of the national holiday celebrating the fortieth anniversary of the Polish People's Republic. In contrast to the 1983 amnesty, neither the length of sentence imposed for "politically motivated offenses" nor people sentenced (or accused) under section 19 of the penal code were excluded from the amnesty.[17] Like the 1983 amnesty, however, it made the release conditional upon "good conduct" until the end of 1985.

The amnesty provided the authorities with a face-saving opportunity to drop charges against the "eleven": four KOR members and seven Solidarity leaders.[18] They were accused of attempting to overthrow the state by force. This charge, which carried a maximum penalty of the death sentence was later reduced to "preparing the overthrow." The KOR members were accused of "undertaking in Warsaw and other towns in Poland, as well as abroad, with the aim of overthrowing the system by force and weakening the defense capability of the Polish People's Republic by breaking its alliance with the Soviet Union, and in agreement with people subject to other proceedings, preparatory activities aimed at implementing this goal."[19]

Fearing that the trial would be politically damaging, the authorities sought ways to release them in the fall of 1983 when they started negotiations with the church on this subject. In early 1984, the United Nations—through its envoy Mr. Emilio de Olivares—became a party to the negotiations. The offer

---

[17] See *Trybuna Ludu* (Warsaw), 22 July 1984.

[18] Among the KOR members were Jacek Kuroń, Adam Michnik, Henryk Wujec, and Zbigniew Romaszewski. They all were accused of plotting the overthrow of the state by force (maximum penalty—ten years in prison). Except for Romaszewski who was arrested in August 1982 (then sentenced to four and one-half years in prison), the others have been detained since 13 December 1981. The seven Solidarity leaders were Andrzej Gwiazda, Seweryn Jaworski, Marian Jurczyk, Karol Modzelewski, Grzegorz Palka, Andrzej Rozpłochowski, and Jan Rulewski.

[19] See "The Indictment against KOR," *Poland Watch* 4 (1983): 34 (An English translation of an abridged version published in *Biuletyn Informacyjny*, Paris, no. 75).

of a "de facto expulsion from Poland for some time and a UN guaranteed return" was rejected by all the prisoners. A subsequent offer of a pledge to give up political activity for a period of two and one-half years was also turned down. After the indictment was read, the trial was twice adjourned until the amnesty under which all the accused were released.

Contrary to what some Solidarity leaders anticipated, the prisons did not again become overcrowded with political prisoners.[20] However, repression continued and a number of opposition activists were again jailed. In 1985, several Solidarity activists were either convicted of activities in an "illegal union" (Władysław Frasyniuk, Bogdan Lis, and Adam Michnik) or were detained (Czesław Bielecki, Bogdan Borusewicz, Zbigniew Bujak, and Tadeusz Jedynak) under the charge of preparing to overthrow "the constitutional order of People's Poland by force" (Vinton Stefanowski, and Swidlicka 1988, 266). The leaders of the Confederation of Independent Poland (Leszek Moczulski, Krzysztof Król, Adam Słomka, and Dariusz Wojcik) were convicted in April 1986. However, repression became more selective and declined overall. Visible social protests also decreased.

The inability to launch strikes and the declining appeal of street demonstrations (because of their apparent ineffectiveness to force political change) shifted the focus of opposition activity to the church. With the banning of Solidarity, the state apparatus and the church remained the main actors on the political scene. Since the imposition of martial law, both of them had been involved in a two-track policy—cooperation at the highest level between the leadership of respective hierarchies and confrontation at lower levels.

The mixture of cooperation and confrontation was not necessarily by design, but more the result of the tolerance by leaders in higher layers of activity carried out at lower layers of their respective hierarchies. Priests tended to be more responsive to demands and expectations of their parishioners. Many of them, in defiance of Glemp's policy of not becoming directly involved in the conflict between the authorities and opposition, strongly identified themselves with the political agenda of underground Solidarity.[21] Similarly, members of a repressive apparatus, who have a natural urge to remove all independent forms of public life, may have been infuriated by the government's policy,

[20] The statement (24 July 1984) signed by Lech Wałęsa and six other Solidarity leaders argued that a return to the Gdańsk Agreements could only guarantee that the "prisons will [not] . . . be filled by the victims of anti-union repression" (*Uncensored Poland*, no. 15 [1984], as quoted in *Poland Watch*, 6 [1986]: 11).

[21] The primate held several meetings with the most activist priests. In his 1983 Christmas message, he called on all priests to moderate their sermons to avoid unnecessary clashes between the state and the church. (See *Uncensored Poland*, London, no. 24, 1983.) Some priests did not obey. For instance, Father Mieczysław Nowak from Ursus, one of the strongholds of legal Solidarity, was transferred by the primate to some obscure rural parish. This triggered massive protests by Ursus parishioners, which were widely publicized in Western media. (See, for example, *New York Times*, 16 February 1984).

which officially respected the church's autonomy. Given the secrecy surrounding the functioning of the security forces, it is impossible to identify which of numerous police actions taken against priests were "spontaneous" and which were directly approved by the government.

Therefore, there is no evidence to support the idea that the killing of Father Popiełuszko was ordered by General Jaruzelski.[22] However, there are grounds to argue that his death was indirectly the result of the campaign to harass priests that was launched by the government in 1983. Its purpose was to intimidate the church and the opposition. Several priests were subjected to police harassment. An advisor and a close friend of Lech Wałęsa, Father Henryk Jankowski, was accused of antistate activity. Cases of attempted arson of priests' houses, breaking of windows in churches, and so forth, were also reported. The underlying motive was the harassment of pro-Solidarity activities.

The murder of Father Jerzy Popiełuszko of the St. Stanisław Kostka parish in Warsaw on 19 October 1984 by three officials of the security forces was the result of exacerbation of the tensions between the church and the state repression apparatus by the government's actions. His outspokenness at regular monthly "masses on behalf of the Fatherland," which began in April 1982 and used to draw enormous crowds, had long been a target of police harassment. In December 1983, he was charged with the production and possession of machine gun ammunition as well as leaflets calling for a national uprising.[23] Between January and July 1984, he was subjected to all sorts of harassment: he was kept under constant police surveillance; his apartment was ransacked several times; he received telephone threats; and he was frequently interrogated. After the amnesty the official press campaign against him continued.[24] These developments created conditions conducive to Father Popiełuszko's murder.

Although there was nothing atypical in the attempts of the repression apparatus to contain the activism of some priests, the authorities' response was not typical for a "normalized" Communist regime. The official reaction was that Father Popiełuszko's abduction and later, as it turned out, his murder, was an antigovernment provocation. It revealed fears that the incident would erode

---

[22] Some opposition activists, for example, Jacek Kuroń (1985), argued that a murder was instigated by the group within the Ministry of Internal Affairs opposed to its chief, General Kiszczak. The fact that one of the officials of the ministry was informed two weeks prior to the killing that Father Popiełuszko would be leaving soon for the Vatican gives some support to this theory. Nonetheless, the trial left many questions unanswered.

[23] There is little doubt that the charges were trumped up. According to the Polish underground press (KOS, no. 46, 1984, quoted in Latynska [1984]), the priest had not lived in the apartment in which these items were found.

[24] It is worth noting that the government spokesman Jerzy Urban, under his pseudonym Jan Rem, in an article published in Tu i teraz 19 September 1984 referred to Father Popiełuszko, as a political fanatic dedicated to inciting hatred toward everything that postwar Poland stood for.

the limited progress that the government had achieved in extending its political base. Bringing to trial the security force officials, an unusual development during periods of "political normalization," reflected the government's determination to demonstrate its innocence and to impose direct controls over internal security activity. In view of the public reaction, sacrificing four individuals to protect the integrity of the repressive apparatus was a small price.

The decision to put the security officials on trial earned General Jaruzelski praise at home and in the West. The trial was only halfway effective, because many questions regarding the possible involvement of other security officials in the murder remained unanswered.[25] From the perspective of hindsight, the Father Popiełuszko case was the high point in the confrontation between the government and the church during the second phase of normalization; subsequently, tensions started to decrease.

Although the Father Popiełuszko case marked the end of the insidious campaign to harass militant priests, it did not lessen the government's reliance on security forces. Their use was less overt, however, as the conditions and circumstances following the amnesty announced on 23 July 1986 demonstrated. The amnesty's objective was to show the government's generosity in not capitalizing on the alleged effectiveness of its internal security forces. The amnesty was conditional on the political prisoners' pledge to refrain from oppositional activity.[26] The amnesty was also extended to those political offenders who would voluntarily surrender to the authorities before 31 December 1986. They were also to detail their activities and pledge "good behavior" in the future. To show the proficiency of the repressive apparatus, three thousand opposition activists were interviewed in the weeks following the amnesty. The interviewers demonstrated extensive knowledge of the interviewees' activities and apparently sought to prove the futility of underground action.

The interviews preceded the announcement of an unconditional release of all political prisoners on 15 September 1986. The statement of the Polish episcopate described the amnesty as a "chance for the closure of a painful period of our history."[27] Contrary to the hopes of the church hierarchy and opposition activists, the amnesty did not lead to a dialogue between the opposition and the government. Contrary to the government's expectations, the decision did not elicit enthusiastic public response. The gratitude was aimed at the church

[25] There is a strong sentiment that more security officials were involved than the four who were brought to trial. General Jaruzelski took over the responsibility of supervising "ideological work" at the ministry from Mr. Milewski (former minister of Internal Affairs), then a member of the Politburo, later dismissed. The death of two security officials involved in the investigation in a car accident raised a spate of new questions about a cover-up hastily arranged by the authorities.

[26] The bill pardoned only those who gave "grounds for the expectation that they will actively join public life in Poland and will not return to crime" (Vinton, Stefanowski, and Świdlicka 1988, 265).

[27] The statement released on September 15 by the press office of the Polish Episcopate (quoted in Vinton, Stefanowski, and Świdlicka [1988], 269.

and at the Western governments that linked the improvement in relations with the improvement in the human rights situation in Poland.

Political changes towards greater liberalization and human rights were not accompanied by similar changes in the economic sphere. To the contrary, political changes moved in the direction opposite to the implemented economic reform measures. A limited withdrawal from the aspiration to control all domains of public life accompanied by a temporary improvement in the economy did not activate the drive toward de-etatization of the economy.

The second phase of normalization witnessed the derailment of economic reform. The great push toward the reform during 1981 and 1982 was followed by a reversal and the increased dominance of ad hoc interventions. The economic system that emerged by 1986 was succinctly described as a "hybrid, often resulting in mutual blockade of old and new components."[28] The new institutions reasserted their direct controls over enterprises. The ministries encouraged centralization under the guise of reform. Public economic policies were a simple continuation of the strategy responsible for the economic crisis. The conspicuous absence of change in economic policies illustrated that pressures toward liberalization in the economy did not acquire as much public support as those in the political sphere.

The regressive evolution of the economic system awakened public opinion only when the government submitted to the Sejm in October 1986 the draft of the legislative package calling for institutional changes in the economic system. In contrast to the usual procedures, the government submitted the draft directly to the Sejm without consulting the independent Commission on Economic Reform, which was in charge of monitoring the implementation of economic reforms. The draft mobilized proreform-minded members of the institutional establishment who had so far remained indifferent to the derailment of the program. Although it sought to remove the discrepancies between the legal foundation of the reform and the actual practice of increasingly centralized controls,[29] it triggered an unexpectedly strong, negative reaction from influential economists and journalists. Bowing to the pressures, the government publicly admitted its mistake and withdrew the draft. This was presented in the official media as evidence of a "democratization" of the political system.

The draft proposed a drastic curtailment of the autonomy of enterprises, workers' councils, and regional authorities. The Polish economist, Tomasz Jeziorański (1986b, 3) gave the following assessment:

[28] The editorial on the question of the second stage of economic reform. *Życie Gospodarcze* 50 (1986): 4.

[29] A de facto recentralization of the economy began in 1983. For instance, the contract prices were frozen, and the portion of national income passing through the state budget, which is the most synthetic measure of recentralization, had been increasing rapidly. See chapter 2.

> Unfortunately, the most depressing aspect of the proposed package is the abandon-
> ment of this [decentralizing] philosophy in favor of the central administration assum-
> ing full responsibility for economic performance. This is an impossible task. History
> has demonstrated it repeatedly. This reorientation cannot be reconciled with authen-
> tic economic coercion of captivated enterprises and their employees. . . . The co-
> ercion will not substantiate, and neither will responsibility, without autonomy.

Judging by numerous articles in professional journals and newspapers, this
view was shared by majority of Polish economists. Interestingly, the proposed
package was in direct conflict with the program of economic reforms adopted
by the 9th Party Congress.[30]

The withdrawal of the package coincided with the establishment of the Social Consultative Council, attached to the Council of State and headed by General Jaruzelski. Jan B. Weydenthal (1988, 271) observed that this "implied
[the government's] recognition that all other attempts to reach the people
through available institutions had failed." However, its political impact was
short-lived. The problem was that the council's prerogatives remained ambiguous. Its institutional responsibilities were not defined. In a sense, the council
was designed as the personal institution of General Jaruzelski. Its role and
significance remained Jaruzelski's whims. He could use it as an extra channel
to provide the views of independent and knowledgeable individuals. However,
nothing compelled him to respond to their advice. Bowing to the request of
some invited members, Jaruzelski promised that recommendations of council
members would be reported uncensored in the mass media.

In an apparent attempt to reach the people, an invitation to participate in the
council was extended to the members of the institutional establishment and the
"moderate" opposition. Many opposition activists reportedly declined; only
a chairman of the church-supported Warsaw's Catholic Intelligentsia Club and
a former legal advisor to Solidarity accepted the invitation under some conditions.[31] The appointed members shared some common traits: many of them
were victims of earlier Communist repression; a substantial proportion of them
were not party members; most of them never occupied highly visible political
positions in the government or party hierarchy; and, a good number of them
had outstanding achievements in their respective professions. Of the fifty-six
members appointed by Jaruzelski, one-third of the total represented officialdom; one-third the realistic and church-oriented opposition; and one-third the

---

[30] The "package" also conflicted with the general tone of Jaruzelski's speeches. See, for instance, his speech at the Katowice Party Conference in October 1986.

[31] Andrzej Świecicki resigned from the chairmanship after accepting Jaruzelski's invitation.
Władysław Siła-Nowicki, an eminent Polish lawyer and defender of a number of opposition activists, requested that council members have access to all information relevant to their discussions
and that the media publish uncensored accounts of the meetings.

independent professionals, many of whom were previously "harmed" by the Communists.

In the short term, the emergence of the council was politically significant for two reasons. First, the government managed to retain the initiative and maintain suspense among the public about the future political course. As one observer noted, "This confirmed the authorities' willingness to make new departures in politics, suggesting both determination and resourcefulness" (Weydenthal 1988, 271) The decision was in line with Jaruzelski's promise that the opponents would not be overpowered but instead would be won over. Second, the idea of the council not only took the opposition by surprise, it planted seeds of discord among the opposition, which had been struggling to organize itself in the wake of political amnesty. The establishment of the council and the full amnesty demonstrated that the government chose a co-optation rather than confrontation strategy vis-à-vis society. In the long-run, the institution had little impact on political dynamics.

Although the government succeeded in checking its opponents, it proved incapable of reversing the economic decline. Its capacity to suppress the opposition was not accompanied by an improvement in the directive capacity of the state in the economic realm. Indeed, given the scope of contraction from 1978 to 1982, the recovery was rather slow and fell short of the objectives set in subsequent plans and programs. Inflation, which the government pledged to get under control by 1985, persisted. In addition, real personal incomes, depressed by about 27 percent in 1982, but which registered a 7 percent increase in 1985, expanded by only 2 percent in 1986.

The most visible signs of political activism were contained, and societal autonomy was curtailed during the second phase. However, the situation did not become normalized in the sense of restoration of control by the state based on fear of repression and persecution. Indeed, the defiance, passive or active, to the state socialist political order became "normalized." The opposition remained unusually vital and large by Communist standards. As one observer succinctly noted: "What has become normal in Poland is not the old political system but the resistance to it" (Ost 1985, 78). Nonetheless, the authorities demonstrated skills in defusing the opposition and social conflicts by introducing measures that loosened the political system.

It is tempting to interpret liberalizing measures introduced by the government as signs of weakness. Clearly, had the government been able to mobilize society by using "traditional" means of state socialism, it would have not followed a policy of limited conciliation. On the other hand, had the opposition been able to mobilize society around its program, the government would have been under strong pressure to resort to more violent means. None of these had been the case, however, because neither the state nor the opposition could rally society. The combined effect of a weak opposition and deteriorating economic performance caused the issue of economic reform to rise to the top of the government's political agenda during the next phase.

PHASE 3: THE "BELATED SEARCH TO BREAK THE DEADLOCK" (1987–1989)

The common feature underlying this period was a failure to infuse viability into the economy, which eventually forced the authorities to negotiate with the opposition. The decision to negotiate was the government's acknowledgment of the failure of normalization. The major events of the third phase of normalization included the debate on the second stage of economic reform; the nationwide referendum on economic reform; and two waves of strikes that eventually led to the fall of the government headed by Zbigniew Messner and a dialogue with Solidarity. While in the civil rights sphere, this phase was characterized by the continuation of the state's withdrawal from controlling areas that did not directly threaten the regime's survival; economic problems exerted increasing pressure on political developments.

The growing recognition that the institutional framework of the old system had been the main impediment to economic recovery triggered debate on economic reform. Various official bodies were charged with the task of submitting theses for public discussion.[32] In spring 1987, the Secretariat of the Commission for Economic Reform submitted a rather extensive list of 174 theses.[33]

"Tezy" did not go significantly beyond the ideas contained in the program "Kierunki" adopted by the 9th Party Congress in 1981. Repetition of the same ideas validated the opinion of those who argued that there had been no first stage. Like "Kierunki," they were the result of compromise between contrasting visions of an economic order: one based on the market and the other on direct intervention. For example, the theses still insisted on the viability of fusing the state and the market mechanism for allocating and coordinating economic activity.

There were, however, two significant differences. First, the theses were much more export oriented. The authors sought to take into account Poland's external indebtedness; the conspicuous absence of debt-servicing considerations in "Kierunki" was rather striking. The "Tezy" called for a radical switch from direct to indirect controls on foreign trade based on exchange rates, tax exemption, and access to foreign exchange earnings. Interestingly,

[32] In addition to the Commission of Economic Reform, various subcommittees of the party-state Commission for the Review and Modernization of the Organizational Structures of the Economy and the State became involved in this task. The subcommittee for the Review of Organizational Structures of the Economy, for instance, presented its own text "Tezy w spawie ksztaltowania struktur organizacyjnych gospodarki" (Theses on shaping organizational structures in the economy) in May 1987.

[33] "Tezy w sprawie II etapu reformy gospodarczej" (Theses on the second stage of economic reform) published in April 1987, supp. no. 102, were grouped into three major categories: the objectives of the second stage (theses 1–27); suggested solutions (28–166); and principles of implementation (167–74).

the reform of foreign trade was consistently implemented during 1987 and 1988, contributing significantly to a 21-percent surge in hard currency exports during the first three quarters in 1988.[34] Foreign trade was the only area in which the reform moved forward by December 1988.

Second, in a marked contrast to "Kierunki," the theses finally overcame the taboo of private entrepreneurship, which was one of the sacrosanct ideological principles of state socialism. The program of the second stage of economic reform adopted in October 1987 promised an end to the discrimination of the private sector. Specifically, it called for the enactment of two major pieces of legislation that would remove direct administrative controls concerning the entry of private firms and of foreign capital. In November 1988, after more than a yearlong debate, the drafts of the law on undertaking economic activity and on joint foreign ventures were submitted to the Sejm. Despite the strong resistance of the Democratic Party and organizations representing handicraft and private service sectors, the proposed law on undertaking economic activity did not impose limits on employment and drastically curtailed the powers of local authorities to refuse the registration of new private firms.[35] This amounted to a genuine change in the rules underlying economic activity of the private sector.[36]

Following the debate, the government prepared the program of the implementation of the second stage of economic reform. The program included a package of measures designed to assure equilibria in the economy through a combination of price increases and supply-stimulating measures, and to liberalize the central planning system by curtailing the powers of the central economic administration and by restructuring the banking system.[37] The economy was to be revived by a viable combination of planning and an effective "self-regulatory market mechanism."[38] It is noteworthy that this was also the objective of the first stage of reform.

[34] The government pursued a very aggressive exchange rate policy designed to keep at least 80 percent of its exports profitable. For instance, as a result of frequent devaluations, the zloty fell against the U.S. dollar by about 60 percent throughout 1987. As of December 1988, the official exchange rate was still below its shadow market or tourist exchange rate.

[35] See *Polityka*, no. 48, 26 November 1988.

[36] Mieczysław Wilczek, minister of Industry in Rakowski's cabinet, was right in arguing that the law amounted to a "historic breakthrough . . . a return to the Polish road to well-being [taken] in the first years in the aftermath of the war." See his interview, *Polityka*, no. 48, 26 November 1988, p. 4.

[37] See the government official documents: "Tezy w sprawie II etapu reformy gospodarczej" (Theses on the second stage of economic reform); and "Tezy w sprawie kształtowania struktur organizacyjnych" (Theses on shaping organizational structures in the economy). For the assessment of economic reform by the Provisional Council and Provisional Coordinating Commission of NSZZ "Solidarność," see Solidarity Provisional Council (1987). The assessment by the "official" Trade Union Confederation (OPZZ) has been presented in Trade Union Confederation (1987).

[38] The term is borrowed from the government's "Tezy w sprawie kształtowania struktur organizacyjnych gospodarki" (Theses on shaping organizational structures in the economy), 1987.

The program warned of inevitable belt-tightening measures during a transition to the new economic system because the equilibrium in the economy was to be obtained initially through demand-suppressing measures.

The program called for price increases, which triggered a negative response from both official trade unions and Solidarity leaders. In the resolution on the program of the second stage, the Council of the "official" Trade Unions' Confederation noted that the realization of the economic reform had been associated with the price increases.[39] Although it accepted the objective of the program (i.e., an economic system "suitably combining the advantages of central planning and market economy"),[40] the council rejected revision of the income-price policy. In an unusually bold statement, the resolution warned that if the government raised prices, the council would demand full compensation.[41]

Solidarity's official statement also advocated market-oriented reforms and equal treatment of all enterprises independently of their ownership. It differed, however, in some important respects from both the government's program and the official trade union "alternative concept." The most crucial difference was that it explicitly recognized the institutional and social forces blocking the implementation of the reform. "Our concept of reforms," Solidarity's experts noted, "differs, however, from that of the authorities; we understand reform to mean fundamental change that reaches to the very root of the problem."[42]

Not surprisingly, Solidarity's experts linked the success of economic reform to democratization of the political environment. They called for the abolishment of the nomenklatura system, which "is the ultimate source of inefficiency."[43] The report argued that by allowing independent social action, that is, the restoration, among others, of trade union pluralism, the institutional counterweight to command planning would emerge. This would overcome social apathy and indifference, bolstering productivity and providing social support for the reform. As a result, Poland would regain access to international financial markets.[44] Like the "official" Trade Union Confederation, Solidar-

[39] See "Uchwala Rady Ogolnopolskiego Porozumienia Zwiazkow Zawodowych z dnia 23 listopada 1987 roku" (Resolution of the Council of the Trade Union Confederation adopted on 23 November 1987), *Punkt Widzenia*, OPZZ, no. 16.

[40] Quoted from Trade Union Confederation (1987) elaborated by experts of the OPZZ, September 1987, 13.

[41] See n. 40, Trade Union Confederation (1987, 3). It is noteworthy that in line with this resolution the official trade union protested against the price increases in March 1988. Rakowski (1987, 19) raises an interesting question whether chairman of the union, Alfred Miodowicz, as a member of the Politburo, objected to the decision at its meetings.

[42] *NSZZ Solidarność on Reforming the Economy*, approved by Lech Wałęsa, Brussels, August 1987, p. 17. Mimeo.

[43] Ibid., 20.

[44] Ibid., 28.

ity leadership pointed to threats to reform and social stability if the government were to rely mainly on the austerity measures.

Although the price-income operation was but one of many measures contemplated by the government, it rose to the peak of the political agenda. More over, it became identified by the public with reform, as the experts of the "official" Trade Union Confederation rightly predicted. A referendum, an unprecedented move to obtain social support by the Communist authorities through direct voting, essentially concentrated on the issue of consumer prices. The program of radical reform that implied drastic price increases gained the approval of the majority of those voting (67 percent). However, according to Polish law, the majority was counted against the total of eligible voters, so the plan was technically defeated.[45] Taking into account that the proposed price-income operation met with strong resistance from not only the opposition but the establishment, it was rather surprising that the government's plan garnered such support.[46] The authorities thus promised the implementation of a less radical variant of the second stage.

In spite of widespread criticism, the government went ahead with the price-income operation, albeit the prices were to be increased less than envisaged in the radical variant of the operation. The 30 percent price increases introduced in February and again in April 1988 were accompanied by a flat monthly wage adjustment of Zł 6,000, the equivalent of approximately 18 percent of the average monthly wage in the state industrial sector in 1987. In addition, enterprise capacity to pass production cost increases to consumers exacerbated inflationary pressures.[47]

The authorities sought to save the ill-designed program by centralizing powers of the government. The new law on emergency powers of the government was adopted by the Sejm on 11 May 1988. It authorized the government to direct ad hoc interventions to "accelerate the processes of decentralization in the management of the national economy."[48] The government was authorized to suspend or change prices, taxes, and enterprise management, and to fuse or diffuse state enterprises, etc. Although one might make a strong argument that the implementation of the decentralizing reform measures might require a con-

[45] The participation rate was 67 percent, and 66 percent voted in favor of the government's plan. Because those not voting were counted as against, the government obtained 44 percent.

[46] The price-income operation was criticized by the influential Consultative Economic Council and the usually loyal to the government, Polish Economic Association.

[47] During the first three quarters of 1988, the prices of consumer products and services increased by 53.6 percent. In September 1988, they were 63.8 percent higher than in September 1987. See Życie Gospodarcze, no. 42 (1988). The irony was that the rate of inflation in 1988 (estimated at 66 percent) amounted to a de facto fulfillment of a radical price variant that was rejected by the Sejm. The government-planned price increases were expected to raise the inflation rate from 20 percent in 1987 to 40 percent in 1988. See the Wall Street Journal, 6 November 1987.

[48] See Dziennik Ustaw (The registrar of acts), no. 13, 12 May 1988, 205.

siderable concentration of power to overcome political and social resistance, the measures actually implemented did not move the economic system toward decentralization. On the contrary, as Marek Dąbrowski (1988, 4) noted: "Under the banner of radical action and 'oxygenification' of the reform, most legislative proposals, which were included in the famous package of amendments [of the acts of economic reform] in the fall of 1986 and rejected because of strong public resistance, were introduced." Instead of creating conditions for enterprise autonomy and marketization, the scope of direct command management was extended. Again, the command-planning system revealed a remarkable capacity to reassert itself.

The second wave of strikes in August/September triggered two policy changes. First, in return for the promise of assistance in ending the strikes, the government invited Lech Wałęsa and his advisors to participate in a series of roundtable discussions.[49] A meeting between Wałęsa, Bishop Jerzy Dąbrowski (whose presence was requested by two sides, Kiszczak and Stanisław Ciosek, Secretary General of PRON) was held on August 31. According to the Polish Press Agency (PAP) communiqué, "the prerequisites for organizing a roundtable meeting and its procedure" were discussed.[50] That was the first meeting between Wałęsa and the government's representatives since 1981. In return for ending the strikes, the government recognized that Lech Wałęsa was not merely a private citizen, although spokesman Jerzy Urban had argued for the last five years that he was. Thus the "unthinkable" happened: Wałęsa was implicitly recognized as the leader of the opposition. The roundtable discussions were to begin in mid-October.[51]

The second change triggered by social resistance to the price-income policy was the dismissal of the government headed by Zbigniew Messner on 19 September 1988. During the August strikes, the Sejm established an Extraordinary Commission to Assess the Implementation of Economic Reform. Its report submitted to the Sejm called for "deep changes in the cabinet" and incorporating the experts "who had been critical of the mode of the reform implementation for a long time."[52] In response, Zbigniew Messner and his government submitted their resignation pending a vote by the Sejm. The Sejm overwhelmingly accepted their resignation.[53] Mieczysław F. Rakowski, deputy prime minister during the Solidarity period in 1980–1981 and then

[49] The possibility of a roundtable meeting with representatives of various social groups was mentioned by the interior minister General Czesław Kiszczak during a television appearance on 26 August 1988. Three days later, Lech Wałęsa stated that if the negotiations were undertaken to solve the "matter of Solidarity," the strikes would be suspended.

[50] See *Uncensored Poland* (London) nos. 16, 17(1988) (double issue).

[51] They actually began in January 1989. In the fall of 1988, many observers doubted whether they would take place at all. See *Radio Free Europe Research: Poland/18*, München, 25 November 1988, pp. 9–10. Mimeo.

[52] Quoted in *Polityka*, 24 September 1988, p. 4.

[53] The results were as follows: 359 accepted the resignation; 17 abstained; and 1 was against.

Politburo member in charge of ideology, was designated to form a new government.

Although the core of the new government was essentially the same as that of the previous government, personnel changes suggested that the fall of the Messner government was a result of its economic policies.[54] The purge affected those who were in charge of the economy. In contrast to Professor Messner's government in which "economic professors" dominated public economic policy making, Rakowski decided to turn to a "businessman" and a "manager" to fill the two most important economic positions in the government. Mieczysław Wilczek, a co-owner of the foreign firm was appointed Minister of Industry, and Dominik Jastrzębski, a director of a state-owned foreign trade enterprise, became Minister of Economic Cooperation with Abroad.

The new government adopted a more aggressive posture toward economic reform and a more confrontational stance toward the opposition. In various policy declarations, the new government committed itself to making radical moves to eradicate command planning. One of its first actions was the withdrawal of the proposed laws from the Sejm on undertaking economic activity and on joint ventures. More "liberalizing" versions were then resubmitted.[55] As was observed earlier, their enactment substantially changed the rules of the economic game by ending the discrimination of the private sector. It was also announced that several steelworks and the Gdańsk shipyard would be closed.[56] In line with the declared goal of marketization, the government also announced that peasants would no longer be compelled to sell their products at fixed prices to state-owned wholesale organizations. In other words, they would be able to choose among consumers on the basis of offered prices. Needless to say, this constituted an important move toward the genuine monetization of the agricultural sector.

The Rakowski government clearly rejected the road to economic reforms through a social anticrisis pact.[57] The approach was based on the conviction

---

[54] Ten cabinet members of the Messner government retained their positions: Aleksander Krawczuk, Culture; General Czesław Kiszczak, Interior; General Florian Siwicki, Defense; Tadeusz Olechowski, Foreign Affairs; General Michał Janiszewski, in charge of the office of the Council of Minsters; Władysław Loranz, Religion; Janusz Kamiński, Transport and Communications; Bogumił Ferensztajn, Construction; Jozef Kozioł (previously deputy prime minister), Natural Environment. *Polityka*, 22 October 1988, p. 6.

[55] The Catholic weekly *Tygodnik Powszechny* (6 November 1988, 1) usually critical of the government's policy, noted that this was a step in "the right direction."

[56] The list of steelworks includes those that were to be closed in the 1970s. The argument of their obsolescence was used to justify the decision to build the Katowice steelworks in the early 1970s.

[57] A term coined by Wałęsa's advisor Professor Bronisław Geremek. See his interview "An Anti-Crisis Pact for Poland?" *Tygodnik Mazowsze*, no. 255, 15 June 1988. For an English text, see *Uncensored Poland*, nos. 16/17, 10 September 1988, pp. 23–25.

that Solidarity was an obstacle to reforms and its support was irrelevant for the revival of the economy. By earmarking the Gdańsk shipyard for closing, Prime Minister Rakowski chose confrontation rather than cooperation. Although Rakowski repeatedly denied that the decision to close the shipyard was made on economic grounds, the decision had clear political implications; it was the birthplace of Solidarity. The dismantling of the Lenin shipyard would symbolize Solidarity's passage to "the dustbin of history." As such, it demonstrated the government's disdain for Solidarity and its commitment to revive the economy through shock therapy.

At the meeting with the Executive Committee of the "official" Trade Union Confederation, Premier Rakowski rejected the suggestion that the case of the Gdańsk shipyard was related to the "former Solidarity."[58] He observed, "I am not responsible for the politicization of decisions having purely economic character."[59] The critics were quick to point out that a number of other gigantic plants built during "socialist modernization" were much more heavily subsidized than the Lenin shipyard.[60]

Thus the case of the Gdańsk shipyard should be assessed in political rather than economic terms. The risk was considerable because it might have provoked another wave of strikes. Thus to reduce it, the government announced a program for its liquidation spread over more than one year that provided a safety net for the released workers. Assuming that Rakowski was serious about restructuring, a smooth closing of the Gdańsk shipyard would enhance his negotiating position when dealing with other large plants usually protected by the local authorities. However, this did not occur and the government again changed its approach to the opposition by agreeing to legalize Solidarity as a precondition for the roundtable negotiations.

The delay in the roundtable negotiations as well as the announced measures to restructure Polish industry indicated that liberalization was not to be extended to the political sphere. The government's objections to the list of Solidarity representatives in the negotiations made well-informed observers increasingly skeptical whether they would ever begin.[61]

Even the furor that the decision to close the Lenin shipyard stirred could not explain a sudden shift in the government's approach to the opposition.[62] It will

[58] *Życie Gospodarcze*, 47, 1988, 2.

[59] *Życie Gospodarcze*, 47, 1988, 2.

[60] In addition, during the first three quarters in 1988, its financial situation significantly improved, and there was a strong surge in international demand. During the first three quarters, the shipyard obtained from the state budget Zł 2.8 billion and paid in taxes Zł 4.8 billion. All obligations to domestic suppliers were paid, and its bank debt fell. Its rentability increased 10.3 percent in 1987 to 40 percent during the first ten months in 1988. The world prices increased in 1988 by about 20–25 percent. All data are from Dryll (1988, 3).

[61] See *Radio Free Europe Research: Poland/18*, Münich, 25 November 1988, p. 10. Mimeo.

[62] The official explanation that this was because of the change in the posture of Solidarity leadership is wanting because the idea of negotiations was first suggested by Solidarity. Lech Wałęsa,

probably remain a well-kept secret of political struggle in Poland in the fall of 1988 as to whether a decision to close Solidarity's birthplace was to test social support for Solidarity. Whatever the immediate reasons, a stormy 10th Plenum of the Central Committee, held in January 1989 in Warsaw, during which Jaruzelski narrowly won approval for negotiating the legalization of Solidarity came as a surprise. As Lech Wałęsa observed, "We were completely taken back by the government's opening."[63] At any rate, a favorable public reaction provided those in favor of legalizing Solidarity in return for political concessions with ammunition to quell opposition of official trade union activists and, probably, of vast segments of the party apparatus.[64] Thus, the view prevailed that economic and political stability would be impossible to maintain without limited power sharing with the opposition.

Whatever the reasons for vicissitudes in Rakowski's position, other deeply rooted developments provided incentives to serious negotiations. First, the two waves of strikes witnessed a grand "comeback" of Solidarity, which had lost much of its support after a full political amnesty in 1986 (Brumberg 1989b). The relegalization of Solidarity topped the list of demands of striking workers.[65]

Second, although the two waves of strikes were limited to a small number of factories,[66] they demonstrated the growing militancy of workers and increasing frustration of the populace. They served as a warning to the ruling elite that striking a compromise with a new generation of militant leaders would be impossible. The fears were succinctly expressed by Secretary of the Central Committee of the Communist party Leszek Miller who said, "It is easy to imagine a wave of anarchy and chaos and the eventual predominance of demagogues."[67]

Third, the authorities looked for political fixes to the persistent inability to revive the economy and gain legitimacy. Bringing the opposition within the confines of the political system offered the hope of legitimacy and increased

---

for instance, expressed a desire to talk with the authorities with no conditions attached in 1987 and 1988, and his advisor Bronisław Geremek called for an anticrisis pact in the spring of 1988. On the other hand, in spite of criticism, the government did not renege on its decision to close the shipyard. It only promised to carry liquidation over a period of several years and to provide a safety net for released workers.

[63] As quoted by Tadeusz Kowalik, *Życie Gospodarcze* 28 (1989).

[64] According to a poll conducted among party members, about 70 percent of respondents supported the decision of the 10th Plenum of the Central Committee of the Communist party to relegalize Solidarity and establish a "socialist parliamentary democracy." See Janusz Reykowski, interview in *Polityka*, 16 (1989): 7.

[65] Solidarity regained the right to legal existence on 17 April 1989.

[66] In 1980, for instance, more than seven hundred enterprises comprised the Interenterprise Strike Committee, whereas during August 1988 only five enterprises proved active (interview with Jacek Merkel, member of the National Executive Commission of NSZZ Solidarność, in *Solidarność News* [Brussels], 132 [16–30 April 1989].)

[67] Quoted in Jackson Diehl, *The Washington Post*, 6 February 1989.

governability. It would demonstrate that the system is legitimate enough to warrant participation in it. They probably expected that Solidarity would fill the gap between political extremes on both the right and left. In all, probably, they did not expect that the elections would bring Solidarity a landslide victory and push aside not only extremists but also party reformers.

The "roundtable" negotiations between the government coalition and the Solidarity opposition, successfully concluded on 7 April 1989 mark the beginning of the first phase of transition from disintegrating totalitarianism to democracy. Its provisions calling for democratic elections, albeit still restricted, promise to be a first step toward accountable government.

CONCLUSION

The late 1970s and the early 1980s witnessed a dramatic collapse of the ability of the ruling elite to use the party-state to maintain its hegemonic position. The state did not succeed in "normalizing" state socialism. As a keen observer of Polish politics noted, "Polish officialdom talks about 'normalization' so much, that all the stark evidence and even published accounts about the population's continued dissatisfaction no longer seem to matter: 'normality,' in the eyes of many, is simply the name for the present reality" (Ost 1985, 76).

The increased political activism by the previously passive masses that led to the emergence of Solidarity represented the greatest ideological and political challenge to the institutions of state socialism. It has produced a "general crisis of the socialist state." The crisis cannot be overcome without reforms opening the political system to the opposition and dismantling state socialism.

The Debt Trap

DURING the 1970s, the continuation of economic growth in Poland became increasingly dependent on external resources. This was best illustrated by the reversal of the relation between the Domestic Net Material Product (DNMP) and the Net Material Product (NMP), a crude measure of the balance of payments' current account. Until 1972 the DNMP had been higher than the NMP, which pointed to the net outflow of resources abroad. The relationship was reversed beginning in 1972. The ratio of the difference between the NMP and the DNMP to the DNMP grew from 0.27 percent (of the DNMP) in 1973 to 5.83 percent in 1976 (Fallenbuchl 1981a, 343). The hard currency debt increased from $1.8 billion in 1970 to $8.4 billion in 1975.

Faced with a growing external deficit, the Polish authorities launched the so-called "economic maneuver" in December 1976. The maneuver was portrayed by state propaganda in military terms as "a change in tactics while advancing." This slogan was embodied in the national plan for the 1976–1980 period, which envisaged a substantial reduction in real consumption and investment growth without a significant slowdown in economic growth. Given the increased dependence of newly built industrial capacities on Western supplies of raw materials and spare parts, the plan unrealistically assumed a substantial increase of exports to hard currency markets while simultaneously reducing imports from these countries (Bozyk 1983). Hence, at the very outset, the adjustment was ill-conceived and ignored the necessity of secondary imports. It was hoped, however, that once investment projects started in the early 1970s were completed, exports would generate sufficient revenues to improve Poland's balance of payments. On paper the policy option chosen was adjustment mainly through expenditure reduction.

Implementation faced the political problem of avoiding another confrontation with the workers. An attempt to cut the purchasing power of the population through an increase in food prices in June 1976 was effectively vetoed by the workers, and the authorities had to back up. Fear of the population's response to austerity measures dramatically reduced the range of expenditure-reducing options available to the authorities. As a result of political impotence to redress imbalances by directly cutting the population's purchasing power, the burden of adjustment fell on hard currency imports and investment. The initial plan was transformed into a series of poorly conceived and uncoordinated policy actions.

In the mid-1970s there was a clear need to reduce foreign borrowing in order to improve the balance between domestic expenditure and income. There was also a need to reduce the debt burden by rescheduling the payments of principals and interest. Had the authorities done so, the Polish pattern would have followed the earlier pattern of other socialist economies in the 1960s. This pattern consisted of two phases. The first was characterized by a simultaneous expansion of investment and trade deficits and the second by a contraction of investment and trade surpluses.[1] However, in Poland the second phase did not succeed the first, and the international debt increased beyond the levels that could be sustained by the Polish economy.

The relationship between interest rates and export growth rates sheds some light on debt sustainability (Cline 1984). Debt is regarded as sustainable if export revenues increase at a rate equal to the interest rate; the debt-servicing ratio remains then unchanged. In other words, to keep up with debt growth, exports must increase at least at the same rate as the interest rate when trade is balanced. If foreign trade is not balanced, exports must expand faster, depending on the size of the deficit and the initial level of indebtedness.

Between 1976 and 1979 the average interest rate was about 10 percent and so was Poland's hard currency export growth. With no new borrowing, the debt would be firmly under control. This was not the case, however. As can be readily seen in table B.1, two problems were related to sustainability of the debt. First, the Polish international debt expanded at an average annual rate of about 30 percent, which by far exceeded annual growth rates of foreign trade. In the period 1976–1979, debt increased almost twice as fast as the hard currency export; the ratio of annual debt to export growth rates varied widely from a maximum of 10.15 in 1976 to a minimum of 2.04 in 1979. Exports exceeded the increase in debt only in 1980. But all hard currency revenues in 1980 were not sufficient to meet payments on principal and interest falling due in 1981. This sluggish hard currency export performance was an indication that development programs had not produced a viable external sector.

The hard currency trade was not balanced, although the deficit was falling. The value of exports amounted to 60 percent of imports in 1976 and 1977 and improved slightly in 1978 and 1979 by increasing to 68 percent and 78 percent respectively. The persistent gap between debt and export growth rates showed that domestic consumption was excessive in relation to productive capabilities of the economy.

Given the levels of imports, hard currency export growth rates were too low either to close the trade gap or to keep debt growth in line with interest rates. This problem persisted despite negative or zero real interest rates between

[1] A contraction of investment activity would (1) reduce import demand for Western capital equipment; (2) free raw materials and intermediate products for export; and (3) weaken inflationary pressures in domestic consumer markets and thereby release some extra consumer goods for export (Stankovsky 1973).

TABLE B.1
Hard Currency Trade and Debt (in Billions of U.S. Dollars, Unless Otherwise Indicated)

	1976	1977	1978	1979	1980
Hard currency debt	11.4	13.9	17.8	21.0	25.1
Debt growth rates (percentage)	44.7	21.9	28.0	12.9	19.5
Export	4.4	4.9	5.5	6.3	8.0
Import	7.4	7.0	7.4	8.1	8.7
Trade balance	−3.0	−2.1	−2.1	−1.8	−0.8
Export growth (percentage)	7.7	11.1	11.2	11.4	27.0
Interest rates[a]	8.0	7.1	10.7	13.0	13.8

Sources: Driscoll (1982); *Mały Rocznik statystyczny* (1983); Fallenbuchl (1985).

[a] Calculated as the sum of the London Interbank Offer Rate (LIBOR) and spreads charged to all Least Developed Countries (LDCs) from data in *World Development Report* (1980, 1985).

1976 and 1978 when the inflation rates in Western economies exceeded interest rates. To close the trade gap, exports would have had to increase by 97 percent in 1976, 70 percent in 1977, 67 percent in 1978, and 66 percent in 1979.[2] Allowing for an increase in convertible currency debt at annual growth rates equal to the interest rates, exports would have had to increase annually by 68 percent in 1976, 43 percent in 1977, 34 percent in 1978, and 28 percent in 1978. The actual interest rates were well below those levels (see table B.1).

The sustainability of debt also depends on its initial level. Comparing annual interest payments on the debt with hypothetical export revenue growth rates equal to import growth, that is, balancing foreign trade, and adjusting for interest rates also demonstrates that the gap between revenues and expenditures would increase from $112 million in 1976 to $312 million in 1977, $696 million in 1978, $1,274 million in 1979, and $1,845 million in 1980.[3] Debt would not increase between 1976 and 1980, assuming that imports were kept at actual historical levels, only if the average annual rate of export growth in nominal terms were about 75 percent as compared with the actual rate of 10.6 percent. Thus, Poland was on the verge of losing control of its international debt position by the mid-1970s.

[2] The growth export rates that would close the trade gap were calculated by using the following formula: $M_t/X_{t-1}(1 + r)$, where M = import; X = export; r = interest rate.

[3] Assuming an interest rate of 10.5 percent, equal to the average for 1976–1980, the total forward value of externally financed deficits would amount to $4.7 billion by the end of 1980. Including the size of the debt in December 1975, which amounted to $8.4 billion, the total debt would be at the level of $13.0 billion instead of $25 billion.

Thanks to a buyer's market prevailing in international financial markets between 1976 and 1980 and favorable attitudes of West European governments, Poland's rapidly deteriorating debt-servicing capacity did not lead to credit rationing.[4] In 1979, for instance, Poland obtained twice as many private credits from Eurocurrency markets as in 1978—$932 million as compared with $435 million. In 1979, a syndicated loan led by Bank of America, initially scheduled for $500 million, was oversubscribed by $50 million (Baird and Delamaide 1982).

The only indication of a worsening external position was higher interest rates (a higher spread over LIBOR) and shorter-term credits. Although East European countries could borrow at a comfortable 5/8 percent over London Interbank Offer Rate (LIBOR) for seven years with three or four years grace, Poland was not able to obtain such favorable terms (Organization of Economic Cooperation and Development 1986, 19). The debt maturity structure deteriorated (shortened) between 1976 and 1980.

Private sources of external financing began drying up in 1980, and the credit curtain fell in 1981. Bank of America, approached by the Polish government to lead a syndicated loan for another $500 million, was able to raise only $375 million. Only pressures from the Western governments allowed Poland to draw $736 million in Eurocurrency markets in 1980.[5] In 1981, Western commercial banks started reducing their exposure in Poland.[6]

Because of deteriorating economic performance, faltering exports, and the skyrocketing costs of debt servicing due to high floating interest rates and shorter maturities, a cash crisis erupted in early 1981. In March 1981, Poland was technically in default and had to enter negotiations to reschedule its international obligations. Belatedly, Poland reached its credit limit.

Thus the balance-of-payments crisis openly erupted in the third year of economic contraction that began in 1979. In retrospect, one may conclude that the economic decline could have been eased had serious adjustment started in 1976. A serious adjustment program would have had to include rescheduling negotiations with both official and private creditors, economic reforms, and reduced consumption. Instead, as John M. Montias succinctly summarized, "the Polish authorities—if they had enough authority to deserve the name—

[4] For a discussion of factors underlying private lending to Eastern Europe, see Eichler (1981).

[5] German banks provided Dm1.2 billion out of which 40 percent was guaranteed by the West German government (Organization for Economic Cooperation and Development 1985). For the discussion of the background of this loan, see Spindler (1984, 81–86). Following the Gdańsk Agreement, the Carter administration granted $600 million worth of Commodity Credit Corporation (CCC) guarantees in September 1980.

[6] The net outflow to private banks of about $1.1 billion was made possible by the Western government official loans of $1.4 billion and the CMEA hard currency loans (mainly Soviet) of $1.7 billion (Goldstein 1983).

reached the edge of disaster in August 1980 without ever having taken one drastic measure to remedy the situation'' (Montias 1982, 19).

An examination of Poland's hard currency imports suggests that credits and export revenues were not grossly misappropriated (see table B.2). Out of total imports from the West of about $58 billion, $42.4 billion or 73 percent was paid for by export proceeds.[7] Total credits provided by Western financial institutions amounted to about $36 billion out of which about $20 billion was paid for in the 1970s. In 1980, Poland's net debt was about $23 billion, credits were $16 billion, and interest and other charges amounted to $7 billion (Szeliga 1982). Credits were used to modernize industry and to sustain production, which required more and more Western industrial inputs.[8] As can be seen from the data in table B.2, 71 percent of Western imports from 1971 to 1980 served to supply current production and to expand industrial capital stock, whereas 29 percent was used to sustain immediate and final consumption.

The distribution of hard currency uses changed in the 1977–1980 period,

TABLE B.2

Composition of Poland's Imports from the West, 1971–1980, (in Billions of U.S. Dollars and Percentages of Total Imports from the West)

	1971–1976	(%)	1977–1980	(%)	1971–1980	(%)
Fuels and energy	1.2	4	2.6	8	3.8	6
Raw materials and industrial inputs	9.5	35	10.1	33	19.7	34
Capital equipment	9.4	35	8.6	28	17.9	31
Agricultural products	5.0	18	7.6	25	12.6	22
Other consumption items	2.0	7	2.0	6	4.0	7
Total	27.1	100	30.9	100	58.1	100
Memorandum Trade deficits	9.0		6.7		15.7	

Sources: Calculated from data in Szeliga (1982, 19); and *Roxznik statystyczny handlu zagranicznego* (1988, 7).

[7] This does not include purchases financed by credits, cost of their servicing, and revenues from invisible transactions the balance of which tended to be favorable.

[8] In contrast to many Third World debt-ridden countries, the crisis was not exacerbated by capital flight (e.g., Mexico) or large-scale embezzlement of foreign credits (the Philippines). In fact, a closer examination of Poland's purchases and credits in the 1970s indicated that loans had not mysteriously evaporated. Although some of them were clearly used to sustain the standard of living beyond the capacity of the Polish economy, the crux of the matter was that in the early 1970s they allowed for significant modernization of Polish industry.

indicating a decrease in export and/or import substitution potential. The productive shares declined, whereas credits to finance current consumption rapidly increased. The share of capital equipment fell from 35 percent during 1971–1976 to 28 percent during 1977–1980, whereas the share of agricultural products and consumer items increased from 21 to 35 percent. The share of industrial inputs also fell thus substantially reducing production. The contraction was larger than indicated by the change in its share because, beginning in 1977, the volume of imports started a downward slide.[9]

The dramatic increase in the shares of credits used to finance purchases of energy and agricultural products, the shortening of maturities, and the greater real cost of international borrowing contributed directly to the deterioration of Poland's capacity to service its international debt. The authorities, fearful of the political consequences of drastic cuts in consumption, sought to generate a convertible currency export surplus through a compression of investment as well as of imports supporting current output.[10]

As can be seen from table B.3, which contains the aggregate data on macroeconomic developments from 1978 to 1981, the authorities sought to shield the population from the impact of crisis. Cuts in the rate of capital formation (accumulation) were very deep, whereas consumption, both individual and

TABLE B.3
Macroeconomic Dis-adjustment, 1978–1981

	1978	1979	1980	1981
Indexes				
NMP	100	97.7	91.8	80.9
DNMP	100	96.3	90.5	81.0
Consumption	100	102.3	103.0	97.7
Accumulaton	100	88.6	73.8	56.9
Share in NMP[a]	100.0	100.0	100.0	100.0
Consumption	59.7	73.9	74.4	79.3
Accumulaton	40.3	26.1	25.6	20.7

Source: Rocznik statystyczny (1983, 1984, 1985).

[9] In 1977, the volume of imports from non-Communist countries fell by 10.9 percent, in 1978 by 2 percent, in 1979 by 4.5 percent, and in 1980 by 7.2 percent. In 1980, the volume of imports stood at 79 percent of their 1976 level. (From data in Rocznik statystyczny handlv zagranicznego 1988:8).

[10] For instance, in 1981 the major victims of import cuts were fuels, machinery, and equipment; thus growing external disequilibrium was only marginally absorbed by the contraction in investment and production activity.

collective, increased. A slower rate of contraction of the DNMP than of the NMP indicated that the growing gap between domestic expenditure and income was filled by the inflow of resources from abroad. External resources artificially extended consumption levels, which exceeded the capabilities of the Polish economy, and thus increased the future debt burden.

This shift toward consumption during a period when debt-servicing cost was rising and when credits earlier drawn began falling due was an indication of inevitable difficulties for future debt management. The link between the expansion of productive capacities and debt-servicing capacity was broken, as was illustrated by the growing discrepancy between debt and capital equipment growth rates.

The net debt increased faster than capital equipment imports by 25 percent from 1972 to 1975 and by 67 percent from 1976 to 1978 (Zoeter 1981). The balance of payments adjustment was not among the most important policy objectives at that time. In view of these data, it is rather startling that the Polish authorities made no attempt to reschedule the debt in 1977 or 1978. The lower debt burden would have offered the much-needed breathing space to finish investment projects and reduce the cost of external adjustment.

The policies pursued in the 1970s could neither close a gap between domestic expenditure and income, filled by the inflow of resources from abroad, nor improve export performance in Western markets. This was not an adjustment but a dis-adjustment strategy. The collapse of import-led development revealed all the drawbacks of the economic system on an unprecedented scale.

The adjustment process in the 1980s did not bring about the structural changes required to generate the economic performance needed to improve its debt-servicing capacity. To the contrary, Poland has found it difficult to sustain convertible currency trade surpluses, which, together with transfers and other invisibles, determine Poland's external capacity. The amounts generated in the 1980s were not sufficient to pay interest on credits. Between 1983 and 1987, Poland's unpaid interest obligations totaled $10.2 billion, which was almost one-fourth of Poland's debt by the end of 1987 (Olechowski and Wojtowicz 1988). The cost of debt servicing amounted to about $1.8 billion per annum from 1984 to 1988 (Aleksandrowicz 1989). In 1988, debt servicing of $1.73 billion accounted for about 24 percent of hard currency revenues.

Faced with inadequate hard currency earnings, the authorities chose to service the debt owed to the Soviet Union, CMEA banks, Arab governments and banks, and nonguaranteed obligations to private Western banks. The debt service obligations guaranteed by Western governments were at the very bottom of the list. The 1988 ratio of actual payments to debts amounted to 6.8 percent for the first group as compared with 0.5 percent for the second group (Aleksandrowicz 1989).

Measured against growing obligations, Poland's debt-servicing capacity has been declining. Although the ratio of debt to hard currency earnings improved slightly in 1988—it fell from 6.4 percent in 1987 to 5.4 percent—its level indicated the nonmanageability of the foreign debt.[11] The improvement was the result of the increase in exports by 17.6 percent in comparison with 1987. In addition, the numerator (i.e., the debt) did not change in 1988, because of the appreciation of the U.S. dollar and payments out of Poland's international reserves. It was estimated that the appreciation lowered the debt by $1.6 billion. The international reserves fell by $0.5 billion. The total of $2.1 billion was offset by the increase in interest arrears, which amounted also to $2.1 billion.

Thus, the stabilization of the hard currency debt was owing to the favorable shifts in foreign exchange rates rather than to the improved earning capacities. The debt remains unsustainable, however. As can be seen from the data in table B.4, the payments falling due in the 1989–1991 period will require a dramatic increase in the hard currency export surplus exceeding by far the historic record levels, even if the balance in "invisibles" is included.

Therefore, the rescheduling negotiations will remain on the political agenda for years to come. As McDonald (1982, 636) observed, "For a debt situation to be sustainable, both the borrowing country and lenders must view it as such." Ultimately, the lenders may have little choice in their policies toward Poland because the costs of debt servicing will approach the costs of debt repudiation.

TABLE B.4
Payments Falling Due, 1989–1993 (in Billions of U.S. Dollars)

	1989	1990	1991	1992	1993
Government-backed loans and interest (mainly Paris Club)	3.6	4.8	4.7	4.4	5.9
Non-guaranteed (mainly London Club)	1.0	1.0	1.9	0.9	0.8
Other (Soviet Union, CMEA banks, Arab countries, and other)	0.7	0.6	0.5	0.6	0.4
Total	5.3	6.4	7.1	5.9	7.1
Memorandum: Ratio of total to hard currency trade surplus in 1988 ($941 million)	5.6	6.8	7.5	6.3	7.5

Sources: Aleksandrowicz (1989, 18); Rubel and Wojtowicz (1989, 13).

[11] The ratio in 1989 was significantly higher than corresponding ratios for major Latin American debtors like Mexico (3.3) and Brazil (3.7). However, in the case of Poland, exports to other CMEA countries are not included. These exports are regarded as "soft" exports—not easily marketable in world markets.

Abbreviations

CAP	Central Annual Plan
CC	convertible currency
CCC	Commodity Credit Corporation
CMEA	Council for Mutual Economic Assistance
CPE	centrally planned economy
DIW	German Institute for Economic Research
DNMP	domestic net material product
FTO	Foreign Trade Organization
GDR	German Democratic Republic
IMF	International Monetary Fund
KOR	Committee for Defense of Workers
LIBOR	London Interbank Offer Rate
MFN	most favored nation
NEP	new economic policy
NIC	newly industrialized country
NMP	net material product
NMP	net material product
NSP	National Socioeconomic Plan
NSZZ	Independent Self-Governing Trade Union
OECD	Organization for Economic Cooperation and Development
OPZZ	"official" Trade Union Confederation
PFAZ	State Fund for Professional Training
PPWW	tax on above-norm payments
PRC	People's Republic of China
PRL	Polish People's Republic
PRON	Patriotic Movement of National Rebirth
PUWP	Polish United Workers' Party
SITC	Standard International Trade Classification
SSS	self-dependent, self-managed, and self-financed
WOG	Large Economic Organizations
WRON	Military Council of National Salvation

Bibliography

Albinowski, Stanisław. 1987. "Cudów (niestety) nie ma" (There are [unfortunately] no miracles). *Życie Gospodarcze* (Warsaw), no. 16.

Aleksandrowicz, Piotr. 1989. "Pod ścianą: Zadłuzenie wonyodewizowe Polski 1988 r." (Against the wall: Poland's hard currency debt 1988). *Gazeta Bankowa*, no. 11.

———. 1987. "Hodowla krasonoludków" (The raising of goblins). *Przegląd Tygodnia* (Warsaw) (December 20–27).

Alton, Thad. 1981. "Production and Resource Allocation in Eastern Europe: Performance, Problems, and Prospects. In *East European Economic Assessments*. Pt. 2: *Regional Assessments*, 348–408. Joint Economic Committee, Cong., Washington, D.C.

Arrow, Kenneth. 1963. "Uncertainty and the Welfare Economics of Medical Care. *American Economic Review* 53(5): 941–73.

Ascherson, Neal. 1981. *The Polish August: The Self-limiting Revolution*. New York: Viking Press.

Baczko, Tadeusz. 1987. "Nieprawidlowosci w systemie motywacji" (Inconsistencies in the motivational system). *Zarządzanie* (Warsaw), no. 6.

Baczyński, Jerzy. 1986. "Z jednej skrajńości w drugą" (From one extreme to another). *Polityka*, no. 16.

———. 1987. "Katorga importowa" (Import drudgery). *Polityka-Eksport-Import*, no. 16.

Baird, Jane, and Darrell Delamaide. 1982. "The Lessons of Poland." *Institutional Investor* (January).

Balassa, B. 1982. "Reforming the New Economic Mechanism in Hungary." World Bank staff working paper, no. 534, Washington, D.C.

———. 1986. "Next Step in the Hungarian Economic Reform." World Bank report no. DRD254, Washington, D.C.

Barry, B., and R. Hardin, eds. 1982. *Rational Man and Irrational Society*. Beverly Hills, Calif.: Sage Publications.

Báuer, Támas. 1978. "Investment Cycles in Planned Economies." *Acta Oeconomica* (Budapest) 21(3): 243–60.

Bautina, Ninel, and Urszula Wojciechowska. 1988. "Wspólny socjalistyczny rynek: Cele i środki realizacji" (Common socialist market: Objectives and means). *Życie Gospodarcze*, no. 35.

Beksiak, Janusz. 1972. *Społeczeństwo gospodarujące* (Economizing society). Warsaw: Polski Wydawmictwa Naukowe.

Bergson, Abraham. 1986. *Essays in Normative Economics*. Cambridge, Mass.: Belknap Press.

Bielasiak, Jack. 1988. "Economic Reform versus Political Normalization." In Marer and Siwiński 1988, 103–14.

Bielecki, C., and J. Majewski. 1988. "Prywatna przedsiębiorczość" (Private entrepreneurship). *Polityka*, no. 16.

Birman, I. 1978. "From the Achieved Level." *Soviet Studies*, no. 2.

Bobek, Józef, and Leszek Zienkowski. 1988. "Z głowy na nogi" (From head back on feet). *Polityka*, no. 44.

Bobrowski, Czesław. 1987. "Wymad nie liczę na przełom liczę na proces" (I don't expect a turnaround, I expect a process). Interviewed. *Życie Gospodarcze*, no. 51.

Boyd, Michael L. 1988. "Agriculture and Debt Crisis." In Marer and Siwiński, eds. 1988.

Bozyk, Paweł. 1983. *Marzenia i Rzeczywistość czyli anatomia polskiego kryzysu* (Dreams and reality: The anatomy of the Polish crisis). Warsaw: Polski Instytut Wydawnicry.

Brabant, Jozef van. 1973. *Bilateralism and Structural Bilateralism in Intra-CMEA Trade*. Rotterdam: Rotterdam University Press.

Brach, Barbara. 1989. "Stan posiadania" (Assets and liabilities). *Życie Gospodarcze*, no. 3.

Brada, Josef, and John Michael Montias. 1984. "Industrial Policy in Eastern Europe: A Three-Country Comparison." *Journal of Comparative Economics* 8:377–419.

Brown, A. A. 1968. "Towards a Theory of Centrally Planned Foreign Trade." In *International Trade and Central Planning*, 57–93. Berkeley: University of California Press.

Brucan, Sylviu. 1983. *The Post-Brezhnev Era*. New York: Praeger.

Brumberg, Abraham. 1989a. "Poland: Danger Ahead." *Washington Post*, 14 June 1989.

———. 1989b. "Poland: State and/or Society." *Dissent* (Winter).

———. 1988. "Poland: The New Opposition." *New York Review of Books*, 18 February 1988.

———. 1987. "A New Deal in Poland?" *New York Review of Books*, 15 January 1987.

Brus, Włodzimierz. 1980. "Political System and Economic Efficiency: The East European Context." *Journal of Comparative Economics* 4(1): 40–55.

———. 1982. "Aims, Methods, and Political Determinants of the Economic Policy of Poland 1970–1980. In *The East European Economies in the 1970's*, Alec Nove, H-H. Hohmann, G. Seidenstecher, eds., 81–105. London: Butterworths.

———. 1988. "The Political Economy of Reforms." In Marer and Siwiński 1988, 65–79.

Brzezinski, Zbigniew. 1983. *Power and Principle: Memoirs of the National Security Advisor, 1977–1981*, New York: Farrar, Straus, and Giroux.

———. 1989. *The Grand Failure: The Birth and Death of Communism in the 20th Century*. New York: Charles Scribner's Sons.

Brzezinski, Zbigniew, and Samuel P. Huntington. 1963. *Political Power: USA/USSR*. New York: Viking Press.

Bugaj, Ryszard. 1988. "Kształt i warunki polskiej przebudowy" (The shape and conditions of Polish reconstruction). *Tygodnik Powszechny* (Cracow), no. 46.

Bunce, Valerie. 1982. "The Political Economy of the Brezhnev Era: The Rise and the Fall of Corporatism." *British Journal of Political Science* 13:129–58.

Carnoy, Martin. 1984. *The State and Political Theory*. Princeton, N.J.: Princeton University Press.

Cave, Jane. 1982. "Worker Response to Martial Law: The December Strikes." *Poland Watch*, no. 1:8–17.

————. 1983. "The Legacy of Martial Law." *Poland Watch* (Washington, D.C.), no. 4:1–20.

Cave, Jane, and Marsha Sosnowska. 1982. "Protest and Resistance." *Poland Watch*, no. 1:63–74.

"Chłopski raport o stanie rolnictwa i warunkach poprawy jego efektywnósci" (Farmer report on the state of agriculture and the conditions to improve its efficiency). 1984. *ład* (28 October 1984).

Clark, Colin. 1957. *The Conditions of Economic Progress*. London: Macmillan.

Cliff, Tony. 1974. *State Capitalism in Russia*. London: Pluto.

Cline, William. 1984. "Managing Global Debt: An Interim Evaluation." Hearing before the Subcommittee on Economic Goals and Intergovernmental Policy, Joint Economic Committee, Cong., Washington, D.C. Mimeo.

Coleman, K. E., and Daniel N. Nelson. 1984. "State Capitalism, State Socialism and the Politicization of Workers." Karl Beck Papers in Russian and East European Studies, paper no. 304, University of Pittsburgh.

Colton, Timothy. 1986. *The Dilemma of Reform in the Soviet Union*. Rev. ed. New York: Council on Foreign Relations.

Comisso, Ellen. 1986. "Introduction: State Structures, Political Process, and Collective Choice in CMEA States." *International Organization*, no. 2:195–238.

Comisso, E., and Laura Tyson. 1986. "Preface." *International Organization*, no. 2.

Crane, Keith. 1987. "An Assessment of the Economic Reform in Poland's State-Owned Industry." Paper presented at conference, The Dimensions of the Polish Economy, 5–6 September 1987 at Witchita State University.

————. 1988. "The Economy Five Years After Martial Law." In Marer and Siwiński 1988, 13–24.

Dąbrowski, Marek. 1988. "Diagnoza niepowodzeń" (Diagnosis of Failure). *Polityka*, no. 40.

Dąbrowski, Zbigniew. 1987. "Inwestycje—fakty i mity" (Investments—Facts and myths). *Rzeczpospolita* (Warsaw), 9 September 1987.

Davie, B. F., and B. F. Duncombe. 1972. *Public Finance*. New York: Holt, Rinehart and Winston.

Dawisha, Karen. 1988. *Eastern Europe, Gorbachev, and Reform*. Cambridge: Cambridge University Press.

Dawisha, Karen, and Phil Hanson, eds. 1981. *Soviet—East European Dilemmas*. London: Holmes and Meier.

Delamaide, Darrell. 1985. *Debt Shock. The Full Story of the World Credit Crisis*. New York: Doubleday.

Dokumenty "okrągłego stolu" (Documents of the roundtable). 1989. Warsaw, 6 April 1989.

Dorosz, A., and M. Puławski. 1984. "Bilans Platniczy Polski 1983–1984" (Poland's balance of payments) 1983–1984. *Polityka Eksport-Import*, no. 3.

Drewnowski, Jan. 1979. "The Central Planning Office on Trial: An Account of the Beginnings of Stalinism in Poland." *Soviet Studies*, no. 1:23–42.

————, ed. 1982. *Crisis in the East European Economy. The Spread of the Polish Disease*. New York: St. Martin's Press.

Driscoll, D. 1982. "Sovereign Debt: The Polish Example." Congressional Research Service, Library of Congress, Washington, D.C., 4 January 1982, report no. 82–25E. Mimeo.

"Drugi etap? Dyskusja" (The Second Stage? Discussion). *Dwadzieścia Jeden Pismo*. Underground publication by Oficyna Wydawnicza Rytm (Warsaw), no. 4 (Summer 1987).

Dryll, Irena. 1988. "Stocznia choe zyć" (The shipyard wants to stay alive). *Życie Gospodarcze*, no. 46.

"Dyrektorzy o reformie" (Business executives' views on economic reform). Summary of the 1984 Central Bureau of Public Opinion Survey. *Polityka* (Warsaw), 12 January 1985, no. 3.

Economic Commission for Europe. 1986–1989. *Economic Survey of Europe*. Prepared annually by the Secretariat of the Economic Commission for Europe. New York: United Nations Publications.

Eichler, Gabriel. 1981. "Country Risk Analysis and Bank Lending to Eastern Europe." In *East European Economic Assessments*. Pt. 2: *Regional Assessments*, 759–75. Joint Economic Committee, Cong., Washington, D.C.

Elster, Jon. 1985. *Making Sense of Marx*. Cambridge: Cambridge University Press; Paris: Éditions de la Maison des Sciences de l'Homme.

Eysymontt, Jerzy, and Wojciech Maciejewski. 1985. "Kryzysy społeczno-ekonomiczne w Polsce. Ujęcie modelowe" (Socio-economic crises in Poland. A modeling approach). *Ekonomista* 1:2–24.

Fallenbuchl, Zbigniew. 1981a. "Poland: Command Planning in Crisis." *Challenge* 5(July/August).

———. 1981b. "Policy Alternatives in Polish Foreign Economic Relations." In Simon and Kanet 1981.

———. 1984. "The Polish Economy Under Martial Law." *Soviet Studies*, no. 4:513–27.

———. 1985. "Sources of Periodic Crises Under the Centrally Planned Socialist System." In *Rhythms in Politics and Economics*, P. M. Johnson and W. R. Thompson, eds., 43–70. New York: Praeger.

———. 1988. "Present State of the Economic Reform." In Marer and Siwiński 1988, 115–30.

———. 1989. "Poland: The Anatomy of Stagnation." In Hardt and Kaufman 1989, 102–36.

Fikus, Dariusz. 1989. "Nomenklatura mości sobie gniazdko: Kto wykupił akcje Igloopolu" (Nomenklatura builds itself a nest: Who purchased stocks of Igloopol). *Gazeta Wyborcza* (Warsaw), 7 June 1989.

Geremek, Bronisław. 1989. "Policies for the Period of Transition." *Solidarność News* (Brussels), 1–15 March 1989.

Gilpin, Robert. 1987. *The Political Economy of International Relations*. Princeton, N.J.: Princeton University Press.

Główczyk, Jan. 1989. "Nierównowaga strukturalna" (Structural disequilibrium). *Życie Gospodarcze*, no. 17.

Goldstein, Elizabeth A. 1982. "Soviet Economic Assistance to Poland, 1980–1981." In *Soviet Economy in the 1980's: Problems and Prospects*, John P. Hardt, ed., 556–74. Vol. 2. Joint Economic Committee, Cong., Washington, D.C.

Gomułka, Stanisław. 1981. "Poland's Macroeconomic Reserves, Constraints, and Prospects in the Early 1980's: Tentative Evaluation." Seminar, Polish Trade and Development, 26–27 March, at the University of Birmingham, England, 26–27 March 1981.

———. 1984. "Poland's Industrialization." Paper presented at international conference, Contemporary Poland in Historical Perspective, 22–25 May 1984, at Yale University.

———. 1985. *Growth, Innovation and Reform in Eastern Europe.* Brighton, England: Wheatsheaf.

Gomułka, Stanisław, and Jacek Rostowski. 1984. "The Reformed Polish Economic System." *Soviet Studies,* no. 3:386–405.

Goode, R. 1984. *Government Finance in Developing Countries.* Washington, D.C.: Brookings Institution.

Gospodarka światowa i gospodarka Polska w 1988 roku (The world economy and the Polish economy in 1988). 1989. Instytut Gospodarki Swiatowej, Szkola Glowna Planowania i Statystyki (Institute of the World Economy, Central School of Planning and Statistics), Warsaw.

Gramsci, A. 1971. *Selections from Prison Notebooks.* New York: International Publishers.

Grinberg, R. 1988. "Discussion: Economists on CMEA, Currency Convertibility." *Izvestiya,* 16 January 1988. (In FBIS-SOV-88-018.)

Grudzińska-Gross, Irena. 1983. "The Politics of Appropriation." *Poland Watch,* no. 4:21–25.

Grosfeld, Irena. 1987. "Modeling Planners' Investment Behavior: Poland, 1956–1981." *Journal of Comparative Economics* 11:180–91.

Haggard, S., and Chung-In Moon. 1986. "Industrial Change and State Power: The Politics of Stabilization and Structural Adjustment in Korea." Paper presented at the annual meeting of the American Political Science Association, 27–31 August 1986, Washington, D.C.

Hardt, John P. 1976. "Stages in the Soviet Economic Development." In *Economic Issues of the Eighties,* N. M. Kameny and R. H. Day, eds., 199–225. Baltimore, Md.: Johns Hopkins University Press.

Hardt, John P., and Jean Boon. 1987. *Poland's Renewal and U.S. Options: A Policy Reconnaissance.* Report prepared for the subcommittee on Europe and the Middle East, House Committee on Foreign Affairs, 5 March 1987, Washington, D.C.

Hardt, John P., and Richard Kaufman, eds. *Pressures for Reform in the Eastern European Economies.* Joint Economic Committee, Cong., Washington, D.C.

Hauser, Ewa. 1984. "Censorship and Law." *Poland Watch,* no. 5:43–62.

Henzler, Marek. 1988. "Trzecia próba" (Third attempt). *Polityka,* no. 53.

Hewett, E. A. 1985. "Gorbachev's Economic Strategy. A Preliminary Assessment." *Soviet Economy* 4:281–94.

———. 1986. "Reform or Rhetoric: Gorbachev and the Soviet Economy." *Brookings Review* (Fall).

Hirschman, Albert O. 1970. *Exit, Voice, and Loyalty: Responses to Decline in Firms, Organizations, and States.* Cambridge: Harvard University Press.

Hirszowicz, Maria. 1980. *The Bureaucratic Leviathan.* New York: St. Martin's Press.

Holzman, Franklyn. 1986. "The Significance of Soviet Subsidies to Eastern Europe." *Comparative Economic Studies*, no. 1:24–35.

Hough, J. 1969. *The Soviet Prefects*. Cambridge: Harvard University Press.

Hudson, C. 1981. "Polish Investment Policy in Confusion." *RFE-RL Background Report/60*, 2 March 1981, Munich.

Hutchings, Raymond. 1983. *The Soviet Budget*. Albany: State University of New York Press.

Jermakowicz, Władysław. 1988. "Reform Cycles in Poland, the USSR, the GDR, and Czechoslovakia." In Marer and Siwiński 1988, 81–92.

Jezierski, Andrzej, and Barbara Petz. 1988. *Historia gospodarcza Polski ludowej* (The economic history of the Polish People's Republic). Warsaw: Polskie Wydawnictesa Naukowe.

Jeziorański, Tomasz. 1986a. "Galimatias" (Jumble). *Życie Gospodarcze*, no. 50.

———. 1986b. "W którym kierunku?" (Where to?) *Życie Gospodarcze*, no. 45.

———. 1986c. "W Sejmie: Ustawa budzetowa" (In the Parliament: Budget 1987). *Życie Gospodarcze*, no. 46.

———. 1987a. "Poparcie i obawy" (Support and fears). *Życie Gospodarcze*, no. 49.

———. 1987b. "Przyspieszenie, jak i kiedy?" (Acceleration, How and When?) *Życie Gospodarcze*, no. 14.

———. 1988. "Jednak koreta planu pięcioletniego" (Finally, the revision of the five year plan). *Życie Gospodarcze*, no. 18.

Józefiak, Cezary. 1986. *The Polish Reform: An Attempted Evaluation*. Forshungsberichte (research report), Vienna Institute for Comparative Economic Studies, no. 116.

———. 1987. *The Structural Changes in the Power Centre and Economic Reform in Poland*. Forshungsberichte (research report), Vienna Institute for Comparative Economic Studies, no. 125.

Kalabiński, Jacek. 1984. "Media War in Poland." *Poland Watch*, no. 5:63–82.

Kaleta, Józef. 1987. "Jak uzdrowić zlotówke?" (How to cure the zloty?) *Odrodzenie* (Crakow), 8 August.

Kaminski, Antoni Z. 1988. "The Privatization of the State: Trends in the Evolution of (Real) Socialist Political Systems." *Asian Journal of Public Administration* 10(1): 27–47.

———. 1989. "Coercion, Corruption, and Reform: State and Society in the Soviet-Type Socialist Regime." *Journal of Theoretical Politics* 1(1): 77–102.

Kamiński, Bartłomiej. 1985. "Dying Command Economy: Solidarity and the Polish Crisis." *Journal of Contemporary Studies* 7(1): 5–35.

———. 1987. "Pathologies of Central Planning." *Problems of Communism* (March/April): 81–95.

———. 1988. "Constraints to Activating Taxation to Direct a Reformed Centrally Planned Economy." University of Maryland. Mimeo.

———. 1989a. "Council for Mutual Economic Assistance: Division and Conflict on Its 40th Anniversary." In Staar 1988, 413–31.

———. 1989b. "Directive Capacity of the Socialist State." *Comparative Political Studies*, 1:66–92.

———. 1989c. "The Economic System and Forms of Government Controls in Poland in the 1980s." In Hardt and Kaufman 1989, 84–101.

Kamiński, Bartlomiej, and Karol Sołtan. 1988. "The Evolutionary Potential of Late Communism." Paper presented at the American Political Science Association convention, 1–4 September 1988, Washington, D.C.

———. 1989. "The Evolution of Communism." *International Political Science Review,* 10(4): 371–91.

Kandal, Terry R. 1989. "Marx and Engels on International Relations, Revolution and Counterrevolution." In *Studies of Development and Change in the Modern World,* M. T. Martin and Terry R. Kandal, eds., 25–76. New York: Oxford University Press.

Karpińska-Mizielińska, Wanda. 1986. "Reforma w oczach kadry" (Reform in the eyes of management). *Życie Gospodarcze,* no. 36.

Karpiński, Andrzej. 1958. *Zagadnienia socjalistycznej industrializacji Polski* (Issues in Poland's socialist industrialization). Warsaw: Państwowe Wydawnictwo Gospodarcze.

Karpiński, Jakub. 1982. *Count-Down, The Polish Upheavels of 1956, 1968, 1970, 1976, 1980.* . . . New York: Karz-Cohl.

Katzenstein, Peter. 1978. *Between Power and Plenty: Foreign Economic Policy of Advanced Industrial States.* Madison: University of Wisconsin Press.

Kelman, Mark. 1987. *A Guide to Critical Legal Studies.* Cambridge: Harvard University Press.

Kennan, George. 1989. *Sketches from a Life.* New York: Pantheon Books.

"Kierunki reformy gospodarczej—projekt: Projekt ustaw o przedsiebiorstwach panstwowych—o samorzadzie przedsiebiorstwach panstwowego" (The direction of the economic reform—project: Project of laws on state-owned enterprises—on self-management of state-owned enterprise). *Trybuna Ludu,* July 1981.

Kittrie, Nicholas N. 1988. "The Undoing of a Monolith: Responding to Diversities in the Eastern Bloc." In *The Uncertain Future: Gorbachev's Eastern Bloc,* Nicholas N. Kittrie and Ivan Volgyes, eds. 1–8. New York: Paragon House.

Kittrie, Nicholas N., and Ivan Volgyes, eds. 1988. *The Uncertain Future: Gorbachev's Eastern Bloc.* New York: Paragon House.

Kleer, Jerzy. 1988. "Czas nadzwyczajny: (Time for urgency). *Polityka* (Warsaw), no. 21.

———. 1989. "Koszty porozumiena: 5 bilionów złotych, 1,5 mld dolarów. Rachunek został na stole" (The cost of the accord: Zl 5 trillion and $1.5 billion. The check is on the table). *Polityka* (Warsaw), no. 18:5–6.

Kleer, Jerzy, and Andrej Mozołowski. 1988. "Godzina prawdy" (The hour of truth). *Polityka,* no. 40.

Knight, Peter. 1983. "Economic Reform in Socialist Countries: The Experience of China, Hungary, Romania and Yugoslavia." World Bank staff working paper, no. 579, Washington, D.C.

Kohn, Martin J., and Nicholas R. Lang. 1977. "The Intra-CEMA Foreign Trade System: Major Price Changes, Little Reform." In *East European Economies Post-Helsinki.* Joint Economic Committee, 95th Cong., Washington, D.C.

Kołodko, Grzegorz W. 1987. "Bez samofinansowania nie ma samodzielności: Rozmowa z doc. Grzegorzem Kołodko" (Without self-financing no autonomy: Interview with Professor Kołodko). *Trybuna Ludu,* 16 June 1987.

Kołodko, Grzegorz W. 1988. "Economic Change and Shortageflation under Centrally Planned Economies." *Journal of Public Finance and Public Choice* 1:15–32.

Komisja Planowania. 1987. "Raport o przebiegu i wynikach wdrazania reformy gospodarczej w 1986 r" (Report on the implementation of economic reform). Summary in *Trybuna Ludu* (Warsaw), 9 July.

Konrad, George. 1984. *Antipolitics*. New York: Harcourt Brace Jovanovich.

Konsultacyjna Rada Gospodarcza (Consultative Economic Council). 1987. "Mechanizm cenowy: nie tylko smiały ale i skuteczny" (Price mechanism: Not only bold but effective). *Życie Gospodarcze* (Warsaw), no. 50.

Korboński, Andrzej. 1981. "Victim or Villain: Polish Agriculture Since 1970." In Simon and Kanet 1981.

———. 1984. "Soviet Policy toward Poland." In Terry 1984.

———. 1988. "Ideology Disabused: Communism without a Face in Eastern Europe. In Kittrie and Volgyes 1988, 39–56.

Kornai, Janos. 1972. *Rush vs. Harmonic Growth*. Amsterdam: North Holland Press.

———. 1980. *Economics of Shortage*. Amsterdam: North Holland Press.

———. 1986a. *Contradictions and Dilemmas: Studies on the Socialist Economy and Society*. Cambridge, Mass.: MIT Press.

———. 1986b. "The Hungarian Reform Process." *Journal of Economic Literature* 24(4).

Kotowicz, Jan. 1987. "Popyt niesterowalny" (Uncontrollable demand). *Życie Gospodarcze*, no. 22.

Kovës, András. 1985. *The CMEA Countries in the World Economy: Turning Inwards or Turning Outwards*. Budapest: Akademiai Kiado.

Kovrig, Bennet. 1988. "Fire and Water: Political Reform in Eastern Europe." In Kittrie and Volgyes 1988, 9–38.

Kowalik, Tadeusz. 1986. "On Crucial Reform of Real Socialism." *Forschungsberichte* (research report), Vienna Institute for Comparative Economic Studies, Vienna, no. 122.

———. 1987. "Jeśli ma się udać . . ." (If it's to succeed). *Zarządzanie* (Warsaw), no. 12.

———. 1989. "Czas przeobrazeń" (The period of transformation). Intervention in a discussion. *Życie Gospodarcze*, no. 18.

Kowalski, Ryszard. 1988. "Droga do normalności" (Road to normality). *Gazeta Bankowa* (Warsaw), no. 1.

Kozłowski, S. 1983. "Ocena gospodarki zasobami naturalnymi" (The assessment of the use of natural resources). *Biuletyn KPZK*, no. 123:26–41.

Krajowa Rada Gospodarcza. 1983. "Krajowa Rada Gospodarcza: Sytuacja gospodarcza w kraju" (Economic situation in the country). Report of the National Economic Council. *Życie Gospodarcze*, no. 20.

Kravis, Irvin. B. 1984. "Comparative Studies of National Incomes and Policies." *Journal of Economic Literature* 1:1–39.

———. 1987. "Krajowa Rada Gospodarcza: Mechanizm cenowy nie tylko smiały ale skuteczny" (The price mechanism not only bold but effective). Report of the National Economic Council. *Życie Gospodarcze*, no. 50.

Kriegsein, Bernhard O. 1987. "A Bilateral Establishment: A Collective Choice Analysis of Austrian Interest Groups." Master's thesis, Department of Economics, University of Maryland, College Park.

Król, Marcin. 1987. "Stowarzyszenia" (Associations). *Tygodnik Powszechny,* 9 August 1987.

Krzak, Maciej K. 1988. "Kapitał zagraniczny w Polsce: Dwie optyki" (Foreign capital in Poland: Two views). *Życie Gospodarcze,* no. 16.

Krzemiński, Adam, and Wiesław Władyka. 1989. "Dwa programy" (Two programs). *Polityka,* no. 19.

Kuczyński, Waldemar. 1983. "Petite Histoire de la Crise Économique en Pologne" (Brief history of the economic crisis in Poland). *Le Temps Moderne* 4:38–54.

Kulesza, Maria. 1987. "Samorzad terytorialny i wlasnosc komunalna" (Territorial self-management and municipal ownership). *Życie Gospodarcze,* no. 23.

Kuroń, Jacek. 1985. "Zbrodnia i polityka" (Crime and politics). *Tygodnik Mazowsze,* no. 107:1–32.

Kuznets, Simon. 1965. *Modern Economic Growth.* New Haven, Conn.: Yale University Press.

Laky, T. 1979. "Enterprises in Bargaining Position." *Acta Oeconomica* 22:45–68.

Landau, Zbigniew. 1985. "Główne tendencje rozwoju gospodarczego Polski" (Main trends in the economic development of People's Poland). In Müller 1985, 17–97.

Lane, David. 1976. *The Socialist Industrial State.* London: George Allen and Unwin.

———. 1985. *The Soviet Economy and Society.* New York: New York University Press.

Lange, Oskar. 1973. "Zasady planowania gospodarczego w socjaliźmie." In *Dzieła* (Collected works). Vol. 2. Warsaw: Państwowe Wydawnictwo Eknomiczne.

Łazowski, Zygmunt, and Jacek Machowski. 1988. "Jak unregulować emigrację zarobkową?" (How to legalize economic emigration?). *Polityka-Eksport-Import,* no. 23 (December).

Leibenstein, Harvey. 1966. "Allocative Efficiency versus X-Efficiency." *American Economic Review* 56(June): 392–415.

Lesiński, Wojciech. 1988. "Z pre-historii reform" (The pre-history of reforms). *Życie Gospodarcze,* no. 36.

Lesz, Mieczysław. 1987. "Co dalej po podwyzce cen?" (What after the increase of prices?) *Życie Gospodarcze,* no. 17.

Lewis, W. Arthur. 1954. *Theory of Economic Growth.* London: Macmillan.

Lindblom, Charles. 1977. *Politics and Markets.* New York: Basic Books.

Lipowski, Adam. 1987. "Plan a rynek" (Plan versus market). *Polityka* (Warsaw), no. 17.

Lowi, Theodore. 1979. *The End of Liberalism.* 2d ed. New York: W. W. Norton.

Luxemburg, Rosa. 1961. *The Russian Revolution and Leninism or Marxism.* Ann Arbor: University of Michigan Press.

McDonald, Donogh C. 1982. "Debt Capacity and Developing Country Borrowing: A Survey of Literature." International Monetary Fund staff paper 29(4): 603–46.

Machowski, Heinrich, and Adam Zwass. 1972. "Polen." In *Die Wirtschaft Osteuropas zu Beginn der 70er Jahre,* H-H. Hohmann, ed., 48–75. Stuttgart.

Madison, James. 1787. "The Federalist Paper #10." In *The Federalist Papers*, introduction by Clinton Rossiter, ed. New York: NAL Penguin, 1961.

Mały Rocznik Statystyczny (Small statistical yearbook). Warsaw: Glowny Urzad Statystyczny (Central Statistical Office).

Marer, Paul. 1972. *Soviet and East European Foreign Trade*. Bloomington: Indiana University Press.

———. 1981. "Economic Performance and Prospects in Eastern Europe: Analytical Summary and Interpretation of Findings." In *East European Economic Assessments*. Pt. 2: *Regional Assessments*, 19–95. Joint Economic Committee, Cong., Washington, D.C.

———. 1984. "The Political Economy of Soviet Relations with Eastern European Relations." In Terry 1984, 155–88.

———. 1987. "Hungary's Foreign Economic Relations in the Mid-1980s: A Retrospective and Predictive Assessment." In *Foreign Economic Relations of East European Economies*, P. Joseph, ed., 231–54. Brussels: NATO.

———. 1988. "The Economies and Trade of Eastern Europe." Discussion paper no. 6, Indiana University, Bloomington.

Marer, Paul, and John M. Montias. 1981. "CMEA Integration: Theory and Practice." In *East European Economic Assessments*. Pt. 2: *Regional Assessments*, 148–195. Joint Economic Committee, Cong., Washington, D.C.

Marer, Paul and Wlodzimierz Siwiński, eds. 1988. *Creditworthiness and Reform in Poland*. Bloomington: Indiana University Press.

Mastny, Vojtech, ed. 1988. *Soviet-East European Survey, 1986–1987: Selected Research and Analysis from Radio Free Europe/Radio Liberty*. Boulder, Colo.: Westview Press.

Meadows, Donnella H., Dennis L. Meadows, Jórgen Randers, and William W. Behren III. 1974. *The Limits to Growth*. New York: New American Library.

Meyer, Alfred G. 1961. "USSR, Incorporated." *Slavic Review* 20(3): 3.

———. 1970. "Theories of Convergence." In *Change in Communist Systems*, Chalmers Johnson, ed., 313–41. Stanford, Calif.: Stanford University Press.

Michnik, Adam. 1986. *Takie czasy. Rzecz o kompromisie* (These times. A piece on compromise). London: Aneks.

———. 1989. Interviewed. *Tygodnik Powszechny*, no. 12.

———. 1990. "Notes on the Revolution." *New York Times Magazine*, 4 March 1990.

Mieszczankowski, Mieczysław. 1987a. "Krótka historia reformy" (Short account of the reform). *Życie Gospodarcze*, no. 20.

———. 1987b. "Hamulce, dylematy, szanse" (Obstacles, dilemmas, opportunities). *Życie Gospodarcze*, no. 22.

———. 1988. "Spuścizna drugiego etapu" (The legacy of the second stage). *Polityka*, no. 47.

Mikołajczyk, Zbigniew J. 1989. "Strukturalne i socjoekonomiczne uwagi na marginesie wynikow '88" (Structural and socioeconomic comments on the results in 1988). *Życie Gospodarcze*, no. 9.

Minc, Hilary. 1946. "Narodowy plan gospodarczy." *Życie Gospodarcze*, no. 18.

Misiak, M. 1986. "Przetargi z fiskusem" (Bargaining with the fiscal authorities). *Życie Gospodarcze*, no. 37.

————. 1987. "Wyniki finansowe przedsiębiorstw w 1986 r" (Financial performance of enterprises in 1986). *Życie Gospodarcze,* no. 10.

Modzelewski, Karol. 1988. "Realizm z wzajemnością" (Realism with reciprocity). *Tygodnik Powszechny,* no. 41.

Montias, J. M. 1976. *The Structure of Economic Systems.* New Haven, Conn.: Yale University Press.

————. 1982. "Poland: Roots of the Economic Crisis." *Aces Bulletin,* no. 3:16–28.

Morąg, Jacek. 1988. "Nauka o drugim obiegu" (Shadow economics). *Gazeta Bankowa,* no. 1.

Morawski, Witold. 1988. "A Sociologist Looks at Public Opinion, Politics, and Reform." In Marer and Siwiński 1988, 93–102.

Morawski, Witold, and Wieslawa Kozek, eds. 1988. *Załamanie porządku etatystycznego* (The collapse of statist order). Institute of Sociology, University of Warsaw, Warsaw.

Moskwa, Antoni, and Tim Kearney. 1984. "The Crises of Development or the Development of Crises." Paper presented at the annual convention of the International Studies Association, Atlanta, Ga., March 1984.

Mujzel, Jan. 1982. In "Piąta bitwa o reformę" (The fifth battle for reform). Intervention in the discussion. *Przeglad Techniczny* (Warsaw), no. 3.

————. 1988. "Jałowa inflacja" (The barren inflation). *Ład,* no. 28.

Müller, Alexsander, ed. 1985. *U zródel polskiego kryzysu: Społeczno-ekonomiczne uwarunkowania rozwoju gospodarczego Polski w latach osiemdziesiątych* (Roots of the Polish crisis: Socio-economic determinants of development of Poland in the 1980s). Warsaw: Państwowe Wydawnictwa Naukowe.

————. 1987. *Structural Change and Economic Reform in Poland.* Forschungsberichte (research report), Vienna Institute for Comparative Economic Studies, Vienna, no. 133.

Musgrave, Richard A. 1959. *The Theory of Public Finance: A Study in Public Economy.* New York: McGraw Hill.

Nagorski, Andrew. 1990a. "The Intellectual Roots of Eastern Europe's Upheaval." *SAIS Review* 10(2): 89–100.

————. 1990b. "A Revolution Born of Ideas." *Newsweek,* 15 January 1990, 22.

Nasilowski, Marian. 1974. *Analiza czynników rozwoju gospodarczego PRL.* Warsaw: Państwowe Wydawnictwo Eknomiczne.

Nove, Alec. 1986. *Socialism, Economics and Development.* London: Allen and Unwin.

Nove, Alec, and Domenico Mario Nuti, eds. 1972. *Socialist Economics.* Harmondsworth, England: Penguin Books.

Nuti, Domenico Mario. 1979. "The Contradictions of Socialist Economies." In *Socialist Registrar.* London: Merlin Press.

————. 1982. "The Polish Crisis: Economic Factors and Constraints." In Drewnowski 1982, 18–64.

————. 1987a. "Financial Innovation under Socialism." Department of Economics, European University Institute, Florence, Italy. Mimeo.

————. 1987b. "Poland: Current Development and Prospects of Economic Reform." In *The Economies of Eastern Europe and Their Foreign Economic Relations,* Philip Joseph, ed., 189–212. Brussels: NATO.

Nuti, Domenico Mario. 1988. "Perestroika: Transition from Central Planning to Market Economy." *Economic Policy* (October): 355–84.

Offe, Claus. 1975. "The Theory of the Capitalist State and the Problems of Policy Formation." In *Stresses and Contradictions in Modern Capitalism*, L. N. Lindberg et al., eds., 125–44. Lexington, Ky.: D. C. Heath.

———. 1984. *Contradictions of the Welfare State*. Cambridge, Mass.: MIT Press.

Oi, Jean. 1986. "Communism and Clientelism: Rural Politics in China." *World Politics*, no. 2:238–66.

Olechowski, Andrzej. 1982. "Katastrofa lub ratunek" (Catastrophe or rescue). *Polityka*, no. 11.

Olechowski, Andrzej, and Grzegorz Wojtowicz. 1988. "O co chodzi wierzycielom?" (What do the creditors want?) *Polityka-Eksport-Import*, no. 34.

Olszewska, Barbara. 1988. "Resjestracje i odmowy" (Registrations and rejections). *Polityka*, no. 42.

Organization for Economic Cooperation and Development. 1986. "East-West Financial Relations: Developments in 1985 and Future Prospects. *Financial Market Trends* (March): 1452.

Osiatyński, Jerzy. 1989. "Zaczely sie schody" (At the bottom of the stairs). A panel discussion. *Życie Gospodarcze*, no. 28.

Ost, David. 1985. "Poland Revisited." *Poland Watch*, no. 7:79–96.

Pakulski, Jan. 1986. "Legitimacy and Mass Compliance: Reflections on Max Weber and Soviet-type Societies." *British Journal of Political Science*, 16:35–56.

Parkin, Frank. 1979. *Marxism and Class Theory: A Bourgeois Critique*. New York: Columbia University Press.

Passent, Daniel. 1988. "Spotkałem optymistę" (I have met an optimist). *Polityka*, no. 40.

Pawlas, J. 1987. "Gospodarka prywatna w Polsce" (Private economy in Poland). *Więź* (Warsaw), no. 9.

Podstawowe dan statystyczne o Polsce, 1946–1988 (Background statistical data about Poland, 1946–1988). 1989. Warsaw: Glowny Urzad Statystyczny.

Polański, Zbigniew. 1986. "Spirala" (The spiral). *Życie Gospodarcze*, no. 39.

Polanyi, Karl. 1957. *The Great Transformation: The Political and Economic Origins of Our Time*. Boston: Beacon Press.

Powiorski, Jan. 1983. "The Poles of '81: Public Opinion on the Eve of Martial Law." *Poland Watch*, no. 3:109–32.

Poznański, Kazimierz. 1986a. "Competition between Eastern Europe and the Developing Countries in the Western Markets for Manufactured Goods." In *East European Economies: Slow Growth in the 1980s*. Joint Economic Committee, Cong., Washington, D.C.

———. 1986b. "Economic Adjustment and Political Forces: Poland Since 1970." *International Organization*, no. 2:455–88.

———. 1988a. "The Competitiveness of Polish Industry and Indebtedness." In Marer and Siwiński 1988, 45–60.

———. 1988b. "The Political Economy of De-Etatization." University of Washington, Seattle. Mimeo.

"Program umacniania złotówki" (Program to strengthen zloty: Summary of the National Bank of Poland report). 1987. *Rynki Zagraniczne*, 6 August 1987.

Prybyla, Jan. 1988. "The Great Malaise: Economic Crisis in Eastern Europe." In Kittrie and Volgyes 1988, 57–82.

Pryor, Frederic L. 1963. *The Communist Foreign Trade System*. Cambridge, Mass.: MIT Press.

Rachwald, Arthur R. 1987. "The Polish Road to the Abyss." *Current History* 86(523): 369–72, 384–85.

Rakowski, Mieczysław F. 1987. "Uwagi na temat niektórych aspektow sytuacji politicznej i ekonomicznej PRL w drugiej polowie lat 1980-tych" (Comments on some aspects of the political and economic situation of the Polish People's Republic in the second half of the 1980s), Warsaw, 8 June–10 October 1987. Typescript.

Reddaway, Peter. 1989. "Is the Soviet Union on the Road to Anarchy?" *Washington Post* (Outlook), 20 August 1989.

Revel, Jean-Francois. 1978. *The Totalitarian Temptation*. New York: Penguin Books.

Rocznik statystyczny (Statistical yearbook). Warsaw: Glowny Urzad Statystyczny (Central Statistical Office).

Rocznik statystyczny handlu zagranicznego (Statistical yearbook of foreign trade). Warsaw: Glowny Urzad Statystyczny (Central Statistical Office).

Rosefielde, Stephen. 1986. "Competitive Market Socialism Revisited: Impediments to Efficient Price Fixing." *Comparative Economic Studies*, no. 3:17–24.

Rubel, A., and G. Wojtowicz. 1989. "Bilans platniczy 1988" (Balance of payments in 1988). *Życie Gospodarcze*, no. 19.

Rutkowski, Jan. 1988. "Planowanie centralne a poziom Życia" (Central planning and standard of living). In Morawski and Kozek 1988, 124–52.

Schelling, Thomas C. 1963. *The Strategy of Conflict Resolution*. New York: Oxford University Press.

Schöpflin, George. 1981. "The Political Structure of Eastern Europe." In Dawisha and Hanson 1981, 61–83.

Sheahan, J. B. 1986. "Alternative Economic Strategies and Their Relevance for China." World Bank staff working papers, Washington, D.C., no. 759.

Siemieńska, Renata. 1984. "Popular Demand and Leadership Responses in Periods of Economic Retreat: A Case Study of Poland." Paper presented at the 25th annual convention of the International Studies Association, 27–31 March, Atlanta, Ga.

Sik, Ota. 1981. *The Communist Power System*. New York: Praeger.

Simon, Maurice D., and Rogez E. Kanet, eds. 1981. *Background to Crisis: Policy and Politics in Gierek's Poland*. Boulder, Colo.: Westview Press.

Skilling, H. Gordon. 1966. "Interest Groups and Communist Politics." *World Politics* 36(1): 1–27.

Smith, Allen H. 1983. *The Planned Economies of Eastern Europe*. New York: Holmes and Meier.

Smolar, Aleksander. 1988. "The Polish Opposition." Woodrow Wilson Center, Washington, D.C. Mimeo.

Sobczak. 1987. In Wieczorkowska 1987, 1.

Solidarity Provisional Council. 1987. "Stanowisko NSZZ 'Solidarność' w sprawie sytuacji i kierunków przebudowy gospodarki polskiej" (NSZZ "Solidarity" position on the situation and restructuring of the Polish economy). 1987. Gdańsk-Warsaw, April 1987. Mimeo.

Sołtan, Karol E. 1987. "Constitutionalism and Democracy." Paper presented at the annual meeting of the American Political Science Association, Chicago.

Spindler, J. Andrew. 1984. *The Politics of International Credit. Private Finance and Foreign Policy in Germany and Japan*. Washington, D.C.: Brookings Institution.

"Sprawozdanie Komitetu Centralnego wygłoszone przez Stanisława Kanię" (A report of the Central Committee [PUWP] read by Stanisław Kanię). *Trybuna Ludu* (Warsaw), 5 July 1981.

Spulber, N. 1957. *The Economics of Communist Eastern Europe*. New York: John Wiley.

———. 1966. *The State and Economic Development in Eastern Europe*. New York: Random House.

Staar, Richard F. 1988. *Communist Regimes in Eastern Europe*. Stanford, Calif.: Hoover Institution Press.

Staniszkis, Jadwiga. 1984. *Self-limiting Revolution*. Princeton, N.J.: Princeton University Press.

———. 1988. "Gospodarka i polityka w okresie transformacji" (The economy and politics during the transformation period). In Morawski and Kozek 1988, 39–88.

Stankovsky, J. 1973. "Determinant Factors of East-West Trade." *Soviet and East European Foreign Trade* 9(2): 141–58.

Stępień, Marian. 1988. "Pluralism." *Polish Perspectives* (Warsaw) 31(3): 5–8.

Strzelecka, Jolanta. 1985. "The Functioning of the Sejm Since December 13, 1981." *Poland Watch*, no. 7:57–74.

Świdlicka, Anna. 1988. "Solidarity Attempts to Regroup." In Mastny 1988, 272–77.

Surdykowski, Jerzy. 1985. "Na smierć i zycie ostatniej reformy" (Life or death of the last reform). *Tygodnik Powszechny* (Cracow), 15 December.

Szeliga, Zygmunt. 1982. "Co się stało z tymi milliardami?" *Polityka-Eksport-Import*, no. 7.

Szumańska, Ewa. 1988. "Ciekawe zjawisko" (An interesting phenomenon). *Tygodnik Powszechny* (Cracow), no. 14–15.

Szyr, Edward et al., eds. *Dwadzieścia lat Polski Ludowej*. Warsaw: Państwowe Wydawnictwa Naukowe.

Tatu, Michel. 1987. *Gorbatchev: L'URSS va-t-elle Changer?* (Gorbachev: Will the USSR change?) Paris: Éditions du Centurion.

Terry, Sarah Meklejohn, ed. 1984. *Soviet Policy in Eastern Europe*. New Haven, Conn.: Yale University Press.

"Tezy dziesiątego zjazdu Polskiej Zjednoczonej Partii Robotniczej (Theses of the PUWP for its 10th congress). *Trybuna Ludu*, 10 February 1986.

"Tezy w sprawie II etapu reformy gospodarczej: Propozycje dyskusji" (Theses on the second stage of economic reform: Proposals for discussion). *Rzeczpospolita*, 17 April 1987, supplement no. 102.

"Tezy w sprawie kształtowania struktur organizacyjnych gospodarki" (Theses on shaping organizational structures in the economy). Prepared by the ad hoc committee to review organizational structures, Party-State Commission for Review and Modernization of Organization Structures of the Economy and State. *Rzeczpospolita*, 12 May 1987.

Trade Union Confederation (OPZZ). 1987. "Alternatywna koncepcja realizacji reformy gospodarczej: Czesc II rozwiniecie" (Alternative approach to economic reform: Part 2 elaboration). Warsaw, September 1987. Mimeo.

Trotsky, Leon. 1965. *The Revolution Betrayed*. New York: Merit Publishers.

Usher, Dan. 1981. *The Economic Prerequisite to Democracy*. New York: Columbia University Press.

Valenta, Jiri. 1984. "Soviet Policy toward Hungary and Czechoslovakia." In Terry 1984, 93–124, 472.

Vernon, Raymond. 1988. "Introduction: The Promise and the Challenge." In *The Promise of Privatization. A Challenge for American Foreign Policy,* Raymond Vinton, ed., 1–22. New York: Council on Foreign Relations.

Vinton, Louisa, Roman Stefanowski, Anna Świdlicka. 1988. "Amnesty at Last." In Mastny 1988, 265–70.

Walendowski, Tadeusz. 1982. "The Polish Church under Martial Law." *Poland Watch*, no. 1:54–62.

Wanless, P. T. 1985. *Taxation in Centrally Planned Economies*. New York: St. Martin's Press.

Warszawski, Dawid. 1984. "The Price of Concessions." *Poland Watch*, no. 6:87–92.

Weber, Max. 1978. *Economy and Society: An Outline of Interpretive Sociology*. Berkeley: University of California Press.

Weydenthal, Jan B. 1988. "New Consultative Council." In Mastny 1988, 270–72.

White, Stephen. 1986. "Economic Performance and Communist Legitimacy." *World Politics*, no. 3:462–82.

White, Stephen, John Gardner, and George Schöpflin. 1982. *Communist Political Systems: An Introduction*. New York: St. Marin's Press.

Wiatr, Jerzy. 1988. "Intra-system Opposition." *Polish Perspectives* (Warsaw), no. 3:9–14.

Wieczorkowska, A. 1987. "Kondycja władzy terenowej: Rozmowa z Prof. Karolem Sobczakiem z Uniwersytetu Warzwskiego" (The state of local authority: Interview with Karol Sobczak of the University of Warsaw). *Życie Gospodarcze*, no. 21.

Wilczynski, J. 1972. *Socialist Economic Development and Reform*. London.

Wildavsky, Aaron. 1979. *Speaking Truth to Power*. Boston: Little Brown.

Wiles, Peter J.D. 1968. *Communist International Economics*. New York: Praeger.

Wilhelm, J. 1979. "Does the Soviet Union Have a Planned Economy? A Comment." *Soviet Studies*, no. 2:268–74.

Wilkin, Jerzy. 1988. "Rolnictwo i gospodarka zywnościowa w roli bufora polskiej gospodarki" (The agriculture and food economy as a buffer of the Polish economy). In *Nasza kondycja i nasze perspektywy* (Our condition and perspectives), 99–107, Department of Economics, University of Warsaw.

Winiecki, Jan. 1987a. *Economic Prospects—East and West. A View from the East*. London: Centre for Research into Communist Economies.

———. 1987b. "The Overgrown Industrial Sector in Soviet-Type Economies: Explanations, Evidence, Consequences." *Comparative Economic Studies* 37(4): 13–36.

———. 1988. "East European Economies: Forced Adjustment Forever?" Institute for International Economic Studies, University of Stockholm, seminar paper no. 413. Mimeo.

Wojciechowska, Urszula. 1987. "Ważna ledcja: VI ankieta Instytutu Gospodarki Narodowej" (Important lesson: The 6th Survey of the Institute of National Economy). *Życie Gospodarcze,* no. 18.

Wojciechowska, Urszula, and M. Żytniewski. 1987. "Deficyt i dotacje w przemysle" (Deficit and subsidies in industry). *Życie Gospodarcze,* no. 12.

"Wojna z narodem widziana od srodka: Wywiad z b. plk. dypl. R. J. Kuklińskim" (War against the nation as seen from the inside: Interview with ex-colonel R. J. Kukliński). 1987. *Kultura* (Paris), no. 4:3–57.

Wolf, Thomas A. 1990. "Foreign Trade in Planned Economies." In *International Economic Policies and Their Theoretical Foundations,* John M. Letiche, ed. 2d ed. New York: Academic Press. In press.

Wolfson, D. J. 1979. *Public Finance and Development Strategy.* Baltimore, Md.: Johns Hopkins University Press.

World Bank. 1986. *Poland: A First Report.* World Bank report no. 6408-POL, 10 October 1986.

World Bank. 1987a. *China: Finance and Investment.* World Bank report no. 6445-CHA, 10 March 1987.

World Bank. 1987b. *Poland: Reform, Adjustment and Growth.* World Bank report no. 6736-POL, 17 August 1987.

World Development Report. New York: Oxford University Press.

Wulf, L., and D. Goldsbrough. 1986. "The Evolving Role of Monetary Policy in China." International Monetary Fund staff paper, 2 June 1986, 209–42.

Zoeter, Joan P. 1981. "Eastern Europe: The Hard Currency Debt." In *East Europe Economic Assessments.* Pt. 2: *Regional Assessments,* 716–31. Joint Economic Committee, Cong., Washington, D.C.

Żychowicz, E. 1987. "Tajemnice zamówien rządowych" (Mystery of government contracts). *Slowo Powszechne,* 13 June 1987.

Index